# Concise
# Dictionary
## of
# Biography

# Concise
# Dictionary
## of
# Biography

Edwin Moore

Goddes & Grosset Ltd 1995

This edition published in 1995 by
Tiger Books International PLC, London

**TIGER BOOKS INTERNATIONAL**
**LONDON**

This edition published in 1993 by
Tiger Books International PLC, London

ISBN 1-85501-370-3

Printed and bound in Slovenia

# A

Abélard, Peter (1079–1142) French theologian and philosopher. He professed the new doctrine of nominalism at Notre Dame in Paris from 1115, and was condemned for heresy twice, in 1121 and in the year he died. When his love affair with his pupil **Héloïse** (1101–64), whose child by him was called Astrolabe, was discovered, Héloïse's uncle had Abélard castrated by thugs. Abélard and Héloïse's letters to each other, with their remarkable mix of intellectual and physical passion, have been much admired.

Achebe, Chinua (1930– ) Nigerian novelist and poet. Regarded as one of Africa's greatest writers in English, Achebe's work focuses on Ibo society and the legacy of colonialism. His works include the novels *Things Fall Apart* (1958), *Arrow of God* (1964) and the poetry collections *Beware Soul Brother* (1972) and *Christmas in Biafra* (1973).

Acheson, Dean [Gooderham] (1893–1971) American lawyer and statesman. As secretary of state under President TRUMAN, he was responsible for formulating and developing several important strands of American foreign policy, notably the MARSHALL Plan for reconstructing war-stricken Europe and the establishment of NATO.

Adams, Ansel [Easton] (1902–84) American photographer, notable for his detailed, deep-focus studies of the American landscape, e.g. his collection *This is the American West* (1960).

**Adams, Richard [George]** (1920– ) English novelist. His best-known work is *Watership Down* (1972), an occasionally grim little fantasy about a colony of rabbits, which has become a modern classic of children's literature. Other novels include *The Plague Dogs* (1977) and *The Girl in a Swing* (1980).

**Addison, Joseph** (1672–1719) English essayist and poet. With his friend Richard STEELE he founded the magazine *The Spectator* in 1711. Addison and Steele used the magazine to promote the virtues of reasonableness, common sense and benevolent moderation, and have been seen by cultural historians as having had a strong influence on the self-perception of the British people.

**Adenauer, Konrad** (1876–1967) German statesman. A member of the Centre Party during the 1930s, he was imprisoned twice by the Nazi regime (1934 and 1944). He became mayor of Cologne in 1945 and a co-founder of the Christian Democratic Union. In his role as chancellor of West Germany (1949–63) he played a major part in world politics.

**Adler, Alfred** (1870–1937) Austrian psychiatrist. He was an associate of FREUD, whose emphasis on sexuality he rejected, founding a school of psychoanalysis based upon the individual's quest to overcome feelings of inadequacy (the "inferiority complex," as it came to be known). His works include *The Practice and Theory of Individual Psychology* (1923).

**Adorno, Theodor [Wiesengrund]** (1903–69) German philosopher, sociologist and music critic. His theorizing on the oppressive nature of all philosophical inquiry, e.g. in *Dialectic of the Enlighten-ment* (1947), is regarded as a significant influence on the 1960s radical movement. Adorno was associated with MARCUSE in the left-wing Frankfurt School of critics.

**Aeschylus** (524–456 BC) Greek dramatist regarded as the founder of Greek tragedy. Seven of his plays survive, including *Prometheus Bound* and the *Oresteia* trilogy. Thought by the Greeks to be less sophisticated than the other two great tragedians, EURIPIDES and SOPHOCLES, his work was re-assessed in the 18th century. SHELLEY was heavily influenced by him, and MARX considered him as one of the two greatest dramatists of all time (with SHAKESPEARE).

**Aga Khan III** [Sultan Sir Mohammed Shah] (1877–1957) spiritual leader of the Ismaili Muslim sect and statesman. He was president of the All-India Muslim League (1906–09) and became president of the League of Nations in 1937. His son Karim (b. 1936), succeeded as **Aga Khan IV**. Like his father, he is a renowned breeder of racehorses.

**Agnew, Spiro [Theodore]** (1918– ) American Republican politician, vice-president (1969–73) in NIXON's administration. A noted critic of the morality of his "effete" liberal opponents, he resigned office following revelations of political corruption and was sentenced to three years' probation.

**Akhmatova, Anna** (1889–1966) Russian poet. An associate of MANDELSTAM, she is regarded as one of the greatest poets of the 20th century. Her masterpiece, *Requiem*, first published in 1963, describes the suffering of the Russian people under STALIN.

**Akihito** *see* **Hirohito**.

**Albee, Edward [Franklin]** (1928– ) American

dramatist. His plays, which are predominantly satires on middle-class life, include *Who's Afraid of Virginia Woolf* (1962) and *A Delicate Balance* (1966).

**Albert, Prince** *see* **Victoria, Queen**.

**Aldrin, Edwin "Buzz"** *see* **Armstrong, Neil**.

**Alexander VI, Pope** *see* **Borgia, Rodrigo**.

**Alexander the Great** (356–323 BC) Macedonian king. The pupil of ARISTOTLE, he inherited the kingdom of Macedon from his father **Philip II** (382–336 BC). He conquered Greece in 336 (razing Thebes in the process), Egypt in 331, and the Persian Empire by 328 (after defeating the Persian king Darius III in battle in 333). He proceeded to extend his conquests to the east and defeated an Indian army in 326. He died in Babylon, and his body was buried in the city he founded, Alexandria.

**Alexandra, Feodorovna** *see* **Nicholas II**.

**Alexandra, Queen** *see* **Edward VII**.

**Ali, Muhammad** [Cassius Clay] (1942– ) American boxer and world heavyweight champion (1964–67, 1974–78, 1978). His licence to box was withdrawn in 1967, after his refusal to be conscripted into the armed forces to serve in Vietnam, service he saw as incompatible with his conversion to Islam (at which he rejected his given "slave" name of Clay). Widely regarded as one of the greatest boxers of all time, he was also much loved for his wit and concern for the plight of the black poor.

**Allen, Woody** [Allen Stewart Konigsberg] (1935– ) American film director, actor and writer, noted for his satirical, often autobiographical films about the (primarily sexual) neuroses of New York intellectuals, e.g. *Annie Hall* (1977) and *Manhattan* (1979).

**Allende [Gossens], Salvador** (1908–73) Chilean

Marxist politician. He was elected president of his country in 1970 (at the fourth attempt), thus becoming the first freely elected Marxist president in Latin America. He was overthrown and killed in the coup that brought PINOCHET to power.

**Amin [Dada], Idi** (1925– ) Ugandan dictator. He wrested power from OBOTE in 1971, and ruled Uganda until 1979 (appointing himself president for life in 1976). He fled Uganda following the Tanzanian army's invasion in 1979, and lived in Saudi Arabia from 1980. He was chairman of the Organization of African Unity (1975–76).

**Amis, Sir Kingsley** (1922– ) English novelist and poet. His first novel, *Lucky Jim* (1954), a satire on academic life, is widely regarded as a comic masterpiece. His later novels also have streaks of anarchic humour, but are much darker in tone, dealing as they do with such issues as the problem of suffering and the nature of God (*The Anti-Death League*, 1966), and modern sexuality (*Stanley and the Women*, 1984). He is the father of **Martin Amis** (1949– ) who is also a novelist.

**Amundsen, Roald** (1872–1928) Norwegian explorer and navigator, leader of the first expedition to reach the South Pole in 1911, whose journey is described in his book *The South Pole* (1913).

**Andersen, Hans Christian** (1805–75) Danish writer. He wrote prolifically in many areas, but is now remembered solely for his fairy tales, e.g. "The Ugly Duckling" and "The Emperor's New Clothes".

**Anderson, Carl David** *see* **Hess, Victor Francis**.

**Anderson, Sherwood** (1876–1941) American novelist and short-story writer. His best-known work is *Winesburg, Ohio* (1919), a collection of naturalistic and gloomy short stories about small-town American life.

**Andrew, Prince** *see* **Elizabeth II**.

**Andropov, Yuri [Vladimirovich]** (1914–84) Soviet statesman, president of the USSR (1983–84). Andropov, a former head of the KGB, was rumoured to be a potential reformer when he succeeded to the Soviet presidency following Brezhnev's death.

**Angelou, Maya** (1928– ) American dramatist, poet and short-story writer, whose works on her upbringing as a poor black female in St Louis, e.g. *I Know Why the Caged Bird Sings* (1970), have established her as one of the leading black writers of the 20th century.

**Anne, Princess** *see* **Elizabeth II**.

**Anne of Cleves** *see* **Henry VIII**.

**Anouilh, Jean** (1910–87) French dramatist. The best known of his plays is his reworking of Sophocles' tragedy *Antigone* (1944), which was produced as a subversive interpretation of Nazi rule in Occupied France. Other notable plays are the *The Waltz of the Toreadors* (1952) and *Beckett* (1959).

**Antonioni, Michelangelo** (1912– ) Italian film director. His films include *L'Avventura* (1959) and *Blow-Up* (1967), the latter being commonly regarded as a landmark of the "Swinging Sixties" English cultural landscape.

**Antony, Mark** [Marcus Antonius] (*c.*83–30 BC) Roman soldier. He fought with Julius Caesar in the Gallic wars, and after Caesar's assassination defeated Brutus and Cassius at the battle of Philipi (42). He then deserted his wife for the Egyptian Queen **Cleopatra** (69–30 BC), their forces being defeated by Augustus at Actium. He killed himself after hearing a false report of Cleopatra's suicide; Cleopatra subsequently also committed suicide.

**Apollinaire, Guillaume** *see* **Delaunay, Robert**.

**Aquinas, Thomas** *see* **Thomas Aquinas**.

**Aquino, [Maria] Corazon** (1933– ) Filipino politician. Following the assassination of her husband Benigno Aquino, the most prominent opponent of MARCOS, she became the leader of the popular movement against Marcos's rule, and was elected President of the Philippines in 1986.

**Arafat, Yasser** (1929– ) Palestinian leader, who helped found the anti-Israeli guerrilla force *Al Fatah*, and became chairman of the Palestine Liberation Organization in 1968. Arafat survived numerous attempts on his life from 1968, primarily from factions within the Palestinian movement, and came to be regarded by many Westerners as a "moderate" spokesman for the Palestinian cause. His leadership of the PLO entered its most crucial phase when he backed Saddam HUSSEIN's 1990 invasion of Kuwait.

**Aragon, Louis** (1897–1982) French poet, essayist and novelist. One of the founders of both Dadaism and Surrealism, his works include the Surrealist novel *Nightwalker* (1926) and several collections of verse. He became a member of the French Communist Party in the late 1920s, for which cause he became a prolific propagandist.

**Arden, John** (1930– ) English dramatist, regarded as one of the leading left-wing playwrights of his generation. His best-known works are the satire *Live Like Pigs* (1958) and the passionately pacifist *Serjeant Musgrave's Dance* (1959).

**Arendt, Hannah** (1906–75) German-born American philosopher. Her best-known work is *The Origins of Totalitarianism* (1951), which argued that the similarities between HITLER's Germany and STALIN's Russia could be traced back to a common 19th-century ancestry. Her other works include *Eichmann in Jerusalem* (1961), *On Revolution* (1963) and *On Violence* (1963).

**Aristotle** (384–322 BC) Greek philosopher. He taught at PLATO's Academy for 20 years, and became tutor to ALEXANDER THE GREAT, and formed his own school (the Lyceum) in Athens in 335. His works, including *Nicomachean Ethics, Poetics* and *Politics*, were re-introduced to the Western world in the Middle Ages via Arabian scholarship, and had a profound and occasionally pernicious influence (due to their unquestioned authority) on almost every field of intellectual inquiry until the Renaissance.

**Armstrong, [Daniel] Louis "Satchmo"** (1900–1971) American jazz trumpeter, singer and leader of many very popular jazz bands, notably the All-Stars. A highly gifted musician and singer with a genius for improvization, Armstrong became one of the best-loved entertainers of the century.

**Armstrong, Neil [Alden]** (1930– ) American astronaut. He commanded the Apollo 11 moon landing mission, in which he became the first man to walk on the moon, followed by the lunar module pilot **Edwin "Buzz" Aldrin** (1930– ). The other member of the mission was the orbiting module pilot **Michael Collins** (1930– ).

**Arp, Jean** *or* **Hans** (1887–1966) German-born French sculptor and painter. One of the founders of Dadaism, Arp's work is characterized by the use of organic forms to create abstract shapes in disparate media.

**Artaud, Antonin** (1896–1948) French stage director, actor and dramatist. He was the creator of the
"Theatre of Cruelty," a form of drama that attempts
to restore humans to their spiritual roots by a
process of communication involving symbolism and
ritualistic gestures rather than language. Artaud's
works include *Manifesto of the Theatre of Cruelty*
(1932) and *The Theatre and its Double* (1938).

**Arthur** (*fl.* 6th century AD) a possibly mythical Celtic
warrior-king of post-Roman Britain, who may have
organized resistance against the Saxon invaders.
He is credited in legend with having won a battle
over the Saxons at "Mount Badon," and is supposed
to have been buried at Glastonbury. Legends of
Arthur and his knights became enormously popular
throughout Europe in the early Middle Ages.

**Ashcroft, Dame Peggy** (1907–91) English actress.
One of the most popular stage and film actresses of
her generation, she is perhaps best known for her
part in the television series *The Jewel in the Crown*
(1983). She won an Oscar for best supporting actress in *A Passage to India* (1984).

**Ashdown, Paddy** [Jeremy John Dunham Ashdown]
(1941– ) English Liberal politician. After service
with the Marines and Special Boat Squadron, he
joined the diplomatic service in 1971 (he was by
then a fluent Mandarin speaker). He was elected
leader of the Liberal and Social Democratic Party in
1988.

**Ashe, Arthur** (1943–93) American tennis player.
The first black tennis player to win the US open
(1968), the Australian open (1970), and the Wimbledon men's competition (1975). An active campaigner
for civil rights, he was forced to retire from profes-

sional tennis in 1979 following a heart attack. He contracted the HIV virus from a blood transfusion after heart by-pass surgery in 1983 and developed full-blown Aids in 1988.

**Ashkenazy, Vladimir [Davidovich]** (1937– ) Russian-born Icelandic pianist and conductor, best-known for his recordings of works by MOZART and Russian composers such as SCRIABIN and RACHMANINOV.

**Ashton, Sir Frederick [William Mallandaine]** (1906–88) Ecuadorian-born British choreographer and co-founder of the Royal Ballet. Ashton's ballets include *Façade* (1931, and *A Month in the Country* (1976).

**Asquith, Herbert Henry** [1st Earl of Oxford and Asquith] (1852–1928) British statesman. He was leader of the Liberal Party (1908–26) and prime minister (1908–16). Regarded as the leader of the conservative wing of the Liberals, he refused to serve under his successor, LLOYD GEORGE (who had engineered Asquith's downfall).

**Astaire, Fred** [Frederick Austerlitz] (1899–1987) American dancer, singer and actor. His partnership with **Ginger Rogers** [Virginia McMath] (1911– ) resulted in a series of classic song-and-dance films, e.g. *Flying Down to Rio* (1933) and *Top Hat* (1935).

**Astor, Nancy Witcher [Langhorne]** [Viscountess Astor] (1879–1964) American-born British politician. She was elected to parliament as a Conservative MP, becoming the first woman to take her seat in Parliament. She was an active campaigner for the temperance movement, and for women's and children's welfare.

**Atatürk, Kemal** [Mustafa Kemal Atatürk] (1881–

1938) Turkish general and statesman, first president of Turkey (1923–38). He introduced wideranging reforms to westernize and secularize Turkish society, and is regarded as the creator of the modern Turkish state.

**Atget, [Jean] Eugène** (1856–1927) French photographer. He began selling his documentary photographs of Paris to museums in his late forties, and became recognized by artists such as BRAQUE as a master at recording the atmosphere of the city.

**Attenborough, Sir David [Frederick]** (1926– ) English naturalist and broadcaster, best known for his highly popular TV series, e.g. *Life on Earth* (1978, on evolution), *The Living Planet* (1983, on the adaptation of life to the environment) and *The Trials of Life* (1989, on animal behaviour). He is Richard ATTENBOROUGH's brother.

**Attenborough, Sir Richard [Samuel]** (1923– ) English film director, producer and actor. Films he has starred in include *Brighton Rock* (1947), *The Angry Silence* (1959) and *Seance on a Wet Afternoon* (1963). Films he has directed include *Oh! What a Lovely War* (1968), *A Bridge Too Far* (1976) and *Gandhi* (1982), the last winning eight Oscars. He is David ATTENBOROUGH's brother. He was created a life peer in 1993.

**Attlee, Clement [Richard]** [1st Earl Attlee] (1883–1967) British statesman. He was leader of the Labour Party (1939–55) and prime minister (1945–51). Attlee's 1945 administration introduced widespread nationalization and a programme of social security reforms (based on the BEVERIDGE Report).

**Auden, W[ystan] H[ugh]** (1907–73) English poet (US citizen from 1946). With such volumes as *Look,*

## Augustine

*Stranger* (1936), he became the leading left-wing poet of his generation (the "Auden generation") but later drifted away from Marxism towards a Christian and socially conservative position. His works include *Collected Shorter Poems* (1966).

**Augustine, Saint** [Augustine of Hippo] (354–430) Latin Church Father. Born in what is now Tunisia, his father was a pagan and he was brought up a Christian by his mother. Reacting against the licentious life he came to lead in Carthage, he converted to Manichaeanism for a while before returning to the Church. He became Bishop of Hippo (396–430) and wrote a spiritual autobiography, *Confessions*, and *City of God*, a major work of Christian apologetics.

**Augustine, Saint** (d.604) Italian monk. With other monks, he was dispatched to Britain in 597 by Pope GREGORY I to convert the Anglo-Saxons to Christianity and impose the authority of Rome on the native Celtic Church. He became the first Archbishop of Canterbury in 601.

**Augustus** [originally Gaius Octavianus] (63 BC–14 AD) Roman emperor. After adoption by his uncle Julius CAESAR in 44 BC, he took the name Gaius Julius Caesar Octavianus. He became the first Emperor of Rome in 31 BC after defeating Mark ANTONY's forces at the naval battle of Actium. A cultured tyrant, he boasted that he had "found Rome brick, and left it marble". He cultivated the arts and was the patron of VIRGIL. He was succeeded by his stepson TIBERIUS.

**Aurelius, Marcus** (121–80) Roman emperor and philosopher. Renowned by his contemporaries for his nobility and learning, he spent much of his reign in war against the incoming "barbarians" in the eastern part of the Empire. He was a devoted follower of Stoic philosophy, which he espouses in his much-admired *Meditations*.

**Austen, Jane** (1775–1817) English novelist. Her six great novels, *Sense and Sensibility* (1811), *Pride and Prejudice* (1813), *Mansfield Park* (1814), *Emma* (1816) and *Northanger Abbey* and *Persuasion* (published posthumously, 1818) are set within the confines of the society in which Jane Austen lived, the well-bred essentially rural middle class of Regency England, and usually feature the quest of young women for suitable husbands. She is renowned for her masterly dialogue, finely tuned satire and moral sense.

**Austin, John Langshaw** (1911–60) English philosopher. He stressed the need for simplicity and use of ordinary language in philosophical speculation, as seen in his posthumously published lectures, *Sense and Sensibilia* and *How to do Things with Words* (both 1962).

**Averroës** [Ibn Rushd] (1126–88) Arab philosopher. Born in Cordoba, he became a judge, scholar and court physician in Morocco. His works, notably his *Commentaries* on ARISTOTLE, which attempted a synthesis of Aristotelian and Islamic philosophy, were profoundly influential on European scholarship.

**Ayckbourn, Alan** (1939– ) English dramatist, noted for such satirical comedies as *Absurd Person Singular* (1973) and *The Norman Conquests* (1974).

**Ayer, Sir A[lfred] J[ules]** (1910–89) English philosopher, whose work is based on "logical positivism" and the rejection of metaphysics. His early

short work *Language, Truth and Logic* (1936) has
been highly influential on British "common-sense"
philosophy. His later work, e.g. *The Problem of
Knowledge* (1956), qualifies and in part rejects the
more strident assumptions of his earlier writing.

**Ayub Khan, Mohammed** (1907–74) Pakistani field
marshal and statesman, president of Pakistan
(1958–69). He was the first commander-in-chief of
his country's army (1951–58), and introduced some
reforms during his presidency. His suspension of
civil liberties and increasingly dictatorial style of
leadership eroded his power base and led to his fall
in 1969.

**Azikiwe, [Benjamin] Nnamdi** (1904– ) Nigerian
statesman, first president of Nigeria (1963–66).
During the Nigerian civil war he joined the (Ibo)
Biafran secessionist government, but accepted the
reunification process once the war was over, when
he (unsuccessfully) stood once more for president.
He has been described as the "father of modern
Nigeria."

# B

**Baader, Andreas** *see* **Meinhoff, Ulrike**.

**Babbage, Charles** (1792–1871) English mathematician. He invented two "calculating machines," the second of which was intended to be operated in a programmatic way by means of punched cards. Babbage's machine is regarded as the precursor of the modern computer.

**Babbitt, Milton [Byron]** (1916– ) American composer. Babbitt became America's foremost exponent of serial twelve-tone music with his advocacy of "total serialization" in all aspects of composition. His works include *Composition for Orchestra* (1941) and *Philomel* (1964).

**Babel, Isaac Emmanuilovich** (1894–1941) Russian short-story writer and dramatist. He joined the Bolshevik forces in the Russian civil war in 1917, serving with the Cossack cavalry. His experiences with the Cossacks form the basis for the stories in his best-known work, *Red Cavalry* (1926). Another notable work is the (also autobiographical) collection of stories on Jewish life in Odessa, *Stories from Odessa* (1924). He died in a Soviet labour camp.

**Bacall, Lauren** *see* **Bogart, Humphrey**.

**Bach, Johann Sebastian** (1685–1750) German composer. A devout Lutheran, he was recognized by his contemporaries as a great organist and by posterity

19

as one of the greatest of all composers. His works include some of the greatest music in several forms, e.g. his six cello suites, choral masterpieces such as the *Saint Matthew Passion*, and works for harpsichord, clavichord and the organ, such as *The Well-Tempered Clavier* and *The Art of Fugue*. Four of his sons were also composers: **Wilhelm Friedemann** (1710–84), **Karl Philipp Emanuel** (1714–88), **Johann Christoph Friedrich** (1732–95), and **Johann [John] Christian** (1735–82), who became a court musician in London, where he was known as "the English Bach," and influenced MOZART.

**Bacon, Francis** (1561–1626) English philosopher and statesman. He served both ELIZABETH I and her successor JAMES VI AND I in various public offices until his conviction and disgrace for bribery in 1621, shortly after being created Viscount St Albans. His writings on philosophy and the need for rational scientific method, particularly in *The Advancement of Learning* (1605) and the *Novum Organum* (1620), are landmarks in the history of human thought, most notably in their insistence on argument based on fact and refusal to accept established authority.

**Bacon, Francis** (1909–92) Irish-born British painter. His works feature twisted and contorted human shapes, often in weird landscapes or spaces. His works include *Figure in a Landscape* (1945) and a series of paintings based on VELÀZQUEZ's portrait of Pope Innocent X.

**Bacon, Roger** (*c.*1214–92) English monk and philosopher, who was known to his contemporaries as *Doctor Mirabilis* for his wide learning and daring speculation, and who acquired the false reputation of being a magician. Like his later namesake, Francis BACON (1561–1626), he advocated the supremacy of practical experience over established authority.

**Baekeland, Leo Hendrik** (1863–1944) Belgian-born American chemist. He made his fortune in the 1890s by selling a photographic process to EASTMAN for $1 million (Baekeland would have settled for $25,000), and subsequently invented the thermosetting resin Bakelite.

**Baez, Joan** (1941– ) American folksinger, renowned for her "protest songs" on civil rights and the Vietnam war in the 1960s. She was closely associated with Bob DYLAN in the peace movement in the mid–1960s. Baez and Dylan made a film together, *Renaldo and Clara* (1978).

**Bailey, David** (1938– ) English photographer, whose work, particularly his fashion photographs of models such as Jean Shrimpton and "personalities" such as Mick JAGGER, were seen as epitomizing the "Swinging 60s" pop culture era in London.

**Baird, John Logie** (1888–1946) Scottish engineer, who invented a mechanically scanned system of television in the mid–1920s. Baird's system was used to transmit pictures (of poor quality) across the Atlantic, and he also produced colour and stereoscopic pictures. Baird's system became redundant in the late 1930s, when it was superseded by an electronic form of scanning.

**Baker, Dame Janet [Abbott]** (1933– ) English mezzosoprano. Baker became one of Britain's most popular opera singers in the 1960s, and had parts created for her by composers such as BRITTEN. She published her memoirs, *Full Circle*, in 1982.

**Bakunin, Mikhail** (1814–76) Russian anarchist. Of aristocratic descent, he engaged in revolutionary activity in Germany in the late 1840s and in France in 1870, and was expelled from the Communist International in 1872. A vigorous controversialist, his ideological enemies included MARX.

**Balanchine, George** (1904–83) Russian-born American choreographer and dancer. The best known of his productions are to music by Russian composers, particularly STRAVINSKY, e.g. *Apollo* (1928). He founded the New York City ballet in 1928.

**Balcon, Sir Michael** (1896–1977) English film producer. One of the most influential of all British producers, Balcon produced such films in the 1930s as the documentary *Man of Aran* (1933) and the thriller *The Thirty-Nine Steps* (1935), but is particularly associated with the great Ealing comedies of the 1940s and 1950s, e.g. *Whisky Galore* (1949) and *The Lavender Hill Mob* (1952).

**Baldwin, James [Arthur]** (1924–87) American novelist, dramatist and essayist. Baldwin's main concern was with the role of blacks in American society, and, to a lesser extent, that of homosexuals. His novels include *Go Tell it on the Mountain* (1953) and *Giovanni's Room* (1956). His polemical work, *The Fire Next Time* (1963), on the oppression of blacks, was much discussed in the 1960s.

**Baldwin, Stanley** [1st Earl Baldwin of Bewdley] (1867–1947) British statesman and Conservative prime minister (1923–24, 1924–29, 1935–37). Notable aspects of his premierships include the passing of a state of emergency during the 1926 General Strike, his refusal to accept Wallis Simpson as Edward VIII's wife (see WINDSOR), which resulted in

the latter's abdication, and his failure to deal with
unemployment and the rise of European totalitarianism.

**Balzac, Honoré de** (1799–1860) French novelist.
His great collection of novels, e.g. *La Cousine Bette*
(1846) and short stories, describes the lives of French
men and women of every class. His name for the
series, *La Comédie humaine* ("the Human Comedy"), is meant to invite comparison with DANTE's
*Divine Comedy*. Balzac was a royalist, a Roman
Catholic, and a reactionary, and has been hailed by
many (including MARX) as the greatest novelist.

**Bancroft, Anne** *see* **Brooks, Mel.**

**Banda, Hastings [Kamuzu]** (1905– ) Malawi statesman, first president of Nyasaland from 1963 and
president of Malawi (formerly Nyasaland) from
1966. Banda, one of the longest-ruling leaders in
the world, was appointed president for life in 1971.
His rule has been autocratic by Western standards,
and he was the only black leader to recognize and
(officially) trade with South Africa.

**Bandaranaike, Mrs Sirimavo Ratwatte Dias**
(1916– ) Sri Lankan stateswoman, prime minister
of Ceylon (later Sri Lanka) (1960–65, 1970–77).
She succeeded her husband S[olomon] W[est]
R[idgeway] D[ias] Bandaranaike (1899–1959)
to the premiership following his assassination. A
socialist and a nationalist, she fostered nationalization, the use of Sinhalese rather than Tamil as
the official language, and Buddhism. She was expelled from parliament in 1980, following "abuse of
power" charges.

**Bankhead, Tallulah [Brockman]** (1903–68) American actress, noted for her sharp wit, beauty and

distinctive low-timbred voice. Her best-known stage role was that of Regina in *The Little Foxes* (1939). She published her memoirs, *Tallulah*, in 1952.

**Banks, Sir Joseph** (1743–1820) English botanist and explorer. He sailed with Cook on his 1768–71 voyage round the world as a representative of the Royal Society, and discovered many species of animals and plants (including a new genus of plants). He also turned Kew Gardens into the most important centre for botanical study.

**Bannister, Sir Roger [Gilbert]** (1929– ) British athlete and doctor, who became the first man to run a mile in four minutes in 1954, the circumstances of which are described in his memoir, *First Four Minutes* (1955). He has also published several papers on neurology.

**Banting, Sir Frederick [Grant]** (1891–1941) Canadian physician. His research into diabetes with the American physiologist **Charles Herbert Best** (1899–1978), initially under the supervision of the Scottish physiologist **John James MacLeod** (1876–1935), resulted in the isolation of the pancreatic hormone insulin, in a form suitable for treating diabetes.

**Barber, Samuel** (1910–81) American composer. Barber is regarded as a "traditional" modern composer working with recognizably 19th-century harmonies and forms. His works include the popular *Adagio for Strings*, an adaptation of a movement from his string quartet (1936).

**Barbirolli, Sir John** (1899–1970) English conductor, cellist and founder of the Hallé Orchestra (1943–68). Barbirolli was particularly associated with the music of modern British composers, particularly DELIUS, ELGAR and VAUGHAN WILLIAMS. Vaughan Williams dedicated his 8th symphony to him.

**Barbusse, Henri** (1873–1935) French novelist and poet. His works are naturalistic, often grim accounts of war and the lives of the poor and the demimonde. His best-known work is the novel *Under Fire* (1916), a strongly pacifist account of trench warfare in World War I.

**Bardeen, John** (1908–91) American physicist and electrical engineer. He won two Nobel prizes, the first in 1956 for research that led to the invention of the transistor, the second in 1972 for research into the theory of superconductivity.

**Bardot, Brigitte** (1934– ) French actress. Starring in such films as *And God Created Woman* (1956), she became the leading "sex symbol" of the 1950s. Few of her films are now seen as of any worth. Since the 1970s, she has lived in virtual seclusion in France, where she devotes herself to animal rights and welfare.

**Barenboim, Daniel** (1942– ) Argentinian-born Israeli concert pianist and conductor. Among his many recordings are complete sets of the MOZART piano concertos and BEETHOVEN's piano sonatas and concertos. He married the cellist Jacqueline DU PRÉ in 1967, and was appointed music director of the Orchestre de Paris in 1975.

**Barnard, Christian [Neethling]** (1922– ) South African surgeon, who performed the first heart transplant in 1967. The patient, Louis Washansky, died not long after the operation.

**Barrie, Sir J[ames] M[atthew]** (1860–1937) Scottish dramatist and novelist, remembered principally for his remarkable fantasy play for children, *Peter Pan* (1904).

**Barrymore, Lionel** (1878–1954) American actor. One of a family of distinguished theatricals, notably his sister **Ethel Barrymore** (1879–1959) and brother **John Barrymore** (1882–1942), Barrymore achieved great popularity as a character actor with his roles in such films as *You Can't Take It With You* (1938) and in the first Dr Kildare series of films. His memoir, *We Barrymores,* was published in 1951.

**Barth, Karl** (1886–1968) Swiss Protestant theologian. Barth's theology was based on an orthodox "theocentric" conception of divine grace and is seen as a reaction against the simplifications of 19th-century liberal theology. Barth was a committed and courageous opponent of Nazism. His theology is summarized in *Church Dogmatics* (1932–62).

**Barthes, Roland** (1915–80) French literary and cultural critic, whose semiological studies on subjects as diverse as washing powder and national monuments, influenced by McLuhan and Saussure, were regarded as necessary reading in the 1960s and 70s. His works include *Writing Degree Zero* (1953) and *Elements of Sociology* (1964).

**Bartók, Béla** (1881–1945) Hungarian composer and pianist. He was a noted collector of folk songs, upon which many of his works are based. His works include the opera *Duke Bluebeard's Castle*, the ballet *The Miraculous Mandarin*, string quartets, and the *Concerto for Orchestra*.

**Basie, Count [William]** (1904–84) American jazz composer and bandleader. He was a jazz pianist of great ability, and his band, featuring singers such as Ella FITZGERALD and SINATRA, became one of the best-loved big bands of their day.

**Bates, H[erbert] E[rnest]** (1905–74) English novelist and short-story writer. His works include two very popular novels, *Fair Stood the Wind for France* (1944), which centres on an RAF bombing crew, and a comic novel featuring the unruly farming family the Larkins, *The Darling Buds of May* (1958).

**Bateson, William** (1861–1926) British geneticist. Although highly unorthodox in some of his viewpoints, e.g. in opposing his "vibratory" theory of inheritance against the now accepted principle of chromosomal carriage of genes, Bateson's work in confirming MENDEL's principles of heredity was of great importance in the study of genetics.

**Batista [y Zaldivar], Fulgencio** (1901–73) Cuban military leader, president of Cuba (1940–44, 1952–59). Initially a reformer who took power during a general strike, his rule became increasingly corrupt and he fled Cuba after the success of the insurrection led by CASTRO in 1959.

**Baudelaire, Charles** (1821–67) French poet. Noted for his fascination with the macabre and alleged Satanism, he became one of the leading Symbolist poets. His works include *Les Fleurs du mal* (1857), a collection of poems renowned for their often perverse nature.

**Bax, Sir Arnold [Edward Trevor]** (1883–1953) English composer, noted for his traditional style of composition and interest in Celtic myth and legend, e.g. his tone poem *Tintagel* (1917). He was Master of the King's Music from 1941.

**Beadle, George Wells** *see* **Tatum, Edward Lawrie.**

**Beaton, Sir Cecil [Walter Hardy]** (1904–80) English society and fashion photographer, stage and costume designer, and writer. Beaton's design credits include *My Fair Lady* (1956), with its famous black-and-white racecourse scene. His society portraits, e.g. of the royal family and GARBO, have a strong period flavour.

**Beatty, Warren** (1938– ) American film actor, producer and director. Films in which he has starred include *Bonnie and Clyde* (1967), *Heaven Can Wait* (1978) and *Reds* (1981).

**Beaumont, Sir Francis** *see* **Fletcher, John**.

**Beauvoir, Simone de** (1908–86) French novelist and essayist whose works explore the female predicament from the standpoint of existential feminism, e.g. her essay *The Second Sex* (1949). Her work was much affected by her lifelong relationship with SARTRE.

**Beaverbrook, Max** [William Maxwell Aitken, 1st Baron Beaverbrook] (1879–1964) Canadian-born British newspaper proprietor and Conservative politician. His newspapers, notably *The Daily Express*, were used as vehicles for Beaverbrook's usually imperialist and often eccentric enthusiasms. In World War I he served as minister of information (1918) and in World War II as minister of aircraft production (1940–41).

**Bechet, Sidney** (1897–1959) American jazz saxophonist and clarinettist. Bechet never learned to read music, but became recognized as one of the greatest soprano saxophone virtuosos of the century. He settled in France in 1951.

**Becket, Thomas à** (1118–70) English saint. Of Norman descent, he became Chancellor of England in 1155 and Archbishop of Canterbury in 1162.

Relations between Becket and **King Henry II** (1133–89) deteriorated due to the former's strong allegiance to Church rather than King, and Becket was murdered by four of the King's knights (Henry had impetuously demanded "Who shall rid me of this turbulent priest?"). Henry made his penance before Becket's tomb in 1173, the year Becket was canonized.

**Beckett, Samuel** (1906–89) Irish dramatist and novelist. He settled in Paris in the 1930s (where he befriended James JOYCE and wrote down *Finnegans Wake* at Joyce's dictation), and wrote in both French and English. His works, generally bleak and existentialist in philosophy, include the play *Waiting for Godot* (1952) and the short novel *Malone Dies* (1951).

**Becquerel, Antoine Henri** *see* **Curie, Marie**.

**Bede, the Venerable, Saint** (*c.*673–735) Anglo-Saxon monk and historian. Prodigiously learned, he settled for life in the monastery at Jarrow in 682. His many works include his Latin *Ecclesiastical History of the English People* (731), which provides an invaluable record of English history.

**Beecham, Sir Thomas** (1879–1961) English conductor, noted for his promotion and dashing interpretation of the works of DELIUS, STRAUSS and SIBELIUS, and for his sharply witty ripostes.

**Beerbohm, Sir [Henry] Max[imilian]** (1872–1956) English parodist, caricaturist and essayist. The parodies of authors such as Henry JAMES and KIPLING in such collections as *A Christmas Garland* (1912) established him as one of the greatest of all parodists, and his caricatures of his contemporaries are also much admired. His only novel, *Zuleika Dobson*

(1911), is a surreal and satirical portrait of Oxford undergraduate life.

**Beethoven, Ludwig van** (1770–1827) German composer. Regarded as the greatest Romantic composer, he became famous throughout Europe in the 1790s as a brilliant pianist with a special gift for improvisation. His works include a violin concerto, nine symphonies, piano sonatas, string quartets, masses, and one of the greatest operas, *Fidelio* (1805), which, is also one of the key works of the Romantic period.

**Begin, Menachem** (1913–92) Polish-born Israeli statesman. He was commander of the Irgun militant Zionist group (1943–48) and prime minister of Israel (1977–84). He and SADAT were awarded the Nobel Peace Prize in 1978, after Egypt and Israel signed a peace treaty.

**Behan, Brendan** (1923–64) Irish dramatist and poet. He was an Irish Republican Army supporter from an early age, and two of his works are directly based on his imprisonment for IRA activity, the play *The Quare Fellow* (1954) and the memoir *Borstal Boy* (1958).

**Behrens, Peter** (1868–1940) German architect. A self-taught architect, his industrial buildings, e.g. the AEG turbine factory (1909) in Berlin, were among the first 20th-century industrial structures to have artistic merit claimed for them. He was a major influence on GROPIUS and LE CORBUSIER.

**Beiderbecke, [Leon] Bix** (1903–31) American jazz cornetist, pianist and composer, who is regarded as one of the few white jazz musicians to have had any significant influence on the development of jazz. He died at 28 of alcoholism.

**Bell, Alexander Graham** (1847–1922) Scottish-born American inventor and scientist. He emigrated to the US in 1871, where he became a professor of vocal physiology in Boston. After several experiments, he succeeded in producing a device for transmitting the voice in 1875, and patented the telephone the following year. He founded the Bell Telephone Company in 1877, and patented the gramophone in 1887.

**Bellini, Giovanni** (*c*.1430–1516) Italian painter. The most prominent of a family of noted artists, including his father **Jacopo** (*c*.1400–*c*.1470) and his brother **Gentile** (*c*.1429–*c*.1507), his classically inspired works include several *Madonnas*. His pupils included TITIAN and GIORGIONE.

**Belloc, [Joseph] Hilaire [Pierre]** (1870–1953) French-born English poet, essayist, historian and Liberal MP. Noted in his own day for his prolific output of all kinds of books, and for his robust Roman Catholicism, anti-imperialism and bucolic nationalism, Belloc is now chiefly remembered as a writer of children's verse, e.g. *The Bad Child's Book of Beasts* (1896).

**Bellow, Saul** (1915– ) Canadian-born American novelist, widely regarded as one of the greatest living writers for his humane yet ironic portrayal of the individual's struggle for identity in the modern world. His novels include *Dangling Man* (1944) and *More Die of Heartbreak* (1987). He was awarded the Nobel prize for literature in 1976.

**Ben Bella, [Mohammed] Ahmed** (1916– ) Algerian statesman. One of the leading figures of his country's independence movement in the late 1940s and 1950s, he was imprisoned twice by the French

31

and became prime minister of Algeria in 1962 shortly after independence. He was deposed in 1965 following a military coup, and was imprisoned until 1980.

**Benes, Eduard** (1884–1948) Czech statesman. One of the founders of Czechoslovakia, with MASARYK, he was minister of foreign affairs (1919–35), prime minister (1921–22) and president (1935–38, 1945–48). He lived in London during the Nazi occupation of his country. A liberal, he resigned from office when the communists took power in Czechoslovakia in 1948.

**Benét, Stephen Vincent** (1898–1943) American poet and short-story writer. His work focuses on people and incidents central to American history and folklore, e.g. his long narrative poem on the Civil War, *John Brown's Body* (1928).

**Ben-Gurion, David** [David Gruen] (1886–1973) Polish-born Israeli statesman. He settled in Palestine in 1906, where he became active in the socialist wing of the Zionist movement. He was the first prime minister of Israel (1948–53) and was prime minister again, 1955–63.

**Benn, Tony** [Anthony Neil Wedgwood Benn, formerly Viscount Stansgate] (1925– ) British politician. Since the late 1970s he has been regarded as one of the leading figures of the radical left in the Labour Party and in British politics generally. He has held several government posts in the past, e.g. minister of technology (1966–70).

**Bennett, [Enoch] Arnold** (1867–1931) English novelist, dramatist and essayist. His novels, which are centred on industrial life in the Staffordshire Potteries, include *The Old Wives' Tale* (1908) and the

Clayhanger trilogy, *Clayhanger* (1910), *Hilda Lessways* (1911) and *These Twain* (1916).

**Bennett, Richard Rodney** (1936– ) English composer and pianist. His works include symphonies, concertos and the opera, *All the King's Men* (1969). He has also written music for films, e.g. *Murder on the Orient Express* (1974).

**Bentham, Jeremy** (1748–1832) English philosopher. Famous for his proposition that the prime aim of political and philosophical inquiry should be the "greatest happiness of the greatest number," expounded in his *Introduction to the Principles of Morals and Legislation* (1789). He bequeathed his body to the University of London (which he founded), where it can be viewed.

**Bentine, Michael** *see* **Milligan, Spike.**

**Bentley, Edmund Clerihew** (1875–1956) English journalist, noted for his invention of the "clerihew," a short comic form of verse consisting of two irregular lines, and for his classic detective novel, *Trent's Last Case* (1913).

**Berberian, Cathy** *see* **Berio, Luciano.**

**Berdyaev, Nikolai Alexandrovich** (1874–1948) Russian philosopher. He was exiled from the USSR in the early 1920s, and spent the rest of his life developing a religious philosophy based on man's free will to choose between good and evil. His books include *The Meaning of History* (1936) and *The Destiny of Man* (1937).

**Berenson, Bernard** (1865–1959) Lithuanian-born American art critic. Berenson became an arbiter of taste for rich collectors in the course of his long career, particularly on Renaissance art. His best-known work is *Italian Painters of the Renaissance*

(1952), but many of his judgments are now regarded as having been seriously compromised by his financial interests.

**Berg, Alban** (1885–1935) Austrian composer. He studied under SCHOENBERG, and adopted his teacher's atonal twelve-tone technique. His works include songs, chamber works and the operas *Wozzeck* (1921) and *Lulu* (1935).

**Bergman, Ingmar** (1918– ) Swedish film and stage director. His films are claustrophobic psychological studies focusing on themes such as man's relations with God and the Devil and highly charged family tensions. The films, which include *The Seventh Seal* (1956), *Wild Strawberries* (1957) and *Cries and Whispers* (1972), have been very influential on many other directors.

**Bergman, Ingrid** (1915–82) Swedish actress. She was regarded as one of the most talented and beautiful actresses of her generation. Her films include several classics, e.g. *Casablanca* (1942) and *Gaslight* (1944).

**Bergson, Henri Louis** (1859–1941) French philosopher. His writings expound his theory of a "vital spirit" moving in the world, bridging the apparent chasm between metaphysics and hard science. His works include *Time and Free Will* (1889) and *Creative Evolution* (1907). He was awarded the Nobel prize for literature in 1927.

**Beria, Lavrenti Pavlovich** (1899–1953) Georgian-born Soviet politician. He rose to power in the 1930s under STALIN, and became head of the secret police (1938–53). He was one of the most feared men in the USSR by the time of his death, which was arranged by his rivals for the succession after

Stalin's death, who had him tried for treason and executed.

**Berio, Luciano** (1925– ) Italian composer. His works, which are based on a system of serialism and often feature electronic components, include *Homage to Joyce* (1958, a tribute to James JOYCE) and *Circles* (1960). From 1950–66 he was married to the American soprano **Cathy Berberian** (1928–83), for whom many of his works were written.

**Berkeley, Busby** [William Busby Enos] (1895–1976) American film director, noted especially for his elaborate, often surreal, dance choreography in such musicals as *42nd Street* (1933) and *The Gang's All Here* (1942).

**Berkeley, Sir Lennox [Randal Francis]** (1903–89) English composer. His early compositions are tonal in construction, but he drifted towards serialism in the 1960s. His works include operas, symphonies, film scores and song cycles, such as *Songs of the Half-Light* (1964).

**Berlin, Irving** [Israel Baline] (1888–1989) Russian-born American songwriter. He began his career as a street singer, and eventually wrote around a thousand songs, many of which achieved world-wide popularity, e.g. "Alexander's Ragtime Band," "God Bless America," and "White Christmas." His songs featured in many highly successful shows, e.g. *Annie Get Your Gun* (1946) and in several film musicals, e.g. *Top Hat* (1935) and *Easter Parade* (1948).

**Berlin, Sir Isaiah** (1909– ) Latvian-born British philosopher and historian. His works focus on the history of ideas, with particular reference to historical determinism, which he regards as discredited. His works include *Karl Marx* (1939), *The Hedge hog and the Fox* (1953, a study of TOLSTOY's deter minism) and *Vico and Herder* (1976).

**Berlioz, Hector** (1803–69) French composer. Re garded as a founder of modern orchestral tech niques, his works include the *Fantastic Symphony* (1830), the cantata *The Damnation of Faust* (1846) and the operas *The Trojans* (1856–59) and *Beatric and Benedict* (1860–62).

**Bernal, J[ohn] D[esmond]** (1901–71) British phys icist. Bernal's most important work was in the field of the structure of complex molecules, in which h used X-ray crystallography. He was a member of th Communist Party from 1923, and one of MOUNTBAT TEN's personal advisers during World War II.

**Bernstein, Leonard** (1918–90) American compose and conductor. He was musical director of the New York Philharmonic (1958–70), and a tireles popularizer of classical music. His works includ *Kaddish Symphony* (1963), chamber and chora music, and several very popular musicals, e.g. *Wes Side Story* (1957).

**Berryman, John** (1914–72) American poet an critic. His works include the verse monologue *Hom age to Mistress Bradstreet* (1956), *Berryman's Son nets* (1967), and *Delusions, etc.* (1972). He wa depressive and an alcoholic, and killed himself b drowning.

**Bertolucci, Bernardo** (1940– ) Italian film direc tor. His films include the sexually explicit *Las Tango in Paris* (1972, starring BRANDO and butter *1900* (1976), a historical epic on the rise and deat of Italian fascism, and *Tragedy of a Ridiculou Man* (1982).

**Best, Charles Herbert** *see* **Banting Sir Frederick**.

**Best, George** (1946– ) Northern Irish soccer player. He signed for Matt BUSBY's Manchester United team while still at school, and soon came to be regarded as one of the world's finest and most entertaining wingers. His playing career slowly folded in a haze of alcohol abuse and general dissipation.

**Bethe, Hans Albrecht** (1906– ) German-born American physicist. Persecuted in Germany for being a Jew, Bethe settled in the US in the mid–1930s, where he became established as a leading theorist in physics. During World War II, he helped develop the atom bomb as director of the theoretical physics division at Los Alamos. He was awarded the 1967 Nobel prize for physics for his work on solar and stellar energy.

**Betjeman, Sir John** (1906–84) English poet and essayist. His deceptively simple poems, which feature a dislike for the cruder excesses of modern commercialism and nostalgia for a quieter, nobler England, were very popular with critics and public alike. His *Collected Poems* were first published in 1958. He also wrote widely on architecture, e.g. *Ghastly Good Taste* (1933), and raised public consciousness about the worth of Victorian architecture. He was appointed poet laureate in 1972.

**Bevan, Aneurin** (1897–1960) Welsh statesman. He was Labour MP for Ebbw Vale for 30 years (1929–60), and was regarded as one of the main spokespeople for the radical socialist opposition during World War II. As minister of health (1945–51) during the postwar ATTLEE administration, he oversaw the formation of the welfare state (*see*

BEVERIDGE). He resigned from the government i
1951 in protest at the reinstatement of charges fo
medical treatment.

**Beveridge, William Henry** [1st Baron Beveridge
(1879–1963) Indian-born English economist. Hi
"Beveridge Report," the *Report on Social Insuranc
and Allied Services* (1942), became the basis for th
welfare state introduced by ATTLEE's postwar ad
ministration.

**Bevin, Ernest** (1881–1951) English trade unionis
and statesman. He helped found the Transport an
General Workers Union (1922) and was minister e
labour (1940–45) in the coalition war governmen
and Labour's foreign secretary (1945–51).

**Bhutto, Zulfikar Ali** (1928–79) Pakistani states
man. He was the first civilian president of Pakista
(1971–73), then prime minister (1973–77). He wa
deposed in a coup and executed, despite worldwid
appeals for clemency. His daughter, **Benazi
Bhutto** (1953– ), became prime minister of Pak
stan in 1988, but was defeated in elections in 199(
She was the first prime minister to give birth to
child while in office.

**Biko, Steve** [Bantu Stephen Biko] (1947–77) Sout
African black radical leader. Biko helped found th
Black People's Convention in order to build conf
dence ("black consciousness") in South Africa
blacks that they could defeat apartheid. His deat
in police custody while awaiting trial was unive
sally regarded as murder, and was widely cor
demned throughout the world.

**Birtwhistle, Sir Harrison** (1934– ) English con
poser. Birtwhistle is regarded, with Maxwell DAVIE
and others, as a leading postwar avant-garde con

poser. His works include the operas *Punch and Judy* (1967) and *Gawain and the Green Knight* (1991).

**Bismarck, Prince Otto von** (1815–98) German statesman. He became prime minister of Prussia (1862–90) and defeated first Austria during the "Seven Weeks' War" (1866) and then France (1870–71). He became the first chancellor of united Germany and was dubbed the "Iron Chancellor".

**Blackett, Patrick Maynard Stuart, Baron** (1897–1974) English physicist. He was awarded the 1948 Nobel prize for physics for his work on cosmic rays and rock magnetism. He discovered the positron in 1933.

**Blake, William** (1757–1827) English poet and artist. He trained as an engraver and for much of his life scraped a precarious living as a book and magazine illustrator. He produced several slim, beautifully coloured books, e.g. *Songs of Innocence* (1789) and *Songs of Experience* (1794) and equally beautiful and innovative watercolours. His main poetic and artistic themes were innocence crippled by cynical experience, and the imprisonment of visionary experience by cynical materialism. He is regarded as one of the greatest English Romantic poets.

**Blériot, Louis** (1872–1936) French aviator and aeronautical engineer. A pioneer in aircraft design, he made the first flight across the English Channel in one of his monoplanes in 1909.

**Bliss, Sir Arthur [Edward Drummond]** (1891–1975) English composer. His works include the choral symphony *Morning Heroes* (1930), music for ballets, e.g. *Miracle in the Gorbals* (1944), and the film score for KORDA's *Things to Come* (1934). He was Master of the Queen's Music (1953–75).

**Bloch, Ernest** (1880–1959) Swiss-born American composer. Bloch was strongly influenced by the Jewish musical tradition in both liturgies and folk music. His works include the symphonies *Israel* (1916) and *America* (1926).

**Blok, Aleksandr Aleksandrovich** (1880–1921) Russian poet. By the time of the Bolshevik Revolution in 1917, which he welcomed, Blok was widely recognized within Russia as one of the country's leading Symbolist poets with a passionate vision of Russia as a great creative force ready to shock the world. "The Twelve" (1918), in which Christ marches at the head of a band of Red Guards, is his best-known poem.

**Blum, Léon** (1872–1950) French statesman. Blum was the first socialist and Jewish prime minister of France (1936–37, 1938, 1946–47). His socialist and humanist beliefs are summarized in his *À l'échelle humaine* (1945), which was written during his imprisonment by the Nazis (1943–45).

**Blunt, Anthony [Frederick]** (1907–83) English art historian. He was one of the most influential art historians of his day, knighted in 1956, and was appointed Surveyor of the Queen's Pictures in 1945, a post he held until 1972. He was stripped of his knighthood in 1979, following the public revelation that he had been a Soviet spy.

**Blyton, Enid [Mary]** (1897–1968) English children's writer. The most famous character in her more than 400 books for young children is Noddy, whose escapades in Toyland with Big Ears, etc., have delighted millions of children. She also wrote adventure stories for older children, featuring heroes such as the "Famous Five." Her work has been much criticized by educationalists as irredeemably politically incorrect and middle-class.

**Boas, Franz** (1858–1942) German-born American anthropologist. His emphasis on linguistic structure and scientific methodology, and respect for individual societies and cultures, e.g. in his much admired studies of North American Indian societies, has been very influential on anthropology. His works include *Race, Language and Culture* (1940).

**Boccioni, Umberto** (1882–1916) Italian painter and sculptor. He became the leading futurist artist of the early 20th century, and one of the movement's principal theorists. Only four of his sculptures survive.

**Bogarde, Sir Dirk** [Derek Jules Gaspard Ulric Niven van den Bogaerde] (1920– ) English actor and author. Films he has starred in include LOSEY's *The Servant* (1963) and VISCONTI's *The Damned* (1969) and *Death in Venice* (1970). He has also written three highly acclaimed volumes of autobiography, *A Postilion Struck by Lightning* (1977), *Snakes and Ladders* (1978) and *An Orderly Man* (1983), and two best-selling novels, *A Gentle Occupation* (1980) and *Voices in the Garden* (1981).

**Bogart, Humphrey [De Forest]** (1899–1957) American actor. Bogart's screen persona (not unlike his true personality) was that of the cynical tough guy with a heart of gold. His films include *Casablanca* (1942) and HAWKS' *To Have and Have Not* (1945) and *The Big Sleep* (1946), the latter two also starring his (fourth) wife **Lauren Bacall** [Betty Joan Perske] (1924– ).

**Bohr, Niels [Henrik David]** (1885–1962) Danish physicist. His greatest achievement was to apply quantum theory to explain the stability of the nuclear model of the atom. He was awarded the 1922 Nobel prize for physics.

**Bokassa, Jean Bedel** (1921– ) president of the Central African Republic (1972–76), who changed his country's name to the Central African Empire and became its self-proclaimed emperor, Bokassa I (1976–79). After his deposition in 1979, his country reverted to its former name.

**Boleyn, Anne** *see* **Elizabeth I; Henry VIII**.

**Bolivar, Simon** (1783–1830) Venezeulan-born revolutionary. Of aristocratic lineage, he fled Venezuela in 1811, returning in 1813 at the head of an army. He eventually overthrew Spanish rule in Venezuela, Ecuador, Colombia and Peru, becoming dubbed "The Liberator" by his admirers in the process. He tried to establish a confederation under his dictatorship against a strong swell of separatist movements in Venezuela and Colombia. Upper Peru was renamed Bolivia in his honour.

**Böll, Heinrich Theodor** (1917–85) German novelist and short-story writer. His works, which are usually critical of the endemic militarism of postwar German society, include the novels *Group Portrait with Lady* (1971) and *The Lost Honour of Katherina Blum* (1974), the latter work being a brave and harrowing account of the excesses of the German gutter press.

**Bolt, Robert [Oxton]** (1924– ) English dramatist and screenwriter. His best-known play is *A Man for All Seasons* (1960, filmed 1967), based on the martyrdom of Sir Thomas More, which won Bolt an

Oscar. His screenplays include LEAN's *Lawrence of Arabia* (1962) and *Dr Zhivago* (1965).

**Bond, Edward** (1934– ) English dramatist and screenwriter. His plays include notoriously violent scenes, e.g. the stoning of a baby in its pram in *Saved* (1965), his justification for the violence being that it is needed for an accurate portrayal of capitalist society. (The furore over *Saved* resulted in the abolition of stage censorship in the UK.) He has also written librettos for opera, e.g. HENZE's *We Come to the River* (1976) and screenplays, e.g. ANTONIONI's *Blow-Up* (1967).

**Bonhoeffer, Dietrich** (1906–45) German Lutheran pastor and theologian. Influenced in his theology by BARTH, he was active in the anti-Nazi Resistance during World War II, was imprisoned in 1943 and hanged by the Gestapo in 1945. His posthumously published *Letters and Papers from Prison* (1955) are among the key spiritual writings of the 20th century.

**Bonnard, Pierre** (1867–1947) French painter and lithographer. Bonnard's work is notable for being intensely colourful, especially in his interior work.

**Booth, William** (1829–1912) English religious leader. Of humble origin, he became a Methodist in the 1840s. Horrified by the poverty and squalor of the English working class, and by such evils as prostitution and child labour, he established a Christian mission in London's East End in the 1860s and founded the Salvation Army in 1878.

**Borel, Emile** (1871–1956) French mathematician and politician. Borel's work in probability theory was highly innovative, resulting in the solution of problems previously intractable. He was a Socialist deputy (1924–36) and joined the French Resistance during World War II.

**Borg, Bjorn** (1956– ) Swedish tennis player. He won five consecutive Wimbledon championship titles (1976–80) and remains one of the most respected tennis players in the world, notably for his great skill, modesty and criticism of ridiculously high prize money.

**Borges, Jorge Luis** (1899–1986) Argentinian short-story writer, poet and critic. Borges is regarded as one of the greatest South American writers, with a remarkable gift for creating short fictions with a beguiling metaphysical content. Collections of his stories include *Fictions* (1944, characteristically described as "games with infinity") and *The Aleph and Other Stories* (1971).

**Borgia, Cesare** (1476–1507) Italian soldier and politician. The son of **Rodrigo Borgia** (1431–1503), he became a cardinal in 1493 after his father became pope, as Alexander VI, in 1492. He attempted to bring Italian affairs under his control, in a never-ceasing atmosphere of intrigue, war and assassination, and was the model for MACHIAVELLI's *Prince*. His sister **Lucrezia** (1480–1519) was a noted patron of the arts and also acquired a reputation for conspiracy.

**Born, Max** (1882–1970) German nuclear physicist. He left Nazi Germany (1933) and became professor of natural philosophy at Edinburgh University (1936–63). With the German physicist **Walther Bothe** (1891–1957), he shared the Nobel prize for physics for his research into the statistical interpretation of quantum physics.

**Bosch, Hieronymous** [Jerome van Aeken *or* Aken]

(*c.*1450–1516) Dutch painter, known for his fantastic and often grotesque allegorical paintings, e.g. *The Garden of Earthly Delights*, which use imagery drawn from folk tales and religious symbolism. His work was collected by Philip II of Spain, and much of it is in the Prado Museum, Madrid. He influenced BRUEGHEL, and surrealists such as DALI claimed him as a precursor.

**Bose, Sir Jagadis Chandra** (1858–1937) Indian physicist and plant physiologist. His research into the response of animal and plant tissue to varied stimuli was particularly innovative. He also invented the crescograph, a device that automatically records plant movements.

**Bose, Subhas Chandra** (1897–1945) Indian nationalist leader. He was president of the Indian National Congress (1938–39) and, in collaboration with the Japanese during World War II, organized the Indian National Army to combat British rule in India.

**Boswell, James** *see* **Johnson, Samuel**.

**Botha, Louis** (1862–1919) South African general and statesman. As general of the Transvaal army, he led the Boer forces against the British during the Boer War. He supported the Allies during World War I, and became first prime minister of South Africa (1910–19).

**Botha, P[ieter] W[illem]** (1916– ) South African politician. He was prime minister (1978–84) and introduced limited reforms of apartheid.

**Botham, Ian** (1955– ) English cricketer. A talented all-rounder, he captained England (1980–81) and scored 5,057 runs in Test matches (including 14 centuries).

**Bothe, Walther** *see* **Born, Max**.

**Bothwell, Earl of** *see* **Mary, Queen of Scots**.

**Botticelli, Sandro** (1444–1510) Florentine painter, best known for such graceful and serene works as *The Birth of Venus* (1482–84) and the *Mystic Nativity* (1500). His work had a revival in the late 19th century through RUSKIN's influence.

**Boughton, Rutland** *see* **Macleod, Fiona**.

**Boulanger, Nadia [Juliette]** (1887–1979) French music teacher, composer and conductor. She was the first woman to conduct a symphony orchestra in London (for the Royal Philharmonic in 1937) and was a highly influential teacher of composition. Her pupils included COPLAND and MILHAUD.

**Boulez, Pierre** (1925– ) French composer and conductor. A follower of SCHOENBERG, he developed a composition style based on total serialism and electronic instruments. He was director of the New York Philharmonic (1971–77).

**Boult, Sir Adrian [Cedric]** (1889–1983) English conductor. He was leader of the BBC Symphony Orchestra (1931–50) and the London Philharmonic Orchestra (1950–57). He published an autobiography, *My Own Trumpet* (1973).

**Bowen, Elizabeth** [Dorothea Cole] (1899–1973) Anglo-Irish novelist and short-story writer. Her novels, e.g. *The Hotel* (1927) and *The Heat of the Day* (1949), are studies of upper middle-class heroines trapped in complex and unhappy relationships. Other works include the posthumously published *Collected Stories* (1980).

**Boycott, Geoffrey** (1940– ) English cricketer. He is regarded as one of England's greatest modern batsmen. He captained Yorkshire (1970–78) and played for England (1964–74, 1977–81), but his erratic and often highly controversial behaviour, e.g. in touring South Africa in 1982, prevented him becoming England's captain.

**Boyle, Robert** (1627–91) Irish scientist. His *Sceptical Chymist* (1661) revolutionized the study of matter, and he later formulated "Boyle's Law," which states that gas pressure will vary inversely with its volume, if the pressure remains constant.

**Bradman, [Sir] Don[ald George]** (1908– ) Australian cricketer. A brilliant batsman, he scored 117 centuries during the 1930s and 1940s. He was Australian captain (1936–48). *See also* FRY, C.B.

**Bragg, Melvyn** (1939– ) English novelist and broadcaster. His novels, frequently set in his native Cumberland, include *The Hired Man* (1969) and *A Place in England* (1970). He is best known as a television presenter of arts programmes.

**Brahms, Johannes** (1833–97) German composer. He regarded himself as firmly in the Classical (as opposed to Romantic) tradition. His works include the great choral *German Requiem* (1869), four symphonies and chamber music.

**Branagh, Kenneth** (1961– ) Irish-born British actor and director. He founded the Renaissance Theatre Company in 1986. His film production of *Henry V* (1990), in which he starred and also directed, was hailed by many critics as comparable with OLIVIER's. He has appeared regularly with his wife, the actress **Emma Thompson** (1959– ), most notably in his film version of Shakespeare's *Much Ado About Nothing* (1993).

**Brancusi, Constantin** (1876–1957) Romanian sculptor (he became a French citizen just before his death). His sculptures, e.g. *Sleeping Muse* (1909) pioneered abstraction in sculpture.

**Brando, Marlon** (1924– ) American actor. His screen performances in *The Men* (1950) and *On the Waterfront* (1954) were highly praised, the latter earning him an Oscar. He also won an Oscar for his role as the Mafia don in COPPOLA's *The Godfather* (1971), which, however, he refused to accept in protest at the oppression of Indians in the US. Other films in which he starred include BERTOLUCCI's *Last Tango in Paris* (1972) and Coppola's *Apocalypse Now* (1979).

**Brandt, Bill** (1904–83) German-born British photographer. He became one of the best-known photojournalists of the 1930s for his compassionate images of the bleak lives of the poor in urban slums and mining communities.

**Brandt, Willy** [Herbert Ernst Karl Frahm] (1913–92) German statesman. He was active in the German Resistance during World War II and became mayor of Berlin (1957–66) and chancellor of West Germany (1969–74). He was awarded the Nobel Peace Prize in 1971.

**Braque, Georges** (1882–1963) French painter. The term "Cubism" (*see* PICASSO) was coined in 1909 to describe his works. He also pioneered the use of collage in modern painting.

**Brassai** [Gyula Halesz] (1899–1984) Hungarian-born French photographer and painter, whose photographs of Parisian low-life and Bohemian society were highly praised in the 1930s. His books include *Paris by Night* (1933) and *Conversations with Picasso* (1964).

**Brattain, Walter** *see* **Shockley, William Bradford.**

**Braudel, Fernand** (1902–85) French historian. His

best-known work, *The Mediterranean and the Mediterranean World* (1949), which focused on socioeconomic trends and the changing relationship between man and the environment rather than on politics or military events, has been very influential on historical studies.

**Bream, Julian [Alexander]** (1933– ) English guitarist and lutenist, who is recognized as one of the finest modern classical guitar players. Several composers, e.g. BRITTEN, have written works for him.

**Brecht, Bertolt** (1898–1956) German dramatist and poet. A Marxist, he devised what he called an "epic" form of theatre, drawing from traditions such as music hall and popular ballads and using "alienation" devices, in order to illustrate that capitalism is evil and communism good. The plays include *Mother Courage* (1941) and *The Caucasian Chalk Circle* (1955).

**Brendel, Alfred** (1931– ) Czech-born Austrian pianist who lives in England and has become one of the world's leading concert pianists.

**Bresson, Robert** (1907– ) French film director. His films, which include *The Trial of Joan of Arc* (1962) and *The Devil, Probably* (1977), are intellectual and complex explorations of religious faith from a Roman Catholic point of view.

**Breton, André** (1896–1966) French poet, essayist and critic. He became a surrealist in the early 1920s. His works include the novel *Nadja* (1928) and *Poems* (1948).

**Breughel** *see* **Brueghel**.

**Brezhnev, Leonid Ilyich** (1906–82) Soviet statesman. He helped organize KHRUSHCHEV's downfall in

1964, and became general secretary of the Communist Party (1977–82) and Soviet president (1977–
82). The period of his rule is now described as the
"period of stagnation" in the USSR.

**Brian, [William] Havergal** (1876–1972) English
composer, frequently described as "post-Romantic."
His more than 30 works include the huge *Gothic
Symphony* (1919–27) and five operas.

**Bridge, Frank** (1879–1941) English composer and
conductor. He is best known for his chamber music,
a few orchestral pieces, and for having been BRIT-
TEN's teacher.

**Bridges, Robert [Seymour]** (1844–1930) English
poet and critic. His works include *The Testament of
Beauty* (1929). He was appointed poet laureate in
1913. Once highly regarded, the critical reputation
of his work declined rapidly in the 1930s.

**Brittain, Vera** *see* **Williams, Shirley**.

**Britten, [Edward] Benjamin** [1st Baron Britten]
(1913–76) English composer and pianist. A pupil of
Frank BRIDGE, his works include the operas *Peter
Grimes* (1945) and *A Midsummer Night's Dream*
(1960), chamber music, orchestral works and song
cycles. His works are noted for their romantic
lyricism, and a prominent theme is the clash between innocence and evil, as in the opera *Billy
Budd* (1951). Many of his vocal works were written
for his long-term companion, the tenor Peter
PEARS. He was created a peer in 1976.

**Brontë, Anne** (1820–49), **Charlotte** (1816–55) and
**Emily** (1818–48) English novelists and poets. The
daughters of an Irish curate in Yorkshire, they
published a book of verse in 1846. Charlotte's *Jane
Eyre*, based on her experiences as a teacher and

governess, was published in 1847, and Anne's *Agnes Grey* and Emily's *Wuthering Heights* followed in 1848. Anne's *Tenant of Wildfell Hall* was published in 1848, in which year Emily died of consumption. Charlotte wrote two more novels: *Shirley* (1849) and *Villette* (1853).

**Brook, Peter [Stephen Paul]** (1925– ) English stage and film director based in Paris. He is regarded as one of the finest experimental directors of the modern era, with productions such as his *Mahabharata* (1988), a nine-hour version of the Indian epic with a multi-cultural cast. His short book, *The Empty Space* (1969), explains his theory of stagecraft.

**Brooke, Rupert [Chawner]** (1887–1915) English poet. He died of cholera while on his way to action in World War I. His war poems, included in *Collected Poems* (1918), were very popular with the public (for a while) with their idealized vision of the nobility of war.

**Brooks, Mel** [Melvin Kaminsky] (1926– ) American comedian, film writer and director. He started his career as a scriptwriter for TV before turning to making fast-moving, irreverent comedy films, e.g. *Blazing Saddles* (1974), *Silent Movie* (1978, with Marcel MARCEAU in the only speaking role), and *Life Stinks* (1991). His wife is the actress **Anne Bancroft** [Anna Maria Italiano] (1931– ) who is noted for her serious acting, e.g. in *The Miracle Worker* (1962), for which she won an Oscar, and *The Graduate* (1968), but who also appears to effect in her husband's films, e.g. *To Be or Not To Be* (1983).

**Brown, George MacKay** *see* **Davies, Sir Peter Maxwell**.

**Brown, Herbert Charles** *see* **Wittig, Georg.**

**Browning, Robert** (1812–89) English poet. Renowned for his innovative experiments in form and narrative skill, his works include *The Ring and the Book* (1869) and *Men and Women* (1855). His wife, **Elizabeth Barrett Browning** (1806–61), whom he married in 1846, was also a major poet. Her works include *Sonnets from the Portuguese* (1850) and *Aurora Leigh* (1857). Their marriage was an idyllic one.

**Brubeck, Dave** (1920– ) American jazz composer and pianist. He studied musical composition with SCHOENBERG and MILHAUD, forming his "Dave Brubeck Quartet" in 1951. "Take Five" is his best-known composition.

**Bruce, Lenny** (1925–66) American comedian. Bruce's satirical and often scabrous humour made him a cult hero of the 1950s. He was imprisoned for obscenity in 1961, and banned from re-entering Britain in 1963. Drug addiction contributed to his death.

**Bruegel** *or* **Brueghel, Pieter (the Elder)** (*c*.1525–69) Flemish painter. His paintings of peasant scenes and allegories show the influence of Bosch. He is best known, however, for his magnificent landscape painting *The Hunters in the Snow* (1565), a key work in the tradition of landscape painting. His sons **Jan Brueghel** (1568–1625) and **Pieter Brueghel (the Younger)** (*c*.1564–1637) were also painters.

**Brunel, Isambard Kingdom** (1806–59) English engineer. He designed the steamships *Great Western* (1838), *Great Britain* (1845) and *Great Eastern* (1858), and in the late 1820s planned and designed the Clifton Suspension Bridge, which was not completed until after his death (1864). His father, **Sir Marc Isambard Brunel** (1769–1849), was a French engineer who fled the Revolution and worked in the USA before settling in England, where he designed a tunnel under the Thames in London.

**Brunelleschi, Filippo** (1377–1446) Italian sculptor and architect. His best-known works are the dome of the cathedral in Florence and the painted wooden *Crucifix* (1412) in the church of Santa Maria Novella.

**Buber, Martin** (1878–1965) Austrian-born Jewish theologian and existentialist philosopher. A Hasidic scholar, his philosophy, which centres on the relationship between man and God, has had a large impact on both Jewish and Christian theology. His works include *I and Thou* (1923) and *Eclipse of God* (1952).

**Buchan, John** [1st Baron Tweedsmuir] (1875–1940) Scottish novelist, statesman and historian. He wrote several best-selling adventure novels, e.g. *The Thirty-Nine Steps* (1915), *Greenmantle* (1916) and *Mr Standfast* (1919). He was created a peer in 1935, and was appointed governor-general of Canada (1935–40).

**Buchman, Frank [Nathan Daniel]** (1878–1961) American evangelist. He founded the Oxford Group and the longer-lived Moral Rearmament, which were intended to provide ideological alternatives to both capitalism and communism. His works include *The Oxford Group and its Work of Moral Rearmament* (1954) and *America Needs an Ideology* (1957).

**Bukharin, Nikolai Ivanovich** (1888–1938) Soviet

statesman. One of the early Bolshevik leaders, he was appointed chairman of the Cominterm in 1926, and supported STALIN against TROTSKY. He was denounced as a Trotskyite in the late 1930s and executed after a show trial. (The character of Rubashov in KOESTLER's novel *Darkness at Noon* is based on Bukharin.)

**Bulganin, Nikolai Aleksandrovich** (1895–1975) Soviet statesman. He became chairman of the council of ministers (1955–58), and drifted into obscurity in the late 1950s following his participation in a failed power play against KHRUSHCHEV.

**Bunche, Ralph Johnson** (1904–71) American diplomat and UN official. The grandson of a slave, he became assistant professor of political science at Howard University, Washington, and became the first black to be awarded the Nobel Peace Prize, in 1950, for his attempt at reconciling Israel and the Arab states (1948–49).

**Bunyan, John** (1628–88) English author. A tinker's son, he became a travelling nonconformist preacher, for which he was imprisoned in 1660 for 12 years. He wrote several devotional works, the most famous being the remarkable allegory *Pilgrim's Progress* (1678–84), which became one of the most influential and popular books of all time.

**Buñuel, Luis** (1900–1983) Spanish-born film director (settled in Mexico from 1947). His first films, *Un chien andalou* (1928) and *L'Age d'or* (1930), were made in collaboration with Salvador DALI, and are regarded as masterpieces of Surrealist cinema. Later films include *The Discreet Charm of the Bourgeoisie* (1972) and *That Obscure Object of Desire* (1977).

**Burgess, Anthony** [John Anthony Burgess Wilson] (1917– ) English novelist, critic and composer. His novels include the still highly controversial futuristic fantasy of juvenile crime *A Clockwork Orange* (1962, filmed by KUBRICK in 1971), *Inside Mr Enderby* (1963), *Earthly Powers* (1980), and the autobiographical *Little Wilson and Big God* (1987).

**Burgess, Guy** (1911–63) English diplomat and spy. Recruited by Soviet Intelligence in the 1930s, he worked for MI5 during World War II and served with PHILBY at the British Embassy in Washington DC after the war. With his fellow agent, **Donald Maclean** (1913–83), he fled to the USSR in 1951.

**Burke, Edmund** (1729–97) Anglo-Irish statesman and philosopher. He entered parliament for the Whig party in 1765 (via a rotten borough) and soon achieved high status for his lively defence of constitutionalism and attacks on government abuses, with his attacks on government policy establishing him as the dominant political thinker of the day. Much admired by even his political opponents, his works include *A Philosophical Inquiry into the Origin of our Ideas of the Sublime and Beautiful* (1756) and a cornerstone of conservative political thought, *Reflections on the Revolution in France* (1790).

**Burnet, Sir Frank Macfarlane** *see* **Medawar, Sir Peter Brian**.

**Burns, Robert** (1759–96) Scottish poet. The son of a farmer, he sprang to fame with his first book of poems, *Poems, Chiefly in the Scottish Dialect* (1786). Renowned as both a lyric poet and a satirist, most of his best poems were written in his twenties, e.g. "The Cotter's Saturday Night" and "To a Mouse". He had many love affairs, and married Jean Armour in 1788. He was said to have "loved mankind in general, and women in particular".

**Burra, Edward [John]** (1905–76) English painter. His favourite medium was watercolour, and his style ranged from early naturalism with strong social comment to, in later years, a dark, private symbolism.

**Burroughs, William S[eward]** (1914– ) American novelist. A friend of GINSBERG and KEROUAC, Burroughs became a heroin addict in the 1940s. His luridly obscene fiction, e.g. *Junkie* (1953) and *The Naked Lunch* (1959), features the squalid, nightmarish underworld of drug addiction.

**Burton, Richard** [Richard Jenkins] (1925–84) Welsh actor. Burton was regarded by his peers and the critics as one of the most talented actors of his generation. Films he starred in include *The Spy Who Came in from the Cold* (1965) and *Who's Afraid of Virginia Woolf?* (1966), the latter also starring Elizabeth TAYLOR, to whom he was married twice (1964–70, 1975–76).

**Busby, Sir Matt[hew]** (1909– ) Scottish footballer and manager of Manchester United (1946–69). Many members of his highly regarded team of 1958 died in a plane crash at Munich. His rebuilt team of "Busby Babes" became the first English team to win the European Cup (1968).

**Bush, Alan Dudley** (1900– ) English composer and pianist. A Marxist, his works include the operas *Wat Tyler* (1950) and *Joe Hill* (1970), several symphonies and choral works. He published his collected essays, *In My Eighth Decade*, in 1980.

**Bush, George [Herbert Walker]** (1924– ) American Republican politician and 41st president of the

US. The son of a wealthy senator, he served in the US Navy (1942–45) during World War II, becoming its youngest pilot, and flew in the Pacific theatre of operations. He became US ambassador to the UN (1971–73), special envoy to China (1974–75) and CIA director (1976). He campaigned against REAGAN for the Republican nomination in 1980 (describing Reagan's monetarist policy as "voodoo economics"), then served under him as vice-president (1980–88). His reputation was damaged by the Iran-Contragate scandal of 1987, and by persistent rumours of CIA involvement in drug running, but he was elected president in 1988, easily defeating the Democrat candidate, **Michael Dukakis** (1933– ), governor of Massachusetts (1974–78, 1982– ). He was defeated by CLINTON in the 1992 presidential election.

**Buthelezi, Chief Gatsha** (1928– ) South African Zulu chief and politician. He helped found the paramilitary organization Inkatha, which is pledged to creating a multiracial democracy in South Africa, but which is claimed by its ANC opponents (*see* MANDELA) to be a major cause of strife in South Africa.

**Butler, R[ichard] A[usten], [Baron]** (1902–82) English Conservative politician. As minister of education (1941–45), he introduced the important Education Act of 1944. He was also chancellor of the exchequer (1951–55), home secretary (1957–62) and foreign secretary (1963–64). He was created a life peer in 1965, and published his memoirs, *The Art of the Possible*, in 1971. His failure to win leadership of the Conservative Party, most notably in 1963 when DOUGLAS-HOME became prime minister, surprised many commentators.

# Byron

**Byron, Lord George Gordon Noel** [6th Baron Byron of Rochdale] (1788–1824) English poet. In his own words, "I awoke one morning and found myself famous", after the publication of his *Childe Harold's Pilgrimage* in 1812, a poetic epic that introduced the Byronic hero to the world: a lonely, handsome, melancholy, flawed man, fatally attractive to women and remarkably similar to his creator. His half-sister had a child generally assumed to be his, and he fled England (and his wife and child) for good in 1816 (staying with SHELLEY for a while), dying of fever in Greece while preparing to fight for Greek independence. His works include many superb lyrics and the long satirical poem *Don Juan* (1819–21).

# C

**Cadbury, George** (1839–1922) English business-man, social reformer and philanthropist. With his brother **Michael Cadbury** (1835–99) he estab-lished the village of Bournville, near Birmingham, for the Cadbury work force. The village came to be seen as a model by many modern architects and town planners.

**Caesar, [Gaius] Julius** (100–44 BC) Roman soldier and historian. He negotiated and formed the "First Triumvirate" with the wealthy politician **Marcus Licinius Crassus** (*c*.114–53 BC) and the statesman and general **Pompey** [Gnaeus Pompeius Magnus] (106–48 BC) in 60, after which he fought in Gaul for nine years, subduing the province in 50, driving the Germans back across the Rhine and invading Brit-ain in 55 and 54. Appointed dictator by the Senate in 49, he defeated Pompey at Pharsalia in 48, and was himself assassinated by a largely aristocratic group of conspirators. His surviving works are the *Commentaries* on the Gallic and Civil wars.

**Cage, John** (1912—92) American composer. Cage's experimental music, e.g. *Water Music* (1952), in which the pianist is required, among other things, to blow whistles under water, and *4 minutes 33 seconds* (1952), in which the performers remain silent and do not touch their instruments, has been derided and admired in about equal proportions.

**Cagney, James** (1899–1986) American film actor.
Cagney's performances as gangsters, e.g. in *The
Public Enemy* (1931) and *Angels With Dirty Faces*
(1938), resulted in him becoming one of the most
imitated persons of the day ("You Dirty Rat," etc.).
He won an Oscar for his performance in the musical, *Yankee Doodle Dandy* (1942).

**Caligula** [Gaius Caesar Augustus Germanicus] (12–
41) Roman emperor (37–41). Nicknamed "Caligula"
("Little Boots") as a child, he ruled moderately at
first but became tyrannical, profligate and murderous, possibly as a result of mental illness. Assassinated by a conspiracy, he was succeeded by his
uncle, CLAUDIUS, one of only two relatives whom he
did not kill (the other was his sister Drusilla, with
whom he may have had an incestuous affair).

**Callaghan, [Leonard] James** [Baron Callaghan of
Cardiff] (1912– ) British Labour statesman who
succeeded Harold WILSON as prime minister (1976–
79). After the passing of a vote of no confidence in
his premiership in the House of Commons, he called
a general election, which Labour lost, and he was
replaced as Labour leader by Michael FOOT. He
published his memoirs, *Time and Chance*, in 1987.

**Callas, Maria** (1923–77) American-born Greek operatic soprano, renowned both for her marvellous
voice and acting skills, which made her one of the
most revered opera singers of the century.

**Calvin, John** (1509–64) French religious reformer.
An ardent reformer, he had to flee from France to
Switzerland, where, in 1536, he published his *Insti-
tutes of the Christian Religion*, a summation of his
Protestant faith and the founding text of Calvinism.
He settled in Geneva, where he established the first

Presbyterian government. After LUTHER, Calvin became the most influential of all the Reformed teachers.

**Calvino, Italo** (1923–85) Cuban-Italian novelist, essayist and critic. His early novels, e.g. *The Path of the Nest of Spiders* (1947), belonged in the Italian realist tradition, while his later, highly complex explorations of fantasy and myth, e.g. *Invisible Cities* (1972), have been compared to Latin American "magic realism."

**Campbell, Sir Malcolm** (1885–1948) English racing driver. He was awarded a knighthood in 1931, the year he set a land speed record of 246 mph, for his achievements in setting land and water speed records. His son, **Donald [Malcolm] Campbell,** (1921–67) held the English water speed record, at a speed of 276 mph, but he died on Lake Coniston while trying to break it.

**Campbell, Mrs Patrick** [Beatrice Stella Tanner] (1865–1940) English actress. She was regarded as one of the finest (and wittiest) actresses of her generation. Among the many roles she created was that of Eliza Doolittle in her friend SHAW's play *Pygmalion*.

**Campbell, [Ignatius] Roy [ston Dunnachie]** (1901–57) South African poet. His verse includes several fine lyric poems and scathing satires on the literary establishment. Collections include *The Flaming Terrapin* (1924), *Adamastor* (1930) and *Flowering Rifle* (1939), the last causing great controversy with its praise of FRANCO (Campbell fought on Franco's side in the Spanish Civil War).

**Campbell-Bannerman, Sir Henry** (1836–1908) British statesman. He was Liberal prime minister (1905–08), and played a major part in healing the rifts within the Liberal party following the Boer War.

**Camus, Albert** (1913–60) French novelist, essayist and dramatist, who is regarded as one of the leading Existentialist writers. His works, which portray man as helpless in the face of an uncaring, absurd universe, include the novels *The Outsider* (1942) and *The Plague* (1947). He joined the French Resistance during the war, and was awarded the Nobel prize for literature in 1957. His study of 20th-century totalitarianism, *The Rebel* (1953), led to a break with SARTRE, who disapproved of the work's condemnation of Communist tyranny.

**Canaletto, Giovanni Antonio Canal** (1697–1768) Venetian painter. An unrivalled architectural painter with an excellent sense of composition, he was commercially successful due to the efforts of Joseph Smith, an English businessman who marketed his works for the tourist trade, and whose collection became part of the Royal Collection. His works include *The Stonemason's Yard* (c.1730) and many views of Venice.

**Capa, Robert** [André Friedmann] (1913–54) Hungarian photographer who became one of the best-known war photographers of the century, with his often dramatic pictures of battlefield incidents, particularly from the Spanish Civil War and the D-Day landings. He was killed by a mine in Vietnam.

**Capek, Karel** (1890–1938) Czech dramatist, novelist and essayist. His best-known play is *R.U.R.* (1920), which introduced the word "robot." With his brother **Josef Capek** (1887–1945), he wrote *The Insect Play* (1921), a prophetic satire on totalitarianism.

**Capone, Al[phonse]** (1899–1947) Italian-born American gangster. Capone, nicknamed "Scarface," established his powerful criminal empire of specializing in bootleg liquor, prostitution and extortion in Chicago during the prohibition era. He was eventually jailed for tax evasion and died of syphilis.

**Capote, Truman** (1924–84) American novelist and socialite. His works include light romances such as *Breakfast at Tiffany's* (1958), and the bleak "faction" documentary novel *In Cold Blood* (1966), a chilling study of murder.

**Capra, Frank** (1897–1991) Italian-born American film director. Capra's comedies, e.g. *Mr Deeds Goes to Town* (1936) and *Mr Smith Goes to Washington* (1939), usually portray an ultimately successful struggle by a decent, everyday American against the flawed political system, and were enormously popular in the 1930s. His other films include *Arsenic and Old Lace* (1944) and *It's a Wonderful Life* (1946). His autobiography, *The Name Above the Title*, was published in 1971.

**Caravaggio, Michelangelo Merisi da** (1573–1610) Italian painter. Noted for his bold, expressive use of chiaroscuro, his religious paintings caused controversy by using everyday people as the models for his Biblical characters. His works include *The Life of St Matthew* and *The Beheading of John the Baptist*. He fled Rome in 1606 after killing a man, and died of malaria.

**Cardin, Pierre** (1923– ) French couturier, who became one of the world's leading fashion designers, and designed clothes for both men and women.

**Carlyle, Thomas** (1795–1881) Scottish historian

and essayist. His early works included translations of GOETHE and *Sartor Resartus* (1833–34), a philosophical reflection on the appearance of things. Hailed by many of his contemporaries as a great social critic and philosopher, he subsequently attacked the materialism of the Industrial Age in such works as *Chartism* (1839) and *Past and Present* (1843).

**Carnap, Rudolf** (1891–1970) German-born American philosopher. Regarded as a leading logical positivist, he attempted to develop a formal language that would remove ambiguity from scientific language. His works include *Introduction to Semantics* (1942) and *The Logical Foundations of Probability* (1950).

**Carné, Marcel** (1909– ) French film director. His films include *Les Visiteurs du soir* (1942) and the highly acclaimed theatrical epic *Les Enfants du paradis* (1944), both of which were filmed during the German occupation of France.

**Carnegie, Andrew** (1835–1919) Scottish-born American industrialist and philanthropist. Carnegie believed that personal wealth should be used for the benefit of all members of society, a view expounded in his *Gospel of Wealth* (1899). His benefactions, notably in the provision of public libraries, have been estimated at around £70 million.

**Carreras, José [Maria]** (1946– ) Spanish lyric tenor. He was born and made his debut in Barcelona, and despite serious illness (he had leukaemia, which responded to treatment) he gained a reputation as one of the finest tenors (with DOMINGO and PAVAROTTI) of the late 20th century.

**Carroll, Lewis** (pseud. of Charles Lutwidge Dodgson) (1832–98) English author, clergyman and mathematician. His most famous works are the two remarkable "Alice" books, *Alice's Adventures in Wonderland* (1865) and *Through the Looking Glass* (1872).

**Carter, Elliot [Cook]** (1908– ) American composer. His works include orchestral pieces, string quartets and cello and piano sonatas. They are regarded as intellectually rigorous and complex, using a wide variety of styles and techniques, from Renaissance music to serialism. His collected writings were published in 1977.

**Carter, Jimmy [James Earl Carter]** (1924– ) American Democratic statesman and 39th president of the US (1977–81). A successful peanut farmer, he became governor of Georgia (1974–77) and defeated Gerald FORD in the 1976 presidential campaign. His administration made significant attempts at linking overseas trade with human rights issues. He was defeated by REAGAN in the 1980 presidential election.

**Cartier-Bresson, Henri** (1908– ) French photographer and film director. His documentary black-and-white photographs were taken on the principle of what he called "decisive moments" of real-life action, without prior composition or preparation, and the full uncropped frame was sacrosanct. His books include *Europeans* (1955) and *Cartier-Bresson's France* (1971). In films, he was closely associated with RENOIR.

**Cartland, Dame [Mary] Barbara Hamilton** (1901– ) English romantic novelist. Over 500 million copies of her upwards of 500 published novels have been sold, making her one of the best-selling authors of all time.

**Caruso, Enrico** (1873–1921) Italian tenor. Born in Naples, he sang most of the great tenor roles in Italian and French opera and is regarded as perhaps the most outstanding operatic tenor of all time. Caruso was also one of the first indisputably great singers to make recordings.

**Carver, Raymond** (1939–88) American poet and short-story writer. His works include *What We Talk About When We Talk About Love* (1981) and *Fire: Essays, Poems, Stories* (1984).

**Cary, [Arthur] Joyce [Lunel]** (1888–1957) Irish-born English novelist. His novels include *Mister Johnson* (1939) and *The Horse's Mouth* (1944).

**Casals, Pablo** (1876–1973) Spanish cellist, pianist and composer. Casals' recordings of Bach's cello suites and of the Dvorak cello concerto are particularly highly regarded.

**Casement, Sir Roger [David]** (1864–1916) British consular official and Irish nationalist. While working for the British colonial service, he exposed the repression of the people of the Congo by its Belgian rulers in 1904. Knighted in 1911, he adopted Irish nationalism shortly afterwards and was hanged for treason in London. The contents of his so-called "Black Diaries," revealing his hidden homosexual life, were leaked by the British government to discredit him.

**Castro [Ruz], Fidel** (1927– ) Cuban statesman, prime minister (1959–76) and president (1976– ). He overthrew BATISTA in a coup in 1959, and shortly afterwards announced his conversion to communism. Castro survived several attempts at his overthrow by exiled opponents and the CIA, e.g. the abortive Bay of Pigs invasion in 1961, but survived by becoming a client of the USSR. Soviet subsidies began to decrease in the late 1980s, and Castro's rule became more beleaguered.

**Catherine II** ("the Great") (1729–96) Russian empress. She became Empress on the death of her husband, Peter III (1728–62), who was murdered by one of her lovers. She consolidated and expanded the Russian Empire by conquest, taking a large portion of Poland in 1772, and scandalized European opinion by having a supposedly legion number of paramours and heading an intrigue-raddled court, while patronizing Enlightenment philosophers such as VOLTAIRE and DIDEROT.

**Catherine of Aragon** *see* **Henry VIII**.

**Catherine of Valois** *see* **Henry V**.

**Cavell, Edith [Louisa]** (1865–1915) English nurse. She treated both German and Allied casualties in Brussels during the German occupation, and was executed by firing squad by the German authorities, who accused her of helping British soldiers to escape to Holland. Her execution was condemned worldwide.

**Caxton, William** (c.1422–91) English printer and translator. His *Recuyell of the Historyes of Troy* (printed at Bruges, 1475), is the first book to be printed in English. Soon afterwards, he began printing books at Westminster in London, with *Dictes or Sayengis of the Philosophres* (1477) being the first dated book to be printed in England.

**Ceausescu, Nicolae** (1918–89) Romanian dictator. He was secretary general of the Romanian Communist Party from 1969, and president of Romania from 1974. His pursuit of a foreign policy independent of the the Soviet Union resulted in his brutal

67

domestic policies being ignored or played down by
Western states. His regime was overthrown by
dissident Communists in 1989, and he and his wife
were executed by firing squad.

**Cecil, William**, 1st Baron Burghley, (1520–98) Eng
lish statesman. He successively served, with great
skill and dexterity, both HENRY VIII and MARY
(converting to Roman Catholicism under Mary)
and was one of the prime architects of ELIZABETH I's
succession. He became Secretary of State (1558-
72) and Lord High Treasurer (1572–98).

**Céline, Louis-Ferdinand [Destouches]** (1894-
1961) French novelist and physician. His master
piece is *Journey to the End of the Night* (1932), a
dark and pessimistic autobiographical account of
the author's wartime and African experiences. A
vicious anti-semite, Céline fled to Denmark after
the Liberation of France, where he was imprisoned
for several years.

**Cervantes [Saavedra], Miguel de** (1547–1616)
Spanish novelist, dramatist and poet. He enlisted in
an Italian force fighting against the Turks, was
wounded, and became the prisoner of an Algerian
corsair (1575–79). When freed, he became a full
time writer. His satirical masterpiece, one of the
world's great novels, *Don Quixote de la Mancha* (in
two parts, 1605 and 1615), describes the picaresque
adventures of the simple-minded gentleman Don
Quixote, his worldly squire, Sancho Panza, and his
horse Rosinante.

**Cézanne, Paul** (1839–1906) French painter. His
early work, influenced by DELACROIX, was Romantic
in style, but from the late 1860s he began painting
from nature. His works include landscapes and still

lifes, and he was very influential on succeeding generations of painters, notably the Cubists.

**Chabrol, Claude** (1930– ) French film director. He was one of the New Wave directors of the 1950s, and was strongly influenced by HITCHCOCK. His films include *Les Bonnes Femmes* (1960) and *Le Boucher* (1970).

**Chadwick, Sir James** (1891–1974) English physicist. He discovered the neutron in 1932, and was awarded the Nobel prize for physics in 1935.

**Chagall, Marc** (1887–1985) Russian-born French painter. Chagall's vividly coloured work features unusual compositions "of images that obsess me," often drawing on symbolism from Russian and Jewish folk art. Highlights of his work include 12 striking stained glass windows in a Jerusalem synagogue (1961) and decorations for the ceiling of the Paris Opera House (1964)

**Chain, Sir Ernst Boris** (1906–79) German-born British biochemist. He prepared penicillin for clinical use, and with FLOREY and Alexander FLEMING, shared the 1945 Nobel prize for physiology or medicine.

**Chaliapin, Fyodor Ivanovich** (1873–1938) Russian operatic bass singer. His performances, particularly in Russian operas such as MUSSORGSKY's *Boris Godunov*, were widely regarded as definitive.

**Chamberlain, [Arthur] Neville** (1869–1940) British statesman and Conservative prime minister (1937–40). He pursued a policy of appeasement towards the totalitarian powers of Germany, Italy and Japan in the 1930s (Winston CHURCHILL being a notable opponent of the policy), which was abandoned when Germany invaded Poland in 1939. He died shortly after illness forced his resignation from Churchill's war cabinet.

**Chandler, Raymond [Thornton]** (1888–1959) American novelist and screenwriter. His detective novels, e.g. *Farewell, My Lovely* (1940), have been widely praised for their witty, street-wise dialogue.

**Chanel, Coco [Gabrielle Bonheur Chanel]** (1883–1971) French couturière and perfumer. She originated the thin, low-waist style for women's dresses exemplified by the "little black dress," and launched a famous range of perfumes, notably Chanel No 5.

**Chaplin, Sir Charlie [Spencer]** (1889–1977) English comedian and film director. He made his film debut in *Making a Living* (1914), in which he introduced the down-at-heel, gentleman-tramp character with a beguiling shuffle, bowler hat and cane that became perhaps the most famous comic creation of the century. Other films include *City Lights* (1931) and *The Great Dictator* (1940). He was knighted in 1975.

**Charlemagne** (*c.*742–814) king of the Franks and Holy Roman emperor. In 771 he became sole ruler of the Frankish kingdom and spent the early part of his reign conquering (and converting to Christianity) the neighbouring Lombard and Saxon kingdoms. He led an army into Spain to fight the Moors in 778, an expedition (he withdrew the same year) that inspired a host of poems and tales of knightly exploits. In 800 he was crowned emperor after crushing a Roman revolt against the Pope. He subsequently settled his court at Aix-la-Chapelle, patronized men of learning, and was on good terms with several Muslim rulers in the east.

**Charles, Prince** [Charles Philip Arthur George

Prince of Wales] (1948– ) heir apparent to ELIZABETH II of the United Kingdom. His interest in alternative methods of healing and cultivation and concern for social harmony resulted in a campaign of vilification against him in Britain's tabloid press. Other notable concerns of his are town planning and vernacular architecture. He married **Lady Diana Spencer** (1961– ) in 1981, and they had two children. They separated in 1992.

**Charles I** (1600–49) king of England, Scotland and Ireland. The son of JAMES VI AND I, he succeeded to the throne in 1625, inheriting a kingdom increasingly riven by political and religious differences. Continuous strife with parliament lasted throughout the 1630s, and in 1639, the Scots rebelled against attempts by the much-hated Archbishop (of Canterbury) Laud (1573–1645) to impose episcopalianism on them. Civil war between Charles and the Long Parliament broke out in 1642, and the royalist forces were defeated at the Battle of Naseby in 1642. He was executed by beheading in 1649.

**Charles II** (1630–85) king of England, Scotland and Ireland. The son of CHARLES I, he succeeded to the throne following the Restoration in 1660. A crypto-Roman Catholic (in which faith he died), he was renowned for his ready wit and patronage of scholars and poets. Tolerant by nature in most things, he had no legitimate offspring but many illegitimate children.

**Charles V** (1500–58) Holy Roman emperor. The founder of the Hapsburg dynasty, he became king of Spain (as Charles I) in 1516, and was crowned Holy Roman emperor at Aachen in 1520. His reign was marked by much political and religious turbulence as Martin LUTHER's Reformation spread and Francis I of France sought to capture territory. He abdicated in 1556.

**Charles VI** *see* **Maria Theresa**.

**Charles, Ray [Ray Charles Robinson]** (1930– ) American singer, pianist and songwriter. Originally a blues/jazz singer, Charles became one of the most popular singers in the world with songs such as "I Can't Stop Loving You."

**Charlton, Bobby** [Robert Charlton] (1937– ) English footballer. One of the "BUSBY Babes" and a survivor of the 1958 Munich air crash, Charlton became one of the most popular forwards of the 1960s, and was capped over 100 times for England. His brother **Jack Charlton** [John Charlton] (1935– ), also an England international, became a national hero in Ireland following his steering of Ireland to the 1990 World Cup finals.

**Charnley, Sir John** (1911–82) English orthopaedic surgeon. He invented an artificial hip joint, and developed methods of hip replacement surgery. He was knighted in 1977.

**Charpentier, Gustave** (1860–1956) French composer. His best-known work is the opera *Louise* (1900), for which he wrote both libretto and music, and which made him a rich man.

**Chatham, William Pitt, 1st Earl of** *see* **Pitt, William**.

**Chaucer, Geoffrey** (*c*.1340–70) English poet. Pensioned in 1367 by King **Edward III** (1312–77), in whose service he was, he subsequently held various posts in the King's gift. His great narrative skill is displayed at its finest in *The Canterbury Tales* (*c*.1387), a masterpiece of wit and humour set in a

London inn, in which various pilgrims (travelling to Canterbury) from all social strata tell each other stories.

**Chekhov, Anton Pavlovich** (1860–1904) Russian dramatist and short-story writer. A qualified physician, he became one of the greatest writers of his age, his works being notable for their wit and dramatic power. The plays include *Uncle Vanya* (1900), *Three Sisters* (1901) and *The Cherry Orchard* (1904). His short stories include several masterpieces, e.g. "My Life" (1896), "The Lady with the Little Dog" (1899).

**Cherenkov, Pavel Alekseievich** (1904– ) Soviet physicist. In the mid–1930s, he discovered the form of radiation known as Cherenkhov radiation, and was awarded the 1958 Nobel prize for physics.

**Chernenko, Konstantin Ustinovich** (1911–85) Soviet statesman. He was a protégé of BREZHNEV, who apparently wished Chernenko to succeed him as president. When ANDROPOV died, Chernenko was appointed his successor as general secretary of the Soviet Communist Party, and was elected state president in 1984. His death was seemingly brought on by emphysema.

**Cherwell, Frederick Alexander Lindemann, Viscount** (1886–1957) German-born British physicist. He was scientific adviser to CHURCHILL during World War II.

**Cheshire, Sir [Geoffrey] Leonard** (1917–92) English philanthropist. He was awarded the Victoria Cross for completing over 100 bombing raids over Germany in World War II, and was the official British observer of the atomic bomb blast at Nagasaki. He subsequently founded the Cheshire Foundation Homes for the incurably sick. He married the philanthropist **Sue Ryder** [Baroness Ryder of Warsaw and Cavendish] (1923– ) in 1959. He was knighted in 1991.

**Chesterton, G[ilbert] K[eith]** (1874–1936) English essayist, novelist, critic and poet. With his friend BELLOC, he became known as a gifted disputant for what they saw as the glory of old, rural Roman Catholic England. Chesterton's novels and "Father Brown" detective stories, e.g. *The Innocence of Father Brown* (1911), and the weirdly anarchic *The Man Who Was Thursday* (1908), are highly entertaining.

**Chevalier, Maurice** (1888–1972) French singer and film actor, who came to be seen as the archetypal romantic Frenchman throughout the world. His films include *Love Me Tonight* (1932) and *Gigi* (1958).

**Chiang Ch'ing** *or* **Jiang Qing** (1913– ) Chinese Communist politician and actress. She married MAO as his third wife in 1939 and became the main force behind the savage purges of the Cultural Revolution in the late 1960s. After Mao's death, her power gradually waned, and she was arrested in 1976 with three confederates (the "Gang of Four") and charged with murder and subversion. She was sentenced to death in 1981, the sentence later being suspended.

**Chiang Kai-shek** *or* **Jiang Jie Shi** (1887–1975) Chinese general and statesman. He was president of China (1928–38, 1943–49), then, after losing the civil war to MAO TSE-TUNG and his Communist forces, fled the mainland to establish the nationalist republic of China in Formosa, of which he became president (1950–57).

**Chichester, Sir Francis [Charles]** (1901–72) English yachtsman and aviator. He made the first solo round-the-world voyage in his yacht *Gipsy Moth IV* (1966–67).

**Chirico, Giorgio de** (1888–1978) Greek-born Italian painter. His dreamlike pictures of open, deserted squares were hailed by the Surrealists as precursors of their own works in the early 1920s.

**Chomsky, Noam [Avram]** (1928– ) American linguist, philosopher and political activist. His innovative work in linguistics is based on the principles that humans are born with an innate capacity for learning grammatical structures and that the linguist must distinguish between "deep" and "surface" grammar. Chomsky has also been a prominent spokesman for left-wing causes, and was a notable opponent of the Vietnam war.

**Chopin, Frédéric [François]** (1810–49) Polish pianist and composer. An infant prodigy, he published his first work at 15 and became the toast of the Paris salons in the 1830s. He toured widely giving performances and became very popular for his emotional, melancholy music, often regarded as quintessentially Polish in mood. His works include over 50 mazurkas, two piano concertos and 25 preludes.

**Chou En-Lai** *or* **Zhou En Lai** (1898–1976) Chinese Communist statesman. He was foreign minister (1949–58) and prime minister (1949–76) of the People's Republic of China. He advocated detente with the US in the early 1970s, and was regarded as a moderate during the chaos of China's Cultural Revolution in the late 1960s.

**Christian X** *or* **Kristian X** (1870–1947) king of

Denmark (1912–47) and of Iceland (1918–44). During the Nazi occupation of Denmark (1940–45), he resolutely opposed their demands for anti-semitic legislation, and was imprisoned in 1943 for speaking out against Nazi ideology.

**Christie, [Dame] Agatha [Clarissa Mary]** (1890–1976) English detective story writer, whose ingeniously plotted novels, e.g. *The Murder of Roger Ackroyd* (1926), established her as one of the greatest writers in the genre.

**Churchill, Sir Winston [Leonard Spencer]** (1874–1965) British Conservative statesman and writer. After an adventurous early life, which included action at the battle of Omdurman (1898) and escape from imprisonment by Louis BOTHA during the Boer War, he held several posts under both Liberal and Conservative governments. He opposed CHAMBERLAIN's policy of appeasement in the 1930s, and served as prime minister (1940–45) in World War II. His works include *The Second World War* (1948–54) and *History of the English-Speaking Peoples* (1956–58). He was awarded the Nobel prize for literature (1953).

**Cicero, Marcus Tullius** (106–43 BC) Roman consul and orator. One of the greatest public speakers and debaters of his day, he exposed the Catiline conspiracy of 63 (directed by Catilina and others against the state) but was subsequently driven into exile. Recalled to Rome in 57, he vacillated between Pompey and CAESAR, and after the latter's death denounced Mark ANTONY in his *Philippics*, following which he was assassinated by Antony's supporters.

**Clair, René** [René Lucien Chomette] (1898–1981) French film director. His films include the comedies *An Italian Straw Hat* (1928, made in France),

*The Ghost Goes West* (1936, made in the UK) and *It Happened Tomorrow* (1944, made in the USA).

**Clapton, Eric** (1945– ) English guitarist, who is widely recognized as one of the most influential rock guitarists. He played with the Yardbirds (1963 –65) and the "super group" Cream (1966–68).

**Clark, Jim** [James Clark] (1936–68) Scottish racing driver. He was World Champion in 1963 and 1965, and was killed in a crash in West Germany. He won 25 Grand Prix events, and is one of the greatest racing drivers of all time.

**Claudel, Paul [Louis Charles Marie]** (1868–1955) French poet, dramatist and diplomat. A devout Roman Catholic, his work includes the plays *Tidings Brought to Mary* (1912) and *The Satin Slipper* (1921). Volumes of poetry include *Five Great Odes* (1910).

**Claudius** (10 BC–54) Roman emperor. A retiring, scholarly man, he was proclaimed Emperor by the palace guards (who found him in hiding) following the death of CALIGULA. He extended the Empire and initiated the conquest of Britain in 43, and extended Roman citizenship. His fourth wife (and niece) Agrippina, was the mother of his successor NERO.

**Cleese, John [Marwood]** (1939– ) English comedy actor and writer. He was one of the main talents involved in the anarchic and highly influential TV comedy series, *Monty Python's Flying Circus* (1969–74). His own subsequent TV comedy series, *Fawlty Towers* (1975, 1980), was also highly successful, as was the film *A Fish Called Wanda* (1988).

**Clemenceau, Georges [Eugène Benjamin]** (1841–1929) French statesman. A leading left-winger, he was an outspoken critic of the French government's war policy in the early days of World War I. He became prime minister (1906–19, 1917–20). His forceful negotiation of the Versailles Treaty (1919) is believed by many to have led directly to World War II.

**Cleopatra** *see* **Antony, Mark**.

**Clinton, Bill** [William Jefferson Davis Clinton] (1946– ) American politician. A lawyer, he became Arkansas attorney general (1974–79), then state governor (1979–81, 1983– ). He was elected the 42nd President of the United States, for the Democratic Party, after defeating George BUSH in the 1992 presidential election. *See also* GORE.

**Clive, Kitty** *see* **Garrick, David**.

**Clive, Sir Robert** [1st Baron Clive of Plassey] (1725–74) English general and administrator in India. He worked for the East India Company (1743–46) before joining the Indian army. Sent to punish the Nawab of Bengal and Calcutta following the death of 146 British civilians in the "Black Hole of Calcutta" (1756), he defeated the Nawab at Plassey (1757) thus strengthening British control, which he sustained against the French as governor of Bengal (1757–60). He was an MP in England (1760–62) and governor of Bengal (1764–67). An opium addict, he committed suicide.

**Cockcroft, Sir John Douglas** (1897–1967) English nuclear physicist. With the Irish physicist **Sir Ernest [Thomas Sinton] Walton** (1903– ), he produced the first laboratory splitting of an atomic nucleus, for which they shared the 1951 Nobel prize for physics.

**Cockerell, Sir Christopher Sydney** (1910– ) English engineer. He invented the hovercraft, the prototype of which first crossed the English Channel in 1959.

**Cocteau, Jean** (1889–1963) French film director, novelist, dramatist, poet and critic. His experimental, surreal films include *The Blood of a Poet* (1932) and *Beauty and the Beast* (1945). The best known of his novels is *Les Enfants Terribles* (1929).

**Coleridge, Samuel Taylor** (1772–1834) English poet and critic. With his friend WORDSWORTH he published *Lyrical Ballads* in 1798, a significant landmark in English poetry in its rejection of a special "poetic" language and advocacy of clear, everyday language (Coleridge's main contribution was "The Rime of the Ancient Mariner"). A radical in his youth, Coleridge became a staunch conservative in politics, for which he was attacked by BYRON. His literary criticism is sometimes obscure in meaning but has many insights into the creative process.

**Colette, [Sidonie Gabrielle]** (1873–1954) French novelist. Her novels, e.g. *Chéri* (1920) and *Gigi* (1944), are often erotic and display a strong sympathy for animals and the natural world.

**Collingwood, R[obin] G[eorge]** (1889–1943) English philosopher, historian and archaeologist. He was an authority on the archaeology of Roman Britain, and developed a historicist approach to philosophy in his *An Essay on Metaphysics* (1940). Other works include *The Principles of Art* (1937) and *Autobiography* (1939).

**Collins, Michael** (1890–1922) Irish Republican politician. A prominent Sinn Fein leader, he negotiated the 1922 peace treaty with Britain that resulted in the establishment of the Irish free State. He was killed in an ambush during the civil war that followed in the Free State.

**Collins, Michael** (1930– ) *see* **Armstrong, Neil**.

**Coltrane, John [William]** (1926–67) American jazz saxophonist. A virtuoso on the tenor and soprano saxophones, he became one of the most influential and popular jazz musicians of his generation.

**Columba, St** (521–97) Irish missionary. Accused of being involved in one of Ulster's many bloody civil conflicts, as penance he fled to the Western Isles of Scotland to proselytise for Christianity. He established a monastic settlement on the island of Iona, from where he and his followers converted many Picts and established churches.

**Columbus, Christopher** (1451–1506) Italian navigator. Under the patronage of Spain, he led an expedition in three ships to seek a western route to the far east. He discovered the New World in 1492, making landfall in the West Indies. He made two subsequent voyages to the New World, in 1493 and 1498, reaching South America on the third trip.

**Compton, Arthur Holly** (1892–1962) American physicist. He was a prominent researcher into X-rays, gamma rays and nuclear energy, and discovered the Compton effect. He was awarded the 1927 Nobel prize for physics.

**Compton, Denis [Charles Scott]** (1918– ) English cricketer, who played for Middlesex and England (1937–57). Regarded as one of the best all-rounders ever in cricket (and a self-taught batter), he broke two records in 1947 by scoring 3,816 runs and 18 centuries in one season.

**Compton-Burnett, Dame Ivy** (1892–1969) English novelist. Her novels—mostly in dialogue and featuring the traumas of upper-middle-class Edwardian family life—include *Brothers and Sisters* (1925) and *Manservant and Maidservant* (1947).

**Connery, Sean [Thomas]** (1930– ) Scottish film actor. He achieved worldwide fame in his role as the Ian FLEMING character James Bond in such movies as *Doctor No* (1962) and *Goldfinger* (1964). Connery gradually became recognized as one of the finest film actors of his time, and won an Oscar for his part as a tough Irish cop in *The Untouchables* (1987).

**Connors, Jimmy** (1952– ) American tennis player. He was Wimbledon champion (1974. 1982) and US champion (1974, 1976, 1978, 1982, 1983).

**Conrad, Joseph** [Teodor Josef Konrad Korzeniowsky] (1857–1924) Polish-born English novelist (English was his third language, after Polish and French). He qualified as a master mariner in the British marine service in 1886. His novels and novellas, which often feature isolated or outcast characters in exotic settings, include *Almayer's Folly* (1895) and *Heart of Darkness* (1902).

**Constable, John** (1776–1837) English painter. Drawing inspiration from nature, he produced works such as *Cloud Studies* (1816–22) and *View on the Stour* (1819), which were initially much more influential in France than England. He became a member of the Royal Academy in 1829. His wife had died the previous year, and his mature work, e.g. *Hadleigh Castle* (1829) became more intense and dramatic.

**Constantine, Learie Nicholas, Baron** (1902–71) West Indian cricketer. Regarded as an exceptionally fine fielder, he was also an outstanding batsman and a dynamic bowler. He was created a life peer in 1969 for his services to race relations.

**Constantine I** (c.274–337) Roman Emperor. He
became the first Christian Emperor in 312, when,
before a battle, he reportedly saw a cross in the sky
inscribed "In this sign conquer". He moved the
imperial capital to Byzantium (which he renamed
Constantinople) in 330. Christianity became the
official religion of the Empire in 324.

**Cook, (Captain) James** (1728–79) English explorer.
During his first expedition to the Pacific of 1768–71
he circumnavigated New Zealand on the *Endeavour* (*see also* BANKS), and charted and claimed the
east coast of Australia for Britain. On his second
voyage (1772–75), he sailed round the northern
coast of Antarctica and discovered New Caledonia.
On his third and last voyage to the Pacific (1776–
79), he was killed by islanders in Hawaii.

**Coolidge, [John] Calvin** (1872–1933) American
Republican statesman. He became 30th president
of the US (1923–29). His election was regarded as a
stabilizing influence in American politics following
years of political scandal. His encouragement of
stock market speculation in the late 1920s may
have contributed to the ensuing economic crash.

**Cooper, Gary** [Frank James Cooper] (1901–61)
American film actor. He specialized in the tall,
silent "integrity" type. His many films include *Mr
Deeds Goes to Town* (1936), *Sergeant York* (1940)
and *High Noon* (1952), the latter two winning him
Oscars.

**Cooper, James Fenimore** (1789–1851) American
novelist. His series of five novels comprising the
"Leatherstocking" tales represent a major landmark
in American fiction, dealing as they do with the
"frontier myth" of America and the adventures of

their hero Natty Bumpo (also called Leatherstocking, Deerslayer, Hawkeye, Pathfinder).

**Copernicus, Nicolaus** (1473–1543) Polish astronomer. He became a canon in 1497, but never took holy orders. He spent several years studying and lecturing throughout Europe before settling in Prussia in 1505. His great work *De Revolutionibus*, which sets out his theory that the earth and planets revolve around the sun, was published in the last year of his life.

**Copland, Aaron** (1900–1990) American composer, pianist and conductor. His work includes the well-known ballet scores *Rodeo* (1942) and *Appalachian Spring* (1944). These and his other works, which include orchestral and chamber works and film scores, often incorporate elements and themes from traditional music such as folk songs.

**Coppola, Francis Ford** (1939– ) American film director and screenwriter. He wrote the screenplay for *Patton* (1970), and subsequently became a very successful director with films such as *The Godfather* (1972) and *Apocalypse Now* (1979).

**Corday, Charlotte** *see* **Marat, Jean Paul**.

**Corman, Roger** (1926– ) American film director and producer. Known primarily in the 1950s and 1960s as a creator of cheap B movies, e.g. *She-Gods of Shark Reef* (1958), he also fostered the careers of many prominent American directors and actors of the 1970s and 1980s, e.g. SCORSESE, Jack NICHOLSON, COPPOLA and DE NIRO. His most highly regarded film is *The Masque of the Red Death* (1964). Corman also makes occasional guest appearances in films, e.g. as the FBI Director in *The Silence of the Lambs* (1990).

**Cosgrave, W[illiam] T[homas]** (1880–1965) Irish

nationalist politician. He became first president of the Irish Free State (1922–32). His son **Liam Cosgrave** (1920– ) became Fine Gael prime minister of the Republic of Ireland (1973–77).

**Courbet, Gustave** (1819–77) French painter. Romantic in style in his youth, he developed a brand of social realism, which was as innovative as it was controversial, in such works as *The Stonebreakers* (1850) and *Burial at Ornans* (1851), which were much criticized for being "distasteful". Later works were less intense and include many landscapes and sea paintings.

**Cousteau, Jacques [Yves]** (1910– ) French oceanographer. He invented the aqualung (1943) and developed techniques of underwater cinematography that, through films such as *The Silent World* (1956) and his long-running TV series, *The Undersea World of Jacques Cousteau* (1968–76), were highly influential in raising public awareness of the world's oceans.

**Coward, Sir Noel [Pierce]** (1899–1973) English dramatist, actor and composer. His witty, sophisticated comedies, e.g. *Private Lives* (1930) and *Blithe Spirit* (1941), were regarded as mildly shocking in their day. He also wrote several amusing songs, e.g. "Mad Dogs and Englishmen." His film roles include the leading role in the patriotic film *In Which We Serve* (1942), and a highly engaging cameo role in *Our Man in Havana* (1959).

**Cowper, William** (1731–1800) English poet. Best known in his own day as an engaging satirist and nature poet, his darker religious poems, e.g. "The Castaway" (1799, published posthumously 1803), are now seen as of more lasting importance.

**Crabbe, George** (1754–1832) English poet. His bitter rural poem *The Village* (1783), which presents a disturbing picture of rural poverty, is a scathing riposte to the more idyllic portrayal of village life given by writers such as GOLDSMITH.

**Cranmer, Thomas** (1489–1556) English prelate. Appointed Archbishop of Canterbury in 1533 (while secretly married), he pronounced the annulment of the marriage of HENRY VIII to Catherine of Aragon in 1533 and was godfather to Queen ELIZABETH I. A moderate Protestant reformer, he was sentenced to die at the stake under MARY I, despite several abject retractions of his beliefs. At the stake, he retracted his retractions and held his hand in the fire saying "This hath offended!".

**Crassus** *see* **Caesar, Julius**.

**Crawford, Joan** [Lucille le Sueur] (1908–77) American film actress. She won an Oscar for her performance in *Mildred Pierce* (1945). The highlight of her later work is the macabre *What Ever Happened to Baby Jane?* (1962), starring with Bette DAVIS.

**Crick, Francis [Harry Compton]** (1916– ) English molecular biologist. With James Dewey WATSON, he discovered the structure of DNA, and was awarded the 1962 Nobel prize for physiology or medicine.

**Crippen, Hawley Harvey** (1862–1910) American doctor who poisoned his wife in London in 1910. He and his mistress, Ethel le Neve, disguised as a boy, fled to Canada, and were arrested on docking at Montreal after the ship's captain had radiotelegraphed their descriptions to Scotland Yard.

**Cripps, Sir [Richard] Stafford** (1889–1952) British Labour statesman. A leading left-winger, with a reputation for being a severe ascetic, he became chancellor of the exchequer (1947-50), and introduced a programme of high taxation and wage restraint to deal with Britain's economic problems.

**Croce, Benedetto** (1866–1952) Italian philosopher and statesman. He initially supported MUSSOLINI, but after 1925 became a leading anti-fascist and advocate of liberal policies. His major work is *Philosophy of the Spirit* (1902–17).

**Cromwell, Oliver** (1599–1658) English soldier and statesman. A Puritan country squire and MP, he was a noted critic of CHARLES I during the 1628–29 Parliament. He displayed a strong grasp of military skill during the opening year of the Civil War (1642), forming his "Ironsides" regiment the following year. He led Parliament's New Model Army to victory at Naseby (1645) and crushed Welsh and Scottish rebellions before signing Charles I's death warrant in 1649. After a murderous conquest of Ireland in 1649, his victory over a second Scottish rebellion in 1651 ended the Civil War. He was nominated "Lord Protector" of the Commonwealth in 1653, and established an authoritarian rule, dissolving parliament when it displeased him. He was buried in Westminster Abbey, his corpse being disinterred and hanged after the Restoration. He was succeeded as Protector for a short while (1658–59) by his son, **Richard Cromwell** (1626–72).

**Cromwell, Thomas** (*c*.1485–1540) English statesman. Of humble origin, he rose to power through the patronage of Cardinal WOLSEY, and became HENRY VIII's chief adviser. He fostered the passing of Reformation legislation, established the king's legal status as head of the Church in England, and oversaw the dissolution of the monasteries. After

Henry's marriage to Anne of Cleves failed (which he had encouraged), the king had him executed.

**Cronin, A[rchibald] J[oseph]** (1896–1981) Scottish novelist and physician. His novels include *The Stars Look Down* (1935) and *Shannon's Way* (1948). His works formed the basis for the hugely popular 1960s and 1990s TV series *Dr Finlay's Casebook*.

**Crosby, Bing** [Harry Lillis Crosby] (1904–77) American singer and actor. His relaxed, jazz-influenced style of singing or "crooning" made him one of the most popular and imitated singers of the century. His recording of BERLIN's "White Christmas" (1942) is often said to be the best-selling record of all time (Crosby had over 80 hits). He also made a series of highly popular "Road to..." series of comedy films with his friend Bob HOPE, e.g. *Road to Rio* (1947).

**Crossman, Richard [Howard Stafford]** (1907–74) English Labour politician. His revelatory diaries of ministerial life in Harold WILSON's 1960s cabinets were published posthumously in three volumes (1975–77), and provide valuable insight into the political life of the period.

**Cumberland, William, Duke of** *see* **George II**.

**cummings, e[dward] e[stlin]** (1894–1962) American poet, novelist and artist. His autobiographical novel *The Enormous Room* (1922) describes his wrongful imprisonment for treason, and his subsequent experimental free verse and distinctive use of typography influenced many other poets.

**Curie, Marie** (1867–1934) Polish-born French chemist. With her husband **Pierre Curie** (1859–1906), also a chemist, and the physicist **Antoine Henri Becquerel** (1852–1908), she was awarded the 1903 Nobel prize for physics for work on radioactivity, thus becoming the first woman to win a Nobel prize. She subsequently became the first person to win two Nobel prizes when her discovery of radium and polonium led to her being awarded the 1911 prize for chemistry.

**Curtin, John Joseph Ambrose** (1885–1945) Australian Labour statesman and prime minister (1941–45). He introduced several significant welfare measures, e.g. unemployment and sickness benefit.

**Cushing, Harvey Williams** (1869–1939) American neurosurgeon, who made significant contributions to neurosurgery, e.g. his identification of the adrenal gland disorder, Cushing's disease.

**Cuthbert, Saint** (c.635–687) Anglo-Saxon monk. A shepherd boy, he was inspired by a vision to become a monk and settled in the tidal island of Lindisfarne in 664, which he later left for a hermit cell. He subsequently became bishop of Hexham, then bishop of Lindisfarne, before returning to his isolated cell.

**Cuvier, Georges, Baron** (1769–1832) French anatomist. Regarded as the founder of palaeontology and of comparative anatomy, he devised a fourfold system of animal classification and made ground-breaking studies of fossils. He was ennobled in 1831 and became minster of the interior in the following year.

**Cyrano de Bergerac, Savinien** (1619–1655) French soldier, poet and dramatist. Most famous in the popular imagination for having an enormous nose and for having (reputedly) fought around a thousand duels, his works include several satires, e.g. *Comical History of the States and Empires* (1661). His life was dramatized by Edmond ROSTAND in the verse drama *Cyrano de Bergerac* (1897).

# D

**Dahl, Roald** (1916–90) English author (of Norwegian parentage) known primarily for his entertaining children's stories, e.g. *Charlie and the Chocolate Factory* (1964) and collections of brutally funny poems. Stories for adults include the collection *Kiss, Kiss* (1960) and the autobiographical *Boy* (1984).

**Daladier, Edouard** (1884–1970) French socialist statesman. He was prime minister (1933, 1934, 1938–40) and signed the Munich Pact of 1938. He denounced the Vichy government in 1943, and was then imprisoned in Germany for the duration of the war.

**Dalai Lama** [Tenzin Gyatso] (1935– ) Tibetan spiritual and temporal leader. He became the 14th Dalai Lama in 1940, and fled Tibet in 1959 following the Chinese invasion of his country in that year. He is widely respected throughout the world for his constant advocation of a peaceful solution, in line with Buddhist principles, to the brutal repression of his country by China. He was awarded the 1989 Nobel Peace Prize.

**Dale, Sir Henry Hallett** (1875–1968) English physiologist. He and **Otto Loewi** (1873–1961) were awarded the 1936 Nobel prize for physiology or medicine for their work on the chemical basis of nerve impulse transmission.

**Dali, Salvador** (1904–89) Spanish surrealist painter.
Influenced by CHIRICO and FREUD, Dali became established as the leading surrealist painter by 1931,
the year in which he painted his *The Persistence of
Memory*, which includes his limp watch faces that
remain the image most characteristic of his "dream
photographs." He made two films with BUÑUEL, and
published three volumes of autobiography, e.g.
*Diary of a Genius* (1966).

**Dallapiccola, Luigi** (1904–75) Italian composer and
pianist. Regarded as the leading Italian exponent of
twelve-tone music, his works include the opera
*Night Flight* (1937–39) and the ballet *Marsia* (1948).
Much of his work, as in his *Songs of Prison* (1938–
41), reflects his concern about political and spiritual
repression.

**Dam, [Carl Peter] Henrik** (1895–1976) Danish
biochemist. He was awarded the 1943 Nobel prize
for physiology or medicine which he shared with
the American biochemist **Edward Doisy** (1893– )
for discovering vitamin K (in 1934).

**D'Annunzio, Gabriele** (1863–1938) Italian poet,
novelist, dramatist and political adventurer. The
sensuous imagery of much of his work has been
widely admired. His novel *The Flame of Life* (1900)
created a public scandal with its thinly disguised
description of his affair with the great French
tragedian **Eleonora Duse** (1858–1924). His oratory was credited with Italy's joining the allies in
World War I. He seized the city of Fiume in 1919,
which he ruled until 1920. He became a supporter of
MUSSOLINI.

**Dante (Alighieri)** (1265-1321) Italian poet, whose
earliest work, *Vita Nuova* (1290-94), tells of his love

for "Beatrice", probably Bice Portinari, a girl whom he hardly knew but who became a symbol of purity and beauty for him. Expelled from Florence in 1309 for political reasons, he spent 20 years in wandering exile, during which he wrote his masterpiece, the *Divine Comedy*, an allegorical description of the poet's journey through Hell, Purgatory and to Paradise. His literary influence was enormous, and resulted in Tuscan becoming the language of literary Italy.

**Danton, Georges Jacques** (1759-94) French revolutionary. After the fall of the monarchy in 1792, he became minister of justice, voted for the death of King LOUIS XVI, and was one of the founders of the Committee for Public Safety. His efforts to moderate the Revolutionary Terror failed, despite his great eloquence. He and several of his followers were outmanoeuvred by ROBESPIERRE and executed.

**Darlan, Jean [Louis Xavier] François** (1881–1942) French admiral and politician who became vice-premier of Vichy France under PÉTAIN. He was assassinated by a French monarchist.

**Darnley, Lord** *see* **Mary, Queen of Scots**.

**Darrow, Clarence Seward** (1857–1938) American attorney. A strong opponent of capital punishment, he conducted many successful and highly publicized defences, notably of murderers and labour leaders, and became the US's most prominent defence counsel. His most famous case was the Tennessee trial of John T. Scopes, a schoolteacher charged with teaching Darwinism (he lost the case, but won a moral victory).

**Darwin, Charles [Robert]** (1809-82) English naturalist. The grandson of the physician and poet

**Erasmus Darwin** (1731-1802), who had published a poem on evolution in 1794, Darwin sailed as a naturalist to South America and the Pacific (1831-36), where his studies among the rich animal and plant life of the area formed the basis for his revolutionary theory of evolution by natural selection, expounded in his *The Origin of Species by Means of Natural Selection* (1859). Darwin's theory rapidly found acceptance not only amongst scientists but among society at large, helped by the forceful arguments of such supporters as the scientist T. H. HUXLEY. Darwin's other works include *The Descent of Man and Selection in Relation to Sex* (1871).

**Daumier, Honoré** (1808-79) French cartoonist, painter and sculptor. One of the most proficient satirists of all time, his caricatures of **Louis Philippe** (1773–1850), King of the French (1830–48), as Gargantua resulted in him spending six months in jail. He was also an innovative lithographer, painter and sculptor, specializing in simple, unsentimental portraits of the life of the poor.

**David, Jacques-Louis** (1748-1825) French painter. His early work was rococo in style, and he won the Prix de Rome in 1775. He became more influenced by neoclassicism, as in the *Oath of the Horatii* (1784). He was the leading artist of the French Revolution and was imprisoned after the death of ROBESPIERRE. He survived to become painter to NAPOLEON and painted *The Coronation of Napoleon* (1805-7).

**Davies, Marion** *see* **Hearst, William Randolph.**

**Davies, Sir Peter Maxwell** (1934– ) English composer. Heavily influenced by medieval music, his works include *Eight Songs for a Mad King* (1969) and the opera *Taverner* (1962–68, revised 1970). With BIRTWHISTLE, he founded the Pierrot Players (later called the Fires of London). Since 1970 he has been based in Orkney, where he frequently collaborates with the Scottish poet, novelist and short-story writer **George Mackay Brown** (1921– ).

**Davis, Bette** [Ruth Elizabeth Davis] (1908–89) American actress, whose electrifying and commanding screen presence made her one of the most highly rated film actresses. Her films include *Of Human Bondage* (1934), *Dangerous* (1935), *Jezebel* (1938), the latter two earning her Oscars, *The Little Foxes* (1941), and *All About Eve* (1950). *See also* CRAWFORD.

**Davis, Sir Colin [Rex]** (1927– ) English conductor. Noted particularly for his interpretations of BERLIOZ, he was conductor of the BBC Symphony Orchestra (1967–71).

**Davis, Miles [Dewey]** (1926–91) American jazz trumpeter, composer and bandleader. He joined the Charlie PARKER Quintet at the age of 19. He became the leading exponent of the "cool jazz" school with his subsequent groups, working with musicians such as COLTRANE.

**Davis, Nancy** *see* **Reagan, Ronald.**

**Davis, Steve** (1958– ) English snooker player. He was the world's leading snooker player for most of the 1980s, renowned for his imperturbability during televised contests.

**Davisson, Clinton Joseph** *see* **Thomson, Sir George Paget.**

**Davy, Sir Humphry** (1778-1829) English chemist. An ingenious experimenter, he discovered many new metals, e.g. sodium and potassium, and developed ground-breaking studies in electrochemistry. His lectures and public experiments at the Royal Institution in London became enormously popular, attracting large crowds. He was knighted in 1812, and invented the "Davy lamp" for miners in 1815.

**Dawes, Charles G[ates]** (1865–1951) American banker. He devised the Dawes Plan of 1924 for German reparation payments after World War I. He was US vice-president (1925–29) and was awarded the 1925 Nobel Peace Prize.

**Day, Doris** [Doris Kappelhoff] (1924– ) American film actress, famous for her light-hearted, girl-next-door image. Her films include *Calamity Jane* (1953) and *The Pajama Game* (1957).

**Day, Sir Robin** (1923– ) English broadcaster and journalist. He presented the popular television current affairs programme *Question Time* (1979–89) and was a notably incisive interviewer of politicians.

**Dayan, Moshe** (1915–81) Israeli general and statesman. He commanded the Israeli forces during the Sinai invasion (1956) and was minister of defence during the Six Day War of 1967. He played an important part in the talks leading to the Israel-Egypt peace treaty of 1979, in which year he resigned from office in protest at what he perceived as BEGIN's intransigence towards the Arabs.

**Day Lewis, Cecil** (1904–72) Irish-born English poet. In the 1930s he was regarded as part of the "Auden generation" of left-wing poets, e.g. *The Magic Mountain* (1933). He became poet laureate in 1968. He also wrote detective novels under the pseudonym "Nicholas Blake," e.g. *A Question of Proof* (1935).

**Deakin, Alfred** (1856–1919) Australian statesman.

He was prime minister (1903–4, 1905–8, 1909–10), and led the movement for Australian federation.

**Dean, Christopher** *see* **Torvill, Jayne.**

**Dean, James [Byron]** (1931–55) American film actor. Dean became a cult figure in the 1950s for his portrayal of troubled, disaffected adolescence in films such as *East of Eden* (1955) and *Rebel Without a Cause* (1955). He died in a car crash.

**Debussy, [Achille] Claude** (1862–1918) French composer. Regarded as the founder of impressionism in music and one of the strongest influences on modern music, his works include the orchestral pieces *Prélude a l'après-midi d'un faune* (1894) and *La Mer* (1905), and the opera *Pelléas et Mélisande* (1902).

**Defoe, Daniel** (1600-1731) English novelist and pamphleteer. Embroiled in many controversies, he was a skilled and prolific propagandist for whichever political faction was paying his wages at the time. His tract *The Shortest Way with the Dissenters* (1702), which satirically argued for the ruthless extirpation of all religious dissenters (Defoe was one himself) was taken at face value by the authorities and he was pilloried and imprisoned. His works include two remarkable novels, *Robinson Crusoe* (1719) and *Moll Flanders* (1722).

**De Forest, Lee** (1873–1961) American electrical engineer. He invented the triode valve in 1907, and made significant contributions to the development of sound and picture transmission.

**Degas, [Hilaire Germain] Edgar** (1834-1917) French painter and sculptor. He met Monet in the 1860s, after which he began exhibiting with the Impressionists. He is especially noted for his paintings and pastel drawings of racehorses and ballet dancers, e.g. *Ballet Rehearsal* (1874).

**de Gaulle, Charles [André Joseph Marie]** (1890–1970) French general, statesman and first president (1958–69) of the Fifth Republic. An opponent of the Vichy regime led by PÉTAIN, he fled to Britain in 1940, where he became the leader of the Free French forces. Elected president of the provisional government in 1945, he resigned in 1946 after disagreement over his executive powers (regarded by him as insufficient). He was asked to form a government in 1958, during the Algerian crisis, and was granted considerable power by the National Assembly following a referendum. He granted independence to France's colonies in Africa (1959–60), oversaw increased economic prosperity, fostered France's independent nuclear deterrent policy and strongly opposed the UK's entry into the Common Market. His party won a large majority in the election following the student riots of 1968. He resigned in 1969, after being defeated on constitutional reform, and retired to Colombey-Les-Deux-Eglises, where he died.

**De Havilland, Sir Geoffrey** (1882–1965) English aircraft designer. He designed several famous aircraft, e.g. the Tiger Moth (1930) and the plywood Mosquito (1941) and the first commercial jet airliner, the De Havilland Comet (1952).

**Deighton, Len** [Leonard Cyril] (1929– ) British thriller writer. His books include *The Ipcress File* (1962) and *Funeral in Berlin* (1965).

**de Klerk, F[rederik] W[illem]** (1936– ) South African statesman. He succeeded P. W. BOTHA as leader of the ruling National party and president (1989) and continued the policy of dismantling apartheid, in 1990 legalizing the African National Congress and organizing MANDELA's release from prison.

**Delacroix, Eugène** (1798-1863) French painter. His early work, while Romantic in subject matter, owes much to classical composition, as in *The Barque of Dante* (1822). He studied CONSTABLE's works, and visited North Africa, which inspired works such as *Women of Algiers* (1834). Other works include murals and portraits, e.g. *Chopin and George Sand* (1838).

**de la Mare, Walter [John]** (1873–1956) English poet and novelist. Much of his work was written for children, e.g. *Peacock Pie* (1913), and the loss of childhood innocence is a major theme in his work. The best of his work, e.g. the poetry collection *The Listeners* (1910) and the novel *Memoirs of a Midget* (1921), has a delicately eerie quality.

**Delaunay, Robert** (1885–1941) French painter. He founded the movement called "Orphism," which was the name given by the French poet **Guillaume Apollinaire** [Apollinaris Kostrowitzky] (1880–1918), to Delaunay's introduction of colour abstraction into his Cubist-style paintings. He influenced many other artists, notably KLEE.

**Delius, Frederick** (1862–1934) English composer. Heavily influenced by traditional folk tunes and drawing much of his inspiration from landscape, his work includes tone poems such as *Over the Hills and Far Away* (1895), the opera *A Village Romeo and Juliet* (1900–1901) and the variations for chorus and orchestra, *Appalachia* (1902). Sir Thomas BEECHAM was a notable champion of his work.

**Delvaux, Paul** (1897– ) Belgian surrealist painter.

Influenced by CHIRICO and MAGRITTE in the mid–1930s, he embarked on a series of paintings, e.g. *Phases of the Moon* (1939), depicting nude girls in dreamlike, architectural settings.

**de Mille, Cecil B[lount]** (1881–1959) American film producer and director. With GOLDWYN, he is credited with creating the mass movie industry of Hollywood. His films, e.g. *The Ten Commandments* (1923), were extravagantly produced epics that achieved enormous success throughout the world.

**Dempsey, Jack** [William Harrison Dempsey] (1895–1983) American boxer. An ex-miner who became one of the most popular boxers of his day, he was world heavyweight champion (1919–26).

**Deng Xiaoping** *or* **Teng Hsiao-p'ing** (1904– ) Chinese Communist statesman. Denounced in the Cultural Revolution of the late 1960s as a "capitalist roader," he was subsequently rehabilitated by CHOU EN-LAI in 1973. He went into hiding after his patron's death in 1976, fearing reprisals from MAO's widow, CHIANG CH'ING, then re-emerged as a powerful figure in the late 1970s. He introduced economic reforms and developed friendly relations with the West, but also sanctioned the Tiananmen Square massacre of dissident students.

**De Niro, Robert** (1943– ) American actor, who is regarded as one of the finest modern screen actors with a remarkable facility for submerging himself in a wide variety of roles. His films include *Taxi Driver* (1976), *King of Comedy* (1982), *The Godfather II* (1974) and *Raging Bull* (1980), the latter two films winning him Oscars.

**Denning, Alfred Thompson, Baron** (1899– ) English judge. Regarded as having a notable concern for individual rights, Denning was also responsible for several controversial judgments and was disinclined to rely on precedent. His books include *The Closing Chapter* (1983).

**Depardieu, Gerard** (1948– ) French actor. Established in the 1970s as a leading man in French films, his strong performances and independent character have made him popular worldwide. His many films including *Danton* (1982), *Jean de Florette* (1987), *Trop Belle Pour Toi* (1990), *Cyrano de Bergerac* (1991), and *Green Card* (1991).

**De Quincey, Thomas** (1785-1859) English essayist and critic. His *Confessions of an English Opium Eater* (1822) describes his opium addiction and poverty in the London slums, where he lived with a young prostitute. His essays, regarded as among the finest in English, include "On Murder Considered as One of the Fine Arts" and "On the Knocking on the Gate in 'Macbeth'."

**Derain, André** (1880–1954) French painter. He was influenced by PICASSO and BRAQUE, and became one of the leading Fauvist painters.

**Desai, Morarji [Ranchhodji]** (1896– ) Indian statesman. He held several ministerial posts under NEHRU, founded the Janata party in opposition to Indira GANDHI's Congress Party, which he defeated in the 1977 general election, and served as prime minister (1977–79).

**Descartes, René** (1596-1650) French philosopher and mathematician. He proposed a dualistic philosophy based on the separation of soul and body, mind and matter, and sought to establish his system on mathematics and pure reason, his most famous dictum being *"Cogito ergo sum,"* usually translated as "I think, therefore I am". He also made important contributions to the disciplines of mathematics and astronomy.

**De Sica, Vittorio** (1902–74) Italian film director and actor. His early films, e.g. *Bicycle Thieves* (1948) are regarded as among the finest Italian neo-realist films for their compassionate insight into the lives of the poor. *The Garden of the Finzi-Continis* (1971) won an Oscar for best foreign film.

**De Valera, Eamon** (1882–1975) American-born Irish statesman. He was sentenced to death by the British government for his part in the 1916 Easter Rising, but was reprieved after US intervention. He became president of Sinn Féin (1917–1926). He opposed the Anglo-Irish Treaty (1921), gave largely symbolic leadership to the anti-treaty forces during the civil war (1922–23), and was imprisoned (1923–24). He became prime minister (1932–48, 1951–54, 1957–59) and president (1959–73).

**Devine, George [Alexander Cassady]** (1910–65) English stage director and administrator. He became one of the most prominent influences on the British stage as artistic director of the English Stage Company at the Royal Court, and fostered the work of new wave dramatists such as OSBORNE and ARDEN.

**De Vries, Hugo [Marie]** (1848–1935) Dutch botanist and geneticist. He rediscovered the genetic principles first put forward by MENDEL, and developed the theory of evolution through the mutation of genes.

**Dewey, John** (1859–1952) American philosopher and educational theorist. His philosophy was firmly in the pragmatist tradition, relying on the defini tion of knowledge as "successful practise" and truth as "warranted assessibility," a view developed in works such *The Quest for Certainty* (1929). He also published radical studies of education theory, e.g. *The School and Society* (1899).

**Diaghilev, Sergei [Pavlovich]** (1872–1929) Russian ballet impresario. His highly successful production of *Boris Godunov* in Paris (1908) led to the founding of his Ballet Russe de Diaghilev in 1911, based in Monte Carlo. He became one of the most influential ballet impresarios, drawing upon the talents of composers such as DEBUSSY and STRAVINSKY and artists such as PICASSO. He was much influenced by Isadora DUNCAN's dancing. *See also* FOKINE.

**Dickens, Charles [John Huffam]** (1812-70) English novelist. He achieved immediate success with *The Posthumous Papers of the Pickwick Club* (1836-37), the first of his 14 great novels, most of which were published in instalments in periodicals. He became immensely popular with both the British and American reading public, with, for example, crowds of New Yorkers waiting at the quayside for the latest instalment of *The Old Curiosity Shop* (1840-41). The novels include *Oliver Twist* (1837), *Martin Chuzzlewit* (1843-44), *David Copperfield* (1849-50), *Bleak House* (1852-53) and *Great Expectations* (1860-61).

**Dickinson, Emily** (1830-86) American poet. A virtual recluse from her late twenties onward, only seven of her *c*.2000 poems were printed in her lifetime. Editions of her remarkable poetry—aphoristic lyrics with highly individual punctuation—began to appear in the 1890s, and she became recognized as a uniquely gifted poet.

**Diderot, Denis** (1713-84) French philosopher. With others, he edited the great *Encyclopédie*, 17 volumes of which appeared under Diderot's overall direction between 1751 and 1772. Diderot's other works include his plays of "bourgeois" life and the intriguing philosophical dialogue, *Rameau's Nephew* (1761). *See also* CATHERINE II.

**Diefenbaker, John George** (1895–1979) Canadian Conservative statesman. He was prime minister (1957–63).

**Dietrich, Marlene** [Maria Magdelene von Losch] (1902–92) German-born American singer and film actress, notable for her strong sexual presence and husky, alluring voice. Her films include *The Blue Angel* (1930, the last film she made in Germany), *Shanghai Express* (1932), *The Devil is a Woman* (1935) and the comedy western *Destry Rides Again* (1939).

**Dior, Christian** (1905–57) French couturier. The extravagance of his New Look design of the late 1940s, with narrow waists and full pleated skirts, proved very popular in the austerity of the postwar period. He later designed the "Sack" dress.

**Dirac, Paul Adrien Maurice** (1902–84) English physicist. He devised a complete mathematical formulation of EINSTEIN's theory of relativity in *The Principles of Quantum Mechanics* (1930), in which he predicted the existence of antimatter. He shared the 1933 Nobel prize for physics with SCHRÖDINGER.

**Disney, Walt[er Elias]** (1901–66) American cartoonist and film producer. His cartoon films of the 1930s and 40s, e.g. *Snow White and the Seven Dwarfs* (1938) and *Bambi* (1942), achieved high critical and popular acclaim. Mickey Mouse and

Donald Duck are two of his most famous cartoon creations. He built Disneyland amusement park in California (1955), and planned Disney World in Florida (1971).

**Disraeli, Benjamin** [1st Earl of Beaconsfield] (1804–81) British statesman and novelist. Although baptised a Christian at thirteen, Disraeli remained proud of his Jewish ancestry and heritage throughout his life. He became a Tory member of parliament in 1837 and wrote the novels *Coningsby* (1844) and *Sibyl* (1845) as manifestos for radical "Young England" Toryism. He became prime minister (1868, 1874-80), and promoted protectionism and a romanticized imperialism that appealed both to Queen VICTORIA and most of the British public, much to the ire of his great rival GLADSTONE.

**Djilas, Milovan** (1911– ) Yugoslav politician. An early associate of TITO, he became vice-president of Yugoslavia (1953–54) and was purged in 1954. He was subsequently imprisoned in 1956 for supporting the Hungarian uprising. He was released in 1966, and "rehabilitated" in 1989. His books include *The New Order* (1957) and *Memoir of a Revolutionary* (1973).

**Dobell, Sir William** (1899–1970) Australian portrait and landscape painter. His prizewinning portrait of a fellow artist, *Joshua Smith* (1943), resulted in a stormy debate between those who supported a more conventional approach to portraiture and the "moderns." A legal battle ensued, which Dobell won.

**Dobzhansky, Theodosius** (1900–75) Russian-born American geneticist. His seminal studies of genetic variation, described in *Genetics and the Evolution-*

*ary Process* (1970), linked Darwin's evolutionary theory with MENDEL's heredity laws.

**Doenitz, Karl** *see* **Dönitz, Karl.**

**Doisy, Edward** *see* **Dam, Henrik.**

**Dolci, Danilo** (1924– ) Italian social reformer. Described as the "GANDHI of Italy," he built schools and community centres in poverty-stricken Sicily, in the teeth of fierce opposition from an unholy alliance of church, state and Mafia. He was imprisoned in 1956 for leading a famous "strike in reverse," organizing the unemployed to repair a road. His books include *Report from Palermo* (1956) and *A New World in the Making* (1965).

**Dollfus, Engelbert** (1892–1934) Austrian statesman. A devout Roman Catholic, he became leader of the Christian Socialist Party and was elected chancellor (1932–34). He opposed the German Anschluss and was assassinated by Austrian Nazis.

**Dolmetsch, Arnold** (1858–1940) French-born British musician and instrument maker. He pioneered the revival of early music played on copies of original instruments.

**Domar, Evsey** *see* **Harrod, Sir Henry Roy Forbes.**

**Domingo, Placido** (1941– ) Spanish tenor who studied in Mexico City. He is regarded as one of the finest modern operatic tenors for his sophisticated vocal technique and considerable acting ability.

**Dominic, St** (*c*.1170-1221) Spanish monk. Noted for his asceticism, he founded the Dominican Order of monks and helped the forces of the Inquisition in their barbarous treatment of the Albigensians in Southern France. He was canonized in 1234.

**Donatello** [Donato di Niccolò di Betto Bardi] (*c*.1386-1466) Florentine sculptor. One of the leading sculptors of the early Renaissance, his most famous work is the huge bronze statue of *David* (1430s). Later works, e.g. *Judith and Holofernes* (1456-60), are less neoclassical in spirit and have more emotional intensity.

**Dönitz** *or* **Doenitz, Karl** (1891–1980) German admiral. He was commander of the German navy (1943–45). As head of the Nazi state following HIT-LER's suicide, he surrendered unconditionally to the Allies, and was sentenced at Nuremberg to ten years imprisonment for war crimes.

**Donleavy, J[ames] P[atrick]** (1926– ) American-born Irish novelist. His works include *The Ginger Man* (1955), a comedy of undergraduate life in Dublin, and *The Beastly Beatitudes of Balthazar B* (1968).

**Donne, John** (1573-1631) English poet and divine. Brought up a Roman Catholic, he converted to Anglicanism in the mid-1590s. After occasional hazardous adventures, such as accompanying Sir Francis DRAKE on his raid on Cadiz, he became Dean of St Paul's in 1621 and was regarded as one of the greatest preachers of his day. His poetry, which includes the *Holy Sonnets* and *Elegies*, displays a love of paradox and self-questioning doubt, and is among the finest metaphysical verse.

**Doré, Gustave** (1832-83) French sculptor, painter and illustrator. Trained as a caricaturist, he became well known for his illustrations to such works as DANTE's *Inferno* (1861) and CERVANTES' *Don Quixote* (1862). His realistic drawings of London slums were used in a government report.

**Dos Passos, John [Roderigo]** (1896–1970) American novelist. His masterpiece is his huge trilogy of

American life, *U.S.A.*, comprising *The 42nd parallel* (1930), *1919* (1932) and *The Big Money* (1936).

**Dostoyevsky, Fyodor Mikhailovich** (1821-81) Russian novelist. Like many Russian intellectuals, he was revolutionary in his youth but converted to a mystical faith in Russian orthodoxy and the "Slav soul" while exiled in Siberia. His exile was preceded by a macabre mock-execution by firing squad, an encounter with death that affected him deeply. His novels are profound explorations of sin and redemption through suffering. They include *Crime and Punishment* (1866), *The Idiot* (1868), *The Possessed* (1872), and *The Brothers Karamazov* (1880).

**Douglas-Home, Sir Alec** [Baron Home of the Hirsel] (1903– ) Scottish Conservative politician. He became the 14th Earl of Home in 1951, renouncing his title in 1963 to contest (and win) the seat of Kinross after succeeding Harold MACMILLAN as prime minister. (The furore over his completely unexpected emergence as party leader resulted in reform of the Tory leadership election process.) After leading the Conservatives to defeat in the 1964 general election, he was replaced by HEATH.

**Doyle, Sir Arthur Conan** (1859–1930) Scottish novelist, short-story writer and physician. His most famous creation is the amateur detective Sherlock Holmes, who solves mysteries by a mixture of deduction and intuitive perception. The stories include the collection, *The Adventures of Sherlock Holmes* (1892), and *The Hound of the Baskervilles* (1902).

**Drake, Sir Francis** (*c.*1540-1596) English navigator and pirate. He became a highly popular hero to the English following his successful depradations upon Spanish ships and settlements in the Caribbean in the early 1570s. He circumnavigated the world (1577-80) and was one of the leading lights in the victory over the Spanish Armada (1588).

**Dreiser, Theodore [Herman Albert]** (1871–1945) American novelist. His early novels, e.g. *Sister Carrie* (1904), are grim naturalistic works with a deterministic view of human behaviour. His later novels, and documentary works such as *America is Worth Saving* (1941), are more optimistic, reflecting his transition from nihilism to socialism. His masterpiece is the doom-laden narrative *An American Tragedy* (1925).

**Dreyer, Carl [Theodor]** (1889–1968) Danish film director. His films, e.g. *The Passion of Joan of Arc* (1928), are concerned with spirituality and martyrdom. His film *Day of Wrath* (1943), which depicts 17th-century witch-hunts, was made during the German occupation of Denmark, of which it was widely seen as an allegory (Dreyer escaped to Sweden).

**Dreyfus, Alfred** (1859-1935) French army officer. Unjustly imprisoned in 1894 on Devil's Island on a trumped-up charge of espionage, the "Dreyfus affair" scandalized much of Europe for the virtually open anti-semitism of the prosecution case. ZOLA's magnificent pamphlet *J'accuse* (1898) was written in his defence, and Dreyfus was released in 1906. He served with distinction in World War I.

**Dryden, John** (1631-1700) English poet, dramatist and critic. One of the most important literary figures of his time, he was also a highly significant contributor to the religious and political controversies of the day. His verse satires, e.g. *Absalom and*

*Achitophel* (1681), the social comedies, e.g. *Marriage à-la-Mode* (1672), and the verse tragedies, e.g. *All for Love* (1678), are among the finest of their kind. He was also the first great English critic, and an outstanding poet. He became poet laureate in 1668, but lost the post in 1688 in the political upheaval surrounding the replacement of King JAMES II by WILLIAM III and Mary.

**Dubcek, Alexander** (1921–92) Czech statesman. As first secretary of the Communist Party (1968–69), he introduced the political reforms of the "Prague Spring" of "socialism with a human face," which ended with the Russian invasion of 1968. From 1970, he worked as a forestry inspector and lumber yard clerk. Following the "Velvet Revolution," which brought HAVEL to the presidency, he was appointed chairman of the federal assembly (1989).

**Dubuffet, Jean** (1901–85) French painter. He devised the concept of "Art Brut" in reaction against "museum art," and made paintings assembled from bits of rubbish, broken glass, etc. His collected works were published in 1967.

**Duchamp, Marcel** (1887–1968) French-born American painter and sculptor. The most famous of his early works is the Cubist-style painting *Nude Descending a Staircase* (1912). He was also one of the early pioneers of Dadaism, and introduced the concept of the "found object" after settling in New York in 1915.

**Dufy, Raoul** (1877–1953) French painter and designer. His early work was much influenced by MATISSE and Fauvists such as DERAIN. The best-known of his works are the bright, colourful paintings of the 1920s, often of seascapes, regattas or racetracks. He also designed ballets and for the theatre.

**Dukakis, Michael** *see* **Bush, George.**

**Dulles, John Foster** (1888–1959) American Republican statesman and lawyer. He was secretary of state (1953–59) under EISENHOWER, and developed the confrontational foreign policy of "brinkmanship" in the Cold War against the USSR.

**Dumas, Alexandre** [*Dumas père*] (1802-70) French novelist and dramatist, whose entertaining Romantic novels, e.g. *The Three Musketeers* (1844) and *The Count of Monte Cristo* (1845) achieved instant and lasting popularity. His illegitimate son, also called **Alexandre Dumas** [*Dumas fils*] (1824-95) also wrote novels and plays, his masterpiece being the play *Camille*, an adaptation of his novel (1848), which caused a sensation when it was staged in 1852, and was the basis for VERDI's *La Traviata* (1853).

**Du Maurier, Dame Daphne** (1907–89) English novelist and short-story writer. Several of her very popular works, e.g. *Jamaica Inn* (1936) and *Rebecca* (1938) have been filmed. Her gift for creating an atmosphere of menace, as in the haunting story "Don't Look Now" (also made into a very successful film) is especially good filmed.

**Duncan, Isadora** (1878–1927) American dancer and choreographer. She was encouraged in her early career by Mrs Patrick CAMPBELL, and developed a free, interpretative style of dancing that was very influential on the development of modern dance (e.g. on DIAGHILEV). Her ardent feminism and unconventional lifestyle alienated many of her contemporaries. Her life was dogged by tragedy; both of her children died in a car crash. A film of her life, *Isadora*, starring Vanessa REDGRAVE, was made in 1968.

**Dunsany, Edward John Moreton Drax Plunkett, 18th Baron** (1878–1957) Anglo-Irish novelist, dramatist and short-story writer. The best of his work, e.g. the fantasy stories in the *Book of Wonder* (1912), is rated a good bit above the usual ruck of "Celtic Twilight" fantasy. His readership and critical reputation increased sharply with the rise of the fantasy market in the 1960s.

**du Pré, Jacqueline** (1945–87) English cellist. She became recognized as one of the world's finest cellists in the 1960s. She married Daniel BARENBOIM in 1967, with whom she frequently performed. Her performing career came to an end in 1973, after she developed multiple sclerosis. Although confined to a wheelchair, she pursued an active teaching career until her death, and gave an acclaimed series of TV masterclasses.

**Dürer, Albrecht** (1471-1528) German engraver and painter. A leading figure of the Northern Renaissance, his work is outstanding in its attention to detail and its emotional content. His later paintings demonstrate his sympathies with Martin LUTHER's reformation, e.g. *Four Apostles* (1526). A superb draughtsman, his albums of engravings were highly influential on other artists.

**Durkheim, Emile** (1858–1917) French sociologist. Regarded as one of the most influential figures in modern sociology, his work was in the Positivist tradition of the 19th-century philosopher, Auguste Comte. He saw the "collective social mind" as the basis for all morality, with religion being seen as society's way of formulating its ideals. His works include *The Rules of Sociological Method* (1895) and *Suicide* (1897).

**Durrell, Lawrence [George]** (1912–90) English poet, novelist and travel writer. His masterpiece is the series of sexual and linguistically elaborate novels comprising the Alexandria Quartet, i.e. *Justine* (1957), *Balthazar* (1958), *Mountolive* (1958) and *Clea* (1960).

**Dürrenmatt, Friedrich** (1921–90) Swiss dramatist, novelist and critic. His plays, e.g. The *Physicists* (1963), exemplify his belief that the world is a chaotic mess, which cannot be sorted out but which equally cannot be accepted for what it is. He has also written several bizarre and ironic detective novels, e.g. *The Pledge* (1958).

**Duse, Eleonora** *see* **D'Annunzio, Gabriele.**

**Duvalier, François** (1907–71) Haitian president (1957–71). Known as Papa Doc, Duvalier's tyrannical rule of Haiti was based on a duality of fear through his supposed Voodoo powers, and, more realistically, his murderous "civil militia" gangs of "Tonton Macoutes." He was excommunicated by the Roman Catholic church (1960–66) and was succeeded by his son, **Jean-Claude Duvalier ("Baby Doc")** (1951– ), who was turned out of office in free elections in 1986.

**Dvorak, Antonin** (1841-1904) Czech composer. Strongly influenced by Czech folk music, his works include *Slavonic Dances, Stabat Mater*, and his most famous composition, *Symphony No. 9 from the New World* (1893), a work including themes from American music which was written while heading the New York Conservatory.

**Dyck, Sir Anthony van** (1599-1641) Flemish
painter. Renowned for his unique and influential
style of portraiture, investing his sitters with character and refinement of detail, he became court
painter to CHARLES I in 1632. Most of his English
works remain in the Royal Collection, including two
portraits of Charles. His album *Iconography* includes etchings of famous contemporaries.

**Dylan, Bob** [Robert Allen Zimmerman] (1941– )
American folk/rock singer and songwriter. Influenced by Woody GUTHRIE, he became the most prominent "protest" folksinger in the 1960s with songs
such as "The Times They Are A-Changin'." He later
took up rock music, for which he was never forgiven
by many of his fans, who got a further shock when
he became a born-again Christian in 1979. His
lyrics are very highly regarded by some critics. *See
also* BAEZ.

# E

**Earhart, Amelia** (1898–1937) American aviator. She was the first woman to make a solo flight across the Atlantic (1932), after which she became a celebrity. She disappeared on a flight across the Pacific while attempting a round-the-world flight.

**Eastman, George** (1854–1932) American inventor of photographic equipment and philanthropist. His invention of the Kodak roll-film camera, which was cheap and easy-to-use, revolutionized the photographic industry, as did his development of colour photography in the late 1920s. He gave away more than $100 million to various charities and institutions.

**Eccles, Sir John Carew** (1903– ) Australian neurophysiologist. He shared the 1963 Nobel prize for physiology or medicine for his work on nerve impulses.

**Eco, Umberto** (1932– ) Italian critic and novelist. Works such as *A Theory of Semiotics* (1972) established him as a leading literary critic. His best known work of fiction is the medieval philosophical whodunit, *The Name of the Rose* (1981).

**Eddington, Sir Arthur Stanley** (1882–1944) English astronomer and physicist. A lifelong Quaker who emphasized the fundamental strangeness of the universe, he published several popular and highly readable books explaining such topics as

EINSTEIN's theory of relativity, e.g. *Mathematical Theory of Relativity* (1923) and *The Expanding Universe* (1933). He also did important work on the nature of the stars, e.g. *The Internal Constitution of the Stars* (1926).

**Eddy, Mary Baker** (1821–1910) American religious leader. A faith healer, she devised a system of healing based on the Bible which she called "Christian Science", and founded the Church of Christ, Scientist, in Boston (1879). As God was good, she argued in *Science and Health with Key to the Scriptures* (1879), physical illness could only be an illusion.

**Eden, Sir [Robert] Anthony** [1st Earl of Avon] (1897–1977) British Conservative statesman. He served several terms as foreign minister and was prime minister (1955–57). He resigned from office following the Suez Crisis, when British and French occupation of Egypt after NASSER's nationalization of the Suez Canal received worldwide condemnation.

**Edison, Thomas [Alva]** (1847–1931) American inventor. One of the most prolific and successful inventors of all time, he patented over a thousand inventions, including the gramophone, the incandescent electric light bulb, and the microphone.

**Edward, Prince** *see* **Elizabeth II**.

**Edward III** *see* **Chaucer**.

**Edward IV** *see* **Henry VI**.

**Edward V** *see* **Richard III**.

**Edward VII** (1841–1910) king of Great Britain and Ireland (1901–10). Queen Victoria's oldest son, in 1863 he married the Danish princess **Alexandra** (1844–1925), and his short reign was preceded by many decades as the leader of fashionable society. He was noted for his charm and was popular with the public. He was succeeded by GEORGE V.

**Edward VIII** *see* **Windsor, Duke of.**

**Edward the Confessor** (*c.*1003–66) Anglo-Saxon king of England. A pious man, he succeeded to the throne in 1042 and founded Westminster Abbey. His death opened up a war of succession, which led to WILLIAM THE CONQUEROR's invasion of 1066 and the overthrow of Edward's successor, HAROLD II.

**Ehrenburg, Ilya Grigorievich** (1891–1967) Soviet novelist and journalist. He was known primarily for his anti-Western works, e.g. the novel *The Fall of Paris* (1941), and for his war reporting, until the publication of his novel, *The Thaw* (1955), which was the first post-Stalin work to criticize Stalinism.

**Ehrlich, Paul** (1854–1915) German bacteriologist. He did significant research into immunology and chemotherapy, and developed a cure for syphilis (1910). He was awarded the 1908 Nobel prize for physiology or medicine.

**Eichmann, [Karl] Adolf** (1906–62) Austrian Nazi leader and war criminal. He was instructed by HITLER in 1942 to bring about the "Final Solution," i.e. the extermination of Europe's Jews, and oversaw the deportation of Jews to death camps. He was captured by US forces at the end of World War II, but escaped to Argentina, from where he was abducted by Israeli agents in 1960. He was tried for crimes against humanity by the Israelis, and executed.

**Eijkman, Christiaan** (1858–1930) Dutch physician. He discovered that beriberi is caused by nutritional deficiency. His research led to the discovery of "essential food factors," i.e. vitamins. He shared the 1929 Nobel prize for physiology or medicine with Sir Frederick HOPKINS.

**Einstein, Albert** (1879–1955) German-born physicist and mathematician. His formulations of the special theory of relativity (1906) and general theory of relativity (1916), and research into quantum theory, mark him as one of the greatest of all thinkers. He was awarded the 1921 Nobel prize for physics. Being Jewish and a pacifist, he was forced to flee Nazi Germany in 1933, and became a US citizen in 1940.

**Eisenhower, Dwight D[avid]** (1890–1969) American general and Republican statesman, known as "Ike." He became supreme commander of the Allied forces in 1943, and 34th president of the US (1953–60). During the Cold War, he adopted a more conciliatory approach to that favoured by DULLES. His memoirs include *Mandate for Change* (1963) and *Waging Peace* (1965).

**Eisenstaedt, Alfred** (1898– ) German-born American photographer. He became one of the world's leading photojournalists in the 1930s, when he pioneered the use of the Leica camera for capturing "storytelling moments." His books include *Witness to Our Time* (1966).

**Eisenstein, Sergei Mikhailovich** (1898–1948) Soviet film director. He served with the Red Army (1918–20) during the Civil War and became one of the most influential directors of all time with films such as *Battleship Potemkin* (1925) and *October* (1928), in which he deployed his theory of montage through skilful cutting .

**Elgar, Sir Edward [William]** (1857–1934) English

composer. A devout Roman Catholic, he became recognized as the leading British composer with works such as the *Enigma Variations* (1899) and the oratorio *The Dream of Gerontius* (1900). He composed many other well-known works, e.g. the five *Pomp and Circumstance* marches (1903–30) and the *Cello Concerto* (1919).

**El Greco** [Domenikos Theotocopolous] (1541–1614) Cretan-born Spanish painter, sculptor and architect. He studied in Italy, where he was a possibly a pupil of TITIAN, although TINTORETTO and MICHELANGELO undoubtedly influenced his work. From 1577 he lived and worked in Toledo in an emotional and spiritually evocative style, his palette containing cold blues and greys at a time when the vogue was for warmer colours. Notable works include *The Burial of Count Orgaz* (1586) and *The Assumption* (1613).

**Eliot, George** [pseud. of Mary Ann Evans] (1819–80) English novelist. Her novels, e.g. *The Mill on the Floss* (1860) and *Middlemarch* (1871–2), deal with the problems of ethical choice in the rapidly changing rural environment of 19th-century England. She lived, unmarried, with her partner, the English writer **George Henry Lewes** (1817–78), from 1854 until his death.

**Eliot, T[homas] S[tearns]** (1888–1965) American-born English poet and critic, whose early work was much influenced by his friend POUND. His early poetry, e.g. *The Waste Land* (1922), is concerned with the breakdown of civilized values in the post-war "Jazz Era." He also wrote verse dramas, e.g. *The Family Reunion* (1939), and published critical works, e.g. *The Sacred Wood* (1920).

**Elizabeth I** (1533–1603) queen of England. The daughter of HENRY VIII and Anne Boleyn, she spent much of her childhood in a dangerous atmosphere and was brought up a Protestant. She was crowned Queen in 1588 after MARY I had died, and instituted a cautious toleration in religious matters. Guided by William CECIL, she established the Church of England over the years 1559–63. She never married, and pursued a shrewd divide-and-rule policy in home and foreign affairs. She survived various plots and PHILIP II's attempt at invasion with his armada in 1588. The later years of her reign saw an astonishing flourishing of literature and one of the great ages of drama.

**Elizabeth II** (1926– ) queen of the United Kingdom from 1952. The daughter of GEORGE VI. She married Prince PHILIP in 1947, and has four children: Prince CHARLES, Princess **Anne** (1950– ), Prince **Andrew** (1960– ) and Prince **Edward** (1964– ). She is regarded as the most formal of all modern European monarchs. Her main personal interests are those traditionally associated with upper-class country life, especially horse racing.

**Ellington, Duke** [Edward Kennedy Ellington] (1899–1974) American jazz composer, pianist and bandleader. Regarded as one of the finest jazz composers, his some two thousand works include "Mood Indigo," "Sophisticated Lady" and "Creole Love Call." His various bands, composed of some of the finest instrumentalists of the time, toured widely.

**Ellis, [Henry] Havelock** (1859–1939) English physician and sexologist. His seven-volume *Studies on the Psychology of Sex* (1897–1928, revised edition 1936) were very influential in bringing the discussion of sexual matters into the realm of open debate (although the work was banned in Britain, except for doctors, until 1953).

**Elton, Charles Sutherland** (1900– ) English ecologist. His field studies of animal communities in their environments raised awareness of the ability of animals to adapt to changing habitats, and popularized such terms as "ecological niche." His works include *The Pattern of Animal Communities* (1966).

**Éluard, Paul** [Eugène Grindel] (1895–1952) French poet. He was part of the Surrealist movement until the late 1930s, and joined the Communist Party in 1942. He joined the French Resistance during the German occupation of France, when his anti-Nazi poems were secretly circulated to raise morale. His postwar poetry, e.g. *The Phoenix* (1951), is more personal and lyrical.

**Emerson, Ralph Waldo** (1803–82) American essayist, philosopher and poet. A Unitarian clergyman, he was influenced by CARLYLE and developed a philosophy of "transcendentalism", based upon the authenticity of the individual conscience against both church and state. He was a strong influence upon THOREAU. His works include *Nature* (1836) and *Essays, First and Second Series* (1841,1844).

**Empson, Sir William** (1906–84) English poet and critic. His *Seven Types of Ambiguity* (1930, written while he was studying mathematics at Cambridge) is regarded as a modern classic of literary criticism for its witty insights.

**Engels, Friedrich** *see* **Marx, Karl**.

**Engler, [Gustav Heinrich] Adolf** (1844–1930) German botanist. His taxonomic classification of plants

in works such as *Syllabus of Plant Names* (1892)
was used as a standard reference for many years by
biologists.

**Epicurus** (341–271 BC) Greek philosopher. He
founded the Epicurean school of philosophy, which
teaches that the highest good and proper study of
mankind is pleasure, and that this can be attained
through a life of simplicity and moderation. He also
taught that everything is a series of atoms that have
come together by chance.

**Epstein, Sir Jacob** (1880–1959) American-born British sculptor of Russian-Polish descent. Much of his
work for public commissions, e.g. *Ecce Homo* (1934),
was widely derided and attacked for indecency. His
portrait busts, e.g. of EINSTEIN and SHAW, were, in
contrast, highly praised.

**Erasmus, Desiderius** (*c*.1466–1536) Dutch humanist. One of the leading scholars of the Renaissance,
he was a strong advocate of tolerance in an intolerant age. His works include *Praise of Folly* (1509),
written partly in tribute to his friend Thomas MORE,
and the first Greek New Testament (1516). The
religious reformers tried to claim as a forerunner,
but he was a firm opponent of LUTHER's intolerant
doctrines.

**Erlanger, Joseph** (1874–1965) American physiologist. With **Herbert Spencer Gasser** (1888–1963),
he shared the 1944 Nobel prize for physiology or
medicine for their work on nerve fibres and the
transmission of nerve impulses.

**Ernst, Max** (1891–1976) German-born French painter.
He was a leading member of both the Dada and
Surrealist movements. He pioneered the use of
collage and photomontage, and developed "frottage"

(pencil rubbings on a variety of surfaces). Birds and petrified cities are prominent subjects in his work.

**Erté** [Romain de Tirtoff] (1892–1990) Russian-born French designer and fashion illustrator, who became one of the most notable exponents of Art Deco style. His designs appeared in magazines such as *Harper's Bazaar* and were used by ZIEGFELD in his "follies."

**Escoffier, Georges Auguste** (1846–1935) French chef, who is regarded as one of the greatest chefs of all time. He invented peach melba in honour of Dame Nellie MELBA.

**Essex, 2nd Earl of** [Robert Devereux] (*c*.1566–1601) English soldier and courtier. A brave but impetuous servitor of Queen ELIZABETH I (who once boxed his ears for turning his back on her), he captured Cadiz in 1596 but fell in and out of favour with Elizabeth, and was imprisoned for concluding an unauthorized truce in Ireland. He eventually launched a desperate attempt at insurrection (against the Queen's advisers, he claimed) in 1601, and was captured and executed.

**Euripides** (480–406 BC) Greek dramatist. He was the youngest of the three great Greek tragedians, the others being AESCHYLUS and SOPHOCLES. His popularity lasted until well until the Byzantine era, and 19 of his (perhaps over 90) plays are extant, the most notable being *Alcestis, Medea, Orestes* and *The Trojan Women.*

**Evans, Sir Arthur [John]** (1851–1941) English archaeologist. His excavations of the palace of Knossos in Crete resulted in the rediscovery of Minoan civilization (so named by Evans after the legendary king Minos).

## Evans

**Evans, Dame Edith [Mary Booth]** (1888–1976)
English actress, notable for her command of a wide
variety of roles. She created the role of Lady
Utterword in SHAW's *Heartbreak House* (1921), and
gave a definitive performance as Lady Bracknell in
WILDE's *The Importance of Being Earnest*. Her most
notable film role was as a lonely old lady in *The
Whisperers* (1967).

**Evans, Sir Geraint [Llewellyn]** (1922–92) Welsh
baritone, who became one of Britain's best known
and popular operatic baritones, with a worldwide
reputation for his skill and warmth.

**Eyck, Jan van** *see* **van Eyck, Jan**.

**Eysenck, Hans [Jürgen]** (1916– ) German-born
British psychologist. Eysenck has been a notable
critic of FREUD's theory of psychoanalysis, which he
regards as having insufficient basis in empirically
derived evidence. His controversial views on the
role of genetic factors in determining intelligence
are expressed in his *Race, Intelligence and Education* (1971).

# F

**Fairbanks, Douglas** [Douglas Elton Ullman] (1883–1939) American film actor and producer, who became one of the leading stars of silent films, starring in such swashbucklers as *The Mark of Zorro* (1920). Mary PICKFORD was his second wife (1920–36). His son, **Douglas Fairbanks Jr** (1909– ), was also an actor starring in swashbucklers, notably *The Prisoner of Zenda* (1937). His first wife was Joan CRAWFORD.

**Falla, Manuel de** (1876–1946) Spanish composer and pianist. His works include the ballet *The Three-Cornered Hat* (1919), the puppet opera *Master Peter's Puppet Show* (1923), song cycles and concertos.

**Faraday, Michael** (1791–1867) English chemist and physicist. He became an assistant to Humphrey DAVY in 1813, and discovered electromagnetic induction and investigated electrolysis. An ingenious and thorough experimenter, he published many papers on physics, and proposed using electric lighting in lighthouses.

**Farouk, King** *see* **Nasser, General Abdel**

**Farquhar, George** (1678–1707) Irish dramatist. His plays, e.g. *The Recruiting Officer* (1706) and *The Beaux' Stratagem* (1707), are both good-natured and satirical, and mark an important transitional stage between the bawdy world of Restoration comedy and the more decorous 18th-century stage.

**Fassbinder, Rainer Werner** (1946–82) German film director. His films include *The Bitter Tears o Petra Von Kant* (1972), *Fear Eats the Soul* (1974 and *The Marriage of Maria Braun* (1979). Fassbind er was influenced by GODARD's political commit ment, and his films do show the underside of th German "economic miracle," but his analysis o oppression is by no means simplistic.

**Faulkner, William [Harrison]** (1897–1962) Ameri can novelist. His first novel, *Soldier's Pay* (1926) was written with Sherwood ANDERSON's encourage ment. His most famous series of works, e.g. *Th Sound and the Fury* (1929), deals with political social, racial and sexual tensions within a fictiona Mississippi county, Yoknapatawpha.

**Fauré, Gabriel [Urbain]** (1845–1924) French com poser and organist. His works include the hauntin *Requiem* (1887), around a hundred lyrical song such as "Après un Rêve," orchestral and pian pieces.

**Fawcett, Dame Millicent** [Millicent Garrett] (1847– 1929) English feminist. She became first presiden of the National Union of Women Suffrage Societie (1897–1919), and opposed the more militant tactic of PANKHURST. Her works include *Political Econom for Beginners* (1870) and *Women's Suffrage* (1912)

**Fellini, Federico** (1920– ) Italian film director. Hi best-known film is *La Dolce Vita* (1960), a cynica portrayal of Roman high society. Other films in clude *8¹/₂* (1963), an autobiographical work con taining fantasy sequences, *Fellini's Roma* (1972) and *Amarcord* (1974).

**Ferdinand V** [Ferdinand the Catholic] (1452–1516 He became king of Castile in 1474, then (a

Ferdinand II) king of Aragon and of Sicily, and (as Ferdinand III) king of Naples. His marriage to **Isabella I of Castile** (1451–1504) in 1469 united the kingdoms of Aragon and Castile. After the expulsion of the Moors from Granada in 1492 (he expelled the Jewish community from Spain in the same year), Ferdinand became the first king of a united Spain. He brought the Inquisition into Spain in 1478, and financed COLUMBUS's voyage to the New World.

**Fermat, Pierre de** (1601–65) French mathematician. The founder of number theory, he initiated, with PASCAL, the study of probability theory. He also devised what has become known as "Fermat's last theorem", a mathematical problem on integers that is still unsolved, and he made discoveries in the field of optics.

**Fermi, Enrico** (1901–54) Italian-born American physicist. With his Jewish wife, he fled to the US in 1938 after being awarded the Nobel prize for physics for his work on radioactive substances and nuclear bombardment. He built the first nuclear reactor at Chicago in 1942.

**Fermor, Patrick Michael Leigh** (1915– ) English travel writer and soldier. His exploits in World War II included the organization of the Cretan Resistance and the capture of a German general. His highly regarded travel books include *Mani* (1958) and *Between the Woods and the Water* (1986).

**Ferrier, Kathleen** (1912–53) English contralto. She created the title role in BRITTEN's *Rape of Lucretia* (1946), and sang at the first Edinburgh Festival in MAHLER's *Song of the Earth* under Bruno WALTER, who became a close friend and described her as "one

of the greatest singers of all time." Her tragically
short singing career ended with her death from
cancer.

**Feydeau, Georges** (1862–1921) French dramatist
noted for his bedroom farces, e.g. *Hotel Paradiso*
(1956).

**Feynman, Richard** (1918–88) American physicist.
He shared the 1965 Nobel prize for physics for his
work in quantum electrodynamics.

**Field, John** (1782–1837) Irish composer and pianist. He settled in Russia (1804–32), then in London
in 1832. He is particularly noted for his 19 *Noc-
turnes*, and was an influence on CHOPIN.

**Fielding, Henry** (1707–54) English novelist and
dramatist. His satirical plays, e.g. *Pasquin* (1736)
and *The Historical Register for 1736* (1737), both of
which included cruelly funny attacks on the WAL-
POLE administration, provoked the British government into passing the strict Licensing Act of 1737 to
censor stage plays. His first novel, *Joseph Andrews*
(1742), is a very funny parody of Samuel RICHARD-
SON's *Pamela*, in which the conventions of male and
female virtue are reversed; the second, *Jonathan
Wild* (1743), re-assails the British government by
presenting the career of a criminal as an allegory of
political vice. His greatest work, *Tom Jones* (1749),
surveys the whole of English society with masterly
insight and compassion. His last novel, *Amelia*
(1751), again stands convention on its head by
having a disfigured heroine. Fielding also wrote
important tracts on social problems, and worked
tirelessly as a magistrate to improve judicial standards (as did his blind brother, who was also a
magistrate).

**Fields, Dame Gracie** [Grace Stansfield] (1898–1979) English singer and comedienne, whose image was "Our Gracie," the earthy, straightforward Northern lass. Her 1930s films, e.g. *Sally in Our Alley* (1931) and *Sing As We Go* (1934), were very popular in England.

**Fields, W. C.** [William Claude Dukenfield] (1880–1946) American comedian, noted for his hard drinking, red nose, gravel voice and antipathy to children and animals. He worked in vaudeville before appearing regularly in ZIEGFELD's *Follies* (1915–21) and many films, e.g. *My Little Chickadee* with Mae WEST (1940). He was a notable Mr Micawber in *David Copperfield* (1934).

**Finney, Albert** (1936– ) English actor. His portrayal of the rebellious young working-class hero of the film *Saturday Night and Sunday Morning* (1960), with its mocking attitude to authority and realistic approach to sex, had a strong impact on British cinema.

**Firbank, [Arthur Annesley] Ronald** (1886–1926) English novelist. His weird and exotic works, characterized by oblique dialogue and fantastic characters, include *Valmouth* (1919) and *Concerning the Eccentricities of Cardinal Pirelli* (1926).

**Fischer, Bobby** [Robert James Fischer] (1943– ) American chess player. He became a grandmaster at 15, and was the first US player to win the world championship (1972) when he won a hotly debated contest against Boris SPASSKY. He became the best-known chess player in the history of the game, partly because of his undoubted genius, but also because of his bizarre charges against opponents, e.g. that he was being bugged.

**Fitzgerald, Edward** (1809–93) English poet. His very free translation of *The Rubáiyát of Omar Khayyám* (1859) has become one of the most quoted poems in the English language, although Fitzgerald's version is more redolent of Victorian doubts and fears than of the bright scepticism of the original.

**Fitzgerald, Ella** (1918– ) American jazz singer, whose highly praised vocal range, rhythmic subtlety and clarity of tone made her one of the most popular singers of her day. She toured widely, notably with BASIE, ARMSTRONG and ELLINGTON.

**Fitzgerald, F[rancis] Scott [Key]** (1896–1940) American novelist and short-story writer. His works are moralistic fables of extravagance and glamour set against the background of 1920s "Jazz Age" High Society. His novels include *The Great Gatsby* (1925) and *Tender is the Night* (1934).

**Flagstad, Kirsten** (1895–1962) Norwegian soprano, noted for her roles in Wagner's operas. She is regarded as one of the finest Wagnerian singers of all time.

**Flaherty, Robert [Joseph]** (1884–1951) American documentary film director. His films include e.g. *Nanook of the North* (1922), about an Eskimo family, and *Man of Aran* (1934), about life on the west coast Irish island of Aran. Although undoubtedly somewhat romantic in his view of his subjects, Flaherty's work set high standards for all following documentary film makers.

**Flaubert, Gustave** (1821–80) French novelist. His masterpiece is his first published novel, *Madame Bovary* (1857), a study of romantic self-deception, adultery and suicide in rural France. Flaubert is especially noted for his meticulously impersonal and objective narrative, and concern for using just the right word.

**Flaxman, John** (1755–1826) English sculptor and designer. A proficient illustrator, his work on the *Iliad* and *Odyssey* (1793) influenced continental artists such as INGRES. He was appointed to the chair of sculpture at the Royal Academy in 1810.

**Fleming, Sir Alexander** (1881–1955) Scottish bacteriologist. He discovered the antiseptic qualities of the bactericidal enzyme lysozome (1922), and made one of the most important medical discoveries ever when he noticed the antibacterial qualities of the substance he dubbed "penicillin." He shared the 1945 Nobel prize for physiology or medicine with CHAIN and FLOREY.

**Fleming, Ian [Lancaster]** (1908–64) English novelist. His series of novels featuring the British secret agent James Bond (*see* CONNERY), *Live and Let Die* (1954) and *Goldfinger* (1964), were enormous popular successes and have all been filmed. The novels have been criticized by some for being slick and amoral in their treatment of sex and violence.

**Fletcher, John** (1579–1625) English dramatist. One of the most popular dramatists of his day, he frequently collaborated with other dramatists, such as SHAKESPEARE, but most notably with **Sir Francis Beaumont** (1584–1616), from 1606–13). Their best-known works are tragicomedies such as *The Maid's Tragedy* (1610–11) and *A King and No King* (1611).

**Florey, Howard Walter, Baron** (1898–1968) Australian pathologist. He shared the 1945 Nobel prize for physiology or medicine with Sir Alexander FLEMING and CHAIN for their work on penicillin.

**Florio**

**Florio, John** *see* **Montaigne**.

**Flynn, Errol** [Leslie Thomas Flynn] (1909–59) Australian-born American film actor. His starring roles in the swashbuckling tradition of FAIRBANKS, included *Captain Blood* (1935) and *The Sea Hawk* (1940), earned him considerable popularity, which was somewhat dimmed in Britain following *Objective Burma* (1944), a film that failed to note any British participation. Flynn was a legendary womaniser and drinker (*see also* NIVEN). The last film he worked on was a ridiculous documentary tribute to Fidel CASTRO, *The Cuban Rebel Girls* (1959).

**Foch, Ferdinand** (1851–1929) French general and marshal of France (1918). He was given command of the Allied forces in March 1918, and, always a believer in attack, led the Allies to victory following the arrival of US troops in July 1918.

**Fokine, Michel** (1880–1942) Russian-born American ballet dancer and choreographer. He choreographed The Dying Swan for PAVLOVA, and, with DIAGHILEV in Paris, created a new comprehensive style of ballet, in which all the elements, dance, music, costume and *mise en scène*, formed a coherent whole. He became a US citizen in 1932.

**Fonda, Henry** (1905–82) American film actor. His performances in such films as John FORD's *Young Mr Lincoln* (1939) and *The Grapes of Wrath* (1940) earned him great accolades. Fonda became seen as the epitome of "decent" America, a man determined to set injustices right. He won an Oscar for his part in *On Golden Pond* (1981), in which he starred with his daughter, **Jane [Seymour] Fonda** (1937– ) Her early film career began with insignificant bimbo roles, but she won recognition as a fine actress in films such as *They Shoot Horses Don't They?* (1969) and *Klute* (1971), the latter earning her an Oscar. She braved public disfavour in the 1960s with her outspoken opposition to the Vietnam war and espousal of radical causes, and subsequently became known primarily as a fitness fanatic with her bestselling "workout" videos and books.

**Fonteyn, Dame Margot** [Margaret Hookham] (1919–91) English ballerina. Regarded as one of the finest classical ballerinas of the century, she partnered NUREYEV at the age of 43.

**Foot, Michael [Mackintosh]** (1913– ) British Labour politician. A leading left-winger, pacifist and CND member, he was secretary of state of employment (1974–76) and leader of the House of Commons (1976–79), and succeeded CALLAGHAN as leader of the Labour Party 1980–83). After losing the 1983 election, Foot resigned as leader and was succeeded by KINNOCK. His many books include biographies of SWIFT and BEVAN.

**Ford, Ford Madox** [Ford Hermann Hueffer] (1873–1939) English novelist, poet and critic. His most important works are the novels *The Good Soldier* (1915) and the tetralogy *Parade's End* (published in one volume 1950). Ford founded the *Transatlantic Review* in 1924, and gave generous encouragement to many writers.

**Ford, Gerald R[udolph]** (1913– ) American Republican statesman and 38th president of the US (1974–77). He replaced AGNEW as NIXON's vice-president in 1973, becoming president the following year, after Nixon's impeachment and resignation. Ford's controversial decision to grant Nixon a free pardon was widely condemned. He barely retained the Republican presidency nomination from REAGAN's challenge, and was defeated by CARTER in the 1977 election.

**Ford, Henry** (1863–1947) American car designer and manufacturer. His Model T Ford, first introduced in 1908, was enormously successful (around 15 million sold) and its production line manufacture, a standard product available in any colour "as long as it's black"), became a role model for much of industry.

**Ford, John** (1586–*c*.1639) English dramatist, notable for such revenge tragedies as *'Tis Pity She's a Whore* and *The Broken Heart* (both 1633). Ford's bleak, objective vision of human suffering and his command of blank verse were highly praised by T. S. ELIOT.

**Ford, John** [Sean Aloysius O'Fearna] (1895–1973) American film director. He is regarded as one of the greatest of all directors for his epic and poetic vision of history, particularly that of the American West, e.g. *Stagecoach* (1939) and *The Searchers* (1956), both starring John WAYNE. Ford's vision of America is expressed strongly in *Young Mr Lincoln* (1939) and *The Grapes of Wrath* (1940), both starring the actor who most exemplified Ford's sense of fundamental American decency, Henry FONDA. Ford's other films include *The Informer* (1935), *How Green Was My Valley* (1941) and *The Quiet Man* (1952).

**Forman, Milos** (1932– ) Czech film director, resident in the US since since 1968. His Czech films include *A Blonde in Love* (1965) and *The Fireman's Ball* (1967). He settled in the US following the ending of the Prague Spring (*see* DUBCEK). His American films include the very successful black comedy *One Flew Over the Cuckoo's Nest* (1975) and *Amadeus*

(1988), the latter being mostly filmed in Prague.

**Forster, E[dward] M[organ]** (1879–1970) English novelist and critic. His novels, e.g. *The Longest Journey* (1907) and *Howard's End* (1910), are mainly concerned with moral and ethical choices, and the personal relationships of educated, middle-class people.

**Fowler, H[enry] W[atson]** (1858–1933) English lexicographer. The second of his two books on English usage, *A Dictionary of English Usage* (1926), was for many years the standard work on the subject.

**Fowles, John** (1926– ) English novelist. The film rights to his first book, *The Collector* (1963), a sinister psychological study of a butterfly collector turned kidnapper, were sold while the book was still in proof stage. His next two novels, *The Magus* (1966) and *The French Lieutenant's Woman* (1969), established him as a major novelist.

**Fox, Charles James** (1749–1806) English Whig statesman. He entered Parliament aged nineteen, and soon acquired a reputation for being a formidable orator. He served in various administrations, and strongly opposed the wars against the American and French revolutionaries. He was also a vigorous opponent of the slave trade.

**Fox, George** (1624–91) English religious leader. Brought up a Puritan, he wandered around England preaching the authenticity of the "inner light" within men that led them to true spirituality, as opposed to the corrupt established religion, and advocated peace and toleration. He founded his Society of Friends (known popularly as "Quakers") in 1647.

**Fragonard, Jean-Honoré** (1732–1806) French painter. One of the greatest exponents of Rococo art, his
early works were historical scenes on a grand scale,
e.g. *Coreseus Sacrificing himself to save Callierhoe*
(1765), but he is best known for his smaller, pictur-
esquely pretty canvases, e.g *The Swing* (1766). His
patrons included Madame de Pompadour and Madame du Barry, and he died in poverty after his style
went out of vogue during the French Revolution.

**Francesca, Piero della** *see* **Piero della Francesca**.

**Francis I** *see* **Maria Theresa**.

**Francis II** *see* **Mary, Queen of Scots**.

**Francis of Assisi, St** [Giovanni Bernardone] (1181–
1226) Italian monk. After a lively youth, he abandoned a military career to care for the poor and
founded a "brotherhood" of friars in 1210, and, in
1212 an order for women, the Poor Clares. He
preached poverty, chastity and obedience to the
Church, and received the stigmata in 1224. He was
canonized in 1228. His works include the *Canticle of
the Sun,* a hymn in praise of God's creation.

**Franck, César [Auguste]** (1822–90) Belgian-born
French composer (of German origin). His best works
were written late in life, e.g. the symphony in D
Minor, a violin sonata, and his string quartet, the
latter written in the year of his death.

**Franck, James** (1882–1964) German-born American physicist. With the German physicist **Gustav
Ludwig Hertz** (1887–1975), he shared the 1925
Nobel prize for physics for work on the quantum
theory, notably on the effects of bombarding atoms
with electrons.

**Franco, Francisco** (1892–1975) Spanish general
and dictator. He led the right-wing rebellion against

the Spanish Republican government during the Spanish Civil War (1936–39). He became leader of the Fascist Falange Party in 1937, and ruled Spain from 1939 until his death. He nominated Prince JUAN CARLOS as his successor.

**Frank, Anne** (1929–45) German-born Dutch Jewish girl. Her journal describing her and her family's experiences while hiding from the Nazis in occupied Amsterdam was published by the family's sole survivor, her father, in 1947. The family was captured in August 1944, and Anne died in Belsen. Her diary is one of the most moving accounts of the terrible suffering of the Jewish people during the war, and was filmed in 1959 as *The Diary of Anne Frank*.

**Franklin, Benjamin** (1706–90) American author, statesman and author. He helped draft the American Declaration of Independence, and played an active role in American political life for most of his long life. Sent to France by the American government in 1776 to seek aid, Franklin's seemingly artless advocacy of social and political change had a powerful influence on French radicals and democrats. His masterpiece is his highly entertaining *Autobiography* (1793). He also invented the lightning conductor.

**Franklin, Rosalind Elsie** (1920–58) British chemist. Her X-ray crystallography research into DNA contributed to the discovery of its structure by James WATSON and CRICK.

**Fraser, [John] Malcolm** (1930– ) Australian Liberal statesman. He was installed as caretaker prime minister (1975–83) following WHITLAM's dismissal, and won the ensuing 1975 election by a large majority.

**Frayn, Michael** (1933– ) English dramatist and novelist, noted for his dry, sardonic humour. Representative novels include *The Tin Men* (1965), a satire on robotics, and *A Very Private Life* (1968), a futuristic, anti-utopian fantasy. His plays include *Noises Off* (1982), which uses the conventions of farce to send up theatrical life.

**Frazer, Sir James George** (1854–1941) Scottish scholar and anthropologist, whose study of religious customs and myth, *The Golden Bough* (1890–1915), influenced FREUD and many 20th-century writers, e.g. T. S. ELIOT and James JOYCE.

**Frederick II** [Frederick the Great] (1712–86) Prussian king. A sickly child, he was brought up under a rigorously military regime by his father, and became King of Prussia in 1740. He expanded Prussian territory during the War of Austrian Succession (1740–48), gaining Silesia, and fought the Seven Years War (1756–63) with great military skill. He was a highly skilled flautist and composer, and patronized the arts and philosophers such as VOLTAIRE.

**Frege, [Friedrich Ludwig] Gottlob** (1848–1925) German mathematician and philosopher. His work received little recognition in his own time, but he is now regarded as having laid the foundations for both modern mathematical logic and the philosophy of language.

**French, Sir John [Denton Pinkstone],** [1st Earl of Ypres] (1852–1925) English field marshal. He commanded the British Expeditionary Force in France (1914–15). He was replaced as commander by HAIG. He became Lord Lieutenant of Ireland (1918–21) during the Anglo-Irish War.

**Freud, Lucian** (1922– ) German-born British painter. The grandson of Sigmund FREUD, he is renowned for his nudes and portraits, often painted from odd angles and in an unsettling, extreme-realist style.

**Freud, Sigmund** (1856–1939) Austrian psychiatrist, who founded psychoanalysis. His works, which include *The Interpretation of Dreams* (1900) and *The Ego and the Id* (1923) have been enormously influential on 20th-century thought. The main tenet of Freudian theory is that neuroses and dreams are repressed manifestations of sexual desire, which is often incestuous, as in the "Oedipus Complex." His stress on the importance of sex was rejected by ADLER and JUNG. His daughter **Anna Freud** (1895–1982) pioneered child psychology in the UK. Her works include *Beyond the Best Interests of the Child* (1973).

**Friedman, Milton** (1912– ) American economist. His controversial monetarist theory of economics, which is based on the thesis that inflation is caused by too much money flowing through an economy, and on the primacy of market forces and consumer choice and the need for minimal government intervention, became the dominant economic theory of the 1980s, even in ex-communist countries, despite much dissent from all quarters ("voodoo economics"—George BUSH). Friedman's many works include *Inflation: Causes and Consequences* (1963). He was awarded the 1976 Nobel prize for economics.

**Friedrich, Casper David** (1774–1840) German Romantic painter. Largely uninfluenced by other artists or trends, his work was highly controversial in its treatment of landscape, e.g. *The Cross on the*

*Mountain* (1808). His works have a melancholy atmosphere: land, sea and sky are fused in crepuscular light or hazy mist, out of which emerge trees and ruins.

**Frisch, Karl von** (1886–1982) Austrian zoologist and ethologist who discovered that bees communicate information on food sources and direction by "dancing" and that they orientate themselves by the direction of light. He shared the 1973 Nobel prize for physiology or medicine with LORENZ and Niko TINBERGEN.

**Frisch, Max** (1911– ) Swiss novelist and dramatist. His works include the BRECHT-influenced plays *Biedermann und die Brandstifter* (1958, translated as *The Fire Raisers*) and *Andorra* (1960), and the novels *Stiller* (1954, translated as *I'm Not Stiller*) and *Homo Faber* (1957).

**Frisch, Otto Robert** (1904–79) Austrian-born British nuclear physicist. He and his aunt, Lise MEITNER, discovered nuclear fission, and their work led directly to the invention of the atom bomb, the development of which Frisch worked on at Los Alamos. He wrote the cheerily entitled *Meet the Atoms* (1947).

**Frisch, Ragnar** *see* **Tinbergen, Jan.**

**Fromm, Erich** (1900–80) German-born American psychoanalyst and social philosopher. Combining elements of Marxism with FREUD's psychoanalysis, Fromm's work is based on the principle that social and economic factors determine human behaviour. His works include *Psychoanalysis and Religion* (1950) and *The Art of Loving* (1956).

**Frost, Robert [Lee]** (1874–1963) American poet. His quiet, lyrical poems, e.g. "Stopping By Woods on a Snowy Evening," have been much admired. Several critics have noted the dark, enigmatic nature of much of his symbolism.

**Fry, C[harles] B[urgess]** (1872–1956) English sportsman, regarded as one of the greatest all-round sportsmen ever. He played for England in athletics, cricket and soccer, played in an FA Cup final for Southampton and, like BRADMAN, hit six consecutive centuries. He was offered the throne of Albania, but declined. His autobiography is *Life Worth Living* (1939).

**Fry, Christopher** (1907– ) English dramatist, whose verse dramas, such as *A Phoenix Too Frequent* (1946) and *The Lady's Not for Burning* (1949), were popular with both critics and public.

**Fry, Elizabeth** (1780–1845) English prison reformer. A Quaker, she became a preacher in 1810. During a visit to Newgate prison in 1813, she was horrified to discover the desperate conditions under which female prisoners and their children were living, and devoted her life to prison reform and improving the lot of prisoners.

**Fuchs, Klaus [Emil Julius]** (1911–88) German-born British physicist. He began work on British atom-bomb research in 1941, becoming a British citizen in 1942, and subsequently worked on the Los Alamos Manhattan project (1943–46). He was jailed in 1950 for 14 years for passing details of atom-bomb research to the Soviet Union, and on his release in 1959 settled in East Germany.

**Fuchs, Sir Vivian Ernest** (1908– ) English explorer and scientist. He led the Commonwealth Trans-Antarctic Expedition (1955–58), which made the first overland crossing of Antarctica, reaching the South Pole in January 1958.

**Fugard, Athol** (1932– ) South African dramatist, whose plays explore the tragedy of racial tension caused by apartheid in South Africa. His works include *Boesman and Lena* (1968) and *Sizwe Bansi is Dead* (1972).

**Fuller, [Richard] Buckminster** (1895–1983) American architect and engineer. He invented the "geodesic dome," a lightweight framework consisting of a set of polygons in the shape of a shell, the best known of which was the US pavilion at the 1967 Montreal exhibition.

**Furtwängler, Wilhelm** (1886–1954) German conductor. He became one of the most popular conductors in Europe in the 1920s and early 1930s, particularly for his highly charged interpretations of Wagner. His popularity outside Germany declined rapidly from the late 1930s, due to his accommodation with the Nazi regime.

**Fuseli, Henry** [Johann Heinrich Füssli] (1741–1825) Swiss-born British painter. He originally trained for the priesthood, took up painting, and settled in England in 1765. His paintings are mannered and Romantic with a sense of the grotesque and macabre, e.g. *The Nightmare* (1781). He was much admired by Surrealists such as DALI.

# G

**Gable, [William] Clark** (1901–60) American film actor. His rugged good looks, sardonic wit and easy-going charm made him one of the most popular film stars of his day. He was voted "King of Hollywood" in 1937. His films include *It Happened One Night* (1934), *Mutiny on the Bounty* (1935) and *Gone With the Wind* (1939), in which he played Rhett Butler to Vivien LEIGH's Scarlett O'Hara. His last film was the downbeat *The Misfits* (1960), in which he starred opposite Marilyn MONROE.

**Gabo, Naum** [Naum Neemia Pevsner] (1890–1977) Russian-born American sculptor. He is regarded as one of the founding fathers of the Constructivist movement in Russia. He also produced innovative kinetic and non-figurative sculptures out of substances such as transparent plastic.

**Gabor, Dennis** (1900–79) Hungarian-born British engineer. He was awarded the 1971 Nobel prize for physics for his invention (in 1947) of the hologram.

**Gaddafi** *or* **Qaddafi, Moammar al-** (1942– ) Libyan statesman and military dictator. Influenced by NASSER, Gaddafi took power in a coup in 1969, and became president in 1977. Regarded almost universally as an unpredictable and often dangerous leader, Gaddafi has openly supported terrorist groups around the world, such as the IRA and Spanish fascists, in what he sees as a holy war against "imperialism" and "Zionism."

Gagarin

**Gagarin, Yuri [Alekseevich]** (1934–68) Soviet cosmonaut, who became, in 1961, the first man in space, when his Vostok satellite circled the earth. He died in a plane crash.

**Gainsborough, Thomas** (1727–88) English painter. He worked as a portrait painter, first in his native Suffolk, then in Bath, before moving to London where he became a member of the Royal Academy. His keen interest in landscape painting pervades most of his work, his sitters often being portrayed in an outdoor setting, e.g. *Mr and Mrs Andrews* (1748). He developed a light, rapid painting style based on a delicate palette and at all times demonstrating his pure delight in painting.

**Gaitskell, Hugh [Todd Naylor]** (1906–63) British Labour politician. He was regarded as being on the right of his party, having introduced, as chancellor of the exchequer (1950–51), national health service charges, which resulted in BEVAN's and WILSON's resignations. He became Labour Party leader (1955–63). His sudden death was followed by Harold Wilson's election to the leadership of the Labour Party.

**Galbraith, John Kenneth** (1908– ) Canadian-born American economist and diplomat. He has been notably critical of the wastefulness of capitalist society in its deployment of resources in activities such as creating consumer needs for superfluous products. His works include *The Affluent Society* (1958) and *The New Industrial State* (1967). He was American ambassador to India (1961–63).

**Galilei, Galileo** (1564–1642) Italian astronomer, mathematician and natural philosopher. As a medical student, he rejected the established Aristotelian doctrines, and by the time he was appointed professor of Mathematics at Padua in 1592 had made a name for himself as an innovative thinker and experimenter, having demonstrated the isochronism of the pendulum and shown that falling bodies of differing weight descend at the same rate. He also developed the refracting telescope, and became convinced of the truth of COPERNICUS's theory that the earth revolved around the sun. Combative by nature, and finally unable to prove the truth of the Copernican theory, he fell out with his old supporter Pope URBAN VIII, who forced him to publicly retract.

**Gallup, George Horace** (1901–84) American statistician. He developed the opinion poll into a sophisticated device, the "Gallup Poll," for testing public opinion, most notably on elections. He founded the American Institution of Public Opinion (1935). His books include *Public Opinion in a Democracy* (1939).

**Galsworthy, John** (1867–1933) English novelist and dramatist. His plays, which are realistic dramas attacking social injustices, include *Strife* (1909) and *Justice* (1910). Public furore over the latter resulted in UK prison reform. His novels include the Forsyte saga trilogy—*The Man of Property* (1906), *In Chancery* (1920), and *Awakening* (1920).

**Galton, Sir Francis** (1822–1911) English scientist and explorer. The cousin of Charles DARWIN, he travelled widely in Africa and made a significant contribution to meteorology, particularly with his work on anticyclones. His most important work was in the study of heredity. Regarded as the founder of eugenics, he published *Hereditary Genius* (1869) and *Natural Inheritance* (1889). He also developed the science of fingerprinting.

**Galway, James** (1939– ) Irish flautist, regarded as one of the finest flautists of the modern era. Equally at home in modern, classical, baroque and (in his early days) the war music of the Orange flute bands, he became a well-known figure through his televised appearances in the 1960s and 1970s.

**Gama, Vasco da** (*c*.1469–1525) Portuguese navigator. He discovered the route to India round the Cape of Good Hope (1497–99), and became Portuguese viceroy in India in 1524.

**Gandhi, Indira** (1917–84) Indian stateswoman and prime minister. The daughter of NEHRU, she became prime minister (1966–77) of India. She instituted a state of emergency in 1975, and lost the ensuing 1977 general election. Her second term of office as prime minister (1980–84) saw much ethnic strife. After ordering Indian soldiers to seize the Sikh Golden Temple at Amritsar, which was occupied by Sikh Punjab separatists, she was assassinated by her Sikh bodyguards. Her son **Rajiv** (1944–91) became prime minister in 1984, and was killed in a suicide bomb attack (the bomber, a woman, was generally assumed to be a Tamil separatist) during the 1991 election.

**Gandhi, Mahatma** [Mohandas Karamchand Gandhi] (1869–1948) Indian nationalist statesman and spiritual leader ("Mahatma" means "Great Soul"). A passionate advocate of non-violent resistance, Gandhi's long campaign against British rule in India, using tactics of civil disobedience through passive resistance and hunger strikes, had great influence on world public opinion. He also struggled for reconciliation between Hindus and Moslems, and championed the cause of the Hindu Harijan caste of "untouchables." He was assassinated by a Hindu extremist, in the wake of India's independence and partition.

**Garbo, Greta** [Greta Lovisa Gustafson] (1905– 90) Swedish-born American film actress. Noted for her austere and remote beauty ("What one sees in other women drunk, one sees in Garbo sober"—TYNAN), her films include *Queen Christina* (1933) and *Ninotchka* (1939). She probably never said "I want to be alone," but she lived in seclusion (in New York) from 1951 to her death.

**García Lorca, Federigo** *see* **Lorca, Federigo García**.

**Garibaldi, Giuseppe** (1807–82) Italian patriot. Condemned to death for his part in attempting to capture Genoa for the patriots in 1834, he escaped to South America, returning to Italy during the year of revolutions, 1848. There, he served with the Sardinians and took part in the defence of Rome against the French, and, in 1860, with a force a thousand strong, took Naples and Sicily for the newly united Italy. He is regarded as the most significant figure in the struggle for Italian independence.

**Garland, Judy** [Frances Gumm] (1922–69) American film actress and singer. She became one of the most loved child stars of the cinema with her performance as Dorothy in *The Wizard of Oz* (1939), and later starred in such films as *Easter Parade* (1948) and *A Star is Born* (1954). She died of drink and drug abuse. Her daughter, **Liza Minnelli** (1946– ), became a star in the 1970s with films such as *Cabaret* (1972).

**Garrick, David** (1717–79) English actor and dramatist. He was a pupil of Samuel JOHNSON at Lichfield and accompanied him to London in 1737. He made his mark as an actor within a few years, his performance as Richard III in 1747 making particular impact. He dominated the English stage for the rest of his life, and was actor-manager of Drury Lane Theatre 1747–76. The farces he wrote are now of little interest, but his letters (published 1831–2) provide fascinating portraits of his contemporaries who were in no doubt as to his acting genius: the actress **Kitty Clive** (1711–85) said of him, "Damn him, he could act a gridiron!".

**Gaskell, Mrs Elizabeth** [Elizabeth Cleghorn Stevenson] (1810–65) English novelist. Her novels about English country life, e.g. *Mary Barton* (1848) and *North and South* (1855), are often concerned (as are DISRAELI's) with the injustices of the "two-nation" society of 19th-century England. Her most popular novel is *Cranford* (1851–3), a gentle and entertaining study of life in a small village. She also wrote a biography (1857) of her friend Charlotte BRONTË.

**Gasser, Herbert Spencer** *see* **Erlanger, Joseph**

**Gaudier-Brzeska, Henri** [Henri Gaudier] (1891–1915) French sculptor. He moved to London in 1912 where he became a leading avant-garde artist and a signatory of the Vorticist Manifesto. He was killed in the trenches during World War I.

**Gauguin, Paul** (1848–1903) French painter. One of the greatest exponents of post-Impressionism, he worked as a stockbroker and exhibited in three Impressionist exhibitions before developing his own simplistic, richly coloured style, as in *The Vision after the sermon, or Jacob wrestling with the Angel*

(1888). His interest in primitive art led to him settling in the South Pacific islands, where despite illness and poverty, he painted some of his most important masterpieces, e.g. *Where do we come from? What are We? Where are we going?*

**Gaulle, Charles de** *see* **de Gaulle, Charles**.

**Gavaskar, Sunil Manohar** (1949– ) Indian cricketer. He was captain of India (1978–83, 1984–85). He was dubbed the "Little Master" for his skill (and stature) and scored 34 test centuries.

**Gay, John** (1685–1732) English dramatist and poet. His masterpiece is *The Beggars' Opera* (1728), a ballad opera inspired by SWIFT's observation that a "Newgate pastoral" might make an "odd, pretty sort of thing". The work was a huge success, its popularity due in part to the fact that characters and incidents in the play were drawn from real life— notably, from the life of the prime minister WALPOLE, who tolerated this play but banned its sequel, *Polly* (1729). The play was said to have made Gay rich, and its producer John Rich gay. BRECHT's *Threepenny Opera* is based on Gay's play.

**Gell-Mann, Murray** (1929– ) American physicist. He introduced the concept of "strangeness" and the quark hypothesis into physics (the word "quark" is taken from JOYCE's *Finnegans Wake)*, and was awarded the 1969 Nobel prize for physics for his research into particle physics. He predicted the existence of the omega-minus particle in his book, *The Eightfold Way* (1964), the title of which refers to the Buddhist path to Nirvana.

**Genet, Jean** (1910–86) French dramatist and novelist. His works, include the plays *The Maids* (1947) and *The Balcony* (1950), and the novels, e.g. *Our*

### Genghis Khan

*Lady of the Flowers* (1944) and *Querelle de Brest* (1947), are often based on Genet's underworld experiences.

**Genghis Khan** [originally Temujin] (*c.*1162–1227) Mongol leader. He united the Mongol tribes and conquered China, establishing an empire that stretched from the Black Sea to the Pacific coast. His adopted name "Genghis" (or "Jinghis") Khan means "universal ruler." His conquests were invariably bloody, although the administrations he set up did maintain law and order, and he is still venerated in Mongolia.

**Gentile, Giovanni** (1875–1944) Italian philosopher and politician. He collaborated with CROCE on both philosophical study and politics, but developed his own variant of idealism, called "actualism," in which only the act of thought is real. He became a long-term supporter of MUSSOLINI and Fascist minister and was assassinated by partisans in Florence.

**George I** (1660–1727) king of Great Britain and Ireland. The elector of Hanover since 1698, he became the first Hanoverian British king in 1714. Unable to speak English and with a marked preference for living in Hanover, he was not the most popular of British monarchs, but was well served by WALPOLE and the Whigs.

**George II** (1683–1760) king of Great Britain and Ireland (1727–60). He was the last British monarch to fight in battle, at Denigen in 1743. The Jacobite rebellion of 1745 was efficiently crushed by his second son **William, Duke of Cumberland** (1721–65), effectively ending any challenge to Hanoverian rule.

**George III** (1738–1820) king of Great Britain and

Ireland (1760–1820). Regarded as the least unattractive of the Hanoverian kings, he had much better relations with his subjects than his predecessors. His American policy—in which he was fully backed by NORTH—proved disastrous, and the Americans established their independence in 1783. He became insane in 1811, after which his son George became Regent.

**George IV** (1762–1830) king of Great Britain and Ireland (1820–30). In the Hanoverian manner, he detested his father, and became Prince Regent in 1811 when his father went insane. A close associate of Whig opposition figures such as FOX, he acquired a public reputation for being dissolute. In 1782, he married the Roman Catholic **Mrs Maria Fitzherbert** (1756–1837); the marriage was not valid in civil law, and he married **Princess Caroline of Brunswick** (1768–1821) in 1795. He subsequently tried to divorce Caroline in an appallingly squalid atmosphere of mutual recrimination and disclosure. When he became king, he dropped his Whig friends and turned to the Tories. He was also a noted patron of the arts.

**George V** (1865–1936) king of Great Britain and Northern Ireland and emperor of India (1910–36). He was the second son of EDWARD VII, and changed the surname of the Royal Family from Saxe-Coburg to Windsor in 1917. He was a very popular monarch, noted particularly for his radio broadcasts. His eldest son was the Duke of WINDSOR, his second GEORGE VI.

**George VI** (1895–1952) king of Great Britain and Northern Ireland (1936–1952) and emperor of India (1936–1947). He was the second son of GEORGE V, and succeeded to the throne following the Duke of WINDSOR's abdication. He achieved great popularity, particularly during World War II. His death was believed by his family to be have been brought on by the pressure of becoming king. He was succeeded by his eldest daughter, ELIZABETH II.

**Géricault, Théodore** (1791–1824) French Romantic painter. Influenced by RUBENS in his early work, his nature style took its inspiration from MICHELANGELO. The realism and baroque dynamism of his masterpiece, *The Raft of the Medusa* (1819), caused almost as much outrage as its political overtones, and his powerful oil sketches, such as *The Derby at Epsom* (1820), had a huge influence on younger painters.

**Gershwin, George** (1898–1937) American composer and pianist. He and his brother, the lyricist **Ira Gershwin** (1896–1983), created several very popular musicals, e.g. *Lady Be Good* (1924) and *Funny Face* (1927). Their black opera, *Porgy and Bess*, (1935) was initially poorly received but soon became acknowledged as a masterpiece of American music. Gershwin was much influenced by jazz, as in his best-known orchestral work *Rhapsody in Blue* (1924).

**Getty, J[ean] Paul** (1892–1976) American industrialist and art collector, renowned for his wealth, miserliness and acquisition of works of art. He made his money in oil (he also inherited $15 million from his father), and was a billionaire by the late 1960s. The J. Paul Getty Museum in Malibu, California, houses his art collection.

**Ghiberti, Lorenzo** (1378–1455) Florentine sculptor. The span of his work covers the late Gothic and early Renaissance periods, of which times he was an outstanding figure. His masterpieces are the two sets of gilded bronze doors for the Baptistry in Florence, on which he worked form 1401 to 1452, giving training and employment to many of the major contemporary artists in his workshops. He also wrote two *Commentaries*, one a history of Italian art and the other an autobiography.

**Ghirlandaio, Domenico** (1449–94) Florentine painter who ran a workshop with his brothers **Benedetto** (1458–97) and **Davide** (1452–1525), where he produced frescos and altarpieces for a number of churches in Florence. He was also a portraitist and included contemporary portraits in his frescos. His son **Ridolfo** (1483–1561) was MICHELANGELO's tutor.

**Giacometti, Alberto** (1901–66) Swiss sculptor and painter. He became a surrealist in 1930, and broke with the movement in 1935. Influenced by SARTRE's existentialism, he began producing his famous thin, elongated, spidery figures, e.g. *Pointing Man* (1947).

**Giap, Vo Nguyen** (1912– ) Vietnamese general. He led the Viet Minh army against the French and commanded the North Vietnamese army against the US during the Vietnam War. His works on military strategy include *People's War, People's Army* (1961).

**Gibbon, Edward** (1737–94) English historian. His masterpiece is his *History of the Decline and Fall of the Roman Empire* (1776–88), a work that, in breadth of narrative and erudite analysis, remains one of the greatest of all historical studies. Gibbon's sceptical and historical tone while describing the rise and establishment of Christianity gave much offence to many of his contemporaries.

**Gide, André** (1869–1951) French novelist. Brought
up a strict Protestant, he decided he was homosexual after reading Oscar WILDE. His novels, e.g.
*Fruits of the Earth* (1897) and *Strait is the Gate*
(1909), are short, fascinating studies of sexual and
social self-deception.

**Gielgud, Sir [Arthur] John** (1904– ) English stage
and film actor and producer. Regarded as one of the
leading Shakespearian actors of the century,
Gielgud, like OLIVIER, also slipped effortlessly into
the acting roles required by such dramatists as
PINTER. His late appearances in several Hollywood
films were regarded as unfortunate by many, although he won an Oscar for *Arthur* (1980).

**Gierek, Edward** (1913– ) Polish Communist statesman. He became leader of the Polish United Workers Party following GOMULKA's resignation in 1971.
He presided over increasing industrial unrest and
the rise of Solidarity (*see* WALESA) and was forced to
resign in 1980.

**Gilbert, Sir W(illiam) S(chwenck)** (1836–1911)
English dramatist and librettist. His collaboration
with the composer **Sir Arthur Sullivan** (1842–
1900) resulted in the "Savoy Operas," e.g. *Trial by
Jury* (1875) and *The Gondoliers* (1889), of which
there are 13 in all, and which have retained their
popularity with critics and public alike for their
bright wit and lively tunes.

**Gill, [Arthur] Eric [Rowton]** (1882–1940) English
sculptor, engraver, typographer and writer. He converted to Roman Catholicism in 1913, and his religious beliefs were profoundly influential in his work,
which includes *The Stations of the Cross* carvings
for Westminster Cathedral (1914–18) and the

*Prospero and Ariel* sculpture (1931) for Broadcasting House. His books include *Art* (1934) and *Autobiography* (1940).

**Gillespie, Dizzy** [John Birks Gillespie] (1917–93) American jazz trumpeter and bandleader, renowned as a virtuoso trumpeter and and for his "bop" sessions with Thelonius MONK and Charlie PARKER.

**Ginsberg, Allen** (1926– ) American poet, regarded as the leading poet of the 1950s "beat generation." His poem *Howl* (1956) includes the claim that Ginsberg's friends were the "best minds" of the 1950s. Ginsberg saw drugs and sex as a liberation, and had much influence on the hippy culture of the 1960s.

**Giorgione** [Giorgio da Castelfranco] (*c*.1477–1510) Venetian painter. Little of his work has survived, although he is one of the most influential painters of his time. The importance of Giorgione's work is in its treatment of landscape; he imbued landscape painting with strong atmosphere and moods to which the detail is subordinated, and his work was much imitated by succeeding artists. His documented works include *The Tempest* and *The Three Philosophers*.

**Giotto di Bondone** (1267–1337) Florentine painter and architect. Little of his work is documented, but his known works show a development of spatial perspective and fully rounded figures that represent a departure from the flat, decorative imagery of the Byzantine era. His works include the fresco *The Life of the Virgin, St Anne and St Joachim* in the Arena Chapel in Padua, and the great *Life of St Francis* in the Church of San Francesco at Assisi (*c*.1290s) has been attributed to him. His work is accepted as the starting point for modern western art.

**Giscard d'Estaing, Valéry** (1926– ) French statesman. He served as minister of finance under DE GAULLE (1962–66) and POMPIDOU (1969–74) and was elected president (1974–81) following the latter's death. He was defeated in the 1984 presidential election by MITTERAND.

**Gissing, George [Robert]** (1857–1903) English novelist. His novels are grimly uncompromising works designed to expose the horrors of social injustice and often have as their central character an artist or hack writer (like Gissing himself) struggling to survive in a sea of indifference and poverty. His novels include *New Grub Street* (1891) and *The Private Papers of Henry Ryecroft* (1903).

**Gladstone, William Ewart** (1809–98) British statesman. He became the leader of the Liberals in 1867, and was subsequently prime minister four times: 1868–74, 1880–5, 1886, and 1892–4. He carried through many reforms, e.g. the disestablishment of the Church of Ireland in 1869, and instituted the secret ballot in 1872, but failed in his objective of giving Ireland Home Rule. He had a long rivalry with his Tory opponent, DISRAELI, whose imperialism he vehemently opposed. He was a devout evangelical, to the extent of seeking out prostitutes to convert.

**Glashow, Sheldon** *see* **Weinberg, Steven**.

**Glass, Philip** (1937– ) American composer. He studied under BOULANGER and SHANKAR and became one of the leading avant-garde composers of the 1970s, noted for his deep interest in Eastern harmonies and use of repeated motifs. His works include *Ein-*

*stein on the Beach* (1976) and *Akhnaton* (1984), and the score for the film *Mishima* (1985).

**Glendower, Owen** *see* **Henry IV**.

**Gluck, Christoph Wilibald von** (1714–87) German composer. He is especially noted for his operas, e.g. *Orfeo and Eurydice* (1762) and *Alceste* (1766).

**Godard, Jean-Luc** (1930– ) French film director. Regarded as one of the most influential New Wave French film directors of the 1950s, his films include *Breathless* (1959) and *Week-End* (1967).

**Goddard, Robert Hutchings** (1882–1945) American physicist. He produced the first successful liquid-fuelled rocket in 1926.

**Gödel, Kurt** (1906–78) Austrian-born American logician and mathematician. His demonstration of the "undecidability" of mathematics, "Godel's theorem," shows the existence of undecidable elements in arithmetic systems.

**Godwin, William** (1756–1836) English novelist and philosopher. His *Enquiry concerning Political Justice* (1793) questioned the validity of established goverment and institutions, notably marriage, and had a strong influence on many radicals, including SHELLEY, who married his daughter Mary (he married Mary WOLLSTONECRAFT in 1797, who died soon after giving birth to Mary). His novel, *The Adventures of Caleb Williams* (1794), is still highly regarded.

**Goebbels, [Paul] Joseph** (1897–1945) German Nazi politician. He joined the Nazi Party in 1924, becoming head of its propaganda section in 1929 and minister of enlightenment and propaganda (1933–45). A ferocious anti-semite, Goebbels drew much of the inspiration for his propaganda techniques from the Bolsheviks. He followed HITLER's suicide with his own, after shooting his wife and children.

**Goering, Hermann** *see* **Göring, Hermann.**

**Goes, Hugo van der** (c.1440–1482) Flemish painter. His major work, on which attribution of others is based, is the Medici commission for the Portinari Altarpiece (1746), now in the Uffizi in Florence, which shows a rich sense of decorative surface texture combined with outstanding perception of space and depth of composition.

**Goethe, Johann Wolfgang von** (1749–1832) German poet, dramatist, novelist, philosopher, scientist and statesman. He was one of the most learned and influential figures of his time. His works include the novels *Die Leiden des jungen Werthers* (*The Sorrows of Young Werther*, 1774), a tale of unrequited love, and *Die Wahlverwandtschaften* (*Elective Affinities*, 1809), the play *Egmont* (1788), and much great poetry. His masterpiece, the verse drama *Faust*, was published in two parts in 1808 and 1832.

**Gogh, Vincent Van** *see* **Van Gogh, Vincent**.

**Gogol, Nikolai Vasilievich** (1809–52) Russian short-story writer, dramatist and novelist. His two greatest works are the play *The Government Inspector* (1836), a scathing satire on Russian bureaucracy and incompetence, and *Dead Souls* (1842), a novel in which the names of dead peasants are bought by a young man scheming for an inheritance.

**Golding, William [Gerald]** (1911–93) English novelist. His first novel, *The Lord of the Flies* (1954), describes the reduction to savagery of a group of schoolboys stranded on an island. This and his second novel, *The Inheritors* (1955), a bleak parable of man's inhumanity, established Golding's reputation as a master novelist. He was awarded the Nobel prize for literature in 1983.

**Goldman, Emma** (1869–1940) Russian-born American anarchist. She was imprisoned several times for agitating against employers and for advocating such measures as resistance to the draft. She was deported to the USSR in 1919 and returned in 1924. Her works include an autobiography, *Living My Life* (1931).

**Goldoni, Carlo** (1707–93) Italian dramatist. He wrote over 250 plays (in French as well as in Italian) and some operas. Around 150 of his plays are comedies, invariably set in his native Venice and frequently featuring satirical attacks on the aristocracy.

**Goldschmidt, Richard Benedikt** (1878–1958) German-born American geneticist, noted for his theory that the pattern and chemical composition of the chromosome molecule determines heredity, rather than the qualities of the individual genes.

**Goldschmidt, Victor Moritz** (1888–1947) Swiss-born Norwegian geneticist. He drew on advances in geology, chemistry and mineralogy to create the modern discipline of geochemistry.

**Goldsmith, Oliver** (1728–1774) Irish poet and essayist. He settled in London in 1756, where he became a hack reviewer and writer for periodicals. His two greatest works are the novel *The Vicar of Wakefield* (1764) a cunningly structured blend of virtue and humour, and his hugely successful play *She Stoops to Conquer* (1773).

**Goldwyn, Samuel** [Samuel Goldfish] (1882–1974)

Polish-born American film producer. Goldwyn became one of the founders of the Hollywood movie business, with DE MILLE and others, with *The Squaw Man* (1914), and formed Metro-Goldwyn-Mayer with Louis B. MAYER in 1924. Among the films he produced are *Wuthering Heights* (1939) and *The Secret Life of Walter Mitty* (1947). His "Goldwynisms" are mostly apocryphal, e.g. "You can include me out."

**Gollancz, Sir Victor** (1893–1967) English publisher and philanthropist. He became a successful publisher in the 1930s, notably of crime fiction, with highly distinctive yellow wrappers on his books. He founded the Left Book Club in 1936, using authors such as KOESTLER and ORWELL, which became a strong influence on left-wing politics. A noted humanitarian, he campaigned for Jewish refugees before the war, and organized aid to Germany after it. His books include *My Dear Timothy* (1952) and *From Darkness to Light* (1959).

**Gomulka, Wladyslaw** (1905–82) Polish Communist statesman. He was general secretary of the Polish United Workers Party (1943–48) but was imprisoned in 1951 for lack of enthusiasm for Soviet dominance of his country. He served again as general secretary (1956–70) and was forced to resign in 1971.

**Goodman, Benny** [Benjamin David] (1909–86) American jazz clarinetist and bandleader. In the 1930s he became one of the first white jazz bandleaders to break racial taboos and hire black players. A highly popular musician, he became known as the "King of Swing."

**Gorbachev, Mikhail Sergeevich** (1931– ) Soviet Communist statesman. He became general secretary of the Soviet Communist party in 1985 in succession to ANDROPOV, and soon began instituting his policies of *glasnost* ("openness") and *perestroika* ("reconstruction"), which resulted in far-reaching social and political reforms that changed Soviet and world history irrevocably. He became "executive president" in 1990, with wide-ranging powers, facing strong opposition from radicals such as YELTSIN and from hard-line Communists. His powers were insufficient to withstand the break-up of the USSR, and he resigned in December 1991.

**Gore, Al[bert]** (1948– ) American politician. A former investigative reporter, tobacco and livestock farmer, and developer, he was elected to the Senate for the state of Tennessee in 1985, and became vice-president of the USA after CLINTON's 1992 presidential victory.

**Göring** *or* **Goering, Hermann [Wilhelm]** (1893–1946) German Nazi politician and military leader. An ace fighter pilot during World War I, he joined the Nazi Party in 1922, becoming head of the SA storm troops in 1923. He served HITLER as Prussian prime minister, minister of the interior and air minister (1933–45), organizing the rebuilding of the Luftwaffe.

**Gorki** *or* **Gorky, Maxim** [Aleksey Maximovich Peshkov] (1868–1936) Russian novelist, dramatist and short-story writer. His best-known works are the autobiographical trilogy *Childhood* (1913), *Among People* (1915) and *My Universities* (1923), and the play *The Lower Depths* (1902). A firm communist, he helped formulate the doctrine of socialist realism in the USSR in the 1930s.

**Gorky, Arshile** [Vosdanig Manoog Adoian] (1904–

48) Armenian-born American painter. Originally a surrealist, his style, characterized by vibrant colours and sinuous, fluid lines, developed into an abstract approach that was influential on the New York Action school of painters.

**Gorton, Sir John Grey** (1911– ) Australian Liberal statesman. He was Liberal prime minister (1968–71), and resigned in 1971 following his defeat on a vote of confidence.

**Goya y Lucientes, Francisco de** (1746–1828) Spanish painter and printmaker. He settled in Madrid in 1775. His major influences were TIEPOLO and VELÀZQUEZ, who inspired his strong, free-flowing and powerful pictorial style, as in his remarkable portraits of the Spanish royal family, to whom he was court painter. Important later works include the etchings *Los Caprichos* (1799) and *Disasters of War* (1810–20), disturbing works inspired by the behaviour of the French army in their invasion of Spain, as are the paintings *May 2nd 1808* and *May 3rd 1808*.

**Grace, W[illiam] G[ilbert]** (1848–1915) English cricketer and physician. One of the first English cricketers to become a national institution, he began playing first-class cricket (for Gloucestershire) in 1864, and had scored a hundred centuries by 1895. He was also noted for his cunning gamesmanship.

**Graham, Billy** [William Franklin Graham] (1918– ) American evangelist. He was ordained a Southern Baptist minister in 1940. His evangelical crusades began in Los Angeles in 1949, and were subsequently taken all over the world, including Eastern Europe. Despite being the friend and confidant of figures such as Richard NIXON, Graham's personal integrity has never been disputed.

**Graham, Martha** (1893–1991) American dancer and choreographer. Regarded as one of the main founders of modern dance, with a distinctively angular and dramatic approach based on strict physical control, she founded her own troupe in 1929, and subsequently founded the Martha Graham School of Contemporary Dance in New York.

**Grahame, Kenneth** (1859–1932) Scottish author. He wrote three children's books, *The Golden Age* (1895), *Dream Days* (1898) and (his masterpiece) *The Wind in the Willows* (1908).

**Grainger, Percy [Aldridge]** (1882–1961) Australian-born American pianist and composer. Like his friends GRIEG and DELIUS, Grainger was a notable enthusiast for folk songs, on which many of his own works are based, e.g. *Molly on the Shore* and *Country Gardens*.

**Gramsci, Antonio** (1891–1937) Italian politician and Marxist theorist. He helped found the Italian Communist Party in 1921, and became its leader in 1924. MUSSOLINI's Fascists banned the party in 1926, and Gramsci spent the next 11 years of his life in prison, being released shortly before his death. Gramsci's prison writings are regarded as among the most important works of socialist theory for their postulation of such concepts as his theory of the all-pervading hegemony of a dominant class in society.

**Grant, Cary** [Archibald Alexander Leach] (1904–86) English-born American film actor. Handsome, debonair and suave, Grant became one of Hollywood's leading stars in light comedy roles such as

*Bringing Up Baby* (1938) and *His Girl Friday* (1940) and in performances in HITCHCOCK thrillers, e.g. *Notorious* (1946) and *North by Northwest* (1959).

**Grant, Ulysses S[impson]** (1822–85) American soldier and 18th US President. Appointed commander of the Union forces in 1864 by LINCOLN, he organized his troops into separate armies striking deep into rebel territory. He was elected President in 1869. Although he established universal suffrage for all citizens regardless of colour, his term was plagued by corruption scandals and he ceased to be President in 1877.

**Granville-Barker, Harley** (1877–1946) English dramatist, producer and critic. The best of his plays are the naturalistic dramas *The Voysey Inheritance* (1905) and *Waste* (1907). His productions of Shakespeare broke new ground in their concern for textual authenticity and disdain for over-elaborate sets. His *Prefaces* to Shakespeare's plays were published in four volumes (1927–45).

**Grappelli, Stéphane** (1908– ) French jazz violinist. With Django REINHARDT, he was a founder of the Quintette de Hot Club de France, which became the leading European jazz group. He is still regarded as the finest jazz violinist ever.

**Grass, Günter [Wilhelm]** (1927– ) German novelist, dramatist and poet. His works include the novel *Die Blechtrommel* (*The Tin Drum*, 1959), a grimly comic satire on the collapse of the Third Reich as seen through the eyes of a boy, and *Die Plebejer proben den Aufstand* (*The Plebians Rehearse the Uprising*, 1966), a satire on BRECHT's dramatic and political theories.

**Graves, Robert [Ranke]** (1895–1985) English poet,

novelist and critic. His works include his classic autobiographical account of World War I soldiering, *Goodbye to all That* (1929), several great love poems, e.g. "She Tells Her Love While Fast Asleep," and historical novels such as *I, Claudius* and *Claudius the God* (both 1934).

**Gray, Thomas** (1716–71) English poet. His best-known poem is "Elegy Written in a Country Churchyard" (1751), a meditation on the graveyard at Stoke Poges, which is one of the most-quoted poems in the English Language.

**Green, Henry** [Henry Vincent Yorke] (1905–73) English novelist. His strange, highly original novels, e.g. *Living* (1929), *Loving* (1945) and *Back* (1946), are noted for their fluid and confident use of the rhythms and expressions of ordinary speech, and have been highly praised by his contemporaries, e.g. WAUGH.

**Greene, [Henry] Graham** (1904–1991) English novelist. He converted to Roman Catholicism in 1926, and his religious beliefs play an important part in his fictional world, the so-called "Graham Greeneland," a seedy, exotic world of spiritually tainted not-quite heroes. Regarded as one of the greatest modern novelists, his division of his work into "entertainments," e.g. *Brighton Rock* (1938), and "serious" works, e.g. *The Heart of the Matter* (1948) is generally disregarded.

**Greene, Robert** (*c.*1558–92) English poet, dramatist and pamphleteer. His tracts on the Elizabethan underworld are valuable for their descriptions of lower-class life and language. He is also of interest for his attack on SHAKESPEARE in his *Groat's Worth of Wit* (1592), in which he warns his fellow university-educated dramatists against the "upstart crow" (the publisher of the tract afterwards apologised publicly for the remark).

**Greer, Germaine** (1939– ) Australian feminist, writer and broadcaster. Her controversial study of the oppression of women in male-dominated society, *The Female Eunuch* (1970), established her as the foremost feminist writer of the 1970s. Later books, e.g. *Sex and Destiny: the Politics of Human Fertility* (1984) display a radical reappraisal of her earlier views.

**Gregory I, St** [Gregory the Great] (*c.*540–640) Roman pope (590–604). Of patrician origins, he became a prefect but relinquished this post and gave his wealth to the poor in order to become a monk (*c.*575). As pope, he organized and greatly expanded the Roman church, including sending St AUGUSTINE to Britain. Tradition has it that he established Gregorian chant, the plainsong used in liturgy.

**Gresham, Sir Thomas** (*c.*1519–79) English financier. He founded the Royal Exchange in London in 1568, and devised "Gresham's Law", the proposition that bad money (i.e. of less intrinsic value) will drive good money out of circulation. He also gave large sums of money to found almshouses.

**Grey, Lady Jane** (1537–54) English Queen. The great-granddaughter of HENRY VII, she was declared queen in 1553 in a move to ensure that the monarch served the Protestant interest, and reigned for ten days. MARY I was crowned queen, and Lady Jane imprisoned and subsequently executed.

**Grieg, Edvard [Hagerup]** (1843–1907) Norwegian composer of Scottish descent. Strongly influenced by Norwegian folk music, his works include music for IBSEN's *Peer Gynt* (1876), orchestral suites, violin sonatas and a string quartet.

**Grierson, John** (1898–1972) Scottish documentary film director and producer, described as the "father of British documentary" for such films as *Drifters* (1929), about the North Sea herring fleet, and *Night Mail* (1936), made for the GPO film unit, where his collaborators included AUDEN and BRITTEN.

**Griffith, Arthur** (1871–1922) Irish nationalist leader. He founded Sinn Fein in 1905, and (with Michael COLLINS) signed the Anglo-Irish Treaty of 1921. He became the first president of the Irish Free State in 1922, following DE VALERA's resignation, and died in office.

**Griffith, D[avid] W[ark]** (1875–1948) American film director and producer. He made over 150 films (mostly one-reelers) before directing his two greatest films, *The Birth of a Nation* (1915) and *Intolerance* (1916). (The latter was necessary after the first, which celebrated the Ku Klux Klan.) Griffith's great skill with such techniques as rapid cutting, soft-focus and fade-outs was highly influential on other film-makers. In 1919, he founded United Artists with CHAPLIN, FAIRBANKS and PICKFORD.

**Gris, Juan** [José Victoriano Gonzàlez] (1887–1927) Spanish painter. He settled in Paris in 1906, where he became an associate of PICASSO and BRAQUE, and one of the leading Cubist painters. He later designed stage sets for DIAGHILEV.

**Gromyko, Andrei Andreyevich** (1909–89) Soviet statesman and diplomat. He was Soviet foreign minister (1957–1985) and a Politburo member (1973–89). Noted for his austerity and bleak demeanour, Gromyko adapted effortlessly to each stage of relations with the West, from Cold War through 1970s detente to the GORBACHEV era. He became a fittingly ceremonial head of state (1985–88) as the old order crumbled.

**Gropius, Walter** (1883–1969) German-born American architect and designer. He founded and directed (1919–28) the highly innovative Bauhus school of architecture and applied arts. Criticized by the Nazis, he moved to the UK in 1934, and emigrated to the US in 1937.

**Grosz, George** (1893–1959) German-born American artist, best known for his bitterly satirical drawings attacking German militarism and capitalism. He fled to the USA in 1932, becoming a citizen in 1938. His later work consists largely of romantic oil paintings.

**Grotius, Hugo** (1583–1645) Dutch jurist, statesman and theologian. His treatise on international law, *De Jura Belli et Pacis* (1625), is regarded as the main foundation of a system of international law, with its appeal to "natural law" and to the social contract.

**Grunewald, Matthias** (*c.*1460–1528) German painter. His few surviving works include religious paintings and altarpieces, the most important of which is the altarpiece commissioned for the monastery at Isenheim (1515). His use of perspective, Gothic imagery, strong colour and an expressionistic style of distortion all combine to produce a powerful and intensely emotional vision of Christ's suffering.

**Guercino, Il** [Giovanni Francesco Barbieri] (1591–1666) Italian Baroque painter. His works are distinguished by their dramatic sense of light and colour, soft, well-rounded forms, and excellent draught-manship. His best-known work is the *Aurora* ceiling fresco (1621–23) in the Villa Ludovisi in Rome.

**Guevara, Che** [Ernesto Guevara] (1928–67) Argentinian-born Communist revolutionary. He joined Fidel CASTRO's forces in the Cuban revolution (1956–59), becoming one of Castro's closest associates. He subsequently led a guerrilla group in Bolivia, where he was killed by government troops. In poster form, he became something of an icon for disaffected Western youth in the late 1960s.

**Guinness, Sir Alec** (1914– ) English stage and film actor. Regarded as one of the most versatile actors of his generation, he appeared as a modern-dress Hamlet in Tyrone GUTHRIE's 1939 production, and became a household name through films such as the comedy, *Kind Hearts and Coronets* (1949), and the war epic, *The Bridge on the River Kwai* (1957). His role as the mystic warrior in *Star Wars* (1977) and its follow-ups reputedly earned him more than all of his previous films put together.

**Gulbenkian, Calouste Sarkis** (1869–1955) Turkish Armenian-born British financier, industrialist, diplomat and philanthropist. He made his fortune in oil deals in the Middle East and endowed the Gulbenkian Foundation for the arts and sciences. His son, **Nubar Sarkis Gulbenkian** (1896–1972), developed a reputation as a socialite but was also a diplomat (as commercial attaché with the Iranian embassy in London) and a philanthropist.

**Gurdjieff, Georgei Ivanovich** (1877–1949) Russian mystic. He attracted disciples to his supposedly Sufi-based regime of spiritual enlightenment through physical discipline. His works include the posthumously published *Meetings with Remarkable Men* (1963).

**Guthrie, Sir [William] Tyrone** (1900–71) English actor and theatrical producer. His productions included a controversial *Hamlet* (1939) in modern dress starring GUINNESS, and several important SHAKESPEARE productions, notably at the Shakespeare Festival in Stratford, Ontario.

**Guthrie, Woody** [Woodrow Wilson Guthrie] (1912–67) American folksinger and writer. His songs, which attack racial bigotry and the economic exploitation of the poor and immigrants, include "This Land is Your Land" and "Pastures of Plenty," and were a strong influence on such 1960s "protest" singers as BAEZ and DYLAN. He published an autobiography, *Bound for Glory* (1943).

# H

**Haber, Fritz** (1868–1934) German chemist, inventor of the Haber process, who was awarded the 1918 Nobel prize for chemistry. He died while fleeing Germany en route to the UK.

**Hadrian** [Publius Aelius Hadrianus] (76–138) Roman soldier and emperor. He was proclaimed emperor by his soldiers. He spent much of his reign travelling through the empire, the boundaries of which he was concerned to make firm, and built Hadrian's Wall in the north of England. A cultured man, he patronized men of learning and founded Adrianopolis.

**Hahn, Kurt** (1886–1974) German educationalist. An admirer of the English "public" system, he fled Germany in 1934 and established a school at Gordonstoun that emphasized physical education and self-reliance. The school's pupils have included Prince PHILIP and Prince CHARLES. The latter will not be sending his sons there.

**Hahn, Otto** (1879–1968) German physical chemist. With MEITNER and others, he undertook significant research into radioactive elements by bombarding uranium with slow neutrons, which led to the discovery of nuclear fission. He was awarded the 1944 Nobel prize for chemistry.

**Haig, Douglas, 1st Earl** (1861–1928) British field marshal. In World War I he was appointed commander in chief of the British forces on the western front (1915–18). The terrible losses of soldiers under his command—the Somme offensive of 1916 resulted in 90,000 British dead—led to fierce criticism of his tactics. Foch assumed overall leadership of the Allies in 1918. In 1921, Haig founded the British Legion to ameliorate the plight of ex-servicemen and their families.

**Haile Selassie** [title of Ras Tafari Makonnen] (1892–1975) emperor of Ethiopia (1930–36, 1941–74). He lived in Britain during the occupation of his country by Italy (1936–41). In the early 1960s, he helped establish the Organization of African Unity in Addis Ababa. The famine of 1973 created unrest, which led to Selassie's deposition in the military coup that resulted in MENGISTU's rise to power. Selassie is worshipped as a god by the Rastafarian cult.

**Haitink, Bernard [Johann Herman]** (1929– ) Dutch conductor, renowned as an interpreter of Bruckner and MAHLER. He has been a regular conductor at Glyndebourne and Covent Garden and was created an honorary KBE in 1977.

**Hakluyt, Richard** (*c.*1552–1616) English geographer, historian and cleric. His books include *Divers Voyages touching the Discovery of America* (1582), which was commissioned by Sir Walter RALEIGH, and *The Principal Navigations, Voyages, and Discoveries of the English Nation* (1589).

**Haldane, J[ohn] B[urdon] S[anderson]** (1892–1964) Scottish biochemist and philosopher. He made significant contributions to the study of enzymes and genetics, and wrote several popular books on science, e.g. *Science and Ethics* (1928) and *Science* *in Everyday Life* (1939). A Marxist, he joined the Communist Party in 1938, resigning in 1956 in disgust at LYSENKO's pseudo-science.

**Hall, Sir Peter [Reginald Frederick]** (1930– ) English stage director and theatre manager. He was director of the Royal Shakespeare Company (1960–68) and of the National Theatre (1973–88). His *Diaries* (1983) are required reading for the history of the modern British stage.

**Halley, Edmund** (1656–1742) English astronomer and mathematician. In 1583, he calculated the orbit of the comet now named after him, and correctly predicted its return in following years. His other discoveries include maps of trade winds and studies of magnetic variation.

**Hals, Frans** (*c.*1581–1666) Dutch painter. His first major work is *The Banquet of the St George Civic Guard* (1616), a lively and innovative group portrait that moved away from formal trends in group portraiture. His fresh, natural spontaneity is demonstrated in his *Laughing Cavalier* (1624). His mature works are more sombre in colour and mood, e.g. *The Regents* and *The Regentesses of the Almshouse* (both *c.*1664).

**Hamilton, Alexander** (1757–1804) American statesman. He founded the Federalist party in 1787 and, as first secretary of the Treasury (1789–95), founded the US federal bank.

**Hamilton, Emma, Lady** (*c.*1765–1815) mistress of Lord NELSON. In 1791 she married her "protector", **Sir William Hamilton** (1730–1803), having previously been the mistress of his nephew and having borne two children by other men (she had also reportedly caused a sensation in 1781 by posing as the goddess Hygeia to promote a charlatan's remedies). She met Nelson in 1793, and bore him a daughter, Horatia, who died in 1888.

**Hammarskjöld, Dag [Hjalmar Agne Carl]** (1905–61) Swedish secretary general of the the United Nations (1953–61). His period of office was a turbulent one, and he died in a plane crash during the Congo crisis. He was posthumously awarded the 1961 Nobel Peace Prize.

**Hammerstein II, Oscar** (1895–60) American songwriter and librettist, best known for his musicals written with Richard RODGERS, e.g. *South Pacific* (1949) and *The Sound of Music* (1959).

**Hammett, [Samuel] Dashiell** (1894–1961) American novelist. Like CHANDLER, he wrote realistic crime novels, based on his own experiences as a Pinkerton detective. His best known are *The Maltese Falcon* (1930) and *The Thin Man* (1932).

**Hammond, Dame Joan** (1912– ) New Zealand operatic soprano. Her recording of PUCCINI's *Turandot* was the first classical record to sell over a million copies.

**Hampden, John** (1594–1643) English parliamentarian. He became a member of parliament in 1621 and became a national hero when prosecuted in 1637 for refusing to pay CHARLES I's unpopular ship-money tax. He raised a regiment for Parliament during the Civil War and died of wounds received in battle.

**Hampton, Lionel** (1913– ) American jazz vibraphonist and bandleader. Hampton began his career with Benny GOODMAN's bands in the late 1930s, and became renowned for his exuberant personality and gift for bringing skilled musicians together in bands of his own.

**Hancock, Tony** [Anthony John Hancock] (1924–68) English comedian. His radio series, *Hancock's Half Hour*, co-starring the English comic actor **Sid James** (1913–76) and scripted by Alan Simpson and Ray Galton, became one of the most popular BBC comedy radio shows ever. The series transferred successfully to television (1956–61), and several films starring Hancock followed, e.g. *The Rebel* (1961). Hancock's comedy persona of a lugubrious misfit closely matched his true personality. His career went into decline, and he killed himself.

**Handel, George Frederick** [Georg Friedrich Händel] (1685–1759) German-born English composer. He became court composer to the Hanover court in 1710, and settled in England in 1711, his former patron becoming GEORGE I in 1714. A highly prolific composer, he wrote over 40 operas, e.g. *Semele*, concertos, oratorios, e.g. the *Messiah* (1742), and chamber and orchestral music, e.g. the *Water Music* (1717).

**Hannibal,** (247–182 BC) Carthaginian general. During the Second Punic War with Rome, he invaded Italy and crossed the Alps in 218, winning two major battles. For 15 years he campaigned in Italy, was never defeated, and was recalled to Carthage in 203 to repel an invasion led by the Roman general **Scipio** [Publius Cornelius Scipio Africanus Major] (237–183 BC). Defeated in 204, Hannibal fled into exile and later committed suicide rather than be given to the Romans.

**Harald Hardrada** *see* **Harold II**.

**Hardie, [James] Keir** (1856–1915) Scottish Labour politician. He was the first leader of the parliamentary Labour Party (1906–7). A committed pacifist, he withdrew from politics following the failure of parties of the Left throughout Europe to oppose World War I.

**Hardy, Godfrey Harold** (1877–1947) English mathematician, noted for his work on analytic number theory. His books include *A Mathematician's Apology* (1940) and *Bertrand Russell and Trinity* (1942).

**Hardy, Oliver** *see* **Laurel, Stan**.

**Hardy, Thomas** (1840–1928) English novelist, short-story writer and poet. His novels are set for the most part in his native Dorset, his "Wessex." The greatest of these are *Far from the Madding Crowd* (1874), *The Return of the Native* (1878), *Tess of the D'Urbervilles* (1891), and *Jude the Obscure* (1896). Censorship of his novels by magazines led to him abandoning the novel form for poetry. He is now ranked, with ELIOT and YEATS, as one of the three great modern poets in English.

**Harlow, Jean** [Harlean Carpentier] (1911–37) American film actress who became one of the screen's main sex symbols of the 1930s, with her tough, wise-cracking "platinum blonde" image. The films include *Hell's Angels* (1930) and *Red Dust* (1932).

**Harold II** (c.1022–1066) English king. He succeeded EDWARD THE CONFESSOR in 1066. He heavily defeated the forces of the Norwegian king **Harald Hardrada** (1015–66) at Stamford Bridge in September, then made a forced march to meet WILLIAM THE CONQUEROR's forces at Hastings, where he was defeated and killed.

**Harriman, W[illiam] Averell** (1891–1986) American diplomat. He was the main negotiator of the nuclear test-ban treaty of 1963, between the US, UK and USSR, and led the US delegation at the

Vietnam peace talks. He was also governor of New York (1955–58).

**Harris, Sir Arthur Travers** (1892–1984), nicknamed "Bomber Harris" for his advocacy of heavy bombing raids on German cities during World War II. Despite much dissent about its morality—and military wisdom—the policy lasted (with CHURCHILL's muted support) from 1942 to the firebombing of Dresden in 1944.

**Harris, Frank** (1856–1931) Irish-born Anglo-American writer and editor, whose best-known work is *My Life and Loves* (1922–27), an entertaining, sexually explicit and thoroughly unreliable autobiography.

**Harrison, George** (1943– ) English singer-songwriter. He played lead guitar for the Beatles (1962–70). His songs with the group include "With a Little Help From My Friends" (i.e. drugs) and "Something." Harrison's work displays a fascination with Eastern religions and mysticism, e.g. "My sweet Lord." He organized the "Concert for Bangladesh" of 1971, the first great rock charity show, and provided the financial backing for several Monty Python films.

**Harrod, Sir Henry Roy Forbes** (1900–78) English economist, noted for his model of economic growth, the Harrod-Domar model of economic growth, socalled because the Polish-born American economist **Evsey Domar** (1914– ) formulated the model independently.

**Hart, Lorenz [Milton]** (1895–1943) American lyricist. His collaborations—around thirty in all—with the composer Richard RODGERS include *The Boys From Syracuse* (1938) and *Pal Joey* (1940).

**Hartley, L[eslie] P[oles]** (1895–1972) English novelist, whose best-known works are the Eustace and Hilda trilogy, i.e. *The Shrimp and the Anemone* (1944), *The Sixth Heaven* (1946), and *Eustace and Hilda* (1947), and *The Go-Between* (1953), a subtle portrayal of social and sexual intrigue in Edwardian England.

**Hartnell, Sir Norman [Bishop]** (1901–79) English couturier. He became court dressmaker in 1938. He designed the WRAC uniform, several functional "utility" designs in the postwar period, and Queen ELIZABETH's coronation robes.

**Harvey, William** (1578–1657) English physician. Court physician to both JAMES VI and CHARLES I, he published his discovery of the circulation of the blood in 1628.

**Hasek, Jaroslav** (1883–1923) Czech novelist and short-story writer. His masterpiece is *The Good Soldier Svejk* (1925), based on his own experiences in the Austro-Hungarian army. He also served in the Bolshevik Red Army as a political commissar.

**Hastings, Warren** (1732–1818) British administrator in India. He went to India in 1750 as an official of the East India Company, became first governor-general of Bengal (1773–85), and established the Company as one of the most powerful forces in India. He resigned office in 1784 and was impeached before the House of Commons in 1788 for corruption. The trial, inspired by the Whig opposition, lasted seven years and resulted in his acquittal.

**Haughey, Charles [James]** (1925– ) Irish Fianna Fáil politician. He became prime minister of the Republic of Ireland (1979–81, 1982 and 1988–92). Regarded by many observers as the supreme living example of a machine politician, his political career has been a notably controversial one. He was acquitted of complicity in alleged gunrunning in the 1970s, and after a series of scandals in the 1980s was forced to resign in 1992.

**Havel, Vàclav** (1936– ) Czech dramatist and statesman. His plays of the 1960s and 1970s, e.g. *The Garden Party* (1963), satirized the brutality and corruption of Czech communism. Following the brief spell of artistic expression during the "Prague Spring," he was imprisoned for several years after the Soviet invasion of 1968. He was a spokesman for Charter 77, the civil rights movement, and was elected his country's president in 1989 but resigned in 1992, before the break-up of Czechoslovakia.

**Hawke, Robert [James Lee]** (1929– ) Australian trades unionist and Labor statesman. After establishing a solid Labor Party base as an advocate for the trades union movement, he became an MP in 1980, and became prime minister after his party's victory in the 1983 election. He resigned in 1992.

**Hawking, Stephen William** (1942– ) English physicist. He has suffered from amyotrophic lateral sclerosis, a rare crippling nervous disease, since the early 1960s, and is confined to a wheelchair. Widely regarded as perhaps the greatest physicist since EINSTEIN, his research into the theory of black holes has been highly acclaimed. His book explaining his theories, *A Brief History of Time* (1988), has had enormous sales.

**Hawkins, Coleman** (1904–69) American jazz tenor saxophonist. His recording of the ballad "Body and Soul" (1939) was regarded as a model of the "swing" style by his peers.

**Hawks, Howard** (1896–1977) American film direc-

tor and producer. His films include a classic "gangster" movie, *Scarface* (1931), and *To Have and Have
Not* (1944) and *The Big Sleep* (1946), both starring
Bogart and Bacall, two great westerns, *Red River*
(1948) and *Rio Bravo* (1959), starring John Wayne,
and the comedy, *Gentlemen Prefer Blondes* (1953),
with Marilyn Monroe.

**Hawthorne, Nathaniel** (1804–64) American novelist and short-story writer. He was born in Salem,
Massachusetts, where his ancestors had helped to
persecute the so-called "Salem witches", and his
consciousness of the dark side of New England
Puritanism profoundly shaped his life and work, as
in his masterpiece, *The Scarlet Letter* (1850), a
psychological novel on the guilt-ridden consequences
of adultery in 17th-century New England.

**Haydn, [Franz] Joseph** (1732–1809) Austrian composer. An innovative and prolific composer, he established the form of both the symphony and the
string quartet. His huge oeuvre includes over 100
symphonies, 84 string quartets, and the oratorio
*The Creation* (1796–98). Beethoven was his pupil
for a while.

**Haydon, Benjamin** (1786–1846) English painter. A
Romantic, he aspired to raise the timbre of British
history painting to the Grand Manner, and was a
friend of the poets Keats and Wordsworth, whose
portraits he painted. His paintings tended to be
awkward and melodramatic, and he was thwarted
in his ambition to decorate the Houses of Parliament with frescos.

**Hayek, Friedrich August von** (1899–1992) Austrian-born British economist. A leading member of
the Austrian school of economics, he opposed the

theories of KEYNES, supporting instead free-market policies and opposing government economic management. His books include *The Pure Theory of Capital* (1941) and *The Road to Serfdom* (1944). He shared the 1974 Nobel prize for economics with MYRDAL.

**Hazlitt, William** (1778–1830) English essayist and critic. Highly influential in his own day, Hazlitt remains one of the most important literary critics, especially valued for his essays on his contemporaries and on SHAKESPEARE. His works include *Characters of Shakespeare's Plays* (1817), *Political Essays* (1818), and *The Spirit of the Age* (1825).

**Healey, Denis [Winston]** (1917– ) English Labour politician. He was chancellor of the exchequer (1974–79) and deputy leader of his party (1980–83). Widely regarded as one of the most impressive modern British politicians, his unexpected defeat by Michael FOOT in the 1980 Labour leadership election has been seen by some as costing Labour the subsequent general election.

**Heaney, Seamus [Justin]** (1939– ) Irish poet and critic. Brought up a Roman Catholic in Northern Ireland, Heaney now lives and works in the Republic of Ireland. His collections of poetry include *Death of a Naturalist* (1966) and *Station Island* (1984). He is regarded by many critics as the finest Irish poet since YEATS.

**Hearst, William Randolph** (1863–1951) American newspaper publisher and politician. In the late 1920s he owned more than twenty-five daily newspapers, most of them noted for their sensationalism, and had become a Hollywood mogul, producing several features starring his mistress, the actress

**Marion Davies** (1897–1961). He served as congressman for New York (1903–7) and built a spectacular castle at San Simeon in California. Orson WELLES' film, *Citizen Kane* (1941), is a thinly fictionalized account of Hearst's life.

**Heath, Edward [Richard George]** (1916– ) British Conservative statesman and prime minister (1970–74). His period of office was marked by much industrial strife, particularly by miners' strikes, and he lost two general elections in 1974. A fervent pro-European, he negotiated Britain's entry into the Common Market in 1973, and lost the leadership of his party to THATCHER, after which he became an outspoken critic of his successor's social and economic policies. He has also been an active and influential figure in world politics. An intensely private man, he is also noted for his devotion to music and sailing.

**Heaviside, Oliver** (1850–1925) English physicist and electrical engineer. Independently of the Irish-American physicist **Arthur Edwin Kennelly** (1861–1939), he predicted the existence of the ionosphere, an ionized gaseous layer in the atmosphere, in 1902.

**Hegel, Georg Wilhelm Friedrich** (1770–1831) German philosopher. His highly influential works include *The Phenomenology of Mind* (1807), which describes how the Absolute is being reached by man's evolving powers of consciousness, and *Science of Logic* (1812–6), which expounds his dialectic of thesis and antithesis into synthesis, which influenced Karl MARX.

**Heidegger, Martin** (1889–1976) German philosopher. He is usually described as an existentialist, despite his disclaimer of the label. His major work is *Being and Time* (1927), a dense and highly obscure work that classifies modes of being and examines human existence. He declared his support for HITLER in 1933, and, through concepts such as "angst," had a great deal of influence on existentialists such as SARTRE.

**Heifetz, Jascha** (1901–87) Lithuanian-born American violinist. He became a US citizen in 1924, and his flamboyant and expressive interpretation of music from BACH to WALTON has been widely acclaimed.

**Heine, Heinrich** (1797–1856) German poet and critic. His masterpiece is his *Book of Songs* (1827), which includes some of the finest lyric poems ever written, many of which, e.g. "The Earl King", have been set to music, notably by SCHUBERT. He had an uneasy friendship with Karl MARX, who observed of Heine that poets were a breed apart. Heine had a healthy (and prophetic) distrust of the intolerance and anti-Semitism of German radicalism.

**Heisenberg, Werner Karl** (1901–76) German theoretical physicist. He was awarded the 1932 Nobel prize for physics for his work on quantum theory. He dismissed Nazi attacks on EINSTEIN, but remained in Germany during World War II. His "uncertainty principle" states that the uncertainty of our knowledge of the values of subatomic variables means that the values cannot be measured simultaneously.

**Heller, Joseph** (1923– ) American novelist. His experiences as a bombardier during World War II formed the basis for his first novel, *Catch–22* (1961), a grim, surrealist satire on military life and logic.

Subsequent novels include *Something Happened* (1974) and *Picture This* (1988).

**Helpmann, Sir Robert** (1909–86) Australian ballet dancer, choreographer and actor. His choreographic work includes *Miracle in the Gorbals* (1944) and *Yugen* (1964). He was the first male principal of the Sadler's Wells Ballet (1933–50), and appears in the ballet films, *The Red Shoes* (1948) and *Tales of Hoffman* (1951).

**Hemingway, Ernest [Millar]** (1899–1961) American novelist and short-story writer, whose laconic narrative style, with its "tough guy" dialogue and macho values, made a big impression on his contemporaries. Major novels include *A Farewell to Arms* (1929), based on his own experiences as an ambulance driver in World War I, and *For Whom the Bell Tolls* (1940), based on his reporting experiences during the Spanish Civil War. He settled in Cuba in 1945, which was the setting for *The Old Man and the Sea* (1952). He was awarded the Nobel prize for literature in 1954. He committed suicide in the US in 1961. *A Moveable Feast* (1964) is an account of life in the expatriate American community in Paris in the 1920s.

**Hendrix, Jimi** [James Marshall Hendrix] (1942– 70) American rock guitarist, singer and songwriter. With his trio, the Jimi Hendrix Experience, he became perhaps the most influential rock guitarist of the 1960s with his loud, exuberant style, e.g. in his *Purple Haze* album. He died of alcohol and drug abuse.

**Henry II** *see* **Becket, Thomas à**.

**Henry IV** (1367–1413) English king. Surnamed Bolingbroke, he became the first king from the

House of Lancaster in 1399. After overthrowing RICHARD II, he suppressed rebellions led by the Welsh national leader **Owen Glendower** [Owain Glyndwr] (c.1359–c.1416) and by the Earl of Northumberland, in the latter of which his rival, Northumberland's son **"Harry" Hotspur** [Sir Henry Percy] (1364–1403), was slain at the Battle of Shrewsbury. He also invaded Scotland (1400) and France (1411–12).

**Henry V** (1387–1422) English king. Reputed to be dissolute in his youth, he inherited the throne in 1413 and defeated the French at the battle of Agincourt in 1415. He conquered Normandy in 1419, married **Catherine of Valois** (1401–37) in 1420, and became Regent of France.

**Henry VI** (1421–71) king of England. The last king of the House of Lancaster, he succeeded as an infant was was crowned king of England in 1429 and of France in 1431. By 1453 he had lost his French territory (except Calais), and his increasing mental instability led in 1454 to the appointment of Richard, Duke of York (*see* RICHARD III) as Protector. The bloody and complex Wars of the Roses then broke out, and Henry was taken prisoner by Richard's forces after a battle at St Albans in 1455. **Edward IV** (1442–83) was proclaimed king in 1461. Henry was briefly restored to the throne in 1470, and was murdered the following year by Edward's men.

**Henry VII** (1457–1509) king of England. The first Tudor king, he succeeded RICHARD III in 1485 after defeating the Yorkist forces at Bosworth. He pursued a policy of peace, notably with France, encouraged commerce, and increased the prosperity of England.

**Henry VIII** (1491–1547) king of England. He inherited the throne in 1509, and acquired a European-wide reputation for his learning and patronage of artists and scholars such as HOLBEIN and ERASMUS. He declared his marriage to **Catherine of Aragon** (1485–1536) invalid (their only child became MARY I), thus precipitating the Act of Supremacy and schism from Rome. He subsequently married **Anne Boleyn** (c.1504–1536), the mother of ELIZABETH I, whom he had executed in 1536. Subsequent wives were **Jane Seymour** (c.1509–1537), who died after giving birth to EDWARD VI; **Anne of Cleves** (1515–57), whom he divorced; **Catherine Howard** (c.1521–42), whom he had beheaded for alleged adultery; and **Catherine Parr** (1512–48), who survived him. Originally violently opposed to LUTHER's Reformation (he was given the title Defender of the Faith by the pope for writing a tract against Luther), Henry established England as a Protestant state. *See also* Thomas CROMWELL, Thomas MORE, WOLSEY.

**Henson, Jim** [James Maury Henson] (1936–90) American puppeteer and film producer. His TV educational series for preschool children, *Sesame Street*, featuring an engaging cast of "muppets," has won wide acclaim since its appearance in 1969. *The Muppet Show* (1976–81), featuring Kermit the Frog and Miss Piggy among others, also achieved enormous viewing figures in over 100 countries. A later series for adults, *The Storyteller* (1987) marked a new, sadly curtailed departure in his extraordinary work. He also made several less critically well-received films, e.g. *Labyrinth* (1986).

**Henze, Hans Werner** (1926– ) German composer. Henze's works, which often reflect his enthusiasm for left-wing causes, include the operas *Elegy for Young Lovers* (1961) and *The Bassarids* (1965), both with librettos by AUDEN, and *We Come to the River* (1975), with libretto by BOND. Other works include the oratorio *The Raft of the Medusa* (1968), a tribute to Che GUEVARA, and symphonies and chamber works.

**Hepburn, Katharine** (1909– ) American film and stage actress, noted for her wit and versatility. She had a long personal and acting relationship with Spencer TRACY, her co-star in *Woman of the Year* (1942) and *Guess Who's Coming to Dinner?* (1967). The latter won her an Oscar, as did *Morning Glory* (1933), *The Lion in Winter* (1968) and *On Golden Pond* (1981).

**Hepworth, Dame [Jocelyn] Barbara** (1903–75) English sculptor. She became one of Britain's leading abstract sculptors in the 1930s, noted for her strong, often monumental carving. Her second husband was Ben NICHOLSON.

**Herbert, Sir A[lan] P[atrick]** (1890–1971) English writer and politician. He was Independent MP for Oxford University (1935–50), and campaigned for reform of the divorce laws. A prolific writer, his works include a collection of mock law cases, *Misleading Cases in the Common Law* (1927), the novel *The Water Gipsies* (1930), and the librettos for several musical revues.

**Herbert, George** (1593–1633) English Anglican priest and poet. His poems were published posthumously as *The Temple: Sacred Poems and Private Ejaculations* (1633). They are among the greatest devotional poems in the language, and are characteristic of Metaphysical poetry in their subtle, paradoxical exploration of spiritual themes. The simple piety of Herbert's life and the intellectual power of his poetry make him one of the most appealing of all English poets.

**Herrick, Robert** (1591–1674) English Anglican priest and poet. His sacred and secular poems were collected in a joint volume published during the Commonwealth period, *Hesperides* and *Noble Numbers* (both 1648). Many of the poems, which are often delicately sensual, are surprisingly direct in their sympathy for the traditional (virtually pagan) customs of English country life. *See also* JONSON.

**Hertz, Gustav Ludwig** *see* **Franck, James.**

**Hertzog, James Barry Munnik** (1866–1942) South African statesman. He founded the Nationalist Party (1913) and advocated noncooperation with Britain during World War I. He became prime minister (1924–39) and founded the Afrikaner Party in 1941.

**Herzog, Werner** (1942– ) German film director. His films include *Aguirre, Wrath of God* (1973), *Wozzeck* (1979) and *Fitzcarraldo* (1982). Bizarre enterprises, e.g. the building of an opera house up the Amazon in *Fitzcarraldo*, are a notable feature of his films.

**Heseltine, Michael** *see* **Thatcher, Margaret Hilda.**

**Hess, Dame Myra** (1890–1965) English pianist. She was also a much acclaimed concert pianist and an influential teacher. Her transcriptions of baroque music, particularly her version of Bach's "Jesu, Joy of man's Desiring," were very popular.

**Hess, [Walter Richard] Rudolf** (1894–1987) German Nazi politician. An early supporter of HITLER, he joined the Nazi Party in 1920 and became its deputy leader (1934–41). In 1941, on the eve of Hitler's invasion of Russia, he flew to Scotland, apparently in the hope of negotiating peace terms with Britain. He spent the rest of his life imprisoned. In 1946 he was transferred to Spandau jail in Berlin.

**Hess, Victor Francis** (1883–1964) Austrian-born American physicist. He shared the 1936 Nobel prize for physics with the American physicist **Carl David Anderson** (1905– ) for his research into cosmic rays.

**Hesse, Hermann** (1877–1962) German-born Swiss novelist, short-story writer and poet. His fiction reflects his fascination with oriental mysticism, spiritual alienation and worldly detachment. His novels, which were blacklisted by the Nazis in 1943, include *Steppenwolf* (1927) and *The Glass Bead Game* (1943). He was awarded the Nobel prize for literature in 1946.

**Heston, Charlton** [John Charlton Carter] (1923– ) American film and stage actor. Renowned principally for his physique, noble profile and commanding presence in such epics as *The Ten Commandments* (1956) and *Ben Hur* (1959), Heston had few screen opportunities to display his considerable acting skills, which appear in WELLES' *Touch of Evil* (1958) and the grimly realistic western *Will Penny* (1967).

**Heyerdahl, Thor** (1914– ) Norwegian anthropologist. His practical demonstration of his theory that South Americans emigrated to Polynesia on rafts of balsa wood, described in his book *The Kon-Tiki Expedition*, caught the public imagination and the book became a huge bestseller. Heyerdahl subsequently launched similar expeditions, e.g. a voyage by raft in 1970 from Morocco to the West Indies.

**Hilbert, David** (1862–1943) German mathematician. He made significant contributions to the study of several fields of mathematics, e.g. to number field theory and algebraic geometry.

**Hillary, Sir Edmund [Percival]** (1919– ) New Zealand explorer and mountaineer. He and the Tibetan sherpa, **Tenzing Norgay** (1914–86), made the first ascent of Mount Everest in 1953. His other exploits include an overland trek to the South Pole in 1958.

**Himmler, Heinrich** (1900–45) German Nazi leader. He was chosen by HITLER to head the SS in 1929, and by 1936 was in command of the German police structure. Through his secret police, the Gestapo, he organized repression first in Germany then in occupied Europe, and oversaw the construction of the Nazi concentration and death camp system and the attempted genocide of the Jews. He committed suicide after his capture by British troops.

**Hindemith, Paul** (1895–1963) German composer and violist. The Nazis banned his works for their dissonance and "impropriety," and he settled in the US in 1939. A highly prolific composer, his works include operas, symphonies, song cycles, ballet and chamber music.

**Hindenburg, Paul von Beneckendorff und von** (1847–1934) German field marshal and statesman. He shared command of the German forces in World War I (1916–18), and became president of Germany (1925–34). He defeated HITLER in the presidential election of 1932, but was persuaded to appoint Hitler chancellor in 1933, after which Hindenburg was a cipher president.

**Hines, Earl [Kenneth] "Fatha"** (1903–83) American jazz pianist, bandleader and songwriter. He became one of the most influential jazz pianists of the 1930s and 1940s, renowned for his virtuoso solos and exuberant style.

**Hirohito** (1901–89) Japanese emperor. He became emperor in 1926 and ruled Japan as a divinity until her defeat in 1945, after which he became a constitutional monarch, known primarily for his marine biology research. He was succeeded as emperor by his son **Akihito** (1933– ).

**Hiss, Alger** (1904– ) American state department official. A highly respected public servant, he was jailed (1950–54) for spying for the USSR. Controversy continues over his conviction.

**Hitchcock, Sir Alfred** (1899–1980) English film director, based in Hollywood from 1940, whose suspenseful thrillers have long been regarded as masterpieces. His films include *Blackmail* (1929), *The Thirty-Nine Steps* (1935), *Rebecca* (1940), *Notorious* (1946) and *Psycho* (1960). In the last film, against all precedent, Hitchcock kills off the heroine in the notorious shower scene long before the end of the film.

**Hitler, Adolf** (1889–1945) Austrian-born German dictator. A failed artist in Vienna before World War I, and a highly decorated soldier by the end of the war, he co-founded the National Socialist Workers' Party in 1919, and was jailed for nine months following his part in the failed Munich coup of 1923, during which time he wrote *Mein Kampf* ("my struggle"), a lurid and viciously anti-semitic "testament" of his belief in the superiority of the Aryan race. He was appointed chancellor by HINDENBURG in 1933 and consolidated his brutal regime through

HIMMLER'S Gestapo. He allied himself temporarily with STALIN in 1939, in which year he invaded Poland, beginning World War II. He invaded Russia in 1941 and killed himself in Berlin in 1945 with Russian troops a few blocks away. Hitler's war resulted in *c.*40 million dead.

**Hobbes, Thomas** (1588–1679) English philosopher. His materialist views were strongly influential on his contemporaries. He was born in the year of the Armada, and once noted that he and "fear came into the world at the same time." Hobbes' most notable work is *Leviathan* (1651), a study of society, observing famously that the life of man outside the constraints of civilized society is "poor, nasty, brutish and short," and concluding that men live best under strong government (CROMWELL became Lord Protector in 1653). A great deal of subsequent political theory consists of attempts to either refute or accommodate Hobbes' bleak conclusions on human nature. He also wrote his autobiography in Latin verse when he was 85.

**Ho Chi Minh** [Nguyen That Tan] (1890–1969) Vietnamese statesman. A Marxist nationalist, he led the Viet Minh forces, with US help, against the occupying Japanese during World War II, and became president of Vietnam (1945–54), during which time he led his forces to victory against French colonial rule. He became president of North Vietnam (1954–69) after the country's partition at the 1954 Geneva conference. In the ensuing civil war (1959–75), he supported the Viet Cong guerrillas in the south with the North Vietnamese army (*see* GIAP).

**Hockney, David** (1937–) English painter and etcher

His work attracted wide acclaim while he was still a student, and he was soon being hailed as a light, witty master of Pop Art. He settled in California in the early 1960s, where his "swimming-pool" paintings, e.g. *A Bigger Splash*, display a fascination for water. Other works, depicting male figures, were described by Hockney as "propaganda for homosexuality." He became very involved with photography in the 1980s, and is now established as one of the world's leading representational painters.

**Hodgkin, Sir Alan Lloyd** (1914– ) English physiologist. With **Sir Andrew Fielding Huxley** (1917– ) and Sir John Carew ECCLES, he shared the 1963 Nobel prize for physiology or medicine for research into nerve impulses.

**Hodgkin, Dorothy** [Dorothy Mary Crowfoot] (1910– ) English chemist. She was awarded the 1964 Nobel prize for chemistry for her work on the molecular structures of penicillin, insulin and vitamin B12.

**Hofstadter, Robert** *see* **Mossbauer, Rudolf Ludwig**.

**Hogan, Ben** [William Benjamin Hogan] (1912– ) American golfer. Regarded as one of the greatest ever golfers, he won over 60 US tournaments. Despite being badly injured in a car crash in 1949, he recovered and won all the major world championships of 1953.

**Hogarth, William** (1697–1764) English artist. He trained as an engraver in the rococo tradition, and by 1720 had established his own illustration business. He then began his series of "conversation pieces", e.g. *A Scene from The Beggar's Opera* (late 1720s). By the 1730s, he was executing some fine portraits, e.g. *Captain Coram* (1740). He also produced remarkable series of paintings following a sequential narrative in the manner of tableaux in a stage play, the best known of which is *Marriage à la Mode* (1742–44). He wrote a treatise on aesthetic principles entitled *The Analysis of Beauty* (1753).

**Hogg, James** (1770–1835) Scottish novelist and poet. He was a self-educated shepherd (nicknamed the "Ettrick Shepherd") who became a leading light of Edinburgh's literary world from 1810. He produced some remarkable works, most notably the novel *The Private Memoirs and Confessions of a Justified Sinner* (1824), a macabre study of religious mania and murder that has gained steeply in reputation since it was published.

**Holbein, Hans (the Younger)** (*c*.1479–1543) German painter. He painted mainly portraits and religious paintings, the most memorable of the latter being the *The Death of Christ* (1521). His portraits were minutely detailed and exactly drawn, as in the painting of *Thomas More as Lord Chancellor* (1527). He also painted *Sir Thomas More and his Family* (1527), thought to be the first ever domestic group portrait. He became court painter to HENRY VIII, and painted the full-length portrait that has come to be the representative image of that monarch.

**Holiday, Billie "Lady Day" [Eleanora]** (1915–59) American jazz singer. She became one of the most influential jazz singers of her time, with her sad, elegiac and subtle interpretations of popular songs. She sang with several bands, e.g. GOODMAN's and BASIE's, and appeared in several films, e.g. *New Orleans* (1947), the latter also featuring ARMSTRONG. Her life was a tragic one, and she died of heroin addiction.

**Holly, Buddy** [Charles Hardin Holley] (1936–59) American rock singer, songwriter and guitarist. One of the most influential of all rock singers, his band, the Crickets, was the first to use the soon to be standard line-up of lead, rhythm and bass guitars, with drums. His songs include several standards, e.g. "That'll Be the Day" and "Peggy Sue." He died in a plane crash.

**Holst, Gustav [Theodore]** (1874–1934) English composer of Swedish descent. His works include operas, e.g. *The Boar's Head* (1924), choral music, e.g. *Ode to Death* (1919), and orchestral music, such as the *St Paul's Suite for Strings* (1913) and his best-known composition, *The Planets* (1917). His own favourite work was the mood-piece *Egdon Heath* (1927), inspired, like much of his music, by the English landscape and by Thomas HARDY.

**Holyoake, Sir Keith Jacka** (1904–83) New Zealand statesman. He served as National Party premier (1957, 1960–72) and became governor general (1977–80).

**Homer** (*c*.800 BC) Greek poet, author of the two great epic poems *The Iliad*, the story of the Greek war against Troy, and *The Odyssey,* which describes the adventures of the Greek hero Odysseus (known to the Romans as Ulysses) on his voyage home from the war. The characters and events of the poems have had a profound influence upon western literature. Homer was reputedly blind and born on the island of Chios, but nothing about him is known for certain (not even his sex; one critic believed Homer was female).

**Homer, Winslow** (1836–1910) American painter. Trained as a lithographer, his first paintings owe something to the directness and detachment of early photography, but he was subsequently influenced by MANET. Clear, bright paintings, such as *Breezing Up* (1876), are typical of his style and show the sea as a favourite theme.

**Honecker, Erich** (1912– ) East German Communist politician. He became first secretary of the Socialist Unity Party in 1971, and became effective leader of the East German state following ULBRICHT's death in 1973. He was appointed head of state in 1976, and fell from power in 1989 following the wide social unrest that followed GORBACHEV's statement that the USSR would no longer intervene in East German affairs. Severely ill with kidney cancer, he was charged in 1990 with treason and corruption following the re-unification of Germany, but because of his illness he did not stand trial and left Germany to live in South America.

**Honegger, Arthur** (1892–1955) French composer (of Swiss parentage). One of the group of Parisian composers dubbed "*Les Six*" (including MILHAUD), his works include the oratorio *King David* (1921), ballet music, symphonies, film scores, and the intriguing orchestral work *Pacific 231* (1924), a musical portrait of a train.

**Hooch** or **Hoogh, Pieter de** (*c*.1629–1684) Dutch painter. His still, peaceful interior and garden-figure compositions are typical of Dutch painting of the time, e.g. *The Courtyard of a House in Delft* (1658). He was an older contemporary of VERMEER, and was probably influenced by the younger artist.

**Hood, Thomas** (1799–1845) English poet. Noted especially for his slight, humorous, skilfully punning verse, e.g., "Faithless Sally Brown", he also

wrote "The Song of the Shirt", a scathing attack on
the appalling working conditions of seamstresses,
and "The Dream of Eugene Aram," a nightmarish
study of a murderer.

**Hooker, Richard** (*c.*1554–1600) English divine. His
*Laws of Ecclesiastical Polity* (1593–97), written in
response to Puritan attacks on Anglican moderation, remains one of the most readable theological
works of its size in English, thanks to Hooker's
beautifully constructed prose and humane tolerance.

**Hoover, Herbert [Clark]** (1874–1964) American
Republican statesman and 31st president of the US
(1929–33). He was appointed by Woodrow WILSON to
oversee food relief for Europe after World War I. He
succeeded COOLIDGE as president in 1929, and was
widely perceived as failing to cope with the crisis of
the Great Depression, which began later that year,
and was heavily defeated by Franklin D. ROOSEVELT
in the 1932 election.

**Hoover, J[ohn] Edgar** (1895–1972) American public servant and founder of the Federal Bureau of
Investigation (1924–1972). He transformed the FBI
into a highly effective federal crime-fighting force in
the 1930s, but also used his organization's considerable powers against anyone perceived as "radical"
in politics. He developed a vast network of surveil-
lance and infiltration by dedicated agents, the latter factor reputedly having the curious effect of
greatly increasing the efficiency of the American
Communist Party.

**Hope, Bob** [Leslie Townes Hope] (1903– ) English-
born American comedian and film actor, renowned
for his snappy wisecracks. His long association with

Bing CROSBY includes the "Road to…" films, e.g. *The Road to Morocco* (1942).

**Hopkins, Sir Frederick Gowland** (1861–1947) English biochemist. He shared the 1929 Nobel prize for physiology or medicine with EIJKMAN for his discovery of "accessory food factors," which came to be called vitamins.

**Hopkins, Gerard Manley** (1844–89) English Jesuit priest and poet. Hopkins converted to Roman Catholicism in 1866. His poems frequently express the keen conflict he felt between his desire to serve God as both priest and poet, and his deeply felt inadequacies, particularly in the "Dark Sonnets" of the mid–1880s, e.g. "No worst, there is none". Other well-known poems are "The Wreck of the Deutschland", inspired by the death of nuns in a shipwreck, and "The Windhover", a spiritually charged celebration of a falcon hovering.

**Hopper, Edward** (1882–1967) American artist. Regarded as the foremost realist American painter, his paintings, which often depict isolated characters in urban scenes, e.g. *Nighthawks*, have a still, introspective and often mysterious quality that is quite distinct from any other artist's work. Hopper's work, never very fashionable, is now seen as having been unjustly obscured by the wave of abstract work from the 1950s onwards.

**Horace** [Quintus Horatius Flaccus] (65–8 BC) Roman poet and satirist. Like his friend VIRGIL, he looked to the literature of Greece for inspiration, but the sardonic, realistic and tightly controlled language of his poems is wholly Roman. His *Odes, Satires* and *Epistles* have been much imitated by other poets, e.g. POPE.

**Hotspur, "Harry"** *see* **Henry IV**.

**Houdon, Jean-Antoine** (1741–1828) French sculptor. He studied in Paris and won the Prix de Rome in 1761. In Rome (1764–68), he achieved initial fame with the figures *L'Ecorche* (1764) and *St Bruno* (1767). He then established his reputation in portrait busts, examples of which are *Gluck* (1775), *Voltaire* and *Benjamin Franklin* (1775). He was also commissioned to do a marble statue of George WASHINGTON (1791) for the Virginia State Capitol in Richmond.

**Housman, A[lfred] E[dward]** (1859–1936) English poet and scholar. His poetic output was small, comprising *A Shropshire Lad* (1896), *Last Poems* (1922) and *More Poems* (1936).

**Howard, Catherine** *see* **Henry VIII**.

**Howard, Sir Ebenezer** (1850–1928) English town planner. Influenced by the visionary ideals of American social reformers such as Ralph Waldo Emerson, Howard introduced the concept of the Garden City, as in his book *Garden Cities of Tomorrow* (1902), with its description of urban communities (limited to populations of around 30,000) surrounded by green belts. Letchworth and Welwyn Garden City in England are based on his concept.

**Howe, Sir Geoffrey** *see* **Major, John**.

**Hoyle, Sir Fred** (1915– ) English astronomer, mathematician, broadcaster and writer. He became the main proponent of the "steady state" theory of the universe, which holds that the universe is basically unchanging (as opposed to the big-bang theory). He also proposed that life on earth is of extraterrestrial origin, and has written several science fiction novels, e.g. *The Black Cloud* (1957), and children's books.

**Hubble, Edwin Powell** (1889–1953) American astronomer. His discovery of galactic "red shift" and other research established the recession of the galaxies and, consequently, the theory of the expanding universe.

**Hughes, Howard [Robard]** (1905–76) American industrialist, aviator and film producer. He greatly extended his inherited oil wealth and produced two classic films, *Hell's Angels* (1930) and *Scarface* (1932), and the offbeat western, *The Outlaw* (1941). He also made several epic flights, including a record round-the-world trip. Hughes became increasingly eccentric after sustaining bad injuries in a plane crash in 1947 and went into seclusion in 1966, running his vast business empire behind a predominantly Mormon ring of "protectors." Wild rumours, and a hoax "authorized" biography resulted from his seclusion.

**Hughes, Ted** [Edward James Hughes] (1930– ) English poet, noted for his violent poetic imagery drawn from the natural world, as in *The Hawk in the Rain* (1957) and *Crow* (1970). He was married (1956–63) to Sylvia PLATH. He was appointed poet laureate in 1984.

**Hugo, Victor** (1802–85) French novelist, dramatist and poet. The production of his play *Hernani* (1830), a highly romantic, unconventional poetic drama, was marked by inflamed squabbles between supporters and opponents of the new, formally looser and more socially challenging drama. The ensuing controversy established Hugo as the leader of the French literary Romantics. His novels include *The Hunchback of Notre Dame* (1831) and *Les Misérables* (1862).

**Hume, David** (1711–76) Scottish philosopher, economist and historian. An empiricist and sceptic, Hume disallowed human speculation much beyond what could be perceived by the senses. His works include *A Treatise of Human Nature* (1739–40), *Essays Moral and Political* (1741–2), *An Enquiry Concerning the Principles of Morals* (1751) and *History of England* (1754–62). His *Dialogues Concerning Natural Religion* (1759) caused much scandal for its explicit ridicule of theism. He has been claimed by some modern economists to have been a proto-monetarist for his discussion of the "hidden hand" guiding market forces.

**Hunt, Leigh** *see* **Keats, John**.

**Hunt, William Holman** (1827–1910) English painter. A founder, with MILLAIS, of the Pre-Raphaelite movement, he was opposed to the frivolity of established trends in contemporary art and sought inspiration in direct study from nature and natural composition. Deeply religious, he made several journeys to the Middle East to paint accurate detail for his Biblical scenes, and his works have a strong moralistic message and symbolic attention to detail, as in *The Light of the World* or *The Awakening Conscience* (1854).

**Hussein, [Ibn Talal]** (1935– ) king of Jordan. He succeeded his mentally ill father in 1953. He lost the West Bank of his country to Israel after the Six Day War of 1967, and has trod an uneasy diplomatic line between friendship with the West and his efforts on behalf of the Palestinians (who form the majority in his country). His position became critical during the Gulf War of 1991, when he came under strong pressure within his country to give military support to Saddam HUSSEIN.

**Hussein, Saddam** (1937– ) Iraqi dictator. He became president of Iraq in 1979, and quickly established a reputation for ruthlessness in the suppression of his opponents within and without the Ba'ath Party. He was given much Western support in his brutal war of attrition against Iran (1980–88) despite incontrovertible proof of his genocidal campaigns against Iraqi Kurds. After his invasion of Kuwait in 1990, UN forces (predominantly US) forced his withdrawal in the Gulf War of 1991.

**Husserl, Edmund** (1859–1938) German philosopher. He founded and became the leading philosopher of phenomenology, the school of philosophy that centres on knowledge of consciousness, rather than the empirical world of "things." His works include *Ideas* (1913).

**Huston, John [Marcellus]** (1906–87) American film director (Irish citizen from 1964). His films include several classics, such as *The Maltese Falcon* (1941), *The Treasure of the Sierra Madre* (1947), both starring BOGART, and *The Man Who Would Be King* (1975). His last film, *The Dead* (1987), from a short story by JOYCE, starred his daughter, the actress **Anjelica Huston** (1951– ).

**Hutton, Sir Leonard ("Len")** (1916–90) English cricketer. A Yorkshire player throughout his long career, he scored a century in his first Test match, against Australia. He became the first professional player to captain England regularly (1952–54).

**Huxley, Sir Andrew Fielding** *see* **Hodgkin, Sir Alan Lloyd**

**Huxley, Sir Julian [Sorell]** (1887–1975) English biologist. He became one of Britain's best-known scientists and humanists, with works such as *The*

*Science of Life* (with H. G. WELLS, 1931), *Evolutionary Ethics* (1947) and *Towards a New Humanism* (1957). He was the first director-general of UNESCO (1946–48). His brother, **Aldous [Leonard] Huxley** (1894–1963) was a novelist, short-story writer and essayist. His early novels and stories, e.g. *Crome Yellow* (1921) and *Point Counter Point* (1928) depict the brittle world of 1920s English intellectual life. His masterpiece is *Brave New World* (1932), a chilling fable of a future totalitarian state. His nonfiction works include *The Doors of Perception* (1954) and *Heaven and Hell* (1956), in which he records the spiritual insights he claims to have received from taking hallucinogenic drugs.

**Huxley, Thomas Henry** (1825–95) English biologist. He became the most prominent scientific defender ("Darwin's Bulldog") of DARWIN's theory of evolution in works such as *Evidence as to Man's Place in Nature* (1863) and in a famous debate with Bishop **Samuel Wilberforce** (1805–73) at Oxford in 1860. He gradually lost his belief in a deity and coined the term "agnostic."

# I

**Ibarruri [Gomez], Dolores ("La Pasionara")** (1895–1989) Spanish Communist politician. A journalist, she was elected to parliament in 1936, and became world-famous for her slogan "They shall not pass" (borrowed from PÉTAIN) during the Spanish Civil War. She lived in exile in the USSR (1939–77) and was re-elected to the Spanish parliament in 1977.

**Ibn Saud, Abdul Aziz** (1880–1953) king of Saudi Arabia. He became the first king of Saudi Arabia (1932–53), and negotiated terms with American oil companies after the discovery of oil in his country (1938), thus becoming a very wealthy man. He had well over a hundred wives and was succeeded by one of his many sons.

**Ibsen, Henrik** (1828–1906) Norwegian dramatist. His great plays fall into three groups: the early verse dramas, which culminated in *Brand* (1866) and *Peer Gynt* (1867); the plays of social realism dealing with such issues as venereal disease, municipal corruption, and female emancipation, e.g. *A Doll's House* (1879), *Ghosts* (1881) and *An Enemy of the People* (1882); the late symbolic plays, in which the realism of the middle period is blended with an introspective, disturbing symbolism that draws upon folk symbolism. *Hedda Gabler* (1890), marked a powerful return to realism in its depiction of the menace of intellectual arrogance. His plays were hugely influential on later dramatists, e.g. SHAW, who wrote the *Quintessence of Ibsenism* (1891).

**Ignatius Loyola, St** (1491–1556) Spanish saint and founder of the Jesuit order. A former soldier who was severely wounded in action, he had a spiritual conversion and founded the Society of Jesus in 1534. He devised a series of spiritual exercises as a training for the new order, and was canonized in 1622.

**Ilyushin, Sergei Vladimirovich** (1894–1977) Russian aircraft designer. He designed many planes, notably bombers and passenger aircraft.

**Ingres, Jean Auguste Dominique** (1780–1867) French painter. He was one of the greatest exponents of neoclassical art. Influenced in his early work by RAPHAEL, he established his reputation with *The Vow of King Louis VIII*. His excellent draughtsmanship influenced DEGAS, MATISSE and PICASSO.

**Ionesco, Eugène** (1912– ) Romanian-born French dramatist. His plays, regarded as masterpieces of the Theatre of the Absurd, include *The Bald Prima Donna* (1950), *The Lesson* (1951) and *Rhinoceros* (1960). Ionesco's hatred of both left and right totalitarianism resulted in him becoming an isolated figure in French intellectual circles.

**Ireland, John [Nicholson]** (1879–1962) British composer. Like DELIUS and HOLST, he was much influenced by English poetry, his works including several song cycles to words by HARDY, HOUSMAN and others. His other works, which were often inspired by a mystical reverence for English landscape, include a piano concerto and the orchestral tone poem, *The Forgotten Rite* (1913).

**Ironside, William Edmund, 1st Baron** (1880–1959) Scottish soldier. His early adventurous exploits included dangerous secret service work in the Boer War (1899–1902). (John BUCHAN used him as the model for the adventurer Richard Hannay.) He became chief of the General Staff at the outbreak of World War II.

**Irving, Washington** (1783–1859) American essayist and historian. His best-known stories are "Rip Van Winkle" and "The Legend of Sleepy Hollow", both of which are included in *The Sketch-Book of Geoffrey Crayon* (1820). He also wrote a five-volume biography of George WASHINGTON (1855–9).

**Isabella I of Castile** *see* **Ferdinand V**.

**Isherwood, Christopher [William Bradshaw]** (1904–86) English-born American novelist and dramatist. His best-known works are the novels *Mr Norris Changes Trains* (1932) and *Goodbye to Berlin* (1939), the latter forming the basis for the film *Cabaret* (1972). He also wrote works in collaboration with AUDEN, e.g. the verse drama *The Ascent of F6* (1936).

**Issigonis, Sir Alec** [Alexander Arnold Constantine Issigonis] (1906–88) Turkish-born (of Greek ancestry) British car designer, settled in Britain from the early 1920s. He began working at Morris Motors in 1936, and designed the Morris Minor, over a million of which were sold between 1948–71. His other famous design was the Mini Minor, of which over 5 million have been sold since its appearance in 1959.

**Ives, Charles Edward** (1874–1954) American composer. His works, which are frequently experimental but based firmly within the American tradition, include five symphonies, chamber music, including the well-known piano sonata, the *Concord Sonata*, and orchestral works.

# J

**Jackson, Glenda** (1936– ) English actress. Jackson's
reputation as an actress, starring in stage, film and
TV with equal facility, was established by the mid–
1960s and continues apace. Highlights include the
films *Women in Love* (1969), *Sunday, Bloody Sunday* (1971) and *Stevie* (1978), and *The Return of the
Soldier* (1982). She became Labour member of parliament for Hampstead in 1992.

**Jackson, Jesse** (1941– ) American Democrat politician, sometimes called "Revd." He was ordained a
Baptist minister in 1968 and became one of Martin
Luther KING's aides, subsequently claiming to have
cradled the dying King in his arms. He founded
what he termed a "Rainbow Coalition" of blacks and
other minority groups and campaigned twice for
the Democratic presidential nomination, in 1984
and 1986.

**Jackson, Michael [Joe]** (1958– ) American pop
singer. The youngest of five brothers (the others are
Jackie, Jermaine, Marion and Tito) who as children
formed the Jackson 5, a rock soul group popular in
the late 1960s and the 1970s. Michael became a solo
performer in the late 1970s, appearing in the film
*The Wiz* (1978), an all-black version of *The Wizard
of Oz*. He became very successful with young teen-
agers in the early 1980s, exploiting the develop-

ment of pop videos, as in *Thriller*(1982). He became famous for undergoing plastic surgery.

**Jacob, François** *see* **Monod, Jacques-Lucien**.

**Jagger, Mick** [Michael Philip Jagger] (1943– ) English singer and songwriter, and lead singer with the Rolling Stones rock group, the original members of which, with Jagger, were the guitarist and co-writer with Jagger of many of their songs, **Keith Richard** (1943– ), bass guitarist **Bill Wyman** (1936– ), drummer **Charlie Watts** (1941– ) and guitarist **Brian Jones** (1944–69). Their carefully marketed image of "Satanic Majesties," and involvement with drugs, ensured high levels of publicity for the group. Several of the Jagger/Richard songs, e.g. the ballad "Ruby Tuesday," have become pop standards. Jagger is also regarded as one of the finest white rock/ blues singers of his generation.

**James V** *see* **Mary, Queen of Scots**.

**James VI and I** (1566–1625) King of Scotland as James VI and king of England and Ireland as James I. The son of MARY QUEEN OF SCOTS, he inherited the Scottish throne in 1567 when his mother was forced to abdicate. He spent his youth amid much conspiracy and made only a token protest at the execution of his mother by ELIZABETH I, whose throne he inherited in 1603. A scholar, he was described by a contemporary as "the wisest fool in Christendom."

**James VII and II** (1633–1701) King of Scotland as James VII and king of England and Ireland as James II. As Duke of York, he became a Roman Catholic in 1672, and survived attempts to disbar him from the succession, becoming king in 1685. A rebellion of 1685, led by James Scott, **1st Duke of**

**Monmouth** (1649–85), the illegitimate son of CHARLES II, was bloodily crushed, but James had to flee to France after WILLIAM III landed in England in 1688.

**James, Henry** (1843–1916) American-born British novelist, short-story writer and critic. James settled in England in 1869 and became a British citizen in 1914, after the outbreak of World War I. Much of his work is concerned with the contrast between American innocence and the older, wiser European culture, e.g. *Daisy Miller* (1879), and with the minutiae of Edwardian upper-class life, e.g. *The Spoils of Poynton* (1897).

**James, M[ontague] R[hodes]** (1862–1936) English scholar and ghost-story writer. His stories, e.g. *Ghost Stories of an Antiquary* (1904), are a mix of dry, scholarly wit with a horrifically reticent undertone of supernatural terror.

**James, Dame P. D.** [Phyllis Dorothy White] (1920– ) English novelist. Her crime novels, particularly those starring her poet/policeman, Inspector Dalgleish, e.g. *Death of an Expert Witness* (1977) and *A Taste for Death* (1986), have been much admired for their wit.

**James, Sid** *see* **Hancock, Tony**.

**James, William** (1842–1910) American philosopher and psychologist. His works include *The Varieties of Religious Experience* (1902), in which he coined the term "stream of consciousness", and *Essays in Radical Empiricism* (1912), which describes his theory of pragmatism.

**Janácek, Leos** (1854–1928) Czech composer. His works, heavily influenced by Czech folk music and culture, include the operas *The Cunning Little Vixen*

(1924) and *The House of the Dead* (1928) and two highly regarded string quartets (1923, 1928).

**Jarry, Alfred** (1873–1907) French dramatist. Regarded as a founder of the Theatre of the Absurd, the first performance of his anarchic farce *Ubu Roi* (1896), a savage and surreal version of *Macbeth*, is memorably described in YEATS' *The Trembling of the Veil* (1926).

**Jeans, Sir James [Hopwood]** (1877–1946) English physicist and astronomer. He wrote several books for the popular market explaining modern scientific theory, e.g. *The Mysterious Universe* (1930) and *The New Background of Science* (1933) and made contributions to the study of quantum theory and stellar evolution.

**Jefferson, Thomas** (1743–1826) American statesman. He was the main creator of the Declaration of Independence in 1776 and became secretary of state (1790–93) under WASHINGTON. He was elected the 3rd president of the United States (1801–9), and founded the University of Virginia. A highly talented man, he designed his own house.

**Jellicoe, John Rushworth, 1st Earl** (1859–1935) English admiral. He was badly wounded during the Boxer Rising of 1900 in Peking, where he served as head of an overland naval expedition. He was appointed Naval commander in chief at the outbreak of World War I and commanded the British fleet at the Battle of Jutland (1916). He was governor-general of New Zealand (1920–24).

**Jenkins, Roy** [Baron Jenkins of Hillhead] (1920– ) Welsh Labour and Social Democrat politician. As Labour home secretary (1965–67) he introduced significant liberalizing reforms in the law, e.g. on homosexuality. With Shirley WILLIAMS, David OWEN and William Rodgers, the so-called "Gang of Four," he resigned from the Labour Party in 1981 to found the Social Democratic Party. He was SDP member for Glasgow Hillhead (1982–87).

**Jenner, Edward** (1749–1823) English physician. In 1775 he began to investigate the traditional belief that catching cowpox gave protection against smallpox, and discovered that vaccination was efficacious in preventing smallpox.

**Jesus Christ** (c.6 BC–c.30 AD) founder of Christianity. *The New Testament* records that he was born in Bethlehem, the son of Joseph and Mary, and Christians have traditionally believed that he is the Son of God, miraculously conceived by Mary, that he gathered together disciples, performed miracles such as raising the dead, was arrested by the authorities and crucified between two thieves, and was resurrected after three days. The Book of Acts describes how the Christian gospel was spread through the Mediterranean world by his disciples, notably **Paul** and **Peter**, the latter being recognized as the founder of the Roman Catholic church.

**Jiang Jie Shi** *see* **Chiang Kai-shek**.

**Jiang Qing** *see* **Chiang Ch'ing**.

**Jinnah, Mohammed Ali** (1876–1948) nationalist leader and Pakistani statesman. He joined the Indian Muslim League in 1916, and worked towards peaceful cooperation between Muslim and Hindu nationalists. By 1940, however, despite GANDHI's urging of nationalist unity, Jinnah was convinced of the need for Indian partition into Hindu and Muslim states. He became the first governor-general of Pakistan (1947–48).

**Joan of Arc** (*c*.1412–31) French patriot. From a peasant family, she had a vision when she was thirteen, urging her to free France from the invading English. She helped raise the siege of Orléans in 1429, and brought Charles VII to Rheims to be crowned king of France. Captured by the English in 1430, she was condemned for witchcraft and burned at the stake. She was canonized in 1920.

**John, King** *see* **Richard I**.

**John XXIII** [Angelo Giuseppe Roncalli] (1881–1963) Italian pope (1958–63). He convened the Second Vatican Council in 1962, which recommended significant liberalizing changes in Roman Catholic practice and liturgy. He was a notable proponent of ecumenicalism and of detente between East and West, as expressed in his encyclical, *Pacem in Terris* of 1963.

**John, Augustus [Edwin]** (1878–1961) Welsh painter. By the beginning of the 20th century, he had acquired a reputation for both superb draughtsmanship and for his mildly shocking "bohemian" lifestyle. He later became known as a portraitist of the good and the great, e.g. HARDY. His sister, **Gwen John** (1876–1939), who became something of a recluse after her conversion to Roman Catholicism in 1913, was also a painter.

**John, Elton** [Reginald Kenneth Dwight] (1947– ) English pop and rock musician. John was particularly popular in the 1960s and 70s with hit songs such as "Daniel" and "Don't Go Breaking My Heart."

**John Paul II** [Karel Jozef Wojtyla] (1920– ) Polish pope (1978– ) Noted for his courage and resistance to both Nazis and Communists, he had been appointed a cardinal in 1967, and gave shrewd and successful advice to his church throughout the growing unrest in Poland. In 1978 he became the first Polish pope and first non–Italian pope for 450 years. His primacy has been notable for both his wide travels throughout the world and for his conservatism in matters such as abortion and the celibacy of the priesthood. He survived an assassination attempt in 1981. Also a dramatist and poet, his works include *The Future of the Church* (1979) and *Collected Poems* (1982).

**Johns, Jasper** (1930– ) American painter, sculptor and printmaker. His work, especially his use of everyday images such as the stars and stripes, was very influential on later Pop Artists such as WARHOL.

**Johns, W[illiam] E[arl]** (1893–1968) English World War I bomber pilot and writer of 96 adventure stories featuring ace pilot Biggles (Sergeant Bigglesworth) and his chums Algy and Ginger. The first Biggles book was *The Camels are Coming* (1932); many of the other titles begin *"Biggles Flies (East, West, etc)*. In all, he published 169 books, 11 of which feature a staunchly feminist World War II version of Biggles, "Worrals of the WAAF." A fine adventure story writer, with a fair share of tolerance and humour, his works remain popular with children.

**Johnson, Amy** (1903–41) English aviator. She was the first woman to fly solo from England to Australia (1930). Her other records include a solo flight from London to Cape Town (1936). She was lost, presumed drowned, after baling out over the Thames Estuary while serving as an Transport Auxiliary pilot in World War II.

**Johnson, Jack** (1878–1946) American boxer. He

became the first black to win the world heavyweight title (1908–15). His reign as champion inspired the phrase "Great White Hope," which was applied to any white boxer thought capable of beating Jackson, who, with his controversial and uncompromising lifestyle, never attracted much white affection or support.

**Johnson, Lyndon B[aines]** (1908–73) American Democrat statesman. Following John F. KENNEDY's assassination in 1963, he became the 36th president of the US (1963–69). His time in office was a troubled one, and the increasing unpopularity of the Vietnam War and Civil Rights agitation overshadowed what he called his "Great Society" reforms, especially in the fields of medical aid for the poor and aged, and in education.

**Johnson, Dr Samuel** (1709–84) English critic, lexicographer and poet. One of the greatest literary figures of the 18th century, his works include the *Dictionary of the English Language* (1755), a highly important edition of SHAKESPEARE (1765), *Lives of the Most Famous Poets* (1779–81), several wonderful essays, e.g. in *The Rambler* (1750–52), and the great verse satires *London* (1738) and *The Vanity of Human Wishes* (1749). His only novel, *Rasselas* (1759), is a melancholic little fable that sums up its author's philosophy thus: "Human life is everywhere a state in which much is to be endured, and little to be enjoyed". Johnson was the great moralist of the age, a devout Christian tormented by self-doubt, a Tory with Jacobite sympathies who once drank a toast to the "next slave rebellion in the West Indies". In 1763 he met **James Boswell** (1740–95), a dissolute Whiggish Scot who mixed with radicals and defended slavery. An unlikely friendship was formed, and Boswell began recording Johnson's conversations. In 1785, after Johnson's death, Boswell published the greatest biography in the language, his *Life of Samuel Johnson, L.L.D.* In 1773, Johnson and Boswell travelled to the Scottish Hebrides, the tour resulting in two books, Boswell's *Journal of the Tour to the Hebrides* (1785), and Johnson's *Journey to the Western Isles* (1775). *See also* GARRICK, VOLTAIRE.

**Joliot-Curie, Irène** (1897–1956) French physicist, daughter of Marie and Pierre CURIE. With her physicist husband, **Frédéric Joliot-Curie** (1900–58), she shared the 1935 Nobel prize for chemistry for their discovery of artificial radioactivity. Both died of cancer, caused by lifelong exposure to radioactivity.

**Jolson, Al** [Asa Yoelson] (1886–1950) Russian-born American singer and actor. The son of a rabbi, Jolson became famous for his "black face" minstrel songs, e.g. "Mammy" and "Sonny Boy." He starred in the first full-length movie with sound, *The Jazz Singer* (1927).

**Jones, Bobby** [Robert Tyre Jones] (1902–71) American golfer. Regarded as one of the greatest golfers of all time, Jones won many major championships, before retiring at the age of 28, still an amateur. In 1930, he won the US and British Opens and the US and British amateur tournaments, a feat unlikely to be repeated.

**Jones, Brian** *see* **Jagger, Mick.**

**Jones, Chuck** [Charles Jones] (1912– ) American cartoon director. His most famous creation is Bugs Bunny, the laconic, subversive rabbit with the catchphrase, "What's Up, Doc?" Jones has won two Oscars for his work.

**Jones, Daniel** (1881–1967) English phonetician. His *English Pronouncing Dictionary* (1917) includes a description of "Received Pronunciation" that, notably through the medium of the BBC, became the standard against which everyday speech was measured.

**Jonson, Benjamin** (1572–1637) English dramatist. After a turbulent early life, during which he served as a soldier in Flanders and killed a fellow soldier in a duel, he began writing his comedies, which are particularly noted for their satirical dialogue and use of the "Theory of Humours" and which established him as one of the great dramatists. The plays include *Bartholomew Fair* (1614), *Volpone* (1616) and *The Alchemist* (1616). He became the first poet laureate in 1616, in which year he published a folio edition of his poetic and dramatic works, setting a highly important precedent: his friend SHAKESPEARE's first folio followed in 1623.

**Joplin, Scott** (1868–1917) American pianist and composer. Joplin's "ragtime" compositions, e.g. *Maple Leaf Rag* (1899), which became enormously popular in the USA, selling over a million copies of sheet music. Longing to be accepted as the first black composer of "serious" music, Joplin grew depressed by the failure of his two operas, and died in a mental home. His music enjoyed a revival in the 1970s, and was used in the hit film *The Sting* (1973).

**Josephson, Brian David** (1940– ) Welsh physicist. He shared the 1973 Nobel prize for physics for his discovery of the "Josephson effect" on electric currents in superconductors.

**Joyce, James [Augustine Aloysius]** (1882–1941) Irish novelist and short-story writer. Educated in Jesuit schools and at Dublin University, he left Ireland in 1902, returning briefly twice. His works include a verse collection, *Chamber Music* (1907), the short-story collection *Dubliners* (1914), and two great novels, *Portrait of the Artist as a Young Man* (1914–15) and *Ulysses* (1922), the last being one of the key novels of the century. His other main work, *Finnegans Wake* (1939), uses Joyce's formidable repertoire of punning and allusive language in an attempt at creating an effect of all actual and possible human experience.

**Joyce, William** (1906–46) American-born British traitor (of Anglo-Irish descent). An ex-member of Mosley's British Union of Fascists, he formed his own pro-Nazi party in 1937, and fled to Germany in 1939, where he broadcast rabid Nazi propaganda to Britain, soon being dubbed "Lord Haw-Haw" by the British public for his affected upper-class accent. he was executed for treason in 1946.

**Juan Carlos** (1938– ) king of Spain from 1975. Nominated by Franco in 1969 as his successor, Juan Carlos carefully steered his country towards democracy and respectability after Franco's death in 1975, despite two attempted coups.

**Julian of Norwich, Dame** (*c*.1342–*c*.1416) English anchorite. Her *Sixteen Revelations of Divine Love* (1393) examines the contradiction between her mystical revelations of the proximity of Christ to her, and the chasm between Christ and man caused by the sins of humanity. T. S. Eliot quotes her on the mystery of sin and redemption in *Four Quartets* ("Little Gidding"): "Sin is behovely [i.e. necessary]

**Jung**

. . . but all manner of things shall be well." Julian
was one of a number of 14th-century English mystical writers, notably **Walter Hilton** (d.1396).

**Jung, Carl Gustav** (1875–1961) Swiss psychiatrist.
He began his career as a follower of FREUD, but split
with him after challenging his concentration on sex.
Jung's theory of the "collective unconscious," a sort
of vast reservoir in the unconscious mind filled with
memories and instincts common to all humans, and
his use of the term "archetype" to denote an image
or symbol drawn from this store, has been highly
influential. His relationship with the Nazi regime
in the 1930s is still a matter of intense debate.

# K

**Kádár, János** (1912–89) Hungarian politician. He fought with the Communist partisans during World War II and became minister of internal affairs in 1948. Imprisoned (1951–54) for "Titoism," he joined NAGY's government during the Hungarian Revolution of 1956, but formed a puppet pro-Soviet government after the Soviet invasion. He served as prime minister (1956–58, 1961–65) and was first secretary of the Communist Party (1956–88). He served a brief period as party president in 1988, being dismissed shortly before his death.

**Kafka, Franz** (1883–1924) Czech-born German novelist and short-story writer. His novels *The Trial* (1925) and *The Castle* (1926), and several of his short stories, notably "Metamorphosis," are established classics of 20th-century literature. The atmosphere of his fiction, in which characters are often trapped in bureaucratic totalitarianism, is oddly prophetic of the coming era (many of his family were to die in HITLER's camps). His unfinished novel, *Amerika* (1927), is a surprisingly light-hearted Chaplinesque affair set in the USA (which he never visited).

**Kaldor, Nicholas, Baron** (1908–86) Hungarian-born British economist. A highly influential economist in the 1960s, particularly in the WILSON administrations, Kaldor advocated expenditure taxes rather than income taxes and was a notable critic of monetarism. His books include *The Scourge of Monetarism* (1982).

**Kandinsky, Wassily** (1866–1944) Russian-born French painter. One of the leading Expressionist painters, he co-founded (with KLEE and MARC) the *Blaue Reiter* ("Blue Rider") group in 1912, and is regarded as the first major abstract artist. His thesis, *On the Spiritual in Art* (1912), was a highly influential work.

**Kant, Immanuel** (1724–1804) German philosopher. His works include *The Critique of Pure Reason* (1781), in which he adopts (in response to HUME's empiricism) an idealist position, arguing that our knowledge is limited by our capacity for perception, and *The Critique of Practical Reason* (1788), in which he expounds his theory of ethics based upon 'categorical imperatives'.

**Kapitza, Piotr Leonidovich** (1894–1984) Russian physicist. He was awarded the 1978 Nobel prize for physics, and made notable contributions to the study of cryogenics. He was dismissed from his post as director of the Institute of Physical Problems in 1946 for refusing to work on the atom bomb, but was reinstated in 1955.

**Karajan, Herbert von** (1908–89) Austrian conductor. By the mid–1930s he was regarded as a brilliant, if dictatorial, conductor of symphonies and operas, whose recordings, notably of BEETHOVEN's symphonies, are held by some critics to be definitive. His membership of the Nazi party from 1933 on is claimed by his admirers, rather unconvincingly, to have been simply a "career move."

**Karamanlis, Konstantinos** (1907– ) Greek politician. He served as prime minister (1955–63), after which he left Greece, returning on the collapse of the military junta to serve again as premier (1974–80), and subsequently became president (1980–85).

**Karpov, Anatoly Yegenyevich** (1951– ) Russian chess player. After FISCHER refused to defend his title, Karpov became world champion by default (1975–85), being displaced by KASPAROV in 1985, in the longest-ever world match (48 games over six months).

**Kasparov, Gary** [Gary Weinstein] (1963– ) Russian chess player. He became world champion in 1985 after defeating KARPOV in a long, exhausting contest. His autobiography, *Child of Change* (1987), depicts himself as a product of GORBACHEV's new glasnost era.

**Kauffmann, Angelica** (1741–1807) Swiss painter. Influenced by neoclassicism, she settled in London in 1776 where her work became very popular, doing portraits from Shakespeare and Homer as well as history paintings. She was a friend of REYNOLDS, whose portrait she painted (GOETHE was another sitter) and a founder of the Royal Academy.

**Kaunda, Kenneth [David]** (1924– ) Zambian politician. He became president of Zambia when his country became independent in 1964. Regarded as a relatively benign dictator by many in the West, his rule was shaken in the continent-wide wave of agitation for reform that followed the release of MANDELA in 1990. Kaunda's opaque philosophy of "African humanism" is expressed in such works as *A Humanist in Africa* (1966).

**Kazan, Elia** [Elia Kazanjoglous] (1909– ) Turkish-born American film and stage director. His films include *On the Waterfront* (1954), *East of Eden* (1954) and *Splendour in the Grass* (1962).

**Kazantzakis, Nikos** (1885–1957) Greek novelist, poet and dramatist. His best-known work is the novel *Zorba the Greek* (1946).

**Keaton, Buster** [Joseph Francis Keaton] (1895–1966) American film comedian and director. Widely regarded as one of the all-time great comedians of the cinema, with his "deadpan" expression and remarkable acrobatic skill, his silent comedy films include *The Navigator* (1924) and *The General* (1926).

**Keats, John** (1795–1821) English poet. He abandoned his apprenticeship as an apothecary to concentrate on poetry in 1816, the year he met the English poet and essayist **Leigh Hunt** (1784–1859), who published the young poet's highly Romantic lyrics in *The Examiner*, the weekly paper Hunt founded in 1808 with his brother **James Hunt** (1774–1848). Keats also became friendly with many of Hunt's friends, including SHELLEY. His poems were savagely attacked by *The Examiner*'s many literary and political rivals. Keats seems to have been deeply affected by the criticism, which was based largely on class spite and cultural snobbery (the "Cockney School" was one sneer), and died of tuberculosis in Rome. Most of his great poems, e.g. "The Eve of St Agnes" and "To a Nightingale", are in *Lamia and Other Poems* (1820).

**Keeler, Christine** *see* **Profumo, John Dennis.**

**Keller, Helen** [Adams] (1880–1968) American writer. She became deaf and blind when 19 months old, and was taught to read and write by the partially sighted Anne Sullivan. Her books include *The Story of My Life* (1902).

**Kelly, Gene** [Eugene Curran Kelly] (1912– ) American dancer, choreographer and film director. Noted for his athleticism and witty dancing style, his films include the musicals *On the Town* (1949) and *Singin' in the Rain* (1952). His "straight" acting films include, notably, *Inherit the Wind* (1960).

**Kelly, Grace [Patricia]** (1929–82) American film actress. Her films include *High Noon* (1952), *High Society* (1956) and *Rear Window* (1954). She married **Prince Rainier III** (1923– ) of Monaco in 1956, and gave up her career.

**Kendrew, Sir John Cowdery** (1917– ) English biochemist. With the Austrian-born British chemist **Max Ferdinand Perutz** (1914– ), he shared the 1962 Nobel prize for biochemistry for work on the molecular structure of the protein myoglobin.

**Kennedy, John Fitzgerald** (1917–63) American Democratic politician, who became 35th president of the US (1961–63). He was the first Roman Catholic and the youngest man elected to the presidency. His brief period of office, cut short by his assassination in Dallas, was subsequently seen by many as a period of hope and social reform, with most of his "New Frontier" legislation being implemented by Lyndon JOHNSON. He gave half-hearted support for the CIA-backed Bay of Pigs invasion of CASTRO's Cuba in 1961, and forced KHRUSCHEV to withdraw Soviet missiles from Cuba in 1962. His brother **Robert ("Bobby") [Francis] Kennedy** (1925–68), who became attorney general (1961–64) and senator for New York (1965–68) and furthered civil rights legislation, was assassinated. Another brother, **Edward [Moore] Kennedy** (1932– ), became a Massachusetts senator in 1962, and was widely regarded as a future president until the "Chappaquidick" incident of 1969, in which a girl passenger in his car was drowned in circumstances that remain obscure.

**Kennelly, Arthur Edwin** *see* **Heaviside, Oliver**.

**Kenyatta, Jomo** (*c.*1893–1978) Kenyan politician. He was jailed for six years (1952–58) for his leadership of the Mau-Mau rebellion. He became prime minister of Kenya on independence in 1963 and president (1964–78).

**Kerenski, Alexsandr Feodorovich** (1881–1970) Russian revolutionary leader. A member of the Social Democratic Party's liberal wing, he became prime minister of the Russian provisional government of 1917, but was unable to unite the squabbling democratic factions and was deposed by LENIN's Bolsheviks in the October Revolution. He fled to France, and lived in the US from 1946. His works include *The Kerensky Memoirs* (1966).

**Kern, Jerome [David]** (1885–1945) American composer and songwriter. A highly prolific writer of music and songs, he had a huge influence on the American musical tradition with works such as the operetta *Show Boat* (1927), in which the songs were integral parts of the dramatic action rather than merely decorative. He wrote over a thousand songs for the stage and for movies in collaboration with, among others, WODEHOUSE and HAMMERSTEIN.

**Kerouac, Jack** [Jean-Louis Lebris de Kérouac] (1922–69) American novelist. One of the "Beat generation" (*see* GINSBERG), his most popular work is the semi-autobiographical novel *On the Road* (1957), a meandering, episodic account of the ramblings across America of a young writer and his friend. His other works include *The Dharma Bums* (1958) and volumes of poetry.

**Kertesz, André** (1894–1985) Hungarian-born American photographer, notable for his documentary photographs of Paris during the 1920s, which were highly praised for their insight into the city's architecture and people. He was one of the first photographers to fully exploit the possibilities of the small Leica cameras, his work was influential on both BRASSAI and CARTIER-BRESSON.

**Keynes, John Maynard, 1st Baron** (1883–1946) English economist. His work, *The Economic Consequences of the Peace* (1919), foretold the terrible consequences that would follow from the Allies demand for war reparations from Germany. In his *General Theory of Employment, Interest and Money* (1936), he argued that unemployment was curable through macroeconomic management of monetary and fiscal policies, and advocated the creation of employment through government schemes (which influenced ROOSEVELT'S "New Deal" policies). He was one of the so-called "Bloomsbury Group" of intellectuals (*see* WOOLF).

**Khomeini, Ayatollah [Ruholla]** (1900–89) Iranian religious leader. A prominent member of the Iranian Shiite Muslim opposition to the Shah of Iran (*see* PAHLAVI) from the early 1960s, he became *de facto* head of the Iranian state after the revolution of 1979. He established a theocratic dictatorship that crushed all dissent, and declared his intention of "exporting" the Shiite revolution to other Islamic countries, thus ensuring Western support for Saddam HUSSEIN in the ruinous Iran-Iraq War (1980–88). He further aroused Western anger by proclaiming a death sentence against Salman RUSHDIE in 1989.

**Khrushchev, Nikita Sergeyevich** (1894–1971) Soviet politician. Following the death of STALIN, whose protégé he was, he became first secretary of the Communist Party (1953–64), and condemned Stalin's crimes and "cult of personality" in his speech (not officially published until 1989) to the party congress of 1956. He became prime minister (1958–64) and promoted peaceful co-existence with the West, where his blunt peasant ways aroused as much admiration as anger. He was deposed in 1964 in the Kremlin coup that brought BREZHNEV to power.

**Kierkegaard, Søren Aabye** (1813–55) Danish theologian and philosopher. Regarded as the founder of existentialism, he rejected the spiritual authority of organized religion and emphasized the centrality of individual choice. His highly influential works include *Either/Or* (1843) and *The Concept of Dread* (1844).

**Kim Il Sung** (1912– ) North Korean marshal and Communist politician. He became prime minister (1948–72) and president (1972– ) of North Korea, establishing a rigorous and increasingly isolated dictatorship, based on Stalinist policies, and a notorious personality cult of himself as the "great leader." His son and proclaimed successor, **Kim Jong II** (1942– ), is officially titled the "dear leader."

**King, Billie Jean** (1943– ) American tennis player. Regarded as one of the finest women players ever, she won a record twenty Wimbledon titles between between 1965 and 1980.

**King, Martin Luther, Jr** (1929–68) American civil rights leader and Baptist minister. Influenced by

GANDHI's policy of nonviolent resistance, he organized opposition to segregationist policies in the Southern US. Over 200,000 people took part in his "March on Washington" in 1963, when he made his "I have a dream" speech. He was awarded the 1964 Nobel Peace Prize, and was assassinated in 1968. *See also* Jesse JACKSON.

**King, William Lyon Mackenzie** (1874–1950) Canadian Liberal statesman. He became leader of the Liberal party (1919–48) and prime minister (1921–26, 1926–30, 1935–48). He was also an authority on industrial relations, and wrote *Industry and Humanity* (1918).

**Kingsley, Charles** (1819–75) English clergyman and novelist. His works include historical novels such as *Hereward the Wake* (1866), but he is best known for his children's story *The Water Babies* (1863), a bizarre fantasy about a young chimney sweep's adventures in an underwater world.

**Kinnock, Neil [Gordon]** (1942– ) Welsh Labour politician. He became MP for Bedwelty in 1970, and established a reputation as a spokesman for left-wing policies such as unilateral nuclear disarmament and abolition of the House of Lords. Elected leader of the Labour Party in 1983 in succession to FOOT, he gradually moderated his policies and had great success in marginalizing the hard left of the party. Attacked by Conservatives and Marxists alike for being a turncoat, Kinnock had by the late 1980s re-established the Labour Party as a mainstream electable force.

**Kinsey, Alfred Charles** (1894–1956) American sexologist and zoologist. He published two controversial studies of American sexual behaviour, *Sexual*

*Behavior in the Human Male* (1948) and *Sexual Behavior in the Human Female* (1953). His evidence that sexual behaviour was much more diverse than generally supposed was initially disbelieved, then gradually accepted as authoritative. His trust in the honesty of his interviewees, however, remains open to question.

**Kipling, [Joseph] Rudyard** (1865–1936) Indian-born English short-story writer, poet and novelist. Born in Bombay, he was sent home to be educated, then returned to India where he soon made a name for himself as a journalist and caustic observer of Anglo-Indian society. He returned to England in 1889, where he achieved celebrity status with his poems of army life, *Barrack-Room Ballads* (1892). Subsequent works include two novels, *The Light That Failed* (1890) and *Kim* (1901), collections of short stories, e.g. *Debits and Credits* (1926), children's books, e.g. *The Jungle Book* (1894) and *Rewards and Fairies* (1910), and many great poems.

**Kissinger, Henry [Alfred]** (1923– ) German-born American statesman. He became NIXON's adviser on national security affairs (1968–73) and shared the 1973 Nobel Peace Prize with the North Vietnamese negotiator **Le Duc Tho** (1911– ) for the treaty ending US involvement in Vietnam. (His policy for winning the war through attrition was a failure, with the bombing of Cambodia in 1969–70 resulting in the victory of the Maoist Khmer Rouge.) He became secretary of state (1973–76), fostered détente with the Soviet Union and China, and helped negotiate peace between Israel and Egypt in 1973.

**Kitchener of Khartoum, [Horatio] Herbert, 1st Earl** (1850–1916) Anglo-Irish field marshal and statesman. He crushed the Dervish revolt in the Sudan at Omdurman (with a savagery condemned by CHURCHILL) and was commander in chief of the British forces during the Boer War of 1901–02, and of the British forces in India (1902–09). He was appointed secretary for war in 1914, and had mobilized Britain's largest-yet army by the time of his death by drowning when his ship hit a mine.

**Klee, Paul** (1879–1940) Swiss painter and etcher. With KANDINSKY and MARC, he was a member of the *Blaue Reiter* group of Expressionists, and developed a style of mainly abstract work characterized by doodle-like (technically very sophisticated) drawings.

**Klemperer, Otto** (1885–1973) German-born conductor. By the late 1920s he was established as a great interpreter of both classical and contemporary works (e.g. BEETHOVEN, his friend MAHLER, and JANÁCEK). Being Jewish, he fled to the US in 1933, where he became director of the Los Angeles Symphony Orchestra, and a US citizen in 1936. He was director of the Budapest Opera (1947–50) and became an Israeli citizen in 1970.

**Knox, John** *see* **Mary, Queen of Scots**.

**Kodály, Zoltán** (1882–1967) Hungarian composer. Like his friend BARTÓK, with whom he collaborated on a plan for a Hungarian folk-music archive, he was much influenced by the traditional music of his country. His works include the comic opera *Hary Janos* (1926) and the *Galanta Dances* (1933).

**Koestler, Arthur** (1905–83) Hungarian-born British author and journalist. While reporting on the Spanish Civil War he was imprisoned and sentenced to death by FRANCO as a Communist agent (which he in fact was), was reprieved and eventually settled in England in 1940. His masterpiece is one of the greatest of all political novels, *Darkness at Noon* (1940), which describes the trial and execution (under STALIN's regime) of an old Bolshevik called Rubashov, who is a fictional composite of several real victims of Stalin, notably BUKHARIN.

**Koffka, Kurt** *see* **Köhler, Wolfgang**.

**Kohl, Helmut** (1930– ) German Christian Democrat statesman. He became chancellor of West Germany (1982–90) and became the first chancellor of reunited Germany after his CDU party won the all-Germany general election of 1990.

**Köhler, Wolfgang** (1887–1967) Estonian-born German-American psychologist. With the German psychologist **Kurt Koffka** (1886–1941) he founded the Gestalt school of psychology. His works include *Gestalt Psychology* (1929).

**Kokoschka, Oskar** (1886–1980) Austrian-born painter and dramatist. One of the leading Expressionist painters, noted particularly for his landscapes and portraits, he fled to Britain in 1938, becoming a British citizen in 1947.

**Kolff, Willem Johan** (1911– ) Dutch-born American physician. He invented the kidney dialysis machine in 1943, invented the artificial kidney in 1975 and also made significant contributions to cardiovascular surgery.

**Korda, Sir Alexander** [Sandor Kellner] (1893–1956) Hungarian-born British film director and producer. He settled in Britain in 1930. He directed *The Private Life of Henry VIII* (1933, with a memorable performance by Charles LAUGHTON), and produced *Things To Come* (1936) and one of the greatest of all films, REED's and WELLES' *The Third Man* (1949).

**Kornberg, Arthur** (1918– ) American biochemist. He shared the 1959 Nobel prize for physiology or medicine with **Severo Ochoa** (1905– ) for his discovery of the DNA enzyme polymerase.

**Kosygin, Aleksei Nikolayevich** (1904–80) Soviet statesman. A notable long-distance survivor in Soviet politics, He became prime minister (1964–80) of the Soviet Union after KHRUSHCHEV's overthrow, resigning in 1980.

**Krebs, Sir Hans Adolf** (1900–81) German-born British biochemist. He shared the 1953 Nobel prize for physiology or medicine with **Fritz Lipmann** (1899–1986) for his work on metabolic cycles, particularly his discovery of the Krebs Cycle.

**Kreisler, Fritz** (1875–1962) Austrian-born American violinist and composer. ELGAR's violin concerto was dedicated to him, and he became one of the most popular violinists of his day. He became a US citizen in 1943. His own compositions include the operetta *Apple Blossoms* (1919).

**Kristian X** *see* **Christian X**.

**Krupp, Alfred Alwin Felix** (1907–67) German industrialist. He took control of the Krupp industrial empire in 1943 by dispensation from HITLER, following the collapse into senility of his father **Gustav Krupp** (1870–1950). He was imprisoned (1947–51) for using slave labour in his factories. He subsequently helped develop Germany's economic postwar economy, and agreed to pay compensation to only some of his ex-slave labourers in 1959.

**Kubrick, Stanley** (1928– ) American film director and producer. His films include the anti-war classic *Paths of Glory* (1957), the black nuclear war comedy

*Dr Strangelove* (1963), the innovative science fiction classic *2001: A Space Odyssey* (1968), and the still highly controversial *A Clockwork Orange* (1971).

**Kundera, Milan** (1929– ) Czech novelist. His masterpiece is *The Unbearable Lightness of Being* (1985), a poignant love story set against the background of repression that followed the Russian invasion of Czechoslovakia in 1968.

**Kurosawa, Akira** (1910– ) Japanese film director. His films include the samurai classics *The Seven Samurai* (1955) and *Yojimbo* (1961), (remade in the west as *The Magnificent Seven* and *A Fistful of Dollars*), and samurai versions of *Macbeth*, titled *Throne of Blood* (1957, T. S. ELIOT's favourite film), and *King Lear*, titled *Ran* (1985). Like John FORD, whom he much admired—Ford to Kurosawa: "You like rain, don't you?"; Kurosawa: "You do know my films!"—Kurosawa was happiest with the epic form, and also had a "family" of actors he used regularly.

**Kuznets, Simon** (1901–85) Russian-born American economist and statistician. He was awarded the 1971 Nobel prize for economics for his research into economic growth and social change, e.g. the "Kuznets cycle" of twenty-year economic cyclical movement. His works include *National Income and its Composition* (1941).

**Kyd, Thomas** (1558–94) English dramatist. His most important work is his revenge tragedy *The Spanish Tragedy* (1588–89), which was popular and influential in its day, serving as a model for SHAKESPEARE's *Titus Andronicus*. Kyd, a close associate of Christopher MARLOWE, died in poverty after being tortured and accused of denying the divinity of Christ.

# L

**Laing, R[onald] D[avid]** (1927–89) Scottish psychiatrist. He became a counterculture guru in the 1960s with his view, expressed in such books as *The Divided Self* (1960) and *The Politics of the Family* (1976), that mental illness was not something to be "treated" but should rather be encouraged by his "anti-psychiatry" as a fulfilling experience, and argued that schizophrenia was an appropriate response to the real madness of the family group and society.

**Lamarck, Jean [Baptiste Pierre Antoine de Monet, Chevalier de]** (1744–1829) French naturalist. In his *Philosophie Zoologique* (1809), he expounded his theory of the evolution of species through the acquisition of inherited characteristics. The theory did not gain general acceptance, but is credited with preparing the ground for DARWIN's theory of evolution. (Lamarckian theory enjoyed a resurgence under 20th-century socialist dictatorships, which approved of his theory for ideological reasons.)

**Lamb, Charles** (1775–1834) English essayist and critic. A much loved friend of HAZLITT, WORDSWORTH and COLERIDGE, his writings display the great charm his friends describe. With his sister, **Mary Anne Lamb** (1764–1847), he wrote a prose version of SHAKESPEARE's plays, *Tales from Shakespeare* (1807), which has retained its popularity. In 1796, in a fit of insanity, Mary killed their mother, and Charles looked after her until his death. His *Specimens of English Dramatic Poets* (1808) was an important contribution to the reassessment of Shakespeare's contemporaries.

**Lambert, Constant** (1905–51) English composer and conductor. Known primarily as a composer of ballet music, including, for DIAGHILEV, *Romeo and Juliet* (1926), he also wrote several jazz-influenced orchestral works, e.g. *The Rio Grande* (1929), a work for chorus, orchestra and piano.

**Lampedusa, Giuseppe Tomasi di** (1896–1957) Italian novelist. His best-known work is *The Leopard* (1958), which describes the decline of aristocratic society in Sicily following the island's annexation by Garibaldi in 1860.

**Lancaster, Sir Osbert** (1908–86) English cartoonist and author of several satirical studies of British architecture, e.g. *Progress at Pelvis Bay* (1936) and *Draynefleete Revealed* (1949). He also invented the "pocket cartoon" while working for *The Daily Express*, which often featured some acid comment on current affairs by the upper-class Maud Littlehampton.

**Land, Edwin Herbert** (1909–91) American physicist and inventor of the Polaroid Land camera, the ability of which to take instant, developed photographs added a new dimension to photography, giving immediate records of objects and events. Land is also noted for his research into the nature of vision, particularly of colour.

**Landau, Lev Davidovich** (1908–68) Russian physicist. He was awarded the 1962 Nobel prize for physics, for his research into theories of condensed matter.

**Landor, Walter Savage** (1775–1864) English poet and essayist, noted for his classically inspired lyrics and epigrams, and for his *Imaginary Conversations* (1824–29), a collection of around 150 imagined dialogues between such people as Francis BACON and Richard HOOKER, and DANTE and Beatrice. DICKENS used him as the model for the bad-tempered yet lovable eccentric Boythorne in *Bleak House*.

**Landseer, Sir Edwin Henry** (1802–73) English painter. A student of HAYDON, he won acclaim while still a child for his animal drawings, which tended towards a gross sentimentality in humanizing animals, particularly dogs, e.g. *The Old Shepherd's Chief Mourner* (1937), a quality that was the source of his widespread popularity. Notable works include *The Monarch of the Glen* (1850) and the lions modelled for Trafalgar Square, London, in 1867.

**Landsteiner, Karl** (1868–1943) Austrian-born American pathologist. He discovered the major human blood groups (A, O, B, AB in 1901 and M and N in 1927), which resulted in the development of blood transfusions. He was awarded the 1930 Nobel prize for physiology or medicine.

**Lane, Sir Allen** (1903–70) English publisher. He founded Penguin Books in 1935, which became one of the most successful—and most imitated—publishing concerns of the century. Initially Penguin specialized in cheap paperback reprints of novels (at sixpence each). Subsequent diversifications included the "Penguin Specials" on current affairs, Penguin Classics and Puffin children's books.

**Lang, Fritz** (1890–1976) Austrian-born American

film director, notable for three classic German films, *Metropolis* (1926), *M* (1931) and *The Testament of Dr Mabuse* (1932). He was offered the job of running the German film industry by GOEBBELS, but fled to the USA in 1933 rather than work for the Nazis (he later claimed that *Dr Mabuse* was an attack on Nazism). He directed many fine films in the US, e.g. the grim film noir, *The Big Heat* (1953).

**Lange, David Russell** (1942– ) New Zealand Labour politician. He became leader of the Labour Party in 1983, and won the 1984 general election decisively on an anti-nuclear defence policy, which led to angry confrontations with other Western powers, notably France and the US. Lange was re-elected in 1987, but resigned, due to ill health, in 1989.

**Lange, Dorothea** (1895–1965) American photographer. Her uncompromising documentary studies of the poverty and suffering of migrant workers during the Depression in the 1930s were highly praised and brought the plight of her subjects into stark public focus.

**Langmuir, Irving** (1881–1957) American chemist. He was awarded the 1932 Nobel prize for chemistry for his work on surface properties. He also developed the gas-filled tungsten lamp and the atomic hydrogen welding process.

**Langtry, Lily** [Emilie Charlotte le Breton] (1853–1929) English actress, nicknamed the "Jersey Lily." One of the great beauties of her day, she became the mistress of the Prince of Wales (later EDWARD VII). She published her (discreet) *Memoirs* in 1925.

**Lankester, Sir Edwin Ray** (1847–1929) English zoologist. He helped found the Marine Biological

Association in 1884, and made important contributions to the study of embryos and protozoa. His works include *Treatise on Zoology* (1900–09).

**Lansbury, George** (1859–1940) English Labour politician, noted for his support for women's suffrage and pacifism. He became the first commissioner of works (1929–31) in Ramsay MACDONALD's administration, and became leader of his party (1931–35) when MacDonald joined the National Government. He resigned when the Labour Party opted for sanctions against fascist Italy in 1935, rather than compromise his pacifist principles. He published his autobiography, *My Life*, in 1928. His daughter, **Angela Lansbury** (1925– ) became a film actress in the 1940s, appearing in such films as *Gaslight* (1944), *The Manchurian Candidate* (1962) and *Bedknobs and Broomsticks* (1972).

**Laplace, Pierre Simon, Marquis de** (1749–1827) French mathematician and astronomer. He formulated the nebular hypothesis in the 1790s, became (briefly) minister of the interior in 1803, and was created a marquis in 1817. He made important studies of the theory of probability.

**Lardner, Ring** [Ringgold Wilmer Lardner] (1885–1933) American journalist and short-story writer, whose stories of American low life, e.g. *What of It?* (1925), are noted for their cynical wit.

**Larkin, Philip [Arthur]** (1922–85) English poet. His early verse, e.g. *The North Ship* (1945), shows the influence of YEATS. His later, far greater poems, owe more to the influence of HARDY, but Larkin's voice, as became apparent in *The Less Deceived* (1955), is all his own: a dark, sardonic lyricism combined with disconcertingly colloquial turns of phrase. Two further volumes, *The Whitsun Weddings* (1964) and *High Windows* (1972), established him as one of the greatest of all modern English poets. He also wrote two novels, *Jill* (1946) and *A Girl in Winter* (1947), and a collection of essays on jazz, *All What Jazz?* (1970).

**Larwood, Harold** (1904– ) English cricketer. His use of "bodyline" tactics in the 1932–33 tour of Australia created great controversy, injuring (seriously) two Australian batsmen and causing diplomatic tension in relations between Australia and the UK. After the war, he emigrated to Australia where he settled very happily. He published two volumes of memoirs, *Bodyline* (1933) and *The Larwood Story* (1965).

**Lasdun, Sir Denys Louis** (1914– ) English architect. Influenced by LE CORBUSIER, his buildings include the University of East Anglia (1968) and the National Theatre (1976). His books include *Architecture in an Age of Scepticism* (1984).

**Lasker, Emanuel** (1868–1941) German chess player. His reign as world champion (1894–1921), is still a record. Being Jewish, he was forced to flee Nazi Germany in 1933.

**Laski, Harold [Joseph]** (1893–1950) English political scientist and socialist propagandist. He joined the staff of the London School of Economics, becoming a professor in 1926. He made his public commitment to Marxism in the early 1930s, and was a highly influential spokesman for Marxism through his position as teacher, writer and Labour Party power-broker (he was party chairman 1945–46), and through his friendships with politicians such as ROOSEVELT. He was, however, widely distrusted, not just by the right but by many non-communists on the Left (ORWELL detested him). His works include *The Rise of European Liberalism* (1936).

**La Tour, Georges Dumesnil de** (1593–1652) French painter. Strongly influenced by CARAVAGGIO, his later works, e.g. *St Sebastian tended by the Holy Women* (*c*.1650), have a monumental air of stillness with figures lit by a single candle.

**Lauda, Niki** [Nikolas Andreas Lauda] (1949– ) Austrian racing driver. He was world champion driver in 1975, 1977 and 1984, and suffered dreadful injuries in the 1976 German Grand Prix. He retired in 1985.

**Lauder, Sir Harry** [Hugh MacLennan] (1870–1950) Scottish music-hall comedian and singer, who made an international career out of his Scottish comedy routines and songs, e.g. "Roamin' in the Gloamin" and "Stop Your Tickling, Jock." Although often reviled in Scotland as a shrewd propagator of the dual myth of the mean Scot in an impossibly romanticized setting of kilts and heather, his status as one of the last great music hall stars is secure.

**Laughton, Charles** (1899–1962) English-born American stage and film actor, renowned for his larger-than-life performances in films such as *The Private Life of Henry VIII* (1932), *Mutiny on the Bounty* (1935) and *The Hunchback of Notre Dame* (1939).

**Laurel, Stan** [Arthur Stanley Jefferson] (1890–1965), English-born American comedian, and **Oliver Hardy** (1892–1957) American comedian. Laurel began his career on the English music-hall stage (understudying CHAPLIN at one point), and Hardy performed with a minstrel troupe before going into films. They formed their Laurel (thin, vacant and bemused one) and Hardy (fat, blustering one) partnership in 1929, and made some very funny films, e.g. *Another Fine Mess* (1930).

**Laval, Pierre** (1883–1945) French statesman. He first entered politics as a socialist, becoming a senator in 1926 and prime minister (1931–32, 1935–36), while gradually moving to the right. He became PÉTAIN's deputy in 1940, was ousted later that year, and served again as prime minister (1942–44), when he sided openly with the Germans. He was executed for treason in 1945 by the victorious Free French.

**Lavoisier, Antoine Laurent** (1743–94) French chemist. Regarded as the founder of modern chemistry, he discovered oxygen and established its role in combustion and respiration. A moderate in politics, he also made important contributions to taxation reform, and was guillotined.

**Law, Andrew Bonar** (1858–1923) Canadian-born Scottish Conservative statesman. He became a Conservative MP in 1900, party leader in 1911, and leader of the House (1916–21). Poor health forced his retirement in 1921, but he became prime minister shortly afterwards (1922–23).

**Law, William** (1686–1761) English divine. His masterpiece is *A Serious Call to a Holy and Devout Life* (1728), which uses sharply drawn portraits ("characters") to illustrate how the Christian life should be lived (and how it should not). Law's beautifully simple prose, and gentle, undogmatic tone, have been highly praised.

**Lawrence, D[avid] H[erbert]** (1885–1930) English novelist, poet and short-story writer. His novels, e.g. *Sons and Lovers* (1913), *The Rainbow* (1915) and *Lady Chatterley's Lover* (1928), caused much controversy for their frank treatment of sex, the latter book not being published in its full four-letter form until 1960.

**Lawrence, Ernest Orlando** (1901–58) American physicist. He was awarded the 1939 Nobel prize for physics for his important contributions to modern physics, including the invention of the cyclotron in 1929.

**Lawrence, Gertrude** [Gertrud Alexandra Dagmar Lawrence-Klasen] (1898–1952) English actress, noted for her long-standing professional relationship with Noel COWARD, many of whose plays, e.g *Private Lives* (1931) had parts written especially for her. Her films include *The Glass Menagerie* (1950).

**Lawrence, Sir Thomas** (1769–1830) English painter. Mainly self-taught, he established his reputation at the age of twenty with a commissioned portrait of *Queen Charlotte* (1789), and quickly became the leading portraitist of his time, succeeding REYNOLDS as court painter in 1792.

**Lawrence, T[homas] E[dward]** (1888–1935) Welsh-born Anglo-Irish soldier and author, known as "Lawrence of Arabia." In World War I, he helped the Arab revolt against the Turks and was instrumental in the conquest of Palestine (1918). He supported Arab independence in the 1920s, and wrote *The Seven Pillars of Wisdom* (1926), a highly controversial memoir.

**Lawson, Nigel** *see* **Major, John**.

**Leach, Bernard Howell** (1887–1979) English potter (born in Hong Kong), who revolutionized the production of pottery by creating reasonably priced, attractively designed studio pottery for use in everyday life. His *A Potter's Book* (1940), describing his philosophy and production methods, remains the standard pottery reference work.

**Leadbelly** [Huddie Ledbetter] (1888–1949) American blues singer. Discovered in a Louisiana prison in 1933, where he was imprisoned for attempted murder, Leadbelly later recorded several songs that soon became recognized as folk/blues classics, e.g. "Rock Island Line" and "Goodnight, Irene."

**Leakey, Louis Seymour Bazett** (1903–72) Kenyan-born British archaeologist and anthropologist, and **Mary Douglas Leakey** (1913– ) English archaeologist. Married in 1936, the Leakeys made several important discoveries about humanity's origins in East Africa. His books include *Olduvai Gorge* (1952); hers include *Disclosing the Past* (1984). Their son, **Richard Erskine Frere Leakey** (1944– ), is also a prominent (Kenyan) archaeologist; his works include *Origins* (1977).

**Lean, Sir David** (1908–91) English film director. His highly acclaimed films include *Brief Encounter* (1945), *Great Expectations* (1946), and the epics *Bridge on the River Kwai* (1957), *Lawrence of Arabia* (1962) and *Dr Zhivago* (1970). After 14 years absence from film-making, Lean made *A Passage to India* (1984), which received distinctly unfavourable reviews for its patronising and insensitive adaptation of the FORSTER novel.

**Leavis, F[rank] R[aymond]** (1895–1978) English literary critic. With his wife, **Queenie Dorothy Leavis** (1906–81), he made a major impact on literary criticism from the 1930s on, through such works as *New Bearings in English Poetry* (1932) and

*The Great Tradition* (1948). The Leavises attacked the modern age of mass culture and advertising, which they saw as destructive of the true "organic" culture of old England, and advocated the close, "practical" study of a severely restricted group of authors, including Henry JAMES and CONRAD.

**Lebrun, Charles** (1619–90) French painter. Having studied with POUSSIN, he settled in Paris in 1646, and established himself in decorative murals with vigorous and grandiose illusionistic works, such as the ceiling of the gallery of the Hotel Lambert. His tapestry designs include *Louis XIV visiting the Gobelins* (1663–75).

**Le Carré, John** [David John Moore Cornwell] (1931– ) English novelist. His novels are sombre anti-romantic narratives of Cold War espionage, and usually have as their chief protagonist a disillusioned, cynical spy. Typical examples are *The Spy Who Came in From the Cold* (1963) and *Smiley's People* (1980).

**Le Corbusier** [Charles Edouard Jeanneret] (1887–1965) Swiss-born French architect and town planner. One of the most influential (and most praised and reviled) architects and planners of the century, his work is characterized by use of reinforced concrete and modular, standardized units of construction (based upon the proportions of the human figure), with the house famously defined as a "machine for living in." His books include *Towards a New Architecture* (1923).

**Lederberg, Joshua** (1925– ) American geneticist. He shared the 1958 Nobel prize for physiology or medicine (with George Beadle and Edward TATUM) for his bacterial research. He demonstrated the sexual reproduction of bacteria, and discovered the process by which genes are transmitted.

**Le Duc Tho** *see* **Kissinger, Henry**.

**Lee Kuan Yew** (1923– ) Singaporean politician. The son of wealthy Chinese parents, he became Singapore's first prime minister (1959– ), establishing a strict regime noted for its economic achievements and Cromwellian authoritarianism.

**Léger, Fernand** (1881–1955) French painter. One of the leading Cubist painters, he was much influenced by industrial imagery and machinery, and has been described as more "tubist" (for his love of cylindrical forms) than Cubist.

**Lehár, Franz** (1870–1948) Hungarian composer and conductor, noted for his operettas, e.g. *The Merry Widow* (1905) and *The Land of Smiles* (1929).

**Leibnitz** or **Leibniz, Gottfried Wilhelm** (1646–1716) German philosopher and mathematician. Renowned for the range and depth of his intellect, he developed a calculus system at the same time as Newton, and made important contributions to many different scientific fields, e.g. optics and probability theory, and posited that the universe was composed of harmonious units, called "monads". His perception of the world as essentially benevolent was ridiculed by Voltaire in *Candide*.

**Leigh, Vivien** [Vivien Mary Hartley] (1913–67) Indian-born English stage and film actress. She became an international star with *Gone With the Wind* (1939), in which she co-starred with Clark Gable and for which she won an Oscar. Her other films include *A Streetcar Named Desire* (1951), which also won her an Oscar. She had a tempestuous marriage (1940–61) with Laurence Olivier.

**Lely, Sir Peter** [Pieter van der Faes] (1618–80) Dutch-born English painter. He settled in England *c*.1643. His early works were landscapes and historical paintings, but he soon turned to portrait painting, in which he was greatly influenced by van DYCK. He painted most of the court of CHARLES II, e.g. the two series *The Windsor Beauties* and *Maids of Honour*. He was knighted in 1680.

**Le Nain, Antoine** (*c*.1588–1648), **Louis** (*c*.1593–1648) and **Matthieu** (1607–77) French painters. All brothers, they established a studio in Paris from *c*.1630, and were founder members of the Academy. Louis was the most significant of the brothers, creating simple and dignified genre paintings of peasant life, e.g. *The Peasant's Meal* (1642).

**Lenin, Vladimir Ilyich** [Vladimir Ilyich Ulyanov] (1870–1924) Russian revolutionary leader and Marxist philosopher. A dedicated Marxist with a striking gift for single-minded, vitriolic polemicism, he became leader of the Bolshevik ("Majority") wing of the Russian Social Democratic Party in 1903. He settled in Switzerland after the failure of the 1905 Revolution, and re-entered Russia with German connivance (in a "sealed" train) in March 1917, after the deposition of Tsar NICHOLAS II. He led the Bolshevik October Revolution, which overthrew KERENSKI's government, and led the Bolsheviks to victory in the Civil War (1918–21). The failure of his economic policy after the war led to the institution of the New Economic Policy of 1921, which fostered limited private enterprise. He was a brilliant demagogue, fully the equal of HITLER, with a comparable repertoire of dehumanizing words and phrases to apply to his enemies (although he was often less coherent than Hitler, e.g. his order to "execute and deport" the prostitutes of Nizhny Novgorod). He survived an assassination attempt in 1918, but suffered increasing ill health. After his death his embalmed corpse was placed in a mausoleum in Red Square for veneration. He left a final "Testament," which condemned STALIN as untrustworthy and gave guarded praise to TROTSKY. His works include *What is to be Done?* (1902) and *Imperialism: the Highest Stage of Capitalism* (1916).

**Lennon, John [Winston]** (1940–80) English rock guitarist, singer and songwriter. With Paul McCARTNEY, George HARRISON and Ringo STARR, he formed the Beatles, the most popular rock group ever. The success of the band was based on the songwriting partnership of Lennon/McCartney, whose songs, e.g. "Please Please Me" and "She Loves You," achieved phenomenal popularity. The group split in 1969, a contributory factor being Lennon's growing partnership with **Yoko Ono** (1933– ), who became his second wife. His subsequent albums included, notably, *Imagine* (1971), the title song of which became the anthem of the declining hippy generation. Lennon was assassinated in New York.

**Lennox, Charlotte** (1720–1804) American-born English novelist and dramatist. Her best-known work is the novel *The Female Quixote* (1752), which was highly praised in its day. Her work was praised by both FIELDING and her friend Dr JOHNSON. Johnson had crowned her with laurel to celebrate the publication of her first novel, *Harriot Stuart* (1751).

**Leonardo da Vinci** (1452–1519) Florentine painter, draughtsman, engineer, musician and thinker. The outstanding genius of his time and of many others, he trained in the studio of VERROCCHIO, where he probably painted the left-hand angel in that artist's *Baptism of Christ* (*c*.1472). Leonardo was a painstaking worker and evolved a technique of thin glazes of oil paint to build up an image of extraordinary translucence and detail, e.g. the far-distance landscapes in *The Annunciation*. His use of this technique was to prove disastrous for the mural of *The Last Supper* (1489) in the refectory of San Maria del Grazie in Milan, which began to deteriorate in his own lifetime. In 1483 he wrote to Duke Sforza of Milan recommending himself as an engineer and musician, and while in Milan painted the two versions of *The Virgin of the Rocks*, which represented a departure from the contemporary stress on strong lighting and outline. He left Milan in 1499 and travelled between Florence and Rome, where he painted the *Mona Lisa* (*c*.1505) for Giulio de Medici. He also composed the beautiful cartoon of *The Virgin and St Anne* (1504–6), which he exhibited as a work of art in its own right. In 1516 he was invited to France, where he remained until his death. His later years were devoted to scientific studies, his sketchbooks detailing models of flying machines, advanced weapons, and other innovative plans.

**Le Pen, Jean-Marie** (1928– ) French politician. He founded the right-wing National Front in 1972, a party identified by most observers as crypto–fascist with its crude anti-immigrant policies. He stood unsuccessfully for the presidency in 1988.

**Lermontov, Mikhail Yurievich** (1814–41) Russian novelist and poet. His masterpiece is his novel *A Hero of our Time* (1840), a brilliant study of a disaffected, Byronic young aristocrat (like many Russians of the time, Lermontov was fascinated by BYRON's life and work). As with PUSHKIN, his life ended prematurely in a duel.

**Lessing, Doris [May]** (1919– ) Iranian-born English novelist and short-story writer, brought up in Rhodesia. Her novels include the Children of Violence quintet, beginning with *Martha Quest* (1952) and ending with *The Five-Gated City* (1969), and the seminal feminist novel *The Golden Notebook* (1962). Her other works include science fiction novels, e.g. *Briefing for a Descent into Hell* (1971), and a stunning analysis of self-deception and political fanaticism, *The Good Terrorist* (1985).

**Lessing, Gotthold Ephraim** (1729–81) German dramatist and critic. His plays include the tragedies *Miss Sara Sampson* (1755), an adaptation of LILLO's *The London Merchant*; *Emilio Galotti* (1772), a study of sexual obsession and oppression; and *Nathan the Wise* (1779), a remarkable plea for religious tolerance (the central character is modelled on MENDELSSOHN's grandfather). Lessing is a significant figure in the development of German Romanticism, and defended SHAKESPEARE against the French neoclassical theorists.

**Lewes, George Henry** *see* **Eliot, George**.

**Lewis, C[live] S[taples]** (1898–1963) English novelist and critic. His works include studies of medieval literature, e.g. *The Allegory of Love* (1936), works of Christian apologetics, e.g. *The Problem of Pain* (1940), and science fiction novels, e.g. *Out of the Silent Planet* (1938). He is best remembered for his enchanting Narnia stories for children, e.g. *The Lion, the Witch and the Wardrobe* (1950).

**Lewis, Norman** (1914– ) English novelist and travel writer. His two travel books include two modern classics, *A Dragon Apparent* (1952), on South-East Asia, and *Golden Earth* (1952), on Burma. His novels include *A Small War Made to Order* (1966), a study of the Bay of Pigs invasion of Cuba, and *The Sicilian Specialist* (1975), a thinly fictionalized account of President KENNEDY's assassination. A staunch champion of tribal peoples, he exposed the genocidal campaign that has been waged against Brazilian Indians.

**Lewis, [Harry] Sinclair** (1885–1951) American novelist. His work is particularly noted for its satirical view of small-town American life, his best-known novels being *Main Street* (1920), *Babbitt* (1922), and *Elmer Gantry* (1927). Lewis was the first American to win the Nobel prize for literature, in 1930.

**Lewis, [Percy] Wyndham** (1884–1957) English painter, novelist and critic. His best-known fictional work is the novel *Apes of God* (1930), a withering satire on his contemporaries. Described by AUDEN AS "that lonely old volcano of the right," he was also a leading member of the Vorticist group of artists.

**Leyden, Lucas van** (1494–1533) Dutch painter and engraver. A child prodigy, he was greatly influenced by Dürer, and he himself subsequently influenced many other artists. Notable works include *The Game of Chess* (c.1510) and his masterpiece, the *Last Judgement* triptych (1526–27).

**Libby, Willard Frank** (1908–80) American chemist. He was awarded the 1960 Nobel prize for chemistry for his role in developing the Carbon–14 radioactive method of dating.

**Lichtenstein, Roy** (1923– ) American painter and

sculptor. He became the leading Pop Art painter of the 1960s with his deadpan, highly coloured reproductions of sections of advertisements and cartoon strips, e.g. *Whaam* (1963).

**Liddell, Eric Henry** (1902–45) Scottish athlete, nicknamed the "Flying Scot." Liddell's refusal to compromise with his sabbatarian principles by running on a Sunday during the 1924 Paris Olympics, followed by his unexpected victory in the 400–metres race, caught the public imagination. Liddell's principled stance is the subject of the award-winning film *Chariots of Fire* (1981). He became a missionary and died in a Japanese prisoner-of-war camp in China.

**Liddell Hart, Sir Basil Henry** (1895–1970) English soldier and military historian, noted for his persistent advocacy of mechanized warfare and the development of air power after World War I. His many works on military strategy, including *Strategy—the Indirect Approach* (1929), were highly influential upon modern military thinkers (including ROMMEL).

**Liebknecht, Karl** *see* **Luxembourg, Rosa.**

**Ligeti, György Sándor** (1923– ) Hungarian composer. He fled to Vienna in 1956, where he soon became established as one of Europe's leading avant-garde composers (with STOCKHAUSEN's encouragement). His works include the large orchestral work *Apparitions* (1958–9) and the *Poème Symphonique* (1962) for a hundred metronomes.

**Lillo, George** (1693–1739) English dramatist. He wrote several plays, of which the most important is the "domestic tragedy," *The London Merchant* (1731), which had great influence throughout Europe:

LESSING did an adaptation, and DIDEROT was also much influenced by the work.

**Limbourg** *or* **Limburg, Jean, Paul** and **Herman de** (all *fl.* 1400–16) Dutch illuminators. In the service of Jean, Duke of Berry, they produced the *Belles Heures* (*c.*1408), and their masterpiece, the unfinished *Les Tres Riches Heures*, one of the greatest illuminated manuscripts of all time.

**Lincoln, Abraham** (1809–65) American statesman. From a poor background, he trained as a lawyer and became an Illinois congressman in 1846, displaying great debating skill in both his profession and in politics. He became the 16th president of the United States in 1861, and led the Union to victory in 1865. Firmly opposed to slavery from his early days, he had been initially reluctant to push through legislation that would endanger the Union, but finally emancipated the slaves in 1863. He was assassinated by **John Wilkes Booth** (1839–65) while attending the theatre.

**Lindbergh, Charles Augustus** (1902–74) American aviator. He became the first man to fly the Atlantic solo and nonstop with his 1927 New York to Paris flight in the monoplane *Spirit of St Louis*, described in his book, *Spirit of St Louis* (1953). The kidnap and murder of his infant son (1932) made world headlines.

**Lipchitz, Jacques** (1891–1973) Lithuanian-born sculptor, of Polish-Jewish parentage, resident in France from 1909 and in the US from 1941. He produced Cubist sculptures from 1916 and created mobile and "transparent sculptures" in the mid–1920s. His later work is often violent and dynamic, symbolic of modern totalitarianism.

**Lipmann, Fritz** *see* **Krebs, Sir Hans Adolf**.

**Lippi, Fra Filippo** (*c.*1406–69) Florentine painter. He took up painting under the influence of MASACCIO, who had decorated the Brancacci Chapel in the Carmine monastery where Filippo was a monk. He later forsook his vows to marry the mother of his son, **Filippino Lippi** (1457–1504), who also became a painter. His lyrical and fluid style invest his paintings with a wistful melancholy, e.g. *Adoration in the Wood*. An innovative painter, he was one of the first artists to explore and develop the *Madonna and Child* theme.

**Liszt, Franz** *or* **Ferencz** (1811–86) Hungarian pianist and composer. Recognized as one of the greatest pianists of his day, he made several important contributions to musical form, e.g. he established the symphonic poem in his Weimar symphonies. His compositions were often highly experimental.

**Littlewood, Joan** (1914– ) English theatre director. Her theatre company, Theatre Workshop, formed in 1945, became one of the major left-wing theatre companies in the British theatre. Littlewood's productions include BRECHT's *Mother Courage* (1955), BEHAN's *The Quare Fella* (1956) and *Oh, What a Lovely War!* (1963), the latter, a bitter musical on World War I, being made into a highly successful film by Richard ATTENBOROUGH (1969).

**Livingstone, David** (1813–73) Scottish missionary and explorer. His discoveries during his African expeditions include Lake Ngami (1849) and the Victoria Falls (1855). He was also a vigorous campaigner against the slave trade, the mechanics of which he exposed in *The Zambesi and its Tributaries* (1865). His last expedition was a search for the source of the Nile, in the course of which he himself was "discovered" by the Welsh-American adventurer **Henry Morton Stanley** (1841–1904). He died in what is now Zambia, his body being conveyed to the coast on a hazardous journey by his followers.

**Lloyd, Clive Hubert** (1944– ) Guyanian-born West Indian cricketer. A very fine batsman and fielder, he captained the West Indies team (1974–78, 1979–85). He retired in 1985, having been on the losing side only twice in 18 tests.

**Lloyd, Harold [Clayton]** (1893–1971) American film comedian. He made hundreds of short silent films, in which he played a bemused, bespectacled everyday young man getting into difficult situations, often involving scarifying stunts on high buildings, e.g. *Safety Last* (1923), which includes the famous sequence of him dangling from a clock face.

**Lloyd George, David**, 1st Earl Lloyd George of Dwyfor (1863–1945) Welsh Liberal statesman. As chancellor of the exchequer (1908–15) he introduced far-reaching reforms in British society, notably the introduction of old age pensions (1908), the National Insurance Act (1911), and the "people's budget" of 1909, the rejection of which by the Lords led to a constitutional crisis and the Parliament Act of 1911. Formerly a pacifist, he became minister of munitions (1915–16) and prime minister (1916–22) of coalition governments. Widely regarded as a brilliant politician, Lloyd George was also widely distrusted. He survived numerous scandals, e.g the Marconi share scandal of 1912, and was a notorious seller of honours to the highest bidder.

**Lloyd Webber, Andrew** (1948– ) English composer. With the librettist **Tim Rice** (1944– ), he composed

Locke

several highly successful musicals, notably *Joseph and the Amazing Technicolour Dreamcoat* (1968), *Jesus Christ Superstar* (1970) and *Evita* (1978). Other successes were *Cats* (1982), adapted from T. S. ELIOT's *Old Possum's Book of Practical Cats*, *Starlight Express* (1984) and *Phantom of the Opera* (1986).

**Locke, John** (1632–1704) English philosopher. He expounded his empiricist philosophy in his enormously influential *Essay Concerning Human Understanding* (1690), and set out his theory of the political nature of man in his *Two Treatises of Government* (1690), in which he sees the social contract as resting on a "natural law", which if rulers ignore they may be overthrown.

**Longfellow, Henry Wadsworth** (1807–82) American poet. Several of his poems, e.g. "The Village Blacksmith", "The Wreck of the Hesperus" and "Excelsior" were among the most popular poems of the 19th century, as were his narrative poems on American legends and folk tales, e.g. *Evangeline* (1849) and *The Song of Hiawatha* (1858). The hypnotic unryhmed rhythms of the latter were much parodied by later writers, e.g. CARROLL.

**Lonsdale, Dame Kathleen** (1903–71) Irish physicist, noted for innovative work in X-ray crystallography. A devout Quaker, she was imprisoned for a month after the outbreak of World War II for refusing to register (even though she would in fact have been exempted) for war work. She became the first woman member to be elected a fellow of the Royal Society (1945).

**Lorca, Federico García** (1899–1936) Spanish poet and dramatist. His dramatic masterpiece is his trilogy of tragedies on the plight of oppressed Spanish women, *Blood Wedding* (1939), *Yarma* (1934) and *The House of Bernarda Alba* (1936). He was killed by Fascist forces near the beginning of the Spanish Civil War.

**Loren, Sophia** [Sophia Scicoloni] (1934– ) Italian actress. A strikingly beautiful woman, she starred in films as diverse as the comedy *The Millionairess* (1960) and the grim war drama *Two Women* (1961).

**Lorenz, Konrad [Zacharias]** (1903–89) Austrian ethologist and zoologist. He shared the 1973 Nobel prize for physiology or medicine (with Niko TINBERGEN and Karl von FRISCH) for his work on animal behaviour. Regarded as the father of ethology, he is best known for his discovery of the "imprinting" of behaviour on young geese and for his (often controversial) works expounding his theories of human and animal behaviour, notably *King Solomon's Ring* (1949) and *On Aggression* (1963).

**Lorenzetti, Ambrogio** and **Pietro** (both *fl.* 1320–48) Sienese painters. Brothers, they developed a style that shows the influence of GIOTTO in the fullness of form and the depth of perspective in their works. Ambrogio was particularly skilled in his use of perspective, as in his most important work, the fresco series on *Good and Bad Government* (1338–39) for the Palazzo Pubblico in Siena.

**Lorre, Peter** [Laszlo Lowenstein] (1904–64) Hungarian stage and film actor. His first major film part, as the pathetic child murderer, in LANG's *M* (1931) established him as a star. His other films include *Casablanca* (1942), *The Maltese Falcon* (1941), and CORMAN's horror comedy *The Raven* (1963).

**Losey, Joseph** (1909–84) American film director,

resident in Britain from 1952. Losey's American films include the thriller *The Prowler* (1951). He moved to Britain after being blacklisted during the MCCARTHY era. His British films include *The Servant* (1963) and *Accident* (1967), both scripted by PINTER and starring BOGARDE, *The Go-Between* (1971) and *Don Giovanni* (1979).

**Lotto, Lorenzo** (*c*.1480–1556) Venetian painter. The contemporary of TITIAN and GIORGIONE, he probably trained in the studio of Giovanni BELLINI, who influenced his early works. His best works are probably his portraits, which have a disturbing quality of intensity and unusual modes of colour and composition, e.g. *Young Man in his Study* (*c*.1528)

**Louis XIV** (1638–1715) king of France. Known as the "Sun King", he inherited the throne at the age of five and became absolute ruler in 1661, after which he declared *"L'état c'est moi."* He also pursued territorial claims throughout Europe, and established the French army as the most powerful in Europe. He was also a noted patron of the arts.

**Louis XVI** (1754–93) king of France. While still dauphin, he married **Marie Antoinette** (1755–93) in 1770 and inherited the throne in 1774. Although inclined to reform and initially popular with the people, Louis was unable to prevent the revolutionaries dictating the course of events that led to himself and Marie being guillotined during the Revolution.

**Louis, Joe** [Joseph Louis Barrow] (1914–81) American boxer, nicknamed the "Brown Bomber." He was world heavyweight champion for a record 12 years, defeating 25 challengers, and the second black champion (after Jack JOHNSON).

**Louis Philippe** *see* **Daumier, Honoré**.

**Lowei, Otto** *see* **Dale, Sir Henry Hallett**

**Lowell, James Russell** (1819–91) American poet, essayist and diplomat. His best-known verse, written in "Yankee" dialect and often inspired by his fervent abolitionism, is contained in *The Biglow Papers* (1848, 1867).

**Lowell, Robert [Traill Spence]** (1917–77) American poet. His verse is intensely personal and marked by occasionally difficult private symbolism. Notable volumes include *Land of Unlikeness* (1944), *Life Studies* (1959) and *Near the Ocean*.

**Lowry, L[aurence] S[tephen]** (1887–1976) English painter. His paintings, which depict thin, dark "matchstick" figures against a background of Northern Industrial life, became very popular in the mid–1960s. Lowry's highly distinctive work, quite unlike that of any other artist, was largely ignored by both critics and public for most of his life.

**Lowry, [Clarence] Malcolm** (1909–57) English novelist and poet. His novels, e.g. *Under the Volcano* (1947), often feature thinly veiled accounts of incidents from his own adventurous life.

**Loyola, St Ignatius** *see* **Ignatius Loyola, St**.

**Lukács, Georg** *or* **György** (1885–1971) Hungarian philosopher. He wrote two important volumes on literary criticism, *Soul and Form* (1910) and *The Theory of the Novel* (1916), before widening his interests to take account of politics after joining the Communist Party in 1918. His study of Marxism, *History and Class Consciousness* (1923), was denounced by the Soviet Communist party, and later by himself. He was minister of culture in NAGY's short-lived government (1956).

**Lumière, Auguste Marie Louis Nicolas** (1862–1954) and **Louis Jean Lumière** (1864–1948) French chemists and cinematographers. They invented the first operational cine camera and projector and a colour photography process. They also produced the first newsreels and probably the first movie, *La Sortie des usines* (1895).

**Lumumba, Patrice** (1925–61) Congolese statesman. He became first prime minister of the the former Belgian Congo in 1960, was deposed later in the year by MOBUTO and assassinated the following year. *See also* TSHOMBE.

**Luther, Martin** (1483–1546) German religious reformer. An Augustinian monk, he was ordained in 1507 and became a lecturer at the University of Wittenberg. A visit to Rome (1510–11) and encounter with the corruption there and the sale of indulgences induced a crisis of faith that led to his proclaiming justification by faith and a break with Rome, after nailing his "95 theses" on the church door of Wittenberg. The Lutheran Reformation, aided by reformers such as **Philipp Melanchthon** (1497–1560) spread rapidly throughout Germany. By the time Luther died, the Protestant Reformation had spread widely, with CALVIN, ZWINGLI and others preaching their variants of the new religion.

**Luthuli** *or* **Lutuli, Chief Albert John** (1898–1967) South African nationalist. He became president of the African National Congress (1952–60), and was awarded the 1961 Nobel Peace Prize for his advocacy of nonviolent resistance to apartheid. He was "banned" by the South African government in 1959, and forbidden to leave Natal for the rest of his life.

**Lutoslawski, Witold** (1913– ) Polish composer and

teacher. He has written extensively, including chamber, piano and vocal music, but is best known for his orchestral works, e.g. *Concerto for Orchestra* (1954) and a *Cello Concerto* (1970).

**Lutyens, Sir Edwin Landseer** (1869–1944) English architect. His buildings, often highly picturesque, include neoclassical mansions and "Arts and Crafts" residences, the Viceroy's House in New Delhi and Liverpool's Roman Catholic Cathedral.

**Luxemburg, Rosa** (1871–1919) Polish-born German revolutionary and socialist theorist. She settled in Berlin in 1898, where she became a member of the Social Democratic Party. With **Karl Liebknecht** (1871–1919) she founded the revolutionary Spartacus League on the outbreak of World War I, and was imprisoned in 1915 for pacifism. She co-founded the German Communist Party after her release in 1918, and was killed with Liebknecht after the failure of the Spartacist-led revolt of 1919.

**Lyly, John** (*c*.1554–1606) English dramatist and prose romance writer. His romances, e.g. *Euphues and his England* (1580), are mostly now unreadable, but were highly popular in Elizabethan times and had some influence on the development of the English novel. The term "Euphuistic" is used to describe his exaggerated use of alliteration and antithesis.

**Lysenko, Trofim Denisovich** (1898–1976) Russian geneticist and agronomist. His doctrinal approach to genetics, which rejected accepted Mendelian principles and advocated LAMARCK's theory of inheritance through acquired characteristics, found favour with STALIN and did severe damage to the development of Soviet biology and agronomy. His influence gradually waned after Stalin's death.

257

# M

**MacArthur, Douglas** (1880–1964) American general. Appointed commander of the US Far East forces in 1941, the Japanese forced him to withdraw from the Philippines in 1942, when MacArthur pledged "I shall return." He was appointed supreme Allied commander in the southwest Pacific in 1942, and gradually rolled back the Japanese forces, accepting their surrender in 1945. He also commanded the UN forces at the beginning of the Korean War (1950–51), being dismissed his command by TRUMAN.

**Macaulay, Dame [Emilie] Rose** (1881–1958) English novelist. Her works include social satires such as *Dangerous Ages* (1921) and later, more spiritual works reflecting her growing Anglican faith, notably *The Towers of Trebizond* (1956).

**Macaulay, Thomas Babington**, 1st Baron Macaulay (1800–59) English historian, statesman and essayist. His writings were very popular with the "middlebrow" reading public of the Victorian era, reflecting as they do, e.g. in *Essays Critical and Historical* (1834), a view of human society as a steady movement from barbarism to the triumph of the enlightened 19th-century middle classes. He became a member of parliament in 1839.

**McCarthy, Joseph R[aymond]** (1908–57) American politician He became a Republican senator in

1946 and embarked upon a populist crusade against supposed communist sympathizers in public life (1950–54) under the TRUMAN administration. McCarthy's wide and increasingly bizarre accusations against innocent people came to an end shortly after being accused, during a televised hearing, of having no shame.

**McCarthy, Mary [Therese]** (1912–89) American novelist, short-story writer and critic. Her most famous novel is *The Group* (1963), which created some controversy due to its open, matter-of-fact treatment of upper-middle-class female sexuality.

**McCartney, Paul** (1942– ) English rock guitarist, singer and songwriter. He was a member of the Beatles (1961–70) with John LENNON, George HARRISON and Ringo STARR. With Lennon, he formed one of the most successful songwriting partnerships of the century. Among the songs credited solely to McCartney is the enormously popular ballad "Yesterday," one of the most recorded songs of the century. After the band's break-up, McCartney formed the group Wings with his wife, **Linda Eastman McCartney**.

**McCullers, Carson [Smith]** (1917–67) American novelist and short-story writer. Her works, many of which were filmed, usually centre on loners and misfits, and include *The Heart is a Lonely Hunter* (1940), *Reflections in a Golden Eye* (1941) and the short-story collection, *The Ballad of the Sad Café* (1951).

**MacDiarmid, Hugh** [Christopher Murray Grieve] (1892–1978) Scottish poet and critic. He was expelled from the Scottish Nationalist Party in the 1930s for Communist sympathies, and expelled shortly after from the Communist Party for Nationalist sympathies. His masterpiece is *A Drunk Man Looks at the Thistle* (1926), an allegory of awakening Scottish consciousness that influenced many Scottish writers. More broadly influential was his *First Hymn to Lenin* (1931), the first great leftist poem of the decade.

**Macdonald, George** (1824–1905) Scottish novelist and poet, remembered chiefly for his children's stories, e.g. *At the Back of the North Wind* (1871), and for two adult fantasy novels, *Phantastes* (1858) and *Lilith* (1895). His work has had a marked influence on modern fantasy writers, e.g. C. S. LEWIS.

**MacDonald, [James] Ramsay** (1866–1937) Scottish statesman. He became the first British Labour prime minister (1924, 1929–31) and was prime minister of the (mostly Conservative) coalition government of 1931–35, which the bulk of the Labour party opposed.

**McEnroe, John [Patrick Jr]** (1959– ) American tennis player. He became Wimbledon singles champion (1981, 1983) and doubles champion (1979, 1981, 1983, 1984), becoming notorious in the process by his loud and foul-mouthed disagreements with umpires.

**McGill, Donald** [Fraser Gould] (1875–1962) English comic postcard artist, renowned for his slightly risqué seaside greeting cards ("I can't see my little Willie"), often featuring gargantuan wives and feeble little men. ORWELL's essay, "The Art of Donald McGill" (1944), examines the appeal of his work.

**MacGonagall, William** (*c.*1830–*c.*1902) Scottish poet, renowned for his memorably awful doggerel verse. A typical example, in its lugubrious tone and morbid subject matter, is "The Tay Bridge Disaster", which commemorates the collapse of the Tay railway bridge in 1879. The poems were published posthumously in *Poetic Gems* (1934) and *More Poetic Gems* (1963).

**Machiavelli, Niccolo** (1469–1527) Italian statesman and political theorist. His treatise on the art of ruling, *The Prince* (1513), takes a dim view of human nature, seeing humanity as essentially corrupt and therefore best ruled by whatever method ensures the stability of the state, even if the method entails merciless cruelty. His treatise caused much outrage, especially in its suggestion that the ruler should maintain a reputation for being virtuous while actually being treacherous and brutal, and his name came to be synonymous on the Elizabethan stage with the devil. His comedy *Mandragola* (*c*.1518) is a notably licentious piece.

**McIndoe, Sir Archibald [Hector]** (1900–1960) New Zealand plastic surgeon. He became one of the world's leading plastic surgeons through his ingenious and caring rebuilding of the faces of badly burned RAF crews at his East Grinstead hospital during World War II.

**Mackenzie, Sir [Edward Montague] Compton** (1883–1972) English novelist. His best-known novels are *Sinister Street* (1914), a semi-autobiographical account of a privileged young man's life at Oxford University and in the London slums, and his series of very popular comic novels set in the Scottish Western Isles, particularly *Whisky Galore* (1947) and *Rockets Galore* (1957).

**Mackintosh, Charles Rennie** (1868–1928) Scottish architect and artist. He designed some of the finest art nouveau buildings, most of which are in Glasgow, notably the Glasgow School of Art (1897–1909) and the Cranston Willow tearooms.

**Maclean, Donald** *see* **Burgess, Guy**.

**Macleod, Fiona** [pseud. of William Sharp] (1855–1905) Scottish writer of Celtic fantasy tales set in the Scottish Western Isles. An operatic version of his eerie "faery" play, *The Immortal Hour* (1900), set to music by the socialist composer **Rutland Boughton** (1878–1960), enjoyed great popularity in the 1920s. The identity of "Fiona Macleod" was kept secret during Sharp's lifetime (Sharp wore a dress while writing in the Fiona persona).

**MacLeod, George** [Baron MacLeod of Fuinary] (1895–1991) Scottish clergyman. Awarded the Military Cross and Croix de Guerre in World War I, he became a pacifist and Church of Scotland minister among the poor in Edinburgh and Glasgow in the 1920s and 30s. Regarded as the leading Scottish churchman of modern times, he founded the Iona Community, restoring the old cathedral and establishing the Community as an international and ecumenical place of worship.

**Macleod, John** *see* **Banting, Sir Frederick**.

**Mac Liammóir, Micheál** (1899–1978) Irish actor, writer and painter. Regarded as one of the finest Irish actors and raconteurs of his generation, with a mesmerizing stage presence, his one-man shows included *The Importance of Being Oscar* (1960), a tribute to Oscar WILDE.

**McLuhan, [Herbert] Marshall** (1911–80) Canadian critic and educator. His studies of mass culture and communication include *The Gutenberg Galaxy*

(1962) and influential *The Medium is the Message* (1967).

**Macmillan, Sir [Maurice] Harold**, 1st Earl of Stockton (1894–1986) English Conservative statesman. He became prime minister (1957–63) in succession to EDEN. Christened "Supermac" by the cartoonist VICKY, he won the General Election of 1959 on the slogan "You've never had it so good" and gained much international respect for his "wind of change" speech in South Africa in 1958. His later years as premier were darkened by the PROFUMO scandal, and his manoeuvres against Rab BUTLER cost the latter the Tory leadership, which went to DOUGLAS-HOME. At the end of his life, he made a notably cutting speech in the House of Lords against THATCHER's privatization policies, "selling the family silver."

**MacMillan, Sir Kenneth** (1929–92) Scottish choreographer. He became the Royal Ballet's principal choreographer in 1977. He had been associated with the company, and its predecessor, the Sadler's Wells Ballet, since the early 1950s. He was also director of the Royal Ballet (1970–77) in succession to ASHTON.

**MacNeice, [Frederick] Louis** (1907–63) Irish poet and scholar. He was one of the leading AUDEN generation of poets, and his collections include *Letters from Iceland* (1937, written with Auden) and *Autumn Journal* (1938).

**Macpherson, James** (1907–63) Scottish poet. His supposed translations of early Scottish Gaelic verse, *Fragments of Ancient Poetry* (1760), *Fingal* (1762) and *Temora* (1763), the latter two allegedly by an ancient bard called Ossian, achieved extraordinary popularity. GOETHE quoted from them in *The Sor-*

*rows of Young Werther*, and NAPOLEON slept with the poems under his pillow. Macpherson certainly used some ancient Gaelic poetry as the basis for the poems, but they are unquestionably largely his own creation.

**Maes, Nicolaes** (1634–93) Dutch painter. He studied with REMBRANDT, and his early genre works show the influence of his teacher in the rich palette of reds and browns and in contrasts of light and shade, e.g. *The Listening Maid* (1656). After the mid–1660s he began to show the influence of van DYCK in his portraits.

**Maeterlinck, [Count] Maurice** (1862–1949) Belgian poet, writer and playwright. Trained as a lawyer, he turned to writing poetry under the influence of the Symbolist poets. His masterpiece is *Pelléas et Mélisande* (1892), the basis for the opera by DEBUSSY (1902). He was awarded the Nobel prize for literature in 1911.

**Magritte, René** (1898–1967) Belgian painter. He became a major surrealist painter in Paris in the 1930s, devising a style dubbed "magic realism" for its incongruous, dreamlike juxtaposition of carefully detailed everyday objects in dreamlike situations, e.g. men in bowler hats raining from the sky.

**Mahler, Gustav** (1860–1911) Austrian composer and conductor. Of Jewish birth, he became a Roman Catholic but remained subject to anti-semitic gibes while conductor of the Vienna State Opera (1897–1907). Regarded as both the last of the great Romantic composers of the 19th century and the first great composer of the modern era, his works include nine symphonies, song cycles, and the great symphonic song cycle, *The Song of the Earth* (1908).

**Mailer, Norman** (1923– ) American novelist and essayist. His first novel, *The Naked and the Dead* (1948), based on his experiences in World War II, was highly successful. Subsequent works include the semi-autobiographical *An American Dream* (1966) and nonfiction works such as *The Executioner's Song* (1977), a gruesome "factional" study of a murderer.

**Major, John** (1943– ) English Conservative politician. He became an MP in 1979 and was appointed a junior minister by THATCHER in 1981. His rise in the late 1980s was spectacular: he replaced **Sir Geoffrey Howe** (1926– ) as foreign secretary in 1989, and later that year replaced **Nigel Lawson** (1932– ) as chancellor. After Thatcher's resignation in late 1990, Major was selected by his colleagues, to most people's surprise, as Tory leader and prime minister. The son of a trapeze artist, his stated aim is to create a "classless society" with consumer rights defined under a "citizen's charter."

**Makarios III** [Mikhail Khristodoulou Mouskos] (1913–77) Cypriot archbishop and statesman. Archbishop of the Orthodox Church in Cyprus, he became first president of Cyprus (1959–77) after independence, with a brief hiatus in 1974 when he was removed from office after a coup by Greek Cypriot extremists forced him to flee to London. He opposed partition, but was powerless to prevent the proclamation of a Turkish state in the north after Turkey's invasion of 1974.

**Malan, Daniel F[rançois]** (1874–1959) South African politician. He became prime minister (1948–54). A fervent believer in a racially divided, hierarchical society dominated by whites, he was responsible for the apartheid legislation that separated South Africa's population into white, coloured and black.

**Malcolm X** [Malcolm Little] (1925–65) American black separatist leader. He abandoned his "slave" surname of Little in the early 1950s, by which time he had become a convert to Elijah Muhammad's Nation of Islam while in jail for burglary. An advocate of violent response to racism, he was murdered by fellow black Muslims in a feud.

**Malenkov, Georgi Maksimilianovich** (1902–88) Soviet politician. He became *de facto* prime minister of the USSR after STALIN's death (whose private secretary he had been in the 1920s). He was deposed by KHRUSCHEV, and dispatched to manage a hydroelectric power plant.

**Mallarmé, Stephane** (1842–98) French symbolist poet. His impressionistic free-verse works include *L'après-midi d'un faune* ("The Afternoon of a Faun" 1876), which was set to suitably sensuous music by DEBUSSY. His literary theorizing, e.g. in *Verse and Prose* (1893), had a strong influence on the development of the Symbolist movement.

**Malory, Sir Thomas** (*fl.* 15th century) Translator, largely from French sources, of *Le Morte d'Arthur* (printed by CAXTON, 1485), a collection of Arthurian legends (*see* ARTHUR). The work includes several episodes, e.g. the quest for the Holy Grail, that have been recycled by generations of writers, e.g. TENNYSON. The author has traditionally been identified with a rather violently inclined Warwickshire knight of that name, but the attribution remains doubtful.

**Malraux, André** (1901–76) French novelist, art historian and politician. He took part in revolutionary movements in China and southeast Asia (1924–27), fought for the republican cause in the Spanish Civil War (1936–39) and was a leader of the resistance movement in France during World War II. He served as minister of information in DE GAULLE's government (1945–46) and as minister of cultural affairs (1959–69). His active life had a great influence on his novels, which include *La Condition humaine* (1933).

**Mandela, Nelson [Rolihlahla]** (1918– ) South African lawyer and nationalist leader. Leader of the banned African National Congress, he was imprisoned in 1964 for life by the South African government. He became an extremely potent symbol of black resistance to the apartheid regime, and his eventual release in 1990 (engineered by DE KLERK) was greeted with international joy, after which he increased his already formidable reputation by his dignified and cautious approach to reform. His second wife, **Winnie Mandela** (1934– ), who had earlier made a notorious speech giving approval to the "necklacing" of black collaborators, was convicted in 1991 of complicity in the murder of a young black activist, with few observers expecting her to go to prison. They separated in 1992.

**Mandelstam, Osip** (1891–1938) Russian poet. The collections published in his lifetime are *Stone* (1913), *Tristia* (1925) and *Poems* (1928). He was denounced for reading a satirical poem about STALIN, and he and his wife, **Nadezhda Mandelstam** (1899–1980), were sent into exile in Siberia, where he died. Nadezhda's two books describing her husband's life and work, *Hope Against Hope* (1971) and *Hope*

*Abandoned* (1974) affirm the resilience of the human spirit.

**Mandeville, Sir John** (*c.*14th century) supposed English author of *The Travels of Sir John Mandeville*, an eventful and mendacious travel book that has charmed countless readers since its first appearance in the 14th century. The work is ostensibly an account of the author's travels in the Holy Land, but is actually a gathering together of unlikely traveller's tales from Africa to India.

**Manet, Edouard** (1832–83) French painter. He had early success at the Salon with *The Guitarist* (1861). Subsequent paintings, however, such as *Le Déjeuner sur l'Herbe* (1863) and *Olympia* (1863) caused outrage due to his direct approach and fresh, painterly style. Manet was by no means a willing leader of the avant-garde, and although pupils such as DEGAS were Impressionists, he never exhibited with them. His later works, e.g. *Argenteuil* (1874), have a light, free atmosphere.

**Manley, Michael [Norman]** (1923– ) Jamaican statesman. He became leader of the socialist People's National Party in 1969, and prime minister (1972–80). He lost two subsequent elections, but won the 1989 election with a much less radical policy programme. He is regarded as a spokesman for the Third World.

**Mann, Thomas** (1875–1955) German novelist and critic, primarily concerned with the role of the artist and the purpose of artistic creation in modern society. His works include *Death in Venice* (1912), *The Magic Mountain* (1930), and *The Confessions of the Confidence Trickster Felix Krull* (1954), a comedy. He was awarded the Nobel prize for literature in 1929 and fled Nazi Germany in 1933.

**Mantegna, Andrea** (1431–1506) Italian painter and prominent figure of the early Renaissance, who was the brother-in-law of Giovanni BELLINI. A proficient draughtsman, he used his knowledge of classical antiquity in his frescos for the Ermetani church in Padua (1448–57), since mainly destroyed. His mastery of foreshortening can be seen in the *trompe l'oeil* figures on the ceiling the bridal chamber of the Ducal Palace in Mantua. His books of engravings were very popular, and influenced many artists, including DÜRER.

**Mao Tse-tung** *or* **Mao Ze Dong** (1893–1976) Chinese Communist statesman and Marxist philosopher. An adherent to SUN YAT-SEN's nationalist policies, he converted to Marxism and was one of the founders of the Chinese Communist Party (1922), and pursued a policy of limited cooperation with CHIANG KAI-SHEK's Kuomingtang until 1927. Mao then established a Soviet-style republic in Kiangsi province (1931–34), until forced by the Kuomingtang into the "Long March" of himself and his followers to northern China (1935–36). Following the Japanese occupation (1937–45), during which Nationalists and Communists collaborated against the Japanese, the Communists won the resumed civil war and Mao established his People's Republic (1949). Mao's dictatorship became the most murderous in all history; as many as fifty million people may have died in his "Great Leap Forward" of collectivization (1958–62), and millions more died in purges, as he sought to break traditional patterns of Chinese family life. In 1966, he launched his "Cultural Revolution" (1966–69), during which his fanatical young

Red Guards were given complete freedom to terrorize the population, in their campaign against "Confucianism" and "bourgeois democracy." The state worship of Mao reached depths remarkable even for the 20th century, with his works, e.g. the notorious *Little Red Book*, being regarded as holy writ. *See also* CHIANG CH'ING.

**Marat, Jean Paul** (1743–93) French revolutionary and journalist. A prominent supporter of DANTON and ROBESPIERRE, and opponent of the moderate Girondists, he made repeated calls for increased executions during the establishment of the Revolution and was stabbed to death in his bath by the Girondist aristocrat **Charlotte Corday** (1768–93), who was guillotined.

**Marc, Franz** (1880–1916) German painter. With KANDINSKY, he founded the *Blaue Reiter* group of expressionist artists. A devoutly religious man, most of his paintings were of animals portrayed in vivid colours, often merging into their backgrounds.

**Marceau, Marcel** (1923– ) French mime artist. Regarded as the world's leading mime artist, his white-faced Bip character has become known worldwide. His films include *Silent Movie* (1976), in which Marceau's is the only speaking part.

**Marciano, Rocky** [Rocco Francis Marchegiano] (1923–69) American boxer. He became world heavyweight champion (1952–56), and never lost a professional fight.

**Marconi, Guglielmo, Marchese** (1874–1937) Italian physicist and electrical engineer. He shared the 1909 Nobel prize for physics for his development of wireless telegraphy. He sent signals across the English Channel in 1898, and across the Atlantic in

1901, and later developed short-wave radio transmissions.

**Marcos, Ferdinand [Edralin]** (1917–89) Filipino politician. He was president of the Philippines (1965–86). An autocratic ruler, he declared martial law in 1972, after which he ruled by oppressive and idiosyncratic decree. He was deposed in 1986 after the popular unrest that brought AQUINO to power, and lived in exile in Hawaii with his wife, **Imelda**, who, after his death, returned to the Philippines and was sued by the Philippines' government for corruption.

**Marcuse, Herbert** (1898–1979) German-born American philosopher. He became prominent in the 1960s as a theorist of the New Left, popular with student activists for his conveniently balanced condemnation of both capitalist and Soviet society. His works include *Eros and Civilisation* (1955) and *Soviet Marxism* (1958).

**Maria Theresa** (1717–80) Queen of Hungary and Bohemia and archduchess of Austria. She married the Holy Roman Emperor **Francis I** (1708–65) in 1736. When her father **Charles VI** (1685–1740) of Austria died in 1740, she inherited the thrones of Hungary and Bohemia, and then had to defend her territories against most of Europe in the Austrian War of Succession (1740–8), and during the Seven Years War (1756–63). She implemented many reforms throughout her realm, and was much admired for her bravery.

**Marie Antoinette** *see* **Louis XVI**.

**Markiewicz, [Constance Georgine] Countess** (1868–1927) Irish nationalist. A member of the Anglo-Irish ruling class, she joined Sinn Fein in 1908 and was sentenced to death for her part in the

1916 Easter Rising, being reprieved in the amnesty of 1917. She became the first woman to be elected to the British Parliament in 1918, when she won a Dublin seat for Sinn Fein, but refused to take her seat.

**Markova, Dame Alicia** [Lilian Alicia Marks] (1910– ) English ballerina. She became a member of DIAGHILEV's Ballet Russe (1924–29) and then of the Vic-Wells Ballet, where she became prima ballerina (1933–35).

**Marks, Simon**, [1st Baron Marks of Broughton] (1888–1964) English businessman. He inherited the Marks and Spencer chain of shops, and, with Israel (later Lord) Seiff, built the chain into one of the most respected retail empires in the world, with a reputation for customer and staff care.

**Marley, Bob** [Robert Nesta Marley] (1945–81) Jamaican singer and songwriter. With his group, the Wailers, he became the world's leading reggae singer. A devout Rastafarian, and large-scale consumer of marijuana, he died from brain cancer. His songs include the haunting ballad "No Woman, No Cry," and the highly political "I Shot the Sheriff."

**Marlowe, Christopher** (1564–93) English dramatist and poet. He was one of the first English dramatists to use blank verse to great dramatic and poetic effect in his plays, the most famous of which are *Tamburlaine the Great* (1590) and his masterpiece, *Doctor Faustus* (1604). He also wrote some very fine classically inspired poetry, e.g. *Hero and Leander*, published posthumously in 1598, and the superb lyric "Come live with me, and be my Love." He was probably an atheist (*see* KYD) and was also probably a secret agent in the employ of the Elizabethan government. He was killed in a tavern brawl. Shakespeare paid tribute to him in *As You Like It*: "Dead Shepherd, now I find thy saw of might: / Who ever lov'd that lov'd not at first sight?"

**Marshall, Alfred** (1842–1924) English economist. His works, e.g. *Principles of Economics* (1890) and *Industry and Trade* (1919), have been of great influence on modern economics. He devised concepts such as "elasticity," "consumer surplus" and "time analysis."

**Marshall, George C[atlett]** (1880–1959) American general and statesman. He was chief of staff of the US army during World War II, and, as US secretary of state, oversaw the economic reconstruction of postwar Europe, through the Marshall Aid Plan, for which he was awarded the 1953 Nobel Peace Prize.

**Marvell, Andrew** (1621–78) English poet. A (passive) supporter of Parliament during the English Civil War, he became member of parliament for Hull in 1659, a position he held until his death. His verse satires were much enjoyed by the wits of the day, even by those whose vices were attacked. His "Last Instructions to a Painter," for example, a coldly brilliant assault on the corruption of the court, was particularly enjoyed by CHARLES II. His strange, metaphysical poems, e.g. "The Garden" and "Upon Appleton House," display an enormous talent for symbolism and metaphor. His poem of 1650 celebrating Oliver CROMWELL's suppression of the Irish rebellion, "An Horatian Ode upon Cromwell's Return from Nature," remains one of the great political poems of all time, with its cool, restrained appreciation of Cromwell's stature.

**Marx, Karl** (1818–83) German philosopher. His theories on class struggle dominated 20th-century political thought from the Bolshevik Revolution to the collapse of the communist regimes of eastern Europe in 1989–91. *Das Kapital*, his study of the economics of capitalism, appeared in 1867; subsequent volumes, edited by **Friedrich Engels** (1820–95)—Marx was unwilling or perhaps incapable of finishing the work—appeared in 1885 and 1895. He also wrote *The Communist Manifesto* with Engels in 1848, and was one of the founders of the "First International" in 1864.

**Marx Brothers** An American comedy group of brothers (of German parents), consisting of **Arthur Marx (Harpo)** (1893–1964), **Milton (Gummo)** (1894–1977), **Herbert Marx (Zeppo)** (1901–79), **Julius Marx (Groucho)** (1895–1977) and **Leonard Marx (Chico)** (1891–1961). Their films, without Gummo, include *Monkey Business* (1932), *Duck Soup* (1933) and *A Night at the Opera* (1937). The anarchic humour of the Marx Brothers' films was enormously popular with both critics and public, with Groucho in particular enjoying a cult status among intellectuals. Groucho wrote several books, including *Groucho and Me* (1959) and a study of US income tax laws.

**Mary I** (1516–58) Queen of England. The daughter of Catherine of Aragon and HENRY VIII, she inherited the throne in 1553 after her half-brother **Edward VI** (1537–53) died and after Lady Jane GREY was deposed. A devout Roman Catholic, she was initially very popular. She gradually reintroduced her religion into England and married PHILIP II in 1554. The last years of her reign were marked by increasing persecution of Protestants, with over 300 being burned at the stake.

**Mary, Queen of Scots** (1542–87) Queen of Scotland. She inherited the throne when a week old, on the death of her father **James V** (1512–42), king of Scotland (1513–42). She was married three times: from 1558 to 1560 to **Francis II** (1544–60), king of France (1559–60); from 1565 to 1667 to **Henry Stewart, Lord Darnley** (1545–67), her cousin; and, from 1567 to 1571, to **James Hepburn, 4th Earl of Bothwell** (1535–78), who is generally credited with Darnley's murder. A Roman Catholic, Mary saw increasing religious strife and political unrest during her reign as Protestant reformers such as **John Knox** (*c.*1514–72) made their mark, and as other factions fought to draw the crown on their side. The marriage to Bothwell—after a token abduction—sealed her fate, and she was forced to abdicate in favour of her son (*see* JAMES VI AND I) and to flee to England in 1567, where she was eventually executed on ELIZABETH I's orders.

**Masaccio** [Tommaso di Ser Giovanni di Mone] (1401–*c.*1428) Florentine painter. A key figure of the early Renaissance, his earliest dated work, the San Giovenale triptych (1422), is painted with revolutionary realism, and displays the influence of DONATELLO. He is the heir to GIOTTO in his rejection of Gothic elegance and decorative detail, and his development of perspective.

**Masaryk, Tomás [Garrigue]** (1850–1937) Czech statesman who founded (with BENES) the modern state of Czechoslovakia in 1918, and became the country's first president (1918–35). His works include *Russia and Europe* (1913). His son, **Jan [Garrigue] Masaryk** (1886–1948), was also a Czech statesman. He became foreign minister of the Czech government in exile in 1941. He returned to Czechoslovakia (with Benes). The circumstances of his death are unknown; he was found dead beneath the open window of his office. It is generally assumed that either he killed himself in grief at the Communist takeover of his country, or he was murdered by the Communists. His biography was written by Karel CAPEK.

**Mascagni, Pietro** (1863–1945) Italian composer. His works include a perennial favourite in opera houses around the world, the one-act *Cavalleria Rusticana* (1890).

**Masefield, John [Edward]** (1878–1967) English poet, whose best-known poem, from *Salt-Water Ballads* (1902) is "I must go down to the sea again." Many later poems, e.g. *The Everlasting Mercy* (1911), caused scandal with their frank treatment of rural themes. He was appointed poet laureate in 1930.

**Mason, James** (1909–84) English stage and film actor. His films include *A Star is Born* (1954), *Georgy Girl* (1966) and his last film, *The Shooting Party* (1984).

**Mastroianni, Marcello** (1924– ) Italian actor. His films include VISCONTI's *White Nights* (1957) and FELLINI's *La Dolce Vita* (1960).

**Mata Hari** [Margarethe Geertruida Zelle] (1876–1917) Dutch spy. A dancer in Paris with many lovers, she became a German spy and was shot for treason.

**Matisse, Henri** (1869–1954) French painter and sculptor. In the period before World War I he became the leading painter of the group mockingly dubbed *Fauves* ("wild beasts"), so called for their love of bright colours and primitive form. A superb draughtsman, he also designed ballet sets for DIAGHILEV.

**Matthews, Sir Stanley** (1915– ) English footballer. Regarded as one of the greatest wingers of all time (the "Wizard of Dribble"), he won 54 international caps in a career that spanned 22 years.

**Maugham, W[illiam] Somerset** (1874–1965) English novelist and dramatist. Trained as a doctor, he used his experiences working in the London slums for his first novel, *Liza of Lambeth* (1897). His best-known novels are *Of Human Bondage* (1915) and *The Moon and Sixpence* (1919), the latter based on the life of the painter Paul GAUGUIN. He was a British secret agent during World War I, and his experiences then form the basis of his spy novel, *Ashenden* (1928).

**Maxwell, [Ian] Robert** [Robert Hoch] (1923–91) Czech-born British newspaper proprietor, publisher and politician. He served with distinction in World War II, winning the Military Cross. He founded the Pergamon Press, specializing (very lucratively) in academic journals. He was a Labour MP (1964–70) and bought the Mirror Group of newspapers. In the late 1980s, he produced an extraordinary and much derided series of laudatory biographies of Communist dictators such as HONECKER and CEAUSESCU, just in time for their downfall. His mysterious death by drowning off the Canary Islands was followed by revelations of his mishandling of his companies' assets, particularly the pension funds.

**Mayer, Louis B[urt]** [Eliezer Mayer] (1885–1957) Russian-born American film producer. He joined with GOLDWYN to form Metro-Goldwyn-Mayer in 1924, and became one of the most powerful of the

Hollywood moguls, producing such films as *Ben Hur* (1926), and fostering the "star system." ("The reason so many people showed up at his funeral was because they wanted to make sure he was dead"—Goldwyn.)

**Mead, Margaret** (1901–78) American anthropologist. Her works, which include *Coming of Age in Samoa* (1928) and *Growing up in New Guinea* (1930), argue that cultural conditioning shapes personality, rather than heredity. The validity of much of her research is still debated.

**Medawar, Sir Peter Brian** (1915–87) Brazilian-born British zoologist. He shared the 1960 Nobel prize for physiology or medicine with the Australian virologist **Sir Frank Macfarlane Burnet** (1899–1985) for his work on immunological tolerance.

**Medici, Lorenzo de'** (1449–92) Florentine aristocrat and statesman. Styled "The Magnificent," he was a poet and a noted patron of the arts. His tomb in Florence was designed by MICHELANGELO.

**Meinhoff, Ulrike** (1934–76) German terrorist. With **Andreas Baader** (1943–77) and others, she founded the "Red Army Faction" in 1970, an ultra-leftist terrorist organization dedicated to using violence to bring about the collapse of West German "capitalist tyranny." She and Baader died in prison, apparently having committed suicide.

**Meir, Golda** (1898–1978) Russian-born Israeli stateswoman, She emigrated to Palestine (1921) from the USA, where she grew up, and was active in the fight for a Jewish state. She was minister of labour (1949–56) and of foreign affairs (1956–66) before becoming Israel's first female prime minister (1969–74).

**Meitner, Lise** (1878–1968) Austrian-born Swedish physicist. She and Otto HAHN discovered the radioactive element protactinium (1918). With her nephew, Otto FRISCH, and others, she discovered the process of nuclear fission in the late 1930s.

**Melanchthon, Philipp** *see* **Luther, Martin**.

**Melba, Dame Nellie** [Helen Porter Mitchell] (1861–1931) Australian soprano. Renowned for her light, pure voice, she became one of the world's leading prima donnas in the late 1880s. ESCOFFIER named an ice cream dish "peach melba" after her.

**Melville, Herman** (1819–91) American novelist, short-story writer and poet. His early experiences as a sailor, including service on a whaler, imprisonment for mutiny, and captivity among cannibals, are reflected in his early novels, e.g. *Typee* (1846) and *Omoo* (1847). His masterpiece is the novel *Moby Dick* (1851), a complex and symbolic narrative in which Captain Ahab leads his whaling crew in a doomed quest for the white whale that bit off his leg. Other notable works include the story "Bartleby the Scrivener," and the short novel *Billy Budd, Foretopman* (published posthumously in 1924), the latter being made into an opera by Benjamin BRITTEN.

**Memling** *or* **Memlinc, Hans** (*c*.1430–1494) German-born Dutch painter, probably a pupil of Rogier van der WEYDEN. His works are influenced by his master in terms of subject and composition, but they have a calmer, more serene quality in contrast to van der Weyden's emotional intensity. He was a prolific and popular artist, and was a successful portraitist. Notable works include *Tommaso Portinari and his Wife* (*c*.1468).

**Menander** *see* **Plautus, Titus Maccius**.

**Mendel, Gregor Johann** (1822–84) Austrian monk who was also a biologist and botanist. By experimenting with generations of pea plants, Mendel discovered that traits such as colour or height had two factors (hereditary units) and that these factors do not blend but can be either dominant or recessive. With no knowledge of genes or cell division, he developed two laws of genetics.

**Mendelssohn, Felix** [Jakob Ludwig Felix Mendelssohn-Bartholdy] (1809–47) German composer. The grandson of the philosopher **Moses Mendelssohn** (1729–86), he became one of the leading Romantic composers. His works include five symphonies, the opera *Elijah* (1846), songs and the overtures *A Midsummer Night's Dream* (1826) and *Fingal's Cave* (1832). His performance of BACH's *St Matthew Passion* resulted in a resurgence of interest in the composer.

**Mendès-France, Pierre** (1907–82) French statesman. He was appointed minister of the national economy by DE GAULLE in 1945, but resigned and joined the opposition the following year. He became prime minister (1954–55), and negotiated the peace treaty that ended the Vietnamese war.

**Mengistu, Mariam Haile** (1937– ) Ethiopian dictator. He participated in the 1974 coup that toppled HAILE SELASSIE, and came to power in the 1977 coup against his erstwhile allies. A Marxist-Leninist, he dealt with subsequent risks of coups by personally shooting any of his colleagues felt to be a danger, and established a relentlessly brutal dictatorship. In 1991, as secessionists closed in on Addis Ababa, he fled to Kenya.

**Menotti, Gian Carlo** (1911– ) Italian-born American composer, who settled in the US in 1928. His operas, for which he also wrote the librettos, include *Amelia Goes to the Ball* (1937) and *Amahl and the Night Visitors* (1951).

**Menuhin, Sir Yehudi** (1916– ) American-born British violinist. An infant prodigy, he performed MENDELSSOHN's violin concerto at the age of 7 with the San Fransisco Symphony Orchestra. He became one of the world's leading virtuosos and founded a school (in 1962) for musically gifted children.

**Menzies, Sir Robert Gordon** (1894–1978) Australian Liberal statesman. He was appointed a privy counsellor in 1937, and was nicknamed "Pig-iron Bob" in 1938 after backing the Australian government's decision to sell pig iron to Japan during the Sino-Japanese war. He became prime minister (1939–41, 1949–66) and a respected arbiter in international affairs, e.g. during the Suez crisis.

**Mercouri, Melina** (1923– ) Greek actress and politician. Her best-known film is *Never on Sunday* (1960). She became an MP in 1974 after the fall of the military junta, which she had bravely criticized and which had forced her into exile, and was appointed minister for culture and science in 1981.

**Meredith, George** (1828–1909) English novelist and poet. His novels, e.g. *The Ordeal of Richard Feverel* (1859) and *The Egoist* (1879), are complex studies of relationships in which the woman's perspective is often the most sympathetically represented. Meredith's strange, intricate dialogue and narration are quite unique. His sonnet sequence *Modern Love* (1862), virtually a novel in verse form, is an intriguing and innovative study of the dissolution of a marriage.

**Messerschmitt, Willy** [Wilhelm Messerschmitt] (1898–1978) German aircraft designer and manufacturer. His planes include two notable fighters, the ME–109, a version of which won the world speed record in 1939, and the first jet combat aircraft, the ME–262.

**Messiaen, Olivier** (1908–92) French composer and organist. His rhythmically complex works, often influenced by birdsong, include *Quartet for the End of Time* (1941, performed before fellow prisoners in a German POW camp) and the massive Hindu-influenced *Turangallia* symphony (1946).

**Messmer, Otto** (1894–1985) American cartoonist. His "Felix the Cat" first appeared in *Feline Follies* (1920) and became the first cartoon superstar. "Felix kept on walking" became an international catchphrase.

**Meynell, Alice** *see* **Thompson, Francis**.

**Michelangelo Buonarotti** (1475–1564) Florentine painter, sculptor, draughtsman, architect and poet, an outstanding figure of the Renaissance. He trained in Florence with GHIRLANDAIO, and Lorenzo de' MEDICI was one of his early patrons. In Rome from 1496–1501 he established his reputation with the sculptures *Bacchus* (1496–7) and *Pietà* (1499). The fresco of *The Battle of Cascina*, commissioned in 1501 for the Palazzo Vecchio, was not completed, but before returning to Rome he executed the powerful sculpture of DAVID (1501–4) for the Florentine Council. From 1505 Pope Julius II was his patron, and it was he who commissioned the ceiling paintings for the Sistine Chapel (1508–12), Michelangelo's masterpiece. The upper part of the ceiling contains images from the Book of Genesis, lower down are the prophets and sybils, and the lunettes and spandels portray characters from the ancestry of Christ and the Virgin. He also worked on the tombs of Lorenzo and Giuliano de Medici, and on the rebuilding of St Peter's. He was also a highly accomplished poet, and wrote many fine sonnets.

**Middleton, Thomas** (*c*.1570–1627) English dramatist. His two powerful tragedies, *The Changeling* (1622) and *Women Beware Women* (1627), are now highly regarded. His other works include the satirical comedy *A Trick to Catch the Old One* (1608) and a political satire, *A Game at Chesse* (1624). The latter almost resulted in his imprisonment. He collaborated with many other dramatists.

**Mies van der Rohe, Ludwig** (1886–1969) German-born American architect. His German pavilion for the 1929 International Exhibition in Barcelona was widely praised, as were his designs for glass skyscrapers. He was director of the Bauhaus (1930–33) and emigrated to the US in 1937. He designed the New York Seagram Tower.

**Milhaud, Darius** (1892–1974) French composer. A member of *"Les Six,"* he was a highly prolific composer. His works, mostly polytonal and often influenced by jazz, include symphonies, operas, songs and string quartets.

**Mill, John Stuart** (1806–73) English philosopher and economist. A follower of BENTHAM, he elaborated the philosophy of the "greater good" in his philosophy of utilitarianism, as expounded in *Utilitarianism* (1861). His other works include *On Liberty* (1859), in which he asserts the freedom of the individual, *Principles of Political Economy* (1848), and his remarkable *Autobiography* (1873), which describes his forced education by his father, the Scottish philosopher **James Mill** (1773–1836).

**Millais, Sir John Everett** (1829–96) English painter. Along with Holman HUNT and ROSSETTI, he founded the Pre-Raphaelite Brotherhood. The Pre-Raphaelites, with their posed, studied tableaux in clashing colours, were unpopular until championed by RUSKIN, whose wife Millais later married. Millais became very successful and gradually shed his Pre-Raphaelite style, becoming president of the Royal Academy in 1896. His works include *The Boyhood of Raleigh* (1870) and the notoriously sentimental *Bubbles* (1870), which was used by Pears Soap in an advertising campaign.

**Miller, Arthur** (1915– ) American dramatist. His tragedies include three classics of the American stage: *Death of a Salesman* (1949), *The Crucible* (1952), a comment on McCarthyism in the USA, and *A View from the Bridge* (1955), inspired by Greek drama. He was married to Marilyn MONROE (1955–61) for whom he wrote the screenplay for her last film, *The Misfits* (1961).

**Miller, [Alton] Glenn** (1904–44) American composer, bandleader and trombonist. His dance band became one of the most popular in the world, with tunes such as "Moonlight Serenade" and "In the Mood." The plane carrying Miller and his band to play for the troops disappeared over the English Channel in 1944.

**Millet, Jean-François** (1814–75) French painter. He earned his living as a portraitist, and exhibited his first major genre painting, *The Winnower*, at the Salon in 1848. In 1850 he exhibited *The Sower* with works by COURBET, and he was labelled a social realist although his work had no direct political import.

**Millett, Kate** (1934– ) American feminist. Her works, notably *Sexual Politics* (1969), are cornerstones of feminist fundamentalism, arguing that society is constructed for the benefit of "male patriarchy," which uses the family as a device for repressing women.

**Milligan, Spike** [Terence Allan Milligan] (1918– ) Indian-born Anglo-Irish comedian. With Peter SELLERS, the Welsh comedian and singer **Harry Secombe** (1921– ) and the Anglo-Peruvian comedian **Michael Bentine** (1921– ), he co-wrote and performed in the radio comedy series *The Goon Show* (1951–59), which became a highly influential comedy series, with its manic wit and surreal invention. Milligan's books include the novel *Puckoon* (1963) and autobiographies, e.g. *Adolf Hitler, My Part in his Downfall* (1971).

**Millikan, Robert Andrews** (1868–1953) American physicist. He was awarded the 1923 Nobel prize for physics for his determination of the charge on the electron, and did significant research on cosmic rays.

**Milne, A[lan] A[lexander]** (1882–1956) English writer and dramatist. His children's books, e.g. *When We Were Very Young* (1924), *Winnie-the-Pooh* (1926) and *The House at Pooh Corner* (1928), are much loved classics of children's literature.

**Milton, John** (1608–74) English poet. One of the most formidably learned of all English poets, Milton had a European-wide reputation by his late twenties. His early poems, e.g. the magnificent elegy *Lycidas* (1637), are steeped in the humanist tradition, which looked to classical literature for ethical principles and modes of expression, and to Scripture and the Christian tradition for faith. He supported Parliament during the Civil War and wrote tracts attacking royalty and episcopacy. His most famous prose work is the tract *Aeropagitica* (1644), a rousing defence of the liberty of free speech. His masterpiece is the great epic poem on the Fall of Man, *Paradise Lost* (1667–74). Other notable works include the verse drama *Samson Agonistes* (1671), i.e. "Samson at the Games", in which the blind hero represents Milton himself in Restoration England, and many great sonnets, e.g. "On His Blindness."

**Minnelli, Liza** *see* **Garland, Judy**.

**Miró, Joan** (1893–1983) Spanish painter. He settled in Paris in 1920, where he became influenced by PICASSO, and exhibited with the Surrealists in 1925. His dreamlike work, depicting highly coloured and curvilinear forms, became increasingly abstract over the years, and was influential on the American Abstract Expressionist painters.

**Mitchell, R[eginald] J[oseph]** (1895–1937) English aircraft designer. He designed the Supermarine Spitfire (1934–36), dying just after its acceptance by the RAF. The Spitfire, arguably the most beautiful plane ever built, went into full production in 1938, and played a significant part in the Battle of Britain. Over 19,000 were produced during World War II.

**Mitterrand, François [Maurice Marie]** (1916– ) French statesman. A member of the Resistance during World War II, he became leader of the Socialist Party in 1971 and the first socialist president of France (1981– ). A shrewd politician, he skilfully marginalized his enemies on both the left and the right throughout the 1980s, reneging on such early policies as nationalization in the process.

**Mobuto, Sese Seko Kuku Ngbendu Wa Za Banga** [Joseph Désiré Mobuto] (1930– ) Zairean dictator. A colleague of LUMUMBA's in the late 1950s, he assumed complete power over the Congo in 1965, changing the country's name to Zaire in 1971. His notoriously corrupt regime—Mobuto is worth £3 or £4 billion—was backed by the Western powers for its supposedly anti-communist virtues.

**Modigliani, Amedeo** (1884–1920) Italian painter and sculptor. His best-known works are his African-influenced sculptures of elongated figures.

**Mohammed** *or* **Muhammad** (*c*.570–*c*.632) Arab prophet and founder of Islam. Born in Mecca, the son of a merchant, he began having revelations, sometime after 600, that he was the last prophet of Allah and His channel of communication with the world. He gathered together a band of followers and established himself at Medina in 622, from where, after several battles, his forces conquered Mecca in 629, and shortly after all Arabia. He died after making a pilgrimage to Mecca.

**Moholy-Nagy, László** *or* **Ladislaus** (1895–1946) Hungarian-born American painter, sculptor and photographer. He taught at the Bauhaus (1923–28) and worked in many different media, notably photography, in which field he won recognition as a leading avant-garde photographer.

**Molière** [pseud. of Jean-Baptiste Poquelin] (1622–73) French dramatist. His great comedies are as popular now as when they were first performed; only SHAKESPEARE's plays have been more widely performed. The plays include *Tartuffe* (1664), a crushing satire on religious hypocrisy, *The Misanthrope* (1666), a study of a cynic in love, and *The Imaginary Invalid* (1673), a hilarious depiction of hypochondria and quack medicine.

**Molotov, Vyacheslav Mikhailovich** [Vyacheslav Mikhailovich Scriabin] (1890–1986) Russian statesman. He joined LENIN's Bolsheviks in 1905 and became one of the few leading Bolsheviks to survive STALIN's purges. He was commissar for foreign affairs (1939–49), negotiated the nonaggression pact with Nazi Germany and attended the founding conference of the UN in 1945. As minister for foreign affairs (1953–56), his reiterated *nyet* to diplomatic overtures became a byword.

**Mondrian, Piet** [Pieter Cornelis Mondriaan] (1872–1944) Dutch painter. He settled in Paris in 1909, where he was influenced by the Cubists and Fauvists, particularly MATISSE. He developed a style of painting based on grids of lines against strong colours, e.g. *Composition in Yellow and Blue* (1929), and co-founded the De Stijl group of Dutch artists.

**Monet, Claude Oscar** (1840–1926) French Impressionist painter. His *Impression: Sunrise* gave its name to the movement. From 1862–63 he studied in Paris, where he met RENOIR and SISLEY, and together they began the direct studies of nature and changing light that was to characterize their works. MANET was an early influence on Monet, but Monet was more interested in experiment with light and colour, e.g. *Women in a Garden* (1867). Other works include the *Haystacks* (1891) and *Rouen Cathedral* (1894) series.

**Monk, Thelonius [Sphere]** (1920–82) American

jazz pianist and composer. He became a member of
Dizzy GILLESPIE's band in 1946 and formed his own
band in 1947, which later included many talented
saxophonists, e.g. COLTRANE. His compositions include "Round Midnight."

**Monmouth, Duke of** *see* **James VII and II**.

**Monod, Jacques-Lucien** (1910–76) French biochemist. He shared the 1965 Nobel prize for physics
with **François Jacob** (1920– ) for their work on
clusters of genes ("operons") round chromosomes.

**Monroe, Marilyn** [Norma Jean Baker *or* Mortenson]
(1926–62) American film actress. She became the
leading "dumb blonde" sex symbol in the movies
with such films as *Gentleman Prefer Blondes* (1953).
Her other films include *Bus Stop* (1956) and the
classic comedy *Some Like It Hot* (1959). Her last
film, *The Misfits* (1961), was written by her third
husband, Arthur MILLER. Her death was apparently
due to an overdose of sleeping pills.

**Montagu, Mrs Elizabeth** (1720–1800) English author. A noted bluestocking, her *Essay on the Writings and Genius of Shakespeare* (1769), a reply to
VOLTAIRE's criticisms of SHAKESPEARE's plays, was
highly regarded by her contemporaries.

**Montaigne, Michel Eyquem de** (1533–92) French
essayist. His essays first appeared in 1580. His
achievement was to establish the essay as a literary
form; his fascinating self-examination of his reflections on incidents in his life and on his favourite
(usually Stoic) authors has had a wide and lasting
influence. His motto was "What do I Know?", with
tolerance and antidogmatic scepticism being the
dominant theme in his work. The essays were translated into English by **John Florio** (*c*.1553–1625) in

1603, and Shakespeare used this translation as one
of the sources for *The Tempest*.

**Montessori, Maria** (1870–1952) Italian educationalist. Her book *The Montessori Method* (1912), which
set out her educational method of encouraging the
child to learn at her or his own pace without restraint, was very influential on modern pedagogy.
She was the first woman in Italy to be awarded a
medical degree.

**Monteverdi, Claudio Giovanni Antonio** (1567–
1643) Italian composer. Court musician to the Duke
of Mantua from 1590 to 1612, he became master of
the chapel of St Mark's in Venice, where he remained until he died. His works include the operas
*Orfeo* (1607) and *The Coronation of Poppea* (1642)
and *Vespers* (1610).

**Montgomery of Alamein, Bernard Law, 1st Vis-
count** (1887–1976) English soldier. In World War
II he was given command of the 8th Army in Egypt
in 1942, and won the Battle of Alamein later that
year against ROMMEL's forces, a victory recognized
by CHURCHILL as a turning point in the war. He later
commanded the Allied land forces on D-Day, and
accepted Germany's surrender on Luneburg Heath.

**Moore, G[eorge] E[dward]** (1873–1958) English
philosopher. A strong influence on his fellow student Bertrand RUSSELL, Moore became one of the
leading philosophers of his day with the publication
of his *Principia Ethica* (1903), an analysis of the
non-analysable nature of good and of the value of
friendship. He regarded philosophy's main concern
as the analysis of everyday life.

**Moore, Henry [Spencer]** (1898–1986) English
sculptor. His monumental sculptures, e.g. *The Ma*

*donna and Child* (1943) at St Matthew's Church, Northampton, often semi-abstract in style but always (after a flirtation with Surrealism) based on organic form, resulted in him becoming the best known of modern sculptors, usually perceived as "the man who makes statues and puts holes in them."

**Moore, Thomas** (1779–1852) Irish poet. His *Irish Melodies* (1807–34), songs of his own composition set to traditional Irish airs, achieved great popularity and are still much loved. They include "The Harp that once through Tara's Halls" and "The Last Rose of Summer". His *Lalla Rookh* (1817), a series of oriental tales in verse, also enjoyed great popularity. He was a friend of BYRON, who praised him extravagantly. Byron gave Moore his unpublished memoirs, which were subsequently bought and burned by their mutual friend and publisher John MURRAY, because of their sexual content.

**More, Hannah** (1745–1833) English writer, who became one of the most prominent and popular members of the bluestocking circle around Dr JOHNSON, a world captured in her good-natured poem *Bas Bleu* (1786). Her works include tragedies, one of which, *Percy* (1777), was produced by her friend GARRICK (earning her over £750). The greater part of her work, however, consisted of "improving" works directed at reforming the morals and domestic economy of the poor. She was a sharp, witty and tough-minded writer who made a lot of money from her books, and left over £30,000 to charity.

**More, Henry** (1614–87) English philosopher. He became the leading light of a small group of Anglican divines known as the Cambridge Platonists.

They were much influenced by humanist thinkers such as ERASMUS, HOOKER and Sir Thomas MORE. Henry More's works include *Divine Dialogues* (1668).

**More, Sir Thomas** (1478–1535) English statesman and Roman Catholic saint. He was HENRY VIII's Lord Chancellor, and his refusal to recognize the annulment of Henry's marriage to Catherine of Aragon and declaration of supremacy over the Church in England led to his execution for treason. More was widely recognized as an honourable man, and his execution revulsed moderate opinion throughout Europe. His greatest work is his fantasy of a supposedly ideally organized state, *Utopia* (1516). More's great friend ERASMUS supervised the printing of *Utopia* (the word means "no place"). More was canonized in 1835, and has always been admired for his firm principles. His involvement in heresy trials, however, and his dispute with William Tyndale (*c.*1495–1536), English translator of the Bible, show a less attractive side of his character.

**Morgan, Thomas Hunt** (1866–1945) American geneticist and biologist. He was awarded the 1933 Nobel prize for physiology or medicine for his research into chromosomes and heredity.

**Morisot, Berthe** (1841–95) French painter. She was a pupil of MANET, whose brother she married. She exhibited in all but one of the Impressionist shows and had 13 paintings at the London Impressionist Exhibition of 1905. Her works include *The Cradle* (1873).

**Moro, Aldo** (1916–78) Italian Christian democrat statesman. He was prime minister (1963–68, 1974–76) and brought the Communist Party into close cooperation with his centre-left coalition shortly before his abduction and murder by the Red Brigade.

**Morris, Desmond [John]** (1928– ) English zoologist. His studies of animal and human behaviour, *The Naked Ape* (1967) and *The Human Zoo* (1968) popularized versions of the theories of behaviourists such as LORENZ and TINBERGEN, were bestsellers in the late 1960s and 70s.

**Morris, William** (1834–96) English poet, romance writer and artist. His best-known romance, *News from Nowhere* (1891), is a utopian (*see* MORE, Thomas) fantasy about a future socialist commonwealth of England. His influence on the arts and crafts movement was immense, as was his influence on the development and character of British socialism.

**Morrison, Herbert Stanley**, Baron Morrison of Lambeth (1888–1965) English Labour politician. He became home secretary (1940–45) in CHURCHILL's World War II cabinet and is credited with having written much of the manifesto that took Labour to power after the war when he became leader of the House of Commons (1945–51).

**Morrison, Jim** (1943–71) American rock singer and songwriter. His band, The Doors, with sombre doom-laden songs such as "The End," became a huge cult after his death (from alcohol and drug abuse).

**Morton, Jelly Roll** [Ferdinand Joseph Lemott] (1885–1941) American jazz pianist, composer and bandleader. Regarded as one of the founders of New Orleans jazz, his band, the Red Hot Peppers, became one of the most popular jazz bands of the mid–1920s, between the ragtime and swing eras.

**Moseley, Henry Gwyn-Jeffries** (1887–1915) English physicist. His research in radioactivity using X-rays led to the discovery of what he called the "atomic numbers" of the elements.

**Mosley, Sir Oswald [Ernald]** (1896–1980) English Fascist leader. First elected to Parliament as a Conservative (1918–22), he became an Independent (1922–24), then a Labour MP (1924, 1929–31), and finally founder and leader of the British Union of Fascists (1932–36). The thuggery and demagoguery of his movement failed to attract much support beyond hoodlums and newspaper tycoons, and he was interned during World War II.

**Mossbauer, Rudolf Ludwig** (1929– ) German physicist. He shared the 1961 Nobel prize for physics with the American physicist **Robert Hofstadter** (1915– ) for his discovery of the "Mossbauer effect," involving gamma radiation in crystals.

**Mountbatten, Louis [Francis Victor Albert Nicholas]**, [1st Earl Mountbatten of Burma] (1900–79) British naval commander and statesman. The great-grandson of Queen Victoria and uncle of Prince PHILIP, he served with distinction in the Royal Navy during World War II, becoming Supreme Allied Commander in South-East Asia (1943–45). He was appointed viceroy of India (1947), and oversaw the transfer of power to the independent governments of India and Pakistan. Regarded as a strong influence on Prince CHARLES, he was murdered by an IRA bomb while sailing off Ireland.

**Moussorgsky, Modest** *see* **Mussorgsky, Modest**.

**Mozart, Wolfgang Amadeus** (1756–91) Austrian musician and composer. A child prodigy, he began composing at the age of five and performed before MARIA THERESA at the age of six. One of the most lyrical of all composers, his works include the operas *The Marriage of Figaro* (1786), *Don Giovanni* (1787), *Cosi fan tutte* (1790) and *The Magic Flute* (1791), over 40 symphonies, concertos, string quartets, sonatas, 18 masses, and the unfinished *Requiem*.

**Mugabe, Robert [Gabriel]** (1924– ) Zimbabwean statesman. He was imprisoned for ten years (1964–74) for his opposition to white rule in Rhodesia (as Zimbabwe then was), being released under Ian SMITH's amnesty of 1974. He became leader of the Zimbabwe African National Union and became prime minister (1980– ) following the end of white minority rule. A Roman Catholic and a Marxist, Mugabe merged his ruling party with the Zimbabwe African People's Union in 1988 to form a one-party state.

**Muir, John** (1838–1914) Scottish-born American environmentalist. Regarded as one of the main founders of environmentalism, his vigorous campaign for a national park in California led to the establishment of Yosemite National Park in 1890. His books include *My First Summer in the Sierra* (1911).

**Mujibur Rahman, Sheik** (1920–75) Bangladeshi politician. He became the first prime minister of Bangladesh (1972–75) following the bloody civil war and secession from Pakistan in 1972, and was subsequently elected president (1975). He assumed dictatorial powers and was assassinated during a military coup.

**Muldoon, Sir Robert [David]** (1921–92) New Zealand statesman. He became National Party prime minister (1975–84), and has held several important international posts, notably with the International Monetary Fund and the World Bank.

**Mulliken, Robert Sanderson** (1896–1986) American chemist and physicist. He was awarded the 1986 Nobel prize for chemistry for his work on molecular structure and on chemical bonding.

**Munch, Edvard** (1863–1944) Norwegian painter. An Expressionist, his works, e.g. *The Scream*, are noted for their strong use of primary colours and emotions.

**Munthe, Axel [Martin Frederik]** (1857–1949) Swedish physicist and psychiatrist. His autobiographical book, *The Story of San Michele* (1929), describing his experiences while practising medicine, became a world bestseller.

**Murdoch, [Keith] Rupert** (1931– ) Australian-born American newspaper tycoon. He inherited an Australian newspaper group from his father and subsequently expanded into Britain, where he turned the *Sun* into Britain's bestselling "sex and sleaze" tabloid. He later bought *The Times* and *The Sunday Times* and the publisher Collins, and established the satellite television network, Sky Television in 1989. The immense losses from the latter enterprise were alleviated by tapping into the reserves of other parts of his empire. His expansion into the US market from the late 1970s necessitated his acquisition of US citizenship in 1985.

**Murillo, Bartolomé Esteban** (1618–82) Spanish painter. From Seville, his early works were influenced by his older contemporary ZURBARÁN. He painted religious and genre scenes popular for their pretty sentimentality.

**Murray, John** (1778–1843) English publisher. His authors included Jane AUSTEN, Thomas MOORE, BYRON, CRABBE and COLERIDGE. He was renowned for his hospitality and generous assistance to authors.

and his premises became a common meeting ground for many of the literary figures of the day.

**Musgrave, Thea** (1928– ) Scottish composer. Her early works were often on Scottish themes, e.g. the chamber opera *The Abbott of Drimock* (1955). Later compositions, often in serial form, include choral works and concertos.

**Mussolini, Benito [Amilcare Andrea]** (1883–1945) Italian dictator. Originally a socialist, he founded his fascist "Blackshirt" party in 1919, and was elected to parliament in 1921, establishing himself as dictator ("Il Duce") in 1922 following a march on Rome. He formed the Axis with HITLER in 1937 and declared war on the Allies in 1940. He was deposed in 1943 and rescued by German paratroops, but was later executed by partisans.

**Mussorgsky** *or* **Moussorgsky, Modest Petrovich** (1839–81) Russian composer who gave up a military career to write music. A chronic alcoholic, he lived in a state of poverty and left much of his work unfinished. His best-known works include the opera *Boris Godunov* and the piano piece "Pictures at an Exhibition" (both 1874).

**Muzorewa, Bishop Abel** *see* **Smith, Ian**.

**Myrdal, [Karl] Gunnar** (1898–1987) Swedish economist. He shared the 1974 Nobel prize for economics with HAYEK, largely for his work on the application of economic theory to the economies of the Third World.

# N

**Nabokov, Vladimir** (1899–1977) Russian-born
American novelist, who wrote in both Russian and
English. His most famous novel is *Lolita* (1955), but
*Pale Fire* (1962) better demonstrates his gift for
narrative and sharp, ironic wit.

**Nader, Ralph** (1934– ) American lawyer and consumer protectionist. His book, *Unsafe at Any Speed*
(1965), which described the woeful standards of car
construction, became a best-seller and resulted in
government legislation on car safety regulations.
Nader and his followers ("Nader's Raiders") publicized many such cases of consumer abuse in the late
1960s and 70s.

**Nagy, Imre** (1896–1958) Hungarian statesman. He
fought with the Bolsheviks during the Russian civil
war and held various ministerial posts in the postwar communist Hungarian government. He was
appointed prime minister (1953–55), and was forced
to resign after attempting to liberalize communist
policies. He became premier again in 1956, and was
replaced by KÁDÁR after the Soviet invasion of that
year. Two years later, he was murdered by Russian
troops. His body was reburied in Budapest in 1989,
with full state honours.

**Namier, Sir Lewis Bernstein** (1888–1960) Polish-
born British historian. A specialist in 18th-century
history, his technique of analysing the minutiae of

the period's characters, events and institutions was enthusiastically followed by his students, resulting in what was called the "Namier school" of history. His works include *The Structure of Politics at the Accession of George III* (1929).

**Nansen, Fridtjof** (1861–1930) Norwegian explorer, scientist and statesman. He traversed Greenland (1888–89) and almost reached the North Pole in 1895, achieving a record latitude. He subsequently organized oceanographic expeditions, and was appointed commissioner for refugees (1920–22) by the League of Nations. He was awarded the 1922 Nobel Peace Prize for his humanitarian work.

**Napoleon I** [Napoleon Bonaparte] (1769–1821) emperor of France (1804–15). Born in Corsica, he became a general of brigade in 1793 and became commander of the French army in Italy in 1796. He became first consul after a coup in 1799. A brilliant and ruthless military leader, he established an empire throughout Europe, defeating coalitions of the other major powers. His invasion of Russia in 1812, and the murderous campaign in the Pyrenees against WELLINGTON's forces, led to the defeat of his armies at Leipzig in 1813 and Allied victory in 1814. Napoleon retired to Elba, from whence, in 1815, he came back to France, beginning the "Hundred Days" campaign which resulted in his defeat at Waterloo, and subsequent banishment to St Helena, where he died. He established the *Code Napoleon*, a system of law that remains largely intact in France.

**Nash, Paul** (1889–1946) English painter. He was an official war artist in both World Wars. He began his career as a landscape painter and flirted briefly with surrealism in the late 1930s. His paintings, which often have a visionary and occasionally abstract quality, include *Totes Meer* ("Dead Sea," 1940–41).

**Nashe, Thomas** (1567–1601) English writer of pamphlets and tracts on various subjects, which were usually satirical and often contain barbs directed against his many literary and religious enemies. He was particularly virulent against the Puritans, and was heavily involved in the so-called "Martin Marprelate" pamphlet war. He also wrote poems, plays, and a striking picaresque novel, *The Unfortunate Traveller* (1594).

**Nasser, Gamal Abdel** (1918–70) Egyptian soldier and statesman. He took a leading part in the coup that deposed **King Farouk** (1920–65) in 1952, and became prime minister in 1954. He became president (1956–70) and precipitated the Suez Crisis by nationalizing the Suez Canal (1956). The US refusal to endorse Britain and France's invasion of Egypt resulted in Nasser acquiring enormous prestige in the Third World. His rule was also marked by the construction of enormously wasteful civic projects, such as the construction of the Aswan Dam, and by two lost wars against Israel.

**Navarrete, Juan Fernandez,** (1526–79) Spanish painter. From 1568 he was court painter to PHILIP II of Spain. Out of the naturalistic Spanish tradition he evolved a unique style reflecting the monumental heroism of his Italian training. His later works, notably *The Burial of St Lawrence* (1579), anticipate the chiaroscuro effects of CARAVAGGIO.

**Navratilova, Martina** (1956– ) Czech-born American tennis player. Regarded as the leading female tennis player of her day, she defected to the US in

1975, becoming a citizen in 1981, and was world champion twice, 1980 and 1984.

**Needham, Joseph** (1900– ) English biochemist and historian. His works include several studies of the philosophy of science, e.g. *The Sceptical Biologist* (1929), and a huge survey of Chinese science, *Science and Civilisation in China* (1954–84).

**Nehru, Jawaharlal** (1889–1964) Indian nationalist leader and statesman. The son of the nationalist lawyer, **Motilal Nehru ("Pandit" Nehru)** (1861–1931), he joined the Indian National Congress in 1919 and was imprisoned many times in the 1930s and 40s for his nationalist views. He became the first prime minister of India (1947–64) following independence and the partition of the subcontinent into India and Pakistan. His daughter Indira GANDHI became prime minister in 1966.

**Neill, A[lexander] S[utherland]** (1883–1973) Scottish educationalist. He established his school at Summerhill in 1927 in order to demonstrate the success of his progressive and anti-authoritarian educational ideas. He wrote many books, e.g. *A Dominie's Log* (1916) promoting his methods.

**Nelson, Horatio**, [Viscount Nelson] (1758–1805) English naval commander. Renowned for his tactics, he became rear-admiral in 1797 after defeating the Spanish fleet at the battle of Cape St Vincent. The following year, he won a striking victory over the French at the battle of the Nile, and was killed by a sniper during his defeat of the French at Trafalgar in 1805. Widely revered by his officers and men, he had a long-standing affair with Emma HAMILTON.

**Nernst, Walther Hermann** (1864–1941) German

physical chemist. He was awarded the 1920 Nobel prize for chemistry for his proposal of the heat theorem, which was formulated as the third law of thermodynamics. The work includes out...

**Nero** (37–68) Roman emperor. He succeeded CLAUDIUS in 54, and soon became infamous for his debauchery and vanity. He has been accused by some of starting the great fire of 64, which destroyed much of Rome, the city subsequently being rebuilt to his specifications. Fearful of conspiracies, he had many people put to death or forced to kill themselves, including PETRONIUS and his old tutor SENECA. Nero committed suicide while awaiting capture by his soldiers.

**Neruda, Pablo** [Ricardo Neftali Reyes] (1904–73) Chilean poet and diplomat, noted for his political verse and for highly personal, cryptic lyrics. He was awarded the Nobel prize for literature in 1971.

**Nerval, Gérard de** (1808–55) French writer, whose life and work influenced both the Symbolist and Surrealist movements. His fantastic short stories, e.g. "Tales and Drolleries" (1852), were particularly influential, and his poem "El Desdichado" is quoted by T. S. ELIOT in *The Waste Land*. He was also noted for his eccentricities, which included taking his pet lobster for walks.

**Nervi, Pier Luigi** (1891–1979) Italian architect and engineer. An exponent of the virtues of reinforced concrete, his designs include the Pirelli skyscraper (1958) in Milan and San Francisco cathedral (1970).

**Newman, Cardinal John Henry** (1801–90) English theologian. An Anglican priest and member of the Oxford Movement, he converted to Roman Catholicism in 1845 and became a cardinal in 1879. His spirited defence of his faith, *Apologia pro Vita*

*Sua* (1864), in response to a critique by KINGSLEY, was much admired by believers and non-believers alike.

**Newman, Paul** (1925– ) American film actor. His films include *Hud* (1963), *Cool Hand Luke* (1967), *Butch Cassidy and the Sundance Kid* (1969) and *The Color of Money* (1986), the last earning him an Oscar. A political activist of the moderate left, he has also raised considerable sums of money for charity through sales of his own-name salad dressing.

**Newton, Sir Isaac** (1642–1727) English scientist, philosopher and mathematician. According to legend, observing the fall of an apple inspired him to discover the law of gravity. He also discovered (independently of LEIBNITZ) the differential calculus, the reflecting telescope, and devised the three laws of motion. A devout Christian, he also spent much time in Bible study. His works include *Principia Mathematica* (1687) and *Opticks* (1703).

**Nicholas II** (1868–1918) Russian tsar (1895–1917). A weak ruler, alternating between bursts of liberalization and repression, his authority was seriously weakened by Russia's defeat in the war with Japan (1904–5). He was deposed by the Bolsheviks in 1917, who later murdered him and his German-born wife, **Feodorovna Alexandra** (1872–1918) and their children.

**Nicholson, Ben** (1894–1982) English painter. Influenced both by Cubism and Wyndham LEWIS's Vorticism in his early career, he became one of Britain's leading abstract artists in the 1950s, receiving many honours from home and abroad.

**Nicholson, Jack** (1937– ) American film actor. One

of CORMAN's many protégés, he made many films before becoming a star with *Easy Rider* (1969). His later, often manic performances include *One Flew Over the Cuckoo's Nest* (1975), for which he won an Oscar, and *The Shining* (1980). He also won an Oscar for *Terms of Endearment* (1983).

**Nicklaus, Jack [William]** (1940– ) American golfer. One of the greatest golfers of all time, he won more major tournaments than any other player in history, including the British Open (1966, 1970, 1978) and the US Open (1967, 1972, 1980).

**Niebuhr, Helmut Richard** (1894–1962) American theologian. His highly influential works on Protestant theology, which call for a radical re-examination of the Christian's role in society, include *Radical Monotheism and Western Culture* (1960). His brother, **Reinhold Niebuhr** (1892–1971), was also a very influential Protestant theologian, whose works include *Moral Man and Immoral Society* (1932).

**Nielsen, Carl [August]** (1865–1931) Danish composer. The first prominent polytonal Danish composer, his works include six symphonies, two operas and concertos.

**Niemeyer, Oscar** (1907– ) Brazilian architect. Influenced by LE CORBUSIER, he designed many extravagantly modernist public buildings in Brazil, notably for the new capital, Brasilia, which were hailed as triumphs of modern architecture and planning. Many of his buildings are now in a state of terminal decay, due to a typically 20th-century failure to match building material and design to climate and environment.

**Niemöller, Martin** (1892–1984) German Lutheran

pastor. A submarine commander in World War I, he was ordained in 1924 and became an outspoken opponent of HITLER and Nazi ideology. He was imprisoned in concentration camps (1937–45), surviving the war despite an order from Hitler at its close for his execution. He became president of the World Council of Churches (1961–68) and a prominent pacifist.

**Nietzsche, Friedrich Wilhelm** (1844–1900) German philosopher and poet, whose works, e.g. *Thus Spake Zarathustra* (1866) and *Beyond Good and Evil* (1886), were highly critical of traditional morality and Christianity ("slave morality") and proclaimed the advent of the superman, the "splendid blonde beast." He has been very influential on many 20th-century writers, e,g, D. H. LAWRENCE, MANN, SARTRE and SHAW. He was claimed by HITLER to be a spiritual forebear of Nazism, but Nietzsche, who despised anti-Semitism, would have rejected this.

**Nijinsky, Vaslav** (1890–1950) Russian ballet dancer and choreographer. He became a protégé of DIAGHILEV, and is regarded as one of the greatest ballet dancers of all time. He choreographed STRAVINSKY's *Rite of Spring* (1913).

**Niven, David** [James David Graham Nevins] (1909–83) Scottish film actor. He arrived in Hollywood in 1935, where he was classed as "Anglo-Saxon Type No. 2008." After a variety of small parts, he appeared with his close friend, Errol FLYNN, in *The Charge of the Light Brigade* (1936). He returned to Britain after war was declared, and gave distinguished service in the army. He returned to Hollywood after the war, where he re-established himself as the model urbane Englishman. He published two highly entertaining volumes of autobiography, *The Moon's a Balloon* (1971) and *Bring on the Empty Horses* (1975) and, oddly, was never honoured by any British government.

**Nixon, Richard Milhous** (1913– ) American Republican politician. He very narrowly failed to defeat KENNEDY in the 1960 presidential election, and became the 37th president of the US in 1969. He became the first president to resign from office, in 1974, following the "Watergate" scandal (and was pardoned by Gerald FORD in 1974). A hate figure of the Left in the early 1970s, his reputation has since undergone considerable reassessment, with more stress being given to his ending of the Vietnam war and rapprochement with China, than to the sleazy aspects of his period in office.

**Nkrumah, Kwame** (1909–72) Ghanaian statesman. He became the first president of Ghana (1957–66) after independence. His rule became increasingly dictatorial and corrupt, and he was deposed while visiting China.

**Nolan, Sir Sidney [Robert]** (1917–92) Australian painter. His paintings draw heavily upon Australian history and folklore, e.g. his series of works based on the figure of the bushranger Ned Kelly.

**North, Frederick, 8th Lord North** [2nd Earl of Guilford] (1732–92) English statesman. As prime minister (1770–82) during the reign of George III, he implemented the king's policy that led to the loss of the American colony. After his resignation he was politically allied with Charles James Fox, previously his opponent.

**North, Sir Thomas** (*c.*1535–*c.*1601) English author, whose translations of works such as Plutarch's

*Lives* (1579) exerted a strong influence on Elizabethan writers, notably SHAKESPEARE, who seems to have largely derived his knowledge of ancient history from North.

**Nostradamus** [Michel de Notredame] (1503–66) French astrologer and physician. He published two books of cryptic prophecies in rhymed quatrains, called *Centuries* (1555–58), which enjoyed a huge vogue throughout Europe and were first published in English in 1672. His work is riddled with fruitful ambiguities and has no literary merit.

**Novalis** [Friedrich Leopold von Hardenberg] (1772–1801) German poet and novelist, who was called the "prophet of Romanticism" in Germany. He wrote two novels, both unfinished, the better known of which is *Heinrich von Ofterdingen* (1802), which involves a symbolic quest for a "blue flower". He also wrote mystical and love poetry, e.g. *Hymns to the Night* (1800), a series of laments on the death of his fiancée. He died of consumption.

**Novello, Ivor** [Ivor Novello Davies] (1893–1951) Welsh songwriter, composer and actor. His songs include "Keep the Home Fires Burning," which was hugely popular with British soldiers during World War I, and "We'll Gather Lilacs." His musicals include *Careless Rapture* (1936) and *The Dancing Years* (1939).

**Nuffield, William Richard Morris, 1st Viscount** (1877–1963) English car manufacturer and philanthropist. He began his business as a bicycle repair man in the early 1890s, and began building cars in the early 20th century. The first Morris car came out in 1913, and he developed a Henry FORD-like system of mass production of cars, notably the

Morris Oxford and the Morris Minor. He gave away a large part of his very large fortune to charitable foundations.

**Nureyev, Rudolf** (1939–93) Russian ballet dancer and choreographer (he defected in 1961 and became an Austrian citizen in 1982). Regarded as the successor to NIJINSKY, he formed a partnership with FONTEYN at the Royal Ballet in London in 1962, and has performed throughout the world. He has also appeared in several films, notably Ken RUSSELL's camp *Valentino* (1977).

**Nyerere, Julius [Kambarage]** (*c.*1922– ) Tanzanian statesman. He became president (1962–85) and negotiated the union of Tanganyika and Zanzibar (1964), which formed Tanzania. Widely regarded as Africa's leading statesman and notably austere in his personal life, he was brought up a Roman Catholic and became attracted to Marxism, which he combined with what he claimed were African values to produce his version of African socialism, which was based on the removal of about nine million peasants—by force—from their ancestral lands into collectives (*ujemaa*, "self-reliance," villages), where they were expected to produce food for the state. The project crashed. Nyerere gave up the presidency in 1985, but retained leadership of his party. His invasion of Uganda in 1978 brought AMIN's dictatorship to an end.

# O

**Obote, [Apollo] Milton** (1924– ) Ugandan politician. He became Uganda's first prime minister (1962–66) after independence, and became president (1966–71) after deposing King Mutesa II. Obote was in turn deposed by AMIN, and became president again (1980–85) after Amin's overthrow. He was deposed again in 1985, and was given political asylum in Zambia.

**O'Brien, Conor Cruise** (1917– ) Irish statesman, critic, historian and dramatist. He was HAMMARSKJÖLD's UN representative in Katanga during the Congo crisis of 1961, about which he wrote the play *Murderous Angels* (1968). A strong opponent of the IRA, he has been described as the "ORWELL of the Right." His other works include a collection of political and literary essays, *Passion and Cunning* (1988).

**O'Casey, Sean** (1880–1964) Irish dramatist. His three early plays, *The Shadow of a Gunman* (1923), *Juno and the Paycock* (1924) and *The Plough and the Stars* (1926) reflect the patriotism that followed the Easter Rising of 1916. Later plays, e.g. *The Silver Tassie* (1928), were less controversial.

**Ochoa, Severo** *see* **Kornberg, Arthur**.

**O'Connell, Daniel** (1775–1847) Irish nationalist. A lawyer, he founded the Catholic Association in 1823 to campaign for Roman Catholic emancipation and for repeal of the Union. In 1830, after the Catholic

Emancipation Act, he took his seat in the House of Commons as member of parliament for County Clare.

**Odets, Clifford** (1906–63) American dramatist. A committed socialist, his masterpiece is *Waiting for Lefty* (1935), a play about a taxi drivers' strike.

**Oistrakh, David Feodorovitch** (1908–74) Russian violinist. A widely admired virtuoso, he made several international tours in the 1950s and 60s. His son, **Igor Davidovitch Oistrakh** (1931– ), has also acquired an international reputation as a violinist.

**Oldenburg, Claes [Thure]** (1929– ) Swedish-born American sculptor. He became one of the leading pop art sculptors in the early 1960s, with his "giant objects," representations of foodstuffs such as hamburgers, and his "soft sculptures," e.g. *Soft Typewriter*.

**Olivier, Laurence [Kerr]**, [Baron Olivier of Brighton] (1907–89) English stage and film actor and director. Regarded as the leading British actor of the modern era, he played all the major SHAKESPEARE roles and became an international film star with *Wuthering Heights* (1939) and *Rebecca* (1939). He produced, directed and starred in films of *Henry V* (1945) and *Hamlet* (1948), and in the 1950s showed his astonishing versatility in roles such as the fading music hall comedian Archie Rice in OSBORNE's *The Entertainer* (1957). He was director of the National Theatre (1962–73). His second wife (of three) was Vivien LEIGH.

**O'Neill, Eugene [Gladstone]** (1888–1953) American dramatist. His early plays, e.g. *Beyond the Horizon* (1920) and *Desire Under the Elms* (1924) established him as one of America's finest dramatists. His greatest plays are *Mourning Becomes Electra* (1931), a tragedy based on Aeschylus's *Oresteia* trilogy, and *Long Day's Journey into Night* (1940–41), a study of family breakdown. He was awarded the Nobel prize for literature in 1936.

**Ono, Yoko** *see* **Lennon, John.**

**Oppenheimer, J[ulius] Robert** (1904–67) American nuclear physicist. He directed the Los Alamos atom bomb project (1943–45). He resigned from the project after the dropping of the bombs on Hiroshima and Nagasaki, and argued for cooperation with the USSR on the control of nuclear weapons. Long regarded as a security risk for his left-wing sympathies, his security clearance was revoked after his refusal to work on the hydrogen bomb.

**Orcagna** [Andrea di Cione Arcangelo] (*fl.*1343–68) Florentine painter, sculptor and architect. His masterpiece is the altarpiece *The Redeemer with the Madonna and Saints* (1354–7) in the church of Santa Maria Novella in Florence. Other important works attributed to him include the remains of *The Triumph of Death, Last Judgement* and *Hell* frescos in Santa Croce.

**Orff, Carl** (1895–1982) German composer. His best-known work is the popular *Carmina Burana* (1937), a "secular oratorio" based on medieval poems. His other works include the opera *Antigone* (1949).

**Ortega, Daniel** (1945– ) Nicaraguan politician. One of the leaders of the Sandinista resistance movement that overthrew Somoza's dictatorship in 1979, he became president of Nicaragua (1985–90). A charismatic figure who pursued socialist policies, Ortega became a notable hate figure for the REAGAN administration, which gave backing to the right-wing "Contra" forces in their guerrilla war against the Sandinistas. Ortega was succeeded as president by Violetta Chamorro, whose centrist party won the 1989 election.

**Ortega y Gasset, José** (1883–1955) Spanish philosopher. His best-known work is *The Revolt of the Masses* (1929), which argued that democracy in the modern era could easily lead to tyrannies of either the left or right. An opponent of FRANCO, he left Spain when Franco came to power, returning in 1946.

**Orwell, George** [Eric Arthur Blair] (1903–50) Indian-born English novelist and essayist. An upper-middle-class socialist, his first published work was *Down and Out in Paris and London* (1933), a description of his often gruesome experiences as a tramp. His other great nonfiction works are *The Road to Wigan Pier* (1937), a study of poverty in northern England, and *Homage to Catalonia* (1939), an account of his experiences with the Republican forces in the Spanish Civil War. His two greatest novels have become classics: *Animal Farm* (1945), a grim allegory of the history of the Soviet Union, and *Nineteen Eighty-Four* (1949), an even grimmer picture of a totalitarian world.

**Osborne, John** [James] (1929– ) English dramatist. His first play, *Look Back in Anger* (1956), gave its name to the "Angry Young Men," a group of young playwrights who replaced the drawing-room comedies of 1950s British theatre with realistic dramas of working-class life. The best known of his later plays are *The Entertainer* (1957), depicting Osborne's view of post-Imperial Britain, and *Luther*

(1961), a psychological study of Martin LUTHER.

**Oswald, Lee Harvey** (1939–63) American alleged assassin of President KENNEDY. He was arrested shortly after Kennedy's murder in Dallas in 1963, and was himself shot dead before he could come to trial by **Jack Ruby** (1911–64), a shady nightclub owner. Oswald repeatedly denied killing Kennedy, whose assassination has spawned many conspiracy theories, the likeliest of which seems to be that an unholy alliance of US Intelligence agents and right-wing Cubans used Oswald as a scapegoat.

**Otway, Thomas** (1652–85) English dramatist, remembered chiefly for one work, the great tragedy *Venice Preserved* (1682), a penetrating study of treason and loyalty.

**Ovid** [Publius Ovidius Naso] (43 BC–*c.* 17 AD) Roman poet. His sensual, witty love poems have always been admired, but his long narrative poem *Metamorphoses*, which describes myths in which characters change their forms, is of much greater significance. It was used as a source book for Greek and Roman mythology by many Renaissance writers, e.g. MARLOWE and SHAKESPEARE.

**Owen, David [Anthony Llewellyn]** (1938– ) English politician. Trained as a doctor, he was a Labour MP from 1966, becoming foreign secretary (1977–79) in CALLAGHAN's cabinet. He resigned from the Labour Party in 1981 to found the Social Democratic Party with JENKINS and others. He refused to accept the merger of the SDP with the Liberal Party in 1987, but dissolved the SDP in 1990 and announced his intention of quitting politics in 1991. He was made a life peer and worked as a UN peace negotiator in the Bosnian conflict of the early 1990s.

**Owen, Robert** (1771–1858) Welsh social reformer, educationalist and industrialist. He bought the New Lanark cotton mills and manufacturers from his father-in-law in 1799, and transformed the site into a model industrial community. He became one of the most influential social reformers of the century, and founded several cooperatives in Britain and America. His works include *A New View of Society* (1813) and *Revolution in Mind and Practice* (1849).

**Owens, Jesse** [James Cleveland Owens] (1913–80) American athlete. One of the finest athletes of his generation, he won four gold medals (for the 100 metres, 200 metres, long jump and 4 x 100 metres relay) in the dramatic setting of the 1936 Berlin Olympics. The great public annoyance this gave HITLER, who was visibly upset on film at this black man defeating his "Aryan" supermen, was much enjoyed worldwide.

**Padarewski, Ignace Jan** (1860–1941) Polish pianist, composer and statesman. Widely regarded as
the greatest pianist of his day, he served as prime
minister for ten months in 1919. He became president of the Polish government in exile in 1940.

**Pahlavi, Mohammed Reza** (1919–80) shah of Iran.
He succeeded his father in 1941 and gradually
established a dictatorship, funded by oil wealth and
guarded by his increasingly brutal "Savak" secret
police. He introduced some social reforms, notably
with regard to women's position in society, but was
forced to flee his country in 1979 as the fundamen-
talists led by KHOMEINI undermined his rule. He
died in Egypt.

**Paine, Thomas** (1737–1809) English-born American political theorist and pamphleteer. He travelled
to America (1774), where he wrote the highly influential pamphlet *Common Sense* (1776), which argued for American independence. The pamphlet's
lucid, expertly argued prose was recognized by
George WASHINGTON as being a significant contribution to the Revolution. Paine returned to England in
1787 and published a defence of democratic principles, *The Rights of Man* (1791–92), in reply to
Edmund BURKE's *Reflections on the Revolution in
France*. In danger of arrest (he was apparently
warned by William BLAKE to escape) he moved to

France where he was elected to the National Convention. He sided with the moderates, was imprisoned by ROBESPIERRE's faction, and released after 11 months, having narrowly escaped execution. He returned to America in 1802, where he alienated many of his former supporters (including BYRON) by publishing *The Age of Reason* (1793), a deist, no-holds-barred attack on Christian revelation.

**Paisley, Ian [Richard Kyle]** (1926– ) Northern Ireland Protestant clergyman and Unionist politician. He formed his Free Presbyterian Church in 1951, and was elected to parliament for North Antrim in 1970. A highly vocal opponent of Irish nationalism and Roman Catholicism, he is nonetheless regarded as a fair and impartial constituency MP.

**Palestrina, Giovanni Pierluigi da** (*c.*1525–1594) Italian composer. One of the greatest Renaissance composers, his compositions are practically all choral church works, including more than 90 masses, hymns, motets and madrigals.

**Palmer, Samuel** (1805–81) English painter and engraver. A painter of pastoral landscapes, *A Hilly Scene* (*c.*1826) is typical of his most intensely creative period, which was spent at Shoreham in Kent. He was a follower of BLAKE, who deeply influenced the visionary mysticism of his work.

**Pankhurst, Emmeline** (1858–1928) English suffragette and feminist. She and her daughter **Dame Christabel Harriette Pankhurst** (1880–1958) founded the Women's Social and Political Union in 1903, a campaigning organization for women's suffrage. With other suffragettes, Emmeline was frequently imprisoned then released under the "Cat and Mouse" act, a government device to avoid the publicity gained by the suffragette hunger strikes. She abandoned her campaign on the outbreak of World War I, and joined the Conservative Party in 1926. Her daughter **Sylvia Pankhurst** (1882–1960) was also a suffragette as well as a pacifist.

**Papandreou, Andreas George** (1919– ) Greek socialist politician. He lived in exile during the military dictatorship, returning to Greece in 1974. He became Greece's first socialist prime minister (1981–89), the last years of his administration being clouded by his public affair with a much younger woman and financial scandals.

**Pareto, Vilfredo** (1848–1923) Italian economist and sociologist. A highly influential economist, his work is regarded as anticipatory of both Fascist and modern welfare economics. His best-known work is *Mind and Society* (1916).

**Parker, Charlie** *or* **Bird** [Charles Christopher Parker] (1920–55) American jazz alto saxophonist. He became the leading exponent of "bop" jazz in the 1940s, and worked closely with Dizzy GILLESPIE. His life ended prematurely through drug and alcohol abuse.

**Parker, Dorothy [Rothschild]** (1893–1967) American journalist, poet and short-story writer, noted for her dry wit and sharply ironic epigrams and satires, many of which were first published in *New Yorker* magazine.

**Parmigiano** *or* **Parmigianino** [Girolamo Francesco Maria Mazzola] (1503–40) Italian Mannerist painter and etcher of precocious talent. His early works were influenced by RAPHAEL and DÜRER. An early masterpiece is *The Vision of St Jerome* (1526–27), and his best-known mature piece is *The Madonna of the Long Neck* (c.1535). His works were widely known through his engravings and etchings.

**Parnell, Charles Stewart** (1846–91) Irish politician. An ardent Home Ruler, he became member of parliament for Cork in 1880 and organized in parliament a masterly campaign of obstruction with the aim of disrupting Parliament and ultimately gaining Home Rule for Ireland. GLADSTONE became a convert to the cause, and in 1889 Parnell successfully sued *The Times* for printing the "Parnell forgeries," letters alleging that Parnell was in favour of violence to achieve his ends. In 1890, Parnell's career began to crumble after he was cited in a divorce case as the lover of "Kitty" O'Shea, whom he subsequently married.

**Parr, Catherine** *see* **Henry VIII**.

**Parsons, Talcott** (1902–79) American sociologist. His writings formed the basis for the functionalist school of sociology. His works include *The Structure of Social Action* (1937) and *Social Structure and Personality* (1964).

**Pascal, Blaise** (1623–62) French theologian, mathematician and physicist. A mathematical prodigy, he made important discoveries in hydraulics and invented a calculating machine. He later made ground-breaking contributions, with FERMAT, on probability theory. He became a convert to Jansenism in 1654 and published *Provincial Letters* (1656–57), a powerful attack on the Jansenists' main enemy, the Jesuits. His posthumously published *Pensées* (1669) contain illuminating and moving thoughts on religious faith.

**Pasolini, Pier Paolo** (1922–75) Italian film director, poet, novelist and critic. His films include *The Gospel According to St Matthew* (1964), a plain and much praised film version of the Gospel using amateur actors, and the bleakly decadent *Saló or the 120 Days of Sodom* (1975), the latter being described by one critic as a "terminal film in every sense." A Marxist in politics, he was an ardent consumer of casual homosexual sex, his last pick-up resulting in his murder.

**Pasternak, Boris [Leonidovich]** (1890–1960) Russian poet and novelist. A highly original and passionate lyric poet, his position under a regime that demanded safe verse praising its achievements forced him to turn to translation for a living; his translations of SHAKESPEARE's plays are still highly valued. His great novel *Dr Zhivago* was first published in Italy in 1958. He was awarded the Nobel prize for literature but was forced to decline it by the Soviet authorities.

**Pasteur, Louis** (1822–95) French chemist. He discovered that fermentation is due to the presence of microorganisms and developed the process of pasteurization to destroy the organisms. He also developed immunization processes against rabies and anthrax. He became first president of the Insitut Pasteur in 1888.

**Pater, Walter [Horatio]** (1839–94) English essayist and critic, noted for his flowery, ornate prose style, described by Oscar WILDE as "the holy writ of beauty". His essay on LEONARDO DA VINCI in *Studies in the History of the Renaissance* (1873) includes his famous description of the Mona Lisa as "older than the rocks among whom she sits."

**Patrick, Saint** (*fl.* 5th century) British missionary.

The son of a British Christian, his place of birth is disputed but may have been in Wales or in Dunbartonshire in Scotland. He was captured and sold into slavery in Ireland as a youth, escaped to France and became a monk. He then returned to Ireland as a missionary and converted many to his faith, and became the patron saint of Ireland. He wrote an autobiography in Latin.

**Patton, George S[mith]** (1885–1945) American general, nicknamed "Old Blood and Guts." A brilliant tank commander, he used his armoured divisions in the cavalry tradition, cutting enemy lines with great speed and daring. In World War II he commanded the Allied invasion of North Africa (1942–43), captured Sicily and Palermo (1943) and led the 3rd US army across France and Germany to the Czech border (1944–45). The film *Patton* (1970) gives a fair picture of the man.

**Paul VI** [Giovanni Battista Montini] (1897–1978) Italian pope. He was elected pope (1963–78) in succession to JOHN XXIII, and continued the trend towards reforms instituted by his predecessor and the Second Vatican Council. His encyclical *Humanae Vitae* (1968), however, reaffirmed the total opposition of the Church towards abortion and "artificial" methods of contraception.

**Paul, Saint** (died *c*.67 AD) Christian apostle and missionary to the Gentiles. A pharisee, he was a notable persecutor of Christians before his "Damascus Road" conversion, after which he became an equally zealous propagator of the faith. Paul's journeys and the arguments raging among the early Christians—and the debate between Paul and PETER, which led to Paul's proselytising among the

Gentiles—are described in the Book of Acts. Many of the Epistles in the New Testament are his. According to tradition, he was executed during the reign of NERO.

**Pauli, Wolfgang** (1900–58) Austrian-born American physicist. He was awarded the 1945 Nobel prize for physics for his discovery of the "exclusion principle" in 1924, and postulated the existence of the neutrino (later established by FERMI).

**Pauling, Linus Carl** (1901– ) American chemist. He was awarded the 1954 Nobel prize for physics for his research into chemical bonding and molecular structure, and the 1962 Nobel Peace Prize for his criticisms of nuclear testing and deterrence. He has published widely in many scientific fields. His book *Vitamin C and the Common Cold* (1970) recommends large daily doses of Vitamin C to build protection against colds.

**Pavarotti, Luciano** (1935– ) Italian tenor. Regarded as one of the most powerful tenor singers of the modern era, and probably the heaviest, he became a leading opera singer and a very popular concert performer in the late 1960s. His recording of "Nessun Dorma," from PUCCINI's opera *Turandot*, became a massive hit after being used as the theme for the 1990 World Cup broadcasts.

**Pavlov, Ivan Petrovich** (1849–1936) Russian physiologist. He was awarded the 1904 Nobel prize for physiology or medicine for his work on the physiology of digestion, and conducted experiments on the conditioning of reflexes, e.g. his conditioning of dogs to salivate in response to metronomes.

**Pavlova, Anna** (1885–1931) Russian ballerina. FOKINE choreographed *The Dying Swan* for her. She also worked with DIAGHILEV, and became one of the most famous ballerinas in the world.

**Peacock, Thomas Love** (1785–1866) English novelist, essayist and poet. His highly entertaining satirical novels consist mostly of ingeniously witty dialogue between characters modelled on Peacock's friends and contemporaries, e.g. BYRON, COLERIDGE and SHELLEY. The novels include *Headlong Hall* (1816), *Nightmare Abbey* (1818), and *Crotchet Castle* (1831).

**Peale, Charles Willson** (1741–1827) American painter. He trained in London under Benjamin WEST, and from 1775 lived in Philadelphia where he painted neoclassical portraits. His works include *The Exhumation of the Mastodon* (1806). Five of his 17 children also became artists.

**Pears, Sir Peter** (1910–86) English tenor. He formed a lifelong personal and professional partnership with Benjamin BRITTEN, whose tenor opera roles, e.g. *Peter Grimes* (1945), were written for Pears, as were several song cycles. He co-founded the Aldeburgh Festival (1948) with Britten.

**Pearse, Patrick** *or* **Padraic [Henry]** (1879–1916) Irish revolutionary. A prominent spokesman for the Gaelic cultural revival, he joined the Irish Revolutionary Brotherhood in 1915 and was executed for his part in the 1916 Easter Rising.

**Pearson, Lester B[owles]** (1897–1972) Canadian Liberal statesman. He became prime minister (1963-68) and was awarded the 1957 Nobel Peace Prize for his role as mediator during the Suez Crisis.

**Peary, Robert Edwin** (1856–1920) American naval commander and Arctic explorer. He is credited with being the first man to reach the North Pole (1909)

**Peel, Sir Robert** (1788–1850) British statesman. He became Home Secretary in 1828 and founded the Metropolitan police (nicknamed "Peelers" or "bobbies"). He became prime minister twice (1834–35, 1841–6). By his last year of office, he had accepted and promoted the free-trade principles that disrupted the Tory party.

**Peierls, Sir Rudolf Ernst** (1907– ) German-born British physicist. With Otto FRISCH, he demonstrated the feasibility of an atom bomb during World War II. He joined the Los Alamos project in 1943.

**Pelé** [Edson Arantes do Nascimento] (1940– ) Brazilian footballer. An inside forward, he is universally recognized as one of the most skilful and entertaining soccer players of all time. He scored over a thousand goals in his professional career.

**Pepys, Samuel** (1633–1703) English diarist and Admiralty official. His diary (written in code) was first published in 1825. The full uncensored version was published in 11 volumes (1970–83), and includes much fascinating detail of life in 17th-century London.

**Percy, Sir Henry** *see* **Henry IV**.

**Perón, Juan Domingo** (1895–1974) Argentinian dictator. Influenced by MUSSOLINI and (to a lesser extent) HITLER, Perón became president (1946–55) through a shrewd mixture of social reform and demagogic appeals to the poor. He was deposed by the army in 1955, and lived in exile in Spain, and was re-elected president (1973–74) on his return. His success was based to a large extent on his first wife, **Eva [Duarte] Perón** (1919–52), an ex-actress nicknamed "Evita," who was an even more skilful player of the populist card and is still venerated in Argentina. His second wife, **Isabelita Perón** [Maria Estela Martinez de Perón] (1931– ), a dancer, was vice-president to her husband (1973–74) and president (1974–76) until ousted by a military coup and imprisoned for five years.

**Perry, Fred[erick John]** (1909– ) English-born American tennis and table-tennis player. He became the world champion table-tennis player in 1929, and became one of the most successful lawn tennis players of the 1930s, winning every major tournament.

**Perugino, Pietro** [Pietro Vannucci] (*c*.1445–1523) Italian painter, possibly a contemporary of LEONARDO DA VINCI in VERROCCHIO's studio in Florence. He took his name from his native Perugia, where he mainly worked. He painted *The Giving of the Keys to St Peter* fresco (*c*.1481) in the Sistine Chapel, Rome, and also produced portraits and altarpieces in the course of his career.

**Perutz, Max Ferdinand** *see* **Kendrew, Sir John Cowdery**.

**Pétain, Henri Philippe Omer** (1856–1951) French soldier and statesman. He was appointed marshal of France in 1918 in recognition of his generalship during World War I, particularly his stubborn defence ("They Shall Not Pass") of Verdun (1916). He became head of the collaborationist Vichy government (1940–44) and was sentenced to death for treason at the end of World War II (later commuted to life imprisonment).

**Peter, Saint** (died *c*.67 AD) Disciple of JESUS CHRIST and Christian apostle. A fisherman, he became one of Jesus's leading disciples and played an equally prominent role in establishing Christianity after the crucifixion. The Book of Acts describes how, at Antioch, he disputed with PAUL the direction of the ministry of the growing church, and is regarded by Roman Catholics as the first pope. He is believed to have been martyred in Rome.

**Peterson, Oscar [Emmanuel]** (1925– ) Canadian jazz pianist and composer. A virtuoso pianist in the mode of his friend Art TATUM, his Oscar Peterson Trio became one of the best-known small jazz groups of the 1950s.

**Petit, Roland** (1924– ) French dancer and choreographer. His innovative work, blending realism with exuberant fantasy, has been highly influential on contemporary dance. His works include a *Carmen* (1949) and dance sequences in several US films, e.g. *Daddy Longlegs* (1955, starring Fred ASTAIRE).

**Petrarch** [Francesco Petrarca] (1304–74) Italian lyric poet and humanist. His love poems are sonnets, madrigals and songs in praise of a woman he called "Laura" (whose identity is unknown), and were strongly influential on other poets. His work popularized the sonnet form, subsequently used to great effect by SHAKESPEARE, and he is recognized as the first major poet of the Renaissance.

**Petronius** [Gaius Petronius Arbiter] (d. c.66 AD) Roman courtier and satirist. His great satirical novel, the *Satyricon*, gives a unique and vivid portrait of the seamy side of Roman life; salacious, funny, and occasionally moving, the work is an important landmark in Western literature. The "Trimalchio's Banquet" scene in the book gave T. S. ELIOT the epigraph for *The Waste Land*. Petronius was ordered to commit suicide by NERO.

**Philby, Kim** [Harold Adrian Russell Philby] (1911–
88) English diplomat, journalist and secret-service
double agent. The most prominent of the Cambridge
School of Treason, he became a Soviet agent in 1933.
He was recruited to the British Secret Service in
1940, and became head of anti-communist espionage (1944–46). He worked in the British embassy
in Washington DC (1949–51) but was asked to leave
by the CIA because of his "previous" communist
sympathies. He worked as a foreign correspondent
(1956–63) before fleeing to the USSR, where he
published *My Silent War* in 1968.

**Philip, Prince**, [Duke of Edinburgh] (1921– ) Greek-
born British naval officer and prince consort. The
nephew of MOUNTBATTEN, he married the then Princes
ELIZABETH in 1947.

**Philip II** (1527–98) king of Spain. He inherited the
Spanish throne in 1556, was the husband (1554–58)
of MARY I and became Philip I of Portugal (1580–98).
A devout Roman Catholic, he strongly supported
the Counter-Reformation and launched the disastrous Armada invasion against ELIZABETH I in 1588.

**Philips, Katherine** (1631–64) English poet. Her
work was much admired by her contemporaries, e.g.
DRYDEN, among whom she was known as the "Match-
less Orinda." Her collected poems were issued posthumously in 1667.

**Piaf, Edith** [Edith Giovanna Gassion] (1915–63)
French singer and songwriter. Nicknamed "Little
Sparrow" for her small size and frail appearance,
her songs, nostalgic and romantic, include the well-
known *"Non, je ne regrette rien."* She died of drug
and alcohol abuse.

**Piaget, Jean** (1896–1980) Swiss psychologist. His

studies of children's intelligence and perception, notably his research on cognitive functions and development, were highly influential on modern educationalists. His works include *The Child's Conception of the World* (1926).

**Picasso, Pablo** (1881–1973) Spanish painter and sculptor. Regarded as the most influential artist of the modern era, he moved to Paris in 1901, where, with BRAQUE, he was the founder of Cubism. His "blue period" (1901–4) works include *The Blue Room* (1901); Cubist works include *Les Demoiselles d'Avignon* (1906–7). He designed costumes and scenery for DIAGHILEV from 1917, exhibited with the surrealists in the mid–1920s, and created his strongest and perhaps best-known image *Guernica* (1937) in response to the fascist bombing of that Basque town during the Spanish Civil War.

**Pickford, Mary** [Gladys Mary Smith] (1893–1979) Canadian-born American film star. She was dubbed "The World's Sweetheart" after the enormous success of such silent films as *Rebecca of Sunnybrook Farm* (1917), and co-founded the United Artists film studio (1919) with Charlie CHAPLIN and D. W. GRIFFITH. Her second husband (1920–35) was Douglas FAIRBANKS.

**Piero della Francesca** (c.1416–92) Italian early Renaissance painter. While working in Florence he was deeply influenced by MASACCIO, who inspired the monumental grandeur of his subsequent works, e.g. *The Compassionate Madonna* (1445). From c.1460 he was working at the Urbino court, where he painted some of his finest works, e.g. *The History of the True Cross* frescos (c.1452–64) and *The Resurrection* (c.1460).

**Piero di Cosimo** (1462–1521) Florentine painter. He painted scenes featuring mythological creatures and animals depicted in a gentle, sympathetic manner. His works include *Death of Procris* and *Mythological Subject*.

**Piggott, Lester [Keith]** (1935– ) English jockey. Regarded as one of the finest flat-racing jockeys of modern times, he won the Derby nine times. He was jailed (1987–88) for tax evasion.

**Pilsudski, Józef Klemens** (1867–1935) Polish soldier and statesman. He became provisional president (1918–21) and, as marshal of Poland (1919–21), held the Bolshevik army's advance into Polish territory in 1920. He was prime minister (1926–28, 1930).

**Pindar** (*c.*518–*c.*438 BC) Greek lyric poet, noted for his odes (based on the choral odes of Greek drama) celebrating victories in the Greek games. His carefully constructed, elaborate poems became influential in late-17th century England, when he was (mistakenly) seen as a much freer poet than HORACE.

**Pinochet [Ugarte], Augusto** (1915– ) Chilean general and dictator. He led the 1973 coup that deposed ALLENDE and became president (1974–90). He ruthlessly suppressed dissent and instituted monetarist economic polities. In 1988, he asked for a public mandate in a plebiscite and was firmly defeated. Pinochet retired from the presidency in 1990, while retaining his military command.

**Pinter, Harold** (1930– ) English dramatist, known for his halting, menacing dialogue and sinister pauses in such plays as *The Birthday Party* (1958) and *The Caretaker* (1960). He has also written several screenplays.

**Piper, John** (1903–92) English artist. His works include a highly acclaimed series of paintings of war-damaged buildings during his period as an official war artist during World War II and the designs for Coventry Cathedral's stained glass. His books include *British Romantic Artists* (1942) and *Buildings and Prospects* (1949).

**Pirandello, Luigi** (1867–1936) Italian dramatist and novelist. His two best-known plays are *Six Characters in Search of an Author* (1921) and *Henry IV* (1922), both of which question theatrical conventions. He was awarded the Nobel prize for literature in 1934.

**Piranesi, Giovanni Battista** (1720–78) Italian artist. He worked in Rome and Venice on frescos, since destroyed, in the International Gothic style. His decorative and detailed works are rich in colour and texture, with excellent draughtsmanship. His works include the haunting painting *The Vision of St Eustace*.

**Pisano, Giovanni** (c. 1245–c. 1314) Pisan sculptor. One of the leading sculptors of his time, his works are expressive and elegant in the Gothic tradition. Most notable are the high-relief facades for the Cathedral at Siena (1248–96) and the baptistry at Pisa (c. 1295). His father **Nicola Pisano** (c. 1220–c. 1284) was also a notable sculptor and instrumental in the development of Christian art towards Roman rather than Gothic influences.

**Pissarro, Camille** (1830–1903) West Indian-born French Impressionist painter. He moved to Paris in 1855, where he met MONET. He was in London from 1870–1 and was influenced by both CONSTABLE and TURNER, as in *Lower Norwood, Snow Scene* (1870).

He helped organize and exhibited in all eight Impressionist exhibitions, a typical work being *Red Roof* (1887). His eldest son **Lucien** (1863–1944) was also a painter in the neo-Impressionist style.

**Pitt, William** [Pitt the Elder, 1st Earl of Chatham] (1707–88) English statesman. He became first minister in 1756, resigning briefly the following year in the face of the king's opposition to his foreign policy, only to be reinstated in a few months and to lead Britain to victory in the Seven Years War (1756–63) with France. He resigned in 1761, and served again 1766–68. His son **William Pitt** (the Younger) (1759–1806) became prime minister in 1783 aged twenty-four, instituted important social and political reforms, worked for good relations with America, and formed a European coalition against Napoleon.

**Pius XII** [Eugenio Pacelli] (1876–1958) Italian pope. He preserved the neutrality of the Church during World War II, in which he maintained diplomatic relations with both Axis and Allies. He pursued a strong anti-communist policy after the war.

**Planck, Max** [Karl Ernst Ludwig] (1858–1947) German physicist. He formulated the quantum theory and was awarded the 1918 Nobel prize for physics.

**Plath, Sylvia** (1932–63) American poet and novelist. She published only two books in her lifetime: *Colossus* (1960), a collection of poems, and a semi-autobiographical novel, *The Bell Jar*. She was married to Ted HUGHES, and committed suicide.

**Plato** (*c*.427–*c*.347 BC) Greek philosopher, who is regarded as the main founder of Western philosophy. Taught by SOCRATES, Plato was in turn ARISTOTLE's tutor. His "Theory of Forms," in which objects

as we perceive them are distinguished from the idea
of the object, have had a strong influence on idealist
philosophy. Plato's speculations are contained in
dialogue form in several works, notably the *Sympo-
sium, Phaedo* and *The Republic*, the last being an
examination of the principles of good government.

**Plautus, Titus Maccius** (*c*.254–*c*.184 BC) Roman
dramatist. His comedies were often adaptations of
lost originals by the Greek dramatist **Menander**
(*c*.342–*c*.292). He wrote about 130 plays, of which 20
are extant, featuring such stock characters as the
wise servant who knows more than his master
(WODEHOUSE's Jeeves is a distant descendant). Many
of Plautus's plots, adaptations themselves, have
been adapted by others (SHAKESPEARE's *Comedy of
Errors* is an adaptation of a Plautus play).

**Poe, Edgar Allan** (1809–49) American short-story
writer, poet and critic. His macabre, highly Gothic
horror stories, e.g. *Tales of the Grotesque and Ara-
besque* (1839), are studies in pathological obsession
with a strong element of sadism, and feature themes
such as premature burial and necrophilia. The best
of the stories, e.g. "The Masque of the Red Death,"
have retained their power, as have the best of his
poems, e.g. "The Raven." His detective stories, e.g.
"The Murders in the Rue Morgue," are influential
early examples of the form.

**Pollaiuolo, Antonio del** (*c*.1431–98) Florentine artist. He ran a workshop with his brother **Piero
Pollaiuolo** (*c*.1441–96), and they collaborated on
many works, including *The Martyrdom of St Sebastian* (1475). Their designs for papal tombs influenced subsequent artists, notably MICHELANGELO.

**Pollock, [Paul] Jackson** (1912–56) American

painter. He became the leading exponent of action painting, a development of Abstract Expressionism, in the late 1940s. Pollock's action paintings consisted of pinned-down canvases covered in paint randomly scattered all over them.

**Pol Pot** *or* **Saloth Sar** [Kompong Thom] (1929– ) Cambodian Communist politician. He led the Communist Khmer Rouge forces that overthrew the Cambodian government in 1976, after which he became prime minister. His pro-Chinese government then instituted a fearful Maoist dictatorship that cost the lives of up to three million people. The Khmer Rouge regime was overthrown by the Russian-backed Vietnamese invasion of 1979, but subsequently fought a guerrilla campaign against the Vietnamese puppet regime, with some success. Most governments in the world gave reluctant recognition to the Khmer Rouge as the legitimate government of Cambodia. Pol Pot's official "retirement" in 1985 is generally regarded as an attempt at sanitizing the Khmer Rouge image.

**Pompey** *see* **Caesar, Julius**.

**Pompidou, Georges [Jean Raymond]** (1911–74) French statesman. He joined DE GAULLE's staff in 1944 and became Gaullist prime minister (1962–68). He was dismissed in 1968 by de Gaulle following the May student riots in Paris. After de Gaulle resigned, Pompidou was elected president (1969–74).

**Pontormo** [Jacopo Carrucci] (1494–1557) Italian painter, who took his name from his native village in Tuscany. He trained under PIERO DI COSIMO, and established his Mannerist style with *Joseph in Egypt* (*c*.1515). His works are characterized by vivid colours and a graceful dynamism conveying strong spirituality and grandeur.

**Pope, Alexander** (1688–1744) English poet. His poetry is generally divided into three (rather arbitrary) periods: an early period in which he made his name as a poet with, especially, the *Essay on Criticism* (1711), a poetic manifesto of neoclassical principles, the nature poems such as *Windsor Forest* (1713), a mock-heroic love poem, *The Rape of the Lock* (1714), designed to reunite two feuding upper-class Roman Catholic families (Pope was himself a Catholic); a middle period in which his translations of HOMER's *Iliad* (1720) and his edition of SHAKESPEARE made him rich; a third period spent at Twickenham where he completed his great satire *The Dunciad* (1728) and philosophical poems such as *An Essay on Man* (1733–34). Pope's reputation suffered a partial eclipse in the 19th century (although BYRON was a vigorous defender). His mastery of the rhymed couplet, his deadly satire and gift for sustaining metaphor place him as one of the greatest English poets.

**Popper, Sir Karl [Raimund]** (1902– ) Austrian-born British philosopher. His book *The Logic of Scientific Discovery* (1934) proposed "falsifiability" as the criterion by which to judge whether or not a particular proposition can be said to be scientific or not, and described psychoanalysis and Marxism as examples of non-falsifiable "pseudosciences." His books, *The Open Society and its Enemies* (1945) and *The Poverty of Historicism* (1957), examine the totalitarian implications of political thought from Plato to Marx.

**Porter, Cole [Albert]** (1893–1964) American songwriter and composer. His highly popular songs, much admired for their wit and lyricism, include "Let's Do It," "Begin the Beguine," and "Night and Day."

**Poulenc, Francis** (1899–1963) French composer. A member of *"Les Six,"* he is particularly noted for his his settings of verses from poets such as Apollinaire (*see* DELAUNAY). Other works include chamber music and sacred choral pieces.

**Pound, Ezra [Weston Loomis]** (1885–1972) American poet and critic. Notable poetry volumes include *Quia Pauper Amaris* (1919) and the unfinished *Cantos* (1925–70). A generous supporter of younger writers, e.g. T. S. ELIOT, HEMINGWAY, he lived in Italy from 1925 and broadcast propaganda against the Allies during World War II. He was committed to a US mental asylum after the war until 1958, when he returned to Italy.

**Poussin, Nicolas** (1594–1665) French painter. He studied antique art in Rome and was influenced by TITIAN and VERONESE, e.g. *The Poet's Inspiration* (*c.*1628). During the 1630s his style became more classical, but his preference was for easel paintings rather than large-scale decorative works. *The Holy Family on the Steps* (1648) marks his achievement of a pure, harmonious classical order.

**Powell, [John] Enoch** (1912– ) English Conservative politician. A professor of Greek at Sydney University when he was 25, he rose from private to brigadier in the course of World War II and was elected to parliament in 1950. An outspoken opponent of immigration into Britain and of the Common Market, he refused to stand for the Conservatives in 1974, advising his supporters to vote Labour, a gesture which some observers credit with giving Labour victory. He was an Ulster Unionist MP (1974–87).

**Powell, Michael** (1905–90) English film producer and director. With the screenwriter **Emeric Pressburger** (1902–88), he made several films that have subsequently been hailed as important works, e.g. *The Life and Death of Colonel Blimp* (1943), *I Know Where I'm Going* (1945), and *The Red Shoes* (1948).

**Presley, Elvis [Aaron]** (1935–77) American rock singer. He became one of the most popular (and controversial) singers in the world in the mid–1950s, with his interpretation of songs such as "Blue Suede Shoes" and "Hound Dog." Condemned by some for the blatant sexual charge in his performances, he became universally recognized as a great popular singer, and an outstanding interpreter of ballads. He died of drug and alcohol abuse, compounded by obesity. He starred in the critically acclaimed western *Flaming Star* (1960).

**Pressburger, Emeric** *see* **Powell, Michael.**

**Priestley, J[ohn] B[oynton]** (1894–1984) English novelist and dramatist. His huge output includes the novel *The Good Companions* (1929) and the plays, *Time and the Conways* (1937) and *An Inspector Calls* (1947). During World War II he made morale-raising broadcasts, which made him one of the best-known literary figures of the time.

**Prior, Matthew** (1664–1721) English poet, diplomat and spy. His first important work, *The Hind and Panther Transvers'd* (1687), was a satire on DRYDEN's defence of Roman Catholicism. Much of Prior's subsequent life was spent immersed in the murky waters of political intrigue and espionage, and earned him a year in jail. The best of his poems are light, mock-serious lyrics, such as "Jinny the Just."

**Profumo, John Dennis** (1915– ) English Conservative politician. He was an MP (1940–63) and secretary of state for war (1960–63), but resigned after admitting misleading the House of Commons about his affair with **Christine Keeler** (1942– ), who was also sexually involved with a Russian diplomat. He became involved with charitable work, for which he was awarded a CBE (1976)

**Prokofiev, Sergei Sergeyevich** (1891–1953) Russian composer and pianist. He left Russia in 1918 and returned in 1936 (he died on the same day as STALIN). His works include seven symphonies, the ballets *Romeo and Juliet* (1935) and *Cinderella* (1944), piano and violin concertos, and the well-known orchestral "fairy tale," *Peter and the Wolf* (1936).

**Psalmanazar, George** (*c.*1679–1763) French-born English literary hoaxer. Little is known for certain of his origins: he arrived in London in 1703, claiming to be a "Formosan", for which country he invented a language and published a travel guide. After years as a hack writer, he renounced his imposture in 1728 and became a highly respected literary figure. Dr JOHNSON called him "the best man he ever knew."

**Puccini, Giacomo** (1858–1924) Italian composer. His operas, e.g. *La Bohème* (1896), *Tosca* (1900) and *Madama Butterfly* (1904), are regarded as the last great lyrical and dramatic works in the tradition of Italian opera.

**Purcell, Henry** (*c.*1659–95) English composer. His works include incidental music for the theatre, songs, church music and six operas, notably *Dido and Aeneas* (1689) and *The Fairy Queen* (1692).

**Pushkin, Aleksandr Sergeyevich** (1799–1837) Russian poet, novelist and dramatist. Widely regarded as Russia's greatest poet, the best known of his works are the historical tragedy *Boris Gudonov* (1825), the verse novel *Eugene Onegin* (1823–31), and the macabre short story "The Queen of Spades." His life ended prematurely in a duel.

**Qaddafi, Moammar al-** *see* **Gaddafi, Moammar al-**.

**Quant, Mary** (1934– ) English fashion designer. Her most famous design was the miniskirt, which became the symbol of "swinging sixties" London.

**Quayle, Sir [John] Anthony** (1913–89) English actor and director. He worked with the Shakespeare Memorial Theatre (1948–56, now the Royal Shakespeare Company), helping to establish its international standing. He appeared in several films, e.g. *Woman in a Dressing Gown* (1957) and *The Guns of Navarone* (1961), but was principally a stage actor, founding his own classical touring company, Compass (1982).

**Quayle, [James] Dan[forth]** (1947– ) American Republican politician. Elected a congressman for Indiana (1977) and senator (1981), BUSH selected him as his presidential running mate (1988) and he was elected vice-president of the USA (1989–93).

**Quine, Willard van Orman** (1908– ) American philosopher and logician. Noted for his criticisms of empiricism, his works include *Set Theory and its Logic* (1963) and *Word and Object* (1961).

**Quisling, Vidkun** (1887–1945) Norwegian Fascist leader. He was installed as prime minister (1942–45) by the Nazis, and was executed for treason after the war. His name is now used to define any person who aids an occupying power to establish its rule.

# R

**Rabelais, François** (c.1494–c.1553) French monk, physician and satirist, noted for his huge, rambling and often licentious prose fantasy *Gargantua and Pantagruel* (1553–62), which includes many fascinating insights into the intellectual currents of the age.

**Rachmaninov, Sergei** (1873–1943) Russian composer and pianist. Influenced by Tchaikovsky, his music was very much in the 19th-century romantic tradition. His works include three symphonies, four piano concertos, the *Rhapsody on a Theme by Paganini* (1934) and many songs.

**Racine, Jean** (1639–99) French dramatist, regarded as the finest of the French tragedians. Several of his plays, e.g. *Andromache* (1667) and *Phaedra* (1677), have been performed in English translations from the late 17th century onwards, but the only productions that have achieved real popularity on the British and American stage are those that have parted radically from Racine's strict neoclassical principles. The full impact of his powerfully restrained language can only be appreciated in French.

**Radcliffe, Mrs Ann** (1764–1823) English novelist, whose Gothic novels. e.g. *A Sicilian Romance* (1790) and *The Mysteries of Udolpho*, were enormously popular in their day.

**Radhakrishnan, Sir Sarvepalli** (1888–1975) Indian philosopher and statesman. His works, which stress the similarities between Western and Hindu culture, include *The Hindu View of Life* (1926) and *An Idealist View of Life* (1932).

**Raeburn, Sir Henry** (1756–1823) Scottish painter. He settled in Edinburgh in 1787, where he established himself as a society portraitist and held a position in Scotland similar to that of REYNOLDS in England. He worked directly onto the canvas, without preliminary studies or sketches, in a bold, original style that occasionally lapsed into superficiality but often retained a freshness, e.g. *The MacNab* (c.1803–13). Another notable work is the delightful *Reverend Walker skating* (c.1784).

**Raleigh, Sir Walter** (1552–1618) English courtier, poet and explorer. He became a favourite of ELIZABETH I after returning from a punitive expedition to punish Irish rebels in 1580, and organized unsuccessful attempts to colonize Virginia with English settlers in the 1580s. In 1595, he travelled to the Orinoco, described in *The Discovery of Guiana*, and participated in the English raid on Cadiz in 1596. He was imprisoned in The Tower after JAMES VI's succession, was released to search for treasure on the Orinoco in 1616, and was executed on his return.

**Raman, Sir Chandrasekhara Venkata** (1888–1970) Indian physicist. He was awarded the 1930 Nobel prize for physics for his discovery of the Raman effect during his researches into the diffusion of light.

**Ramanujan, Srinivasa** (1887–1920) Indian mathematician. A self-taught prodigy with considerable intuitive powers, he sent a large number of theorems to Godfrey HARDY, who arranged for him to study at Cambridge University. He became the first Indian to be elected a Fellow of the Royal Society (1919).

**Rambert, Dame Marie** [Cyvia Rambam] (1888–1982) Polish-born British ballet dancer, teacher and producer. After working with DIAGHILEV and NIJINSKY, she settled in Britain in 1917. She formed the Ballet Club in 1931, which, renamed the Ballet Rambert in 1935, became the most influential ballet company in Britain.

**Ramphal, Sir Shridath Surrendranath, "Sonny"** (1928– ) Guyanan statesman. As secretary-general of the Commonwealth (1975–89), he took an active and influential role in world affairs.

**Ramsay, Allan** (1713–84) Scottish painter. The son of the poet **Allan Ramsay** (c.1685–1758), he settled in London in 1737, where he became a popular portrait painter. His works include *The Artist's Wife* (c.1755) and the coronation portrait of *George III*.

**Ramsey, Sir Alf[red]** (1922– ) English footballer and manager of the England national team that won the World Cup in 1966.

**Ranjitsinhji [Vibhaji], Prince [Kumar Shri]** (1872–1933) Indian maharajah and cricketer, nicknamed the "Black Prince" of cricket, he batted for Sussex (with C. B. FRY) and England. After service in World War I commanding Indian troops, he became maharajah of Nawanagar in 1918, and was noted for his progressive rule.

**Raphael** [Raffaello Sanzio] (1483–1520) Italian painter from Urbino, a leading figure of the High Renaissance. He is thought to have studied under PERUGINO, and was deeply influenced by the works of MICHELANGELO and LEONARDO DA VINCI during a trip to Florence *c.*1504. By the age of twenty-five, his reputation was such that he was summoned to Rome by Pope Julius II, where he painted the School of Athens fresco (*c.*1509). He spent the rest of his career in Rome, where he enjoyed great success. His fully human portrayals of the Madonna and Holy Family are imbued with a deep religious feeling as he combined Christian ideals with the grace and grandeur of classical antiquity.

**Rasputin, Grigori Efimovich** (*c.*1871–1916) Russian monk. Notably licentious when young, he became a monk and, claiming to have healing powers, became a cult figure among the Russian aristocracy, and a member of the royal household in 1907. He achieved considerable influence over the Tsarina Alexandra (*see* NICHOLAS II), and was assassinated in 1916.

**Rattigan, Sir Terence [Mervyn]** (1911–77) English dramatist. Many of his plays, e.g. the melodramas of middle-class hypocrisy and crisis, *The Browning Version* (1948) and *The Deep Blue Sea* (1952), have become firm favourites. He also wrote *Ross* (1960), a psychological study of T. E. LAWRENCE.

**Ravel, Maurice** (1875–1937) French composer. Influenced by FAURÉ and DEBUSSY, he became one of the leading impressionist composers of his time. His works include the overture *Schéhérazade* (1899) the small orchestral piece *Boléro* (1928) and several works for piano and for the ballet.

**Ravi Shankar** (1920– ) Indian sitar player and composer. Regarded as one of India's greatest modern musicians, he became world-famous after teaching George HARRISON to play the sitar in the 1970s and made several very popular international tours

Another pupil was Philip GLASS. He wrote and performed the music scores for Satyajit RAY's *Apu* trilogy of films.

**Ray, Man** (1890–1976) American photographer and painter. A founder (with DUCHAMP) of New York Dadaism, he moved to Paris in 1921 where he became a leading exponent of Surrealist photography.

**Ray, Satyajit** (1921–92) Indian film director. His films, popular in art houses the world over, include the *Apu* trilogy of life in rural India, i.e. *Pather Panchali* (1955), *Aparajito* (1956) and *Apu Sansar* (1959), and *The Chess Players* (1977).

**Reagan, Ronald [Wilson]** (1911– ) American film actor, Republican statesman and 40th president of the US (1981–89). He appeared in around fifty films, including *Bedtime for Bonzo* (1951), which co-starred a chimpanzee, and (his last) the fine thriller *The Killers* (1964). He was president of the Screen Actors Guild (1947–52, 1959–60). His second wife, the actress **Nancy Davis** (1923– ), whom he married in 1952, is often credited with transforming the liberal trade unionist into a conservative. Reagan became governor of California in 1967, and defeated CARTER in the 1980 presidential election. He pursued strong monetarist deflationary economic policies, revoked as much liberal social legislation as he could, and adopted a doctrinaire anti-communist foreign policy, which reached its limits in his crusade against Nicaragua's Sandinista government.

**Redgrave, Sir Michael [Scudamore]** (1908–85) English stage and film actor. One of the finest actors of his generation, with a distinctively intellectual approach to his craft, his stage roles included Hamlet (1949–50) and Uncle Vanya (1963). His films include *The Lady Vanishes* (1938), *The Browning Version* (1951), and *The Go-Between* (1971). His daughter, **Vanessa Redgrave** (1937– ), became a highly successful stage and film actress, winning an Oscar for *Julia* (1977). She is also noted for her political activism and was a leading campaigner for the Workers' Revolutionary Party.

**Reed, Sir Carol** (1906–76) English film director. His films include *The Third Man* (1949), written by Graham GREENE and starring Orson WELLES, a bleak thriller set in postwar Vienna that is one of the most highly praised films ever made. Other films include the spy comedy (from a Greene novel) *Our Man in Havana* (1959).

**Reinhardt, Django** [Jean Baptiste Reinhardt] (1910–53) Belgian guitarist. A French-speaking gipsy, he formed the Quintette de Hot Club de Paris with GRAPPELLI, which became the most highly regarded jazz group in Europe.

**Reith, John Charles Walsham**, [1st Baron Reith of Stonehaven] (1889–1971) Scottish engineer, who was appointed first manager of the British Broadcasting Company (later Corporation) in 1922. Renowned for his high moral purpose, and criticized by some for his autocracy, he did much to shape the BBC into an institution of great influence. The annual BBC Reith Lecture was instituted in 1947 in his honour.

**Rembrandt Harmensz, van Rijn** (1606–69) Dutch painter, draughtsman and etcher. Born in Leyden, he trained in Amsterdam where he developed a CARAVAGGIO-like style, as in *The Stoning of St Stephen* (1625). He established a reputation as a portraitist with *The Anatomy Lesson of Dr Tulp* (1632) and was subsequently in great demand, painting more than 40 commissions in two years. In 1634 he married Saskia van Uylenburgh and painted the confident *Self-portrait with Saskia*. He reached the peak of his baroque style in 1636 with *The Blinding of Samson*, and later works are less dramatic, although more spiritually and psychologically perceptive, as in *Supper at Emmaus* (1648). His remarkable series of self-portraits, painted over 40 years, reveals the spiritual development of his work. He died alone and in poverty, and it was to be around 50 years before his genius was recognized.

**Renoir, Jean** (1894–1979) French film director. The son of the impressionist painter Pierre Auguste RENOIR, his films, often described as "humanist" for their compassion and sense of humanity's unity, include two classics of the cinema, *La Grande Illusion* (1937) and *La Régle du jeu* (1939). He fled the German occupation of France to the US in 1941, where he became a naturalized American.

**Renoir, Pierre Auguste** (1841–1919) French Impressionist painter. He trained in Paris, where he met MONET and SISLEY. He exhibited in the first three Impressionist exhibitions, and thereafter pursued his own version of Impressionism, giving more value to perspective, solidity of form and preliminary sketches, e.g. *The Bathers* (c.1884–7). Other notable works include *Mme Charpentier and her Children* (1876) and *Moulin de la Galette* (1876).

**Resnais, Alain** (1922– ) French film director. One of the best known of the French "New Wave" directors, his films include the romance *Hiroshima mon amour* (1959) and the experimental, "Surrealist" *Last Year* *in Marienbad* (1961), the latter attracting praise and derision in about equal amounts.

**Reynolds, Albert** (1933– ) Irish politician. Elected in 1977 as a Fianna Fáil member, he held several posts under HAUGHEY but was sacked by him (1991). He eventually succeeded as *taoiseach* (prime minister) (1992) and was faced almost immediately by a constitutional crisis concerning abortion.

**Reynolds, Sir Joshua** (1723–92) English painter and art theorist. He trained in London and worked as a portraitist in his native Devon. He visited Italy in 1750–52 and developed his theories—published as *Discourses*—on the Grand Manner from his studies of Renaissance and Baroque painting and classical sculpture. On his return to London, he began to organize his sitters in the poses of classical sculpture, e.g. *Commodore Keppel* (1753). As first president of the Royal Academy he set high standards in portraiture.

**Rhine, Joseph Banks** (1895–1980) American psychologist. He founded parapsychology, the study of ESP and related mental phenomena, such as telekinesis. His claim that his experiments in thought transference produced results better than could have been obtained by chance, has not been accepted by scientists. His works include *New Frontiers of the Mind* (1937).

**Ribbentrop, Joachim von** (1893–1946) German Nazi diplomat. He served HITLER as foreign minister (1938–45), signing the German-Soviet treaty with MOLOTOV, and was convicted and hanged for war crimes at Nuremberg.

**Rice, Tim** *see* **Lloyd Webber, Andrew**.

**Richard, Cliff** [Harry Roger Webb] (1940– ) Indian-born English pop singer and film actor. His first hit record, with his backing group the Drifters (renamed the Shadows) was "Move It" in 1958, since when he has become an institution in British popular music. His films include the musicals *The Young Ones* (1961) and *Summer Holiday* (1962), and the satirical *Expresso Bongo* (1959).

**Richard, Keith** *see* **Jagger, Mick**.

**Richard I** [Richard the Lionheart] (1157–99) king of England (1189–99). He went out on the third crusade in 1190 to the Holy Land, where he won a series of victories over the Saracens. He made peace with SALADIN and set out to return to England, but was imprisoned by the Emperor Henry VI, and was ransomed for a huge sum of money by the English people. He returned to England, where he forgave his brother John for trying to thwart his ransom, and was subsequently killed fighting in France. A gifted poet and a brave soldier, Richard was one of the most admired men of his day. He was succeeded by his brother, **King John** (1167–1216).

**Richard II** (1367–1400) king of England. He inherited the throne in 1377, and his reign was much disturbed by civil unrest, such as the poll tax riot of 1380, and by turbulent coalitions of barons. He was forced to abdicate in favour of Henry Bolingbroke (subsequently HENRY IV) in 1399 and was murdered in Pontefract Castle.

**Richard III** (1452–85) King of England. The Duke of Gloucester, he became Protector in 1483 and the guardian of **Edward V** (1470–83) following the death of HENRY VI. He was crowned in 1483, having executed or neutralized all other contenders (Edward, with his brother Richard, Duke of York, the "Princes in the Tower," being later murdered in captivity by persons unknown). Now regarded generally as a capable administrator, Richard was reviled—perhaps justly—as a tyrant by Tudor historians following Richard's defeat and death at the hands of Henry Tudor's forces (*see* HENRY VII) at Bosworth.

**Richards, Sir Gordon** (1904–86) English jockey. He rode 4,870 winners and was champion jockey 26 times. He won 14 Classic races (the Derby once).

**Richards, Viv** (1952– ) Antiguan-born West Indian cricketer. He was captain of the West Indies (1985–91), and was regarded as one of the best batsmen and fielders in modern cricket. He retired in 1991.

**Richardson, Sir Ralph [David]** (1902–83) English stage and film actor. Ranked with GIELGUD and OLIVIER as among the finest British actors of the 20th century, Richardson became a leading actor in the 1930s, equally at home with the classics and modern roles. Notable film roles include Buckingham in Olivier's film of *Richard III* (1955), the head of the secret service in *Our Man in Havana* (1960) and God in *Time Bandits* (1981). (The critic Kenneth TYNAN had long before observed that Richardson was the actor best suited to play God.)

**Richardson, Samuel** (1689–1761) English novelist. All his novels were written in epistolary form, and all were hugely popular. The first was *Pamela; or Virtue Rewarded* (1740), in which a servant girl achieves an upwardly mobile marriage by resisting seduction (the work was attacked by FIELDING in his parody *Shamela* for its dubious morality). Richardson subsequently published *Clarissa Harlowe* (1747–48) and *Sir Charles Grandison* (1753–54). Fielding was not alone in feeling unease at the occasional moral ambiguity in Richardson's novels. However, Fielding's sister Sarah (also a novelist) and Dr JOHNSON were convinced of Richardson's superiority to other novelists for his insights into human (especially female) character, and for his insights into the darker aspects of human nature.

**Richthofen, Manfred, Baron von** (1882–1918) German fighter pilot, nicknamed the "Red Baron." He commanded the 11th Chasing Squadron ("Richthofen's Flying Circus") in World War I, and was credited with shooting down 80 allied aircraft. He was killed in action, probably by ground fire.

**Rilke, Rainer Maria** (1875–1926) Prague-born Austrian poet. His lyrical, mystical poems, in e.g. *Duino Elegies* (1922) and *Sonnets to Orpheus* (1923), are regarded as amongst the finest religious verse of the 20th century.

**Rimbaud, Arthur** (1854–91) French poet. An early Symbolist, he stopped writing poetry at the age of nineteen after a torrid affair with VERLAINE (described in *A Season in Hell*, 1873). Some of the pieces in his collection of hallucinatory, vivid prose poems, *Les Illuminations* (1884), were set to music by BRITTEN.

**Rivera, Diego** (1886–1957) Mexican painter. He is especially noted for his murals, which combine traditional Mexican and Indian themes with Marxist-Leninist didacticism. His mural for the Rockefeller Center (later replicated in Mexico) was destroyed because it included a portrait of LENIN.

**Robeson, Paul [Le Roy]** (1898–1976) American bass singer and actor. He qualified as a lawyer before becoming a highly popular stage actor in the

1920s. Notable performances include *Showboat* (1927) and *Othello* (1940). His warm, sensitive recordings of spirituals and folk songs were also very popular. A noted advocate of civil rights for blacks, he came under strident attack in the US for supposed Communist sympathies and spent much of his life from the early 1960s in seclusion.

**Robespierre, Maximilien Marie Isidore de** (1758–94) French lawyer and revolutionary. He was elected to the National Assembly (1789) at the beginning of the French Revolution and to the Paris Commune (1791). He became leader of the Jacobin group, and as a member of the Committee of Public Safety (1793–94), he launched the Reign of Terror. A rigid man possessed by the idea of the state as paramount, he used terror of the guillotine rigorously in pursuit of his vision, in the process antagonizing his political opponents, who organized his denunciation and execution—by guillotine.

**Robinson, Joan Violet** (1903–83) English economist. She became one of the leading theorists of the "Cambridge School" of economists, and developed, following KEYNES, macroeconomic theories of growth and distribution. Her works include *Introduction to Modern Economics* (1973).

**Robinson, John [Arthur Thomas]** (1919–83) English Anglican prelate and theologian. His best-selling book, *Honest to God* (1963), inspired by the thinking of (predominantly German) theologians, created much public controversy with its portrayal of God as an inner presence rather than an external "father in the sky."

**Robinson, Mary** (1944– ) Irish barrister, politician and president (1990– ) of the Republic of Ireland.

Notably liberal in her policies, she won wide support from parties opposed to her conservative Fianna Fáil opponent.

**Robinson, Sir Robert** (1886–1975) English chemist. He was awarded the 1947 Nobel prize for chemistry for his work on plant extracts. He also made significant contributions to the study of plant pigments.

**Robinson, "Sugar" Ray** [Walker Smith] (1920–89) American boxer. A highly skilled boxer, he was world welterweight champion (1946–51) and world middleweight champion five times from 1951 to 1960.

**Robson, Dame Flora** (1902–84) English stage and film actress. She was especially noted for her historical roles, e.g. as Queen Elizabeth in the highly patriotic film *Fire over England* (1937).

**Rochester, John Wilmot, 2nd Earl of** (1647–80) English poet and courtier. Renowned (and feared) at the court of CHARLES II for his savage wit and supposedly limitless depravity, his verse is among the most sexually explicit in English. A representative (and very fine) poem is his "Satyr Against Mankind", (1675), with its memorable image of man as, in death, a "reasoning engine" huddled in dirt. He may have made a deathbed conversion to Christianity.

**Rodgers, Richard [Charles]** (1902–79) American composer. With the librettist Lorenz HART, he created musicals such as *The Boys from Syracuse* (1938) and *Pal Joey* (1940). After Hart died, Rodgers collaborated with HAMMERSTEIN on several more successful musicals, e.g. *Oklahoma* (1943) and *The Sound of Music* (1959).

**Rodin, Auguste** (1840–1917) French sculptor. He came to prominence in a whirlwind of publicity over *The Age of Bronze* (1875–6), a male nude figure that he was accused of casting from life. It was bought by the state, which commissioned a never-completed bronze door, entitled *The Gates of Hell*, for a planned museum of art. Figures from the door were expanded into some of his most famous pieces, e.g *The Thinker* and *The Kiss*. Rodin was responsible for reviving sculpture as an independent art form rather than as an embellishment or decoration for buildings or monuments.

**Rogers, Ginger** *see* **Astaire, Fred**.

**Rogers, Richard** (1933– ) Italian-born English architect. His designs include the Lloyds building (1979) in London, a steel and glass confection that typifies the controversial nature of his frontiersmanship approach to architectural technology.

**Rogers, Will[iam Penn Adair]** (1879–1935) American humorist and actor, nicknamed the "cowboy philosopher." A highly skilled rodeo performer, he came to exemplify, for many Americans, the common man in rhetorical arms against injustice and governmental stupidity. He appeared in several John FORD movies, most notably *Judge Priest* (1934).

**Rolls, Charles Stewart** (1877–1910) English motor car manufacturer and aviator. He joined Henry ROYCE in car manufacture in 1906, and made the first nonstop double flight across the English Channel in 1910, shortly before his death in a plane crash.

**Romero y Galdames, Oscar Arnulfo** (1917–80) Salvadorean Roman Catholic prelate. Appointed archbishop in 1977 he was a conservative both in theology and politics, and became an outspoken opponent of the murderous campaigns of the El Salvador government's semi-official death squads, for which he was assassinated.

**Rommel, Erwin** (1891–1944) German soldier. After distinguished service in World War I, he became a Nazi supporter in the 1920s. During World War II, he commanded the Afrika Korps in North Africa, earning the nickname the "Desert Fox" for his brilliant tactics, but was defeated at El Alamein by MONTGOMERY's troops. He committed suicide after the discovery of his complicity in the July assassination attempt on HITLER (*see* STAUFFENBERG).

**Roosevelt, Franklin D[elano]** (1882–1945) American Democratic statesman. He became 32nd president of the US (1933–45) after defeating HOOVER in 1933, and, in order to deal with the crisis of economic collapse, instituted far-reaching "New Deal" reforms in US society, e.g. his massive Public Works Administration programme of public spending and establishment of basic social security measures. He was a popular and highly effective leader during World War II, dying shortly after the Yalta summit meeting with CHURCHILL and STALIN. His wife, **[Anna] Eleanor Roosevelt** (1884–1962), was an active and popular First Lady, supporting her husband during his illness with polio and writing several books, e.g. *It's Up to the Women* (1933) and *The Moral Basis of Democracy* (1940). After his death she worked with the UN as US representative to the General Assembly (1946–52) and as chairman of the Human Rights Commission (1947–51).

**Roosevelt, Theodore** (1858–1919) American Republican statesman. A notably bellicose figure who organized a corps of irregular soldiers, dubbed "Roosevelt's Rough Riders," during the Spanish-American War (1898), he became 26th president of the US (1901–9) after President McKinley's assassination. He legislated against big business monopolies, intervened forcefully during the Panama civil war to protect the construction of the Panama Canal, and won the 1906 Nobel Peace Prize for mediating the end of the Russo-Japanese war. He split the Republican presidential vote in 1912 by standing as a Progressive (letting Woodrow WILSON in).

**Rossetti, Christina Georgina** (1830–94) English poet, noted for her reflective, occasionally melancholic religious poems. She also wrote verse for children, and the remarkable verse fairy story *Goblin Market* (1882). Her brother **Dante Gabriel** (1828–82) was both a poet and an artist, who with Holman HUNT and MILLAIS, founded the Pre-Raphaelite school of painting.

**Rossini, Gioacchino Antonio** (1792–1868) Italian composer, noted especially for his light operas, e.g. *The Barber of Seville* (1816), *The Thieving Magpie* (1817) and *William Tell* (1829). His other works include the *Stabat Mater* (1841).

**Rostand, Edmond** (1868–1918) French dramatist and poet. His best-known work is the verse drama *Cyrano de Bergerac* (1897). *See* CYRANO DE BERGERAC.

**Rostropovich, Mstislav** (1927– ) Russian cellist. One of the outstanding cellists of modern times, he has also given many recitals as a pianist, often accompanying his wife, the soprano **Galina Vishnevskaya** (1926–), in song recitals. He made public his support of SOLZHENITSYN in 1970, and left the USSR in 1975.

**Rothko, Mark** [Marcus Rothkovitch] (1903–70) Russian-born American painter. Having passed through Expressionism and Surrealism, in the late 1940s he adopted the Abstract Expressionist style of painting for which he became famous, creating large canvases with almost luminous rectangles of colour.

**Rothschild, [Nathaniel Mayer] Victor, 3rd Baron** (1910–90) English zoologist and banker. A member of the European-wide Rothschild dynasty of bankers and intellectuals, he succeeded to his father's title in 1937. After distinguished service in British Intelligence during World War II, he became a prominent scientist and also served on various government committees. He was in charge of the government's central policy review staff (1971–74). His works include *A Classification of Living Animals* (1961).

**Rous, Francis Peyton** (1879–1970) American pathologist. With the Canadian-born surgeon **Charles Brenton Huggins** (1901– ), he shared the 1966 Nobel prize for physiology or medicine for his innovative cancer research. Much of his work, e.g. his discovery of the Rous Sarcoma Virus, had been done over fifty years previously.

**Rousseau, Henri Julien ["Le Douanier"]** (1844–1910) French painter. He worked in the Paris Toll Office, which earned him his soubriquet, and took up painting when he retired in 1885. His naive style remained unaffected by all trends, and he defied conventions of colour and perspective in his exotic imaginary landscapes and painted dreams, e.g. *The Dream* (1910).

**Rousseau, Jean-Jacques** (1712–78) Swiss-born

French philosopher. His most notable fictional works are the novels *Julie, or the New Héloïse* (1761) and *Emile* (1762), the former describing a highly improbable menage à trois, the latter being a didactic work on how to educate children (whom he saw as naturally good). These works and others, notably the political tract *The Social Contract* (1762), which begins with the famous statement "Man is born free, and is everywhere in chains", were profoundly influential on the intellectual ferment that led to the French Revolution (*see also* VOLTAIRE). His very frank 12 volumes of autobiography, *Confessions*, were published posthumously in 1781–88 and set a fashion for this style of reminiscence.

**Roussel, Albert** (1869–1937) French composer. His early works were influenced by Impressionist and 18th-century composers. His later works, e.g. the choral piece *Evocations* (1912), show the influence of oriental music.

**Rowlandson, Thomas** (1756–1827) English caricaturist and printmaker. He worked as a portraitist for a time, then began his famous watercolour caricatures and book illustrations. His popular series of engravings included *The Comforts of Bath* (1798) and *The Tour of Dr Syntax in search of the Picturesque* (1812, 1820 and 1821).

**Royce, Sir [Frederick] Henry** (1863–1933) English engineer. In partnership with Charles ROLLS, he founded the car firm Rolls-Royce in 1906. The Rolls-Royce marque, e.g. the Silver Ghost (1907), became a modern symbol of wealth and of first-rate engineering design.

**Rubbra, [Charles] Edmund** (1901–86) English composer. A traditionalist composer, Rubbra found much of his inspiration in English lyric poetry, and in his religious beliefs (originally an Anglican, he converted to Roman Catholicism in 1948). His works include 11 symphonies.

**Rubens, Sir Peter Paul** (1577–1640) Flemish painter and diplomat. He went to Italy in 1600, studying the works of TITIAN and VERONESE in Venice before entering the service of the Duke of Mantua. He became court painter to the Spanish viceroys in Antwerp in 1609. He was already famous when he painted his masterpiece, the triptych *Descent from the Cross* (1611–14). In 1629 he was sent to England to negotiate peace with CHARLES I, who knighted him, and while there he painted *Peace and War*.

**Rubinstein, Artur** (1888–1982) Polish-born American pianist. An outstanding concert pianist, he was particularly noted for his CHOPIN recitals. He became a US citizen in 1946.

**Ruby, Jack** *see* **Oswald, Lee Harvey.**

**Ruisdael** *or* **Ruysdael, Jacob van** (*c.*1628–82) Dutch landscape painter. His atmospheric landscapes, e.g. *Landscape with Ruins*, and seascapes are outstanding, particularly in their depiction of clouds, and anticipate CONSTABLE's work. His uncle **Salomon van Ruysdael** (*c.*1600–70), also a landscape painter, was possibly his tutor.

**Rushdie, [Ahmed] Salman** (1947– ) Indian-born British novelist. His first major success was *Midnight's Children* (1981), a fantasy on post-independence India. After the publication of *Satanic Verses* (1988), Ayatollah KHOMEINI of Iran pronounced a death sentence for blasphemy on Rushdie, who has had to go into hiding.

**Rusk, [David] Dean** (1909– ) US secretary of state

(1961–69). Notable for being a firm Cold Warrior and a strong supporter of the Vietnam War, which he saw as a crusade against communism, he served under KENNEDY and JOHNSON.

**Ruskin, John** (1819–1900) English art critic. His works include *Modern Painters* (1843–60), *The Seven Lamps of Architecture* (1849), *The Stones of Venice* (1851–53), *Unto This Last* (1860) and *Sesame and Lilies* (1865, 1871). Ruskin was an enthusiast for Gothic art, the Pre-Raphaelite movement and TURNER, and was, like CARLYLE, a strong critic of the values and ugliness of Industrial England.

**Russell, Bertrand [Arthur William]** 3rd Earl Russell (1872–1970) British philosopher, mathematician and political reformer. He studied mathematics at Cambridge under WHITEHEAD, and published his *Principles of Mathematics* in 1903. With Whitehead, he wrote *Principia Mathematica* (1910–13). His other works include *Problems of Philosophy* (1912) and *A History of Western Philosophy* (1945). Russell became the best-known philosopher of his time, making notable contributions to mathematical and philosophical theory, e.g. in set theory and, with the help of his student, WITTGENSTEIN, logical positivism. He was a pacifist during World War I and a noted campaigner against nuclear weapons. He was awarded the 1950 Nobel prize for literature.

**Russell, Ken** (1927– ) English film director. He is especially noted for his film biographies of musicians, which began with a film for television on ELGAR (1962) and (on DELIUS) *A Song of Summer* (1968), and progressed through increasingly bizarre works such as (on Tchaikovsky) *The Music Lovers* (1970) to the lunatic *Lisztomania* (1975).

**Ruth, Babe** [George Herman Ruth] (1895–1948) American baseball player. Regarded as the finest all-rounder in the history of baseball, as pitcher with the Boston Red Sox (1914–19) and batter for New York Yankees (1920–34), his total of 714 home runs was unsurpassed until 1974. He finished his career as coach for the Brooklyn Dodgers.

**Rutherford, Ernest** [1st Baron Rutherford of Nelson] (1871–1937) New Zealand physicist. He was awarded the 1908 Nobel prize for chemistry for his work in the radioactive transformation of atoms. In 1911, he deduced the existence of the atom's structure, and was the first scientist to split the atom.

**Rutherford, Dame Margaret** (1892–1972) English actress. Notable for her engaging portrayal of eccentrics, she portrayed Agatha CHRISTIE's Miss Marple in several films in the 1960s.

**Ruysdael** *see* **Ruisdael**.

**Ryder, Sue** *see* **Cheshire, Sir Leonard.**

**Ryle, Gilbert** (1900–76) English philosopher. He became one of the leading "linguistic" philosophers of his generation, asserting that philosophy's function is to disentangle the misconceptions caused by linguistic conception. His works include *The Concept of Mind* (1949) and *Plato's Progress* (1966).

**Ryle, Sir Martin** (1918–84) English astronomer. He was awarded the 1974 Nobel prize for physics for his work in the field of radio astronomy, which, in the 1960s, led to the conclusion that the universe is not in a "steady state." He was astronomer royal (1972–82).

# S

**Sabin, Albert Bruce** (1906– ) Polish-born American microbiologist. He developed the Sabin polio vaccine in the mid–1950s, which, due to its effectiveness and oral administration, supplanted the SALK vaccine.

**Sadat, [Mohammed] Anwar El** (1918–81) Egyptian statesman. He succeeded NASSER as president in 1970. After the 1973 war with Israel, he signed a peace treaty with BEGIN, for which they were awarded the 1978 Nobel Peace Prize. He was assassinated by Islamic fundamentalist soldiers during a military parade.

**Sade, Donatien Alphonse François, Marquis de** (1740–1814) French soldier and novelist. He was condemned to death in 1772 for acts of unspeakable depravity, escaped, was recaptured and spent most of the rest of his life in prison. His highly licentious works include several novels, of which the least difficult to read is *Justine* (1791). The term "sadism" derives from the dominant theme in his life and work, the desire to inflict pain in the pursuit of (usually sexual) pleasure. He was released from prison during the French Revolution and was appointed a judge, but was soon back in prison for being too lenient in sentencing. His main contribution to the Revolution was a memorably evil speech in praise of MARAT's blood lust. He died insane.

**Sakharov, Andrei Dimitrievich** (1921–89) Russian physicist and dissident. Regarded as one of the greatest nuclear physicists, he developed the Russian hydrogen bomb in the 1950s. He subsequently campaigned for international control of nuclear weapons and for civil rights in the Soviet Union, and was awarded the 1975 Nobel Peace Prize. He was sent into internal exile in 1980, and released on GORBACHEV's intervention in 1986. He was elected to the Congress of People's Deputies in 1989.

**Saladin** [Salah al-Din al-Ayyubi] (1137–93) Sultan of Egypt and Syria. A Kurd, he became *de facto* leader of the Arab world during the Crusades, defeating the Christian army at the battle of Tiberias (1187) and capturing strongholds along the Syria coast. The crusaders fought back under Richard the Lionheart (*see* RICHARD I), recapturing Acre and other cities. Saladin, a wise and tolerant ruler, was much admired by his Christian opponents. (DANTE put him in the outer circle of Hell, describing him as "Great Saladin, aloof and alone").

**Salam, Abdus** *see* **Weinberg, Steven.**

**Salazar, António de Oliveira** (1889–1970) Portuguese dictator. A former professor of economics, he was prime minister (1932–68), during which time he gradually assumed dictatorial powers. He retired in 1968.

**Salk, Jonas Edward** (1914– ) American physician and microbiologist. He developed the Salk vaccine (by inoculation) against polio (later supplanted by the SABIN vaccine).

**Saloth Sar** *see* **Pol Pot.**

**Sanger, Frederick** (1918– ) English biochemist. He was awarded two Nobel prizes for chemistry (1958,

1980), the first for his work on protein structure and the sequence of amino acids, the second for his work on the structure of nucleic acids.

**Santayana, George** (1863–1952) Spanish-born American philosopher, critic and poet. His works include *The Life of Reason* (1905–6) and *Realms of Being* (1927–40).

**Sapir, Edward** *see* **Whorf, Benjamin Lee.**

**Sappho** (b. *c.*650 BC) Greek poet. The Greeks regarded her as one of the greatest of all lyric poets, but only tantalizingly short fragments of her poetry have survived, e.g. her magical little hymn to the Evening Star.

**Sartre, Jean-Paul** (1905–80) French philosopher, novelist and dramatist. His attempts at reconciling Existentialist philosophy with Marxism are now of historical interest only. His novels, however, e.g. *Nausea* (1938), are highly readable. Several of his plays, e.g. *The Flies* (1943) and *Huis clos* (1944, in English *No Exit*) are frequently performed.

**Satie, Erik [Alfred Leslie]** (1866–1925) French composer (his mother was a Scottish composer). Satie's cool, simple, classically inspired compositions, e.g. "Three Pieces in the form of a pear" (1903, for two pianos), often had very odd titles, and were influential on DEBUSSY and RAVEL. COCTEAU helped bring his work to a wider public, and collaborated with him on a ballet commissioned by DIAGHILEV, *Parade* (1917), for which PICASSO designed the sets.

**Sato Eisaku** (1901–75) Japanese Liberal-Democrat prime minister (1964–72). He was awarded the 1974 Nobel Peace Prize for his opposition to the nuclear arms race.

**Saussure, Ferdinand de** (1857–1913) Swiss linguist. Regarded as one of the founders of modern linguistics, he established the "structuralist" approach to language as a social phenomenon, focusing on the arbitrary relationship between the word as "linguistic sign" and the thing it signifies. His works include *Course in General Linguistics* (1916).

**Savage, Michael Joseph** (1872–1940) Australian-born New Zealand Labour politician. He became the first Labour prime minister of New Zealand (1935–40).

**Schlesinger, John [Richard]** (1926– ) English film director. His films include *Billy Liar* (1963), *Midnight Cowboy* (1969) and *Sunday, Bloody Sunday* (1971).

**Schlick, Moritz** (1882–1936) German philosopher. One of the founders of the "Vienna Circle" logical positivist school, his works include *Problems of Ethics* (1930). He was murdered by one of his students.

**Schmidt, Helmut [Heinrich Waldemar]** (1918– ) West German Social Democrat statesman and chancellor. A former leader in the Hitler Youth, he won the Iron Cross during the war. He succeeded Willy BRANDT as chancellor (1974–82) and fostered relations with East Germany, resigning from politics in 1983.

**Schnabel, Artur** (1882–1951) Austrian pianist and composer. Noted in particular for his interpretations of BEETHOVEN, SCHUBERT and MOZART, he settled in the USA from 1939, after the Nazi seizure of Austria.

**Schoenberg** *or* **Schönberg, Arnold [Franz Walter]** (1874–1951) Austrian composer (US citizen from 1941). His early works, e.g. the huge choral and orchestral *Gurrelieder* (1900), are lush chromatic compositions in the late Romantic tradition. He then began composing atonal works, such as the second string quartet (1908), and eventually developed his serial or "twelve-tone method" style of composition in such works as *Suite for Piano* (1924). He settled in the US in 1933, where he recovered his Jewish faith, an experience mirrored in his powerfully moving *Kol Nidre* (1938).

**Schopenhauer, Arthur** (1788–1860) German philosopher. Renowned for his pessimistic outlook on life, he reacted strongly against the Idealist tradition in philosophy, emphasizing the active role of the will as the creative (and irrational) force in human thought. His works include *The World as Will and Idea* (1819).

**Schrödinger, Erwin** (1887–1961) Austrian physicist. He shared the 1933 Nobel prize for physics (with DIRAC) for his formulation of his wave equation, which was the starting point for the study of wave mechanics in quantum theory. He fled from Germany to Britain in 1933, when the Nazis came to power.

**Schubert, Franz [Peter]** (1797–1828) Austrian composer. His works include nine symphonies, the eighth (in B minor) being the "Unfinished" (1822), string quartets, and other chamber music. His songs, as in the song cycles *Die schöne Müllerin* and *Die Winterreise*, are regarded as some of the finest ever written, include settings of lyrics by HEINE and GOETHE, and others.

**Schumacher, Ernst Friedrich** (1911–77) German-born British economist. His book, *Small is Beautiful* (1973), became a founding text of the conservationist movement, with its critique of Western industrialism and advocacy of local, small-enterprise development.

**Schumann, Robert Alexander** (1810–56) German composer. Noted for his espousal of Romantic values in music, his works include four symphonies, songs, and much fine piano music. His wife **Clara Schumann** (1819–96) was also a pianist and composer.

**Schuschnigg, Kurt von** (1897–1977) Austrian statesman. A staunch opponent of HITLER, he succeeded DOLLFUSS as Christian Socialist chancellor in 1934, and was imprisoned by the Nazis (1938–45).

**Schweitzer, Albert** (1875–1965) Alsatian medical missionary, theologian, musician and philosopher. In 1913, he founded a missionary hospital at Lambaréné, Gabon, which attracted worldwide interest for Schweitzer's avowed aim of helping Africa in the spirit of "atonement" rather than benevolence. He was awarded the 1952 Nobel Peace Prize. His works include *The Quest of the Historical Jesus* (1906) and *On the Edge of the Primeval Forest* (1922).

**Scipio** *see* **Hannibal**.

**Scorsese, Martin** (1942– ) American film director. Born into a poor Italian-American family in New York, his original intention was to become a priest. His films include *Taxi Driver* (1976), *Raging Bull* (1980) and *Goodfellas* (1990), these three films starring the actor most associated with Scorsese's work, Robert DE NIRO.

**Scott, C[harles] P[restwich]** (1846–1932) English journalist. He became editor of *The Manchester*

*Guardian* in 1872, which he transformed into one of the most respected newspapers in the world. Although his politics were Liberal (he was a Liberal MP, 1895–1906) his insistence on journalistic integrity ("Comment is free, facts are sacred") became proverbial. He was a strong opponent of the Boer War and supported women's suffrage.

**Scott, Sir Peter [Markham]** (1909–89) English naturalist and artist. The son of Robert SCOTT, his support and publicity for the conservation lobby was notably influential, particularly through his television documentaries and many books. He founded the Severn Wild Fowl Trust in 1948. His books include an autobiography, *The Eye of the Wind* (1961).

**Scott, Robert Falcon** (1868–1912) English explorer. He led two Antarctic expeditions (1901–4, 1910–12). He died with four companions on his last expedition, returning from the South Pole after having reached it a month after AMUNDSEN. He was the father of Sir Peter SCOTT.

**Scott, Sir Walter** (1771–1832) Scottish novelist and poet. His early, highly Romantic narrative poems, set in the Scottish past, e.g. *The Lady of the Lake* (1810) and *The Lord of the Isles* (1815), established his popularity with both the reading public and the literary world, BYRON being particularly generous in his praise. His historical novels (a genre he refined and made into an art form), particularly *Waverley* (1814), *The Heart of Midlothian* (1818) and *Ivanhoe* (1819), were enormously influential and spawned a host of imitators, e.g. Fenimore COOPER. Scott's re-creation (or invention) of Scottish Highland culture, e.g. making the kilt respectable and glorifying the Highland virtues of courage and loyalty, was also of enormous influence, and inspired similar undertakings throughout Europe.

**Scriabin** *or* **Skryabin, Alexander Nikolayevich** (1872–1915) Russian composer and pianist. His compositions often involved extra-musical effects, e.g. *Prometheus* (1909), a piece for piano accompanied by coloured light projected on a screen. He envisaged all the arts coming together in one great apocalyptic future performance (by himself).

**Seaga, Edward** (1930– ) American-born Jamaican politician. He became prime minister (1980–89) when his Labour Party defeated MANLEY's National Party in the 1980 general election, and lost power to Manley's party in 1989.

**Searle, Ronald [William Fordham]** (1920– ) English cartoonist and writer. Recognized at the outset of his career as a prodigious talent by Max BEERBOHM, he is known primarily as the creator of the monstrous St Trinian's schoolgirls, who feature in several of his works, e.g. *Back to the Slaughterhouse* (1951). Regarded, particularly in the US and France, as one of the finest graphic artists of the 20th century, he still lacks official recognition in Britain. His haunting book *To the Kwai—and Back: War Drawings 1939–45* (1986), a record of his experiences as a Japanese prisoner of war, also received scant notice.

**Secombe, Harry** *see* **Milligan, Spike**.

**Sedley, Sir Charles** (1639–1701) English poet and dramatist. He was a friend of both DRYDEN and ROCHESTER, and, like the latter, was involved in many sordid incidents; he was once fined for indecent exposure, but reformed to some extent when the roof fell in on him during a tennis match. His three plays are the tragedy *Antony and Cleopatra* (1677) and two comedies, *The Mulberry Garden* (1668) and *Bellamira* (1687). His lyrics include the magical "Love still has something of the sea," and several other very fine poems, collected in the posthumously issued *Miscellaneous Works* (1702).

**Segovia, Andrés** [Marquis of Salobreña] (1894–1987) Spanish guitarist. An internationally recognized virtuoso, he initiated a revival of interest in the classical guitar, with composers such as FALLA writing works for him.

**Sellers, Peter** (1925–80) English actor and comedian. One of the founders of the Goon Show (*see* Spike MILLIGAN), he became an international star with KUBRICK's black nuclear comedy *Dr Strangelove* (1963), in which he played three parts. He achieved further popularity as Inspector Clouseau in such films as *The Pink Panther* (1963).

**Seneca** [Lucius Annaeus Seneca] (*c*.4 BC–65 AD) Roman dramatist and Stoic philosopher. The violent rhetoric of his verse tragedies (which often have a supernatural content) was very influential on Elizabethan dramatists such as SHAKESPEARE. Like PETRONIUS, he was ordered to commit suicide by NERO (who had been his pupil).

**Senghor, Léopold Sédar** (1906– ) Senegalese politician and poet. A classics teacher in Paris in the 1930s, he helped develop the concept of "negritude" with other black writers, which chiefly involved writing (in French) polemical works celebrating African culture. (His poems were extravagantly praised by Western Marxists, notably SARTRE.) He became the president of Senegal (1960–80), maintaining his power by a shrewd mixture of persecution (holding French support by labelling all his opponents as Marxists) and conciliation of the Muslim majority.

**Sennett, Mack** [Michael Sinnott] (1880–1960) Canadian-born American film director and producer. After working for D. W. GRIFFITH, he formed his Keystone Studio in 1912, where he produced the manic "Keystone Cop" comedies, which achieved international success. He also produced Charlie CHAPLIN's first films.

**Serling, Rod** (1924–75) American television dramatist. An ex-paratrooper, his TV plays include the much acclaimed *Requiem for a Heavyweight* (1956, broadcast live). He also created and introduced the innovative fantasy series *The Twilight Zone* (1959–64), episodes of which often had rather beguiling titles, e.g. "Deathshead Revisited."

**Seurat, Georges** (1859–91) French painter, a leading neo-Impressionist. He developed the system of pointillism in which the painting is built up from tiny areas of pure colour. His works include *The Parade* (1887–88) and *The Circus* (1891).

**Seymour, Jane** *see* **Henry VIII**.

**Shackleton, Sir Ernest Henry** (1874–1922) Anglo-Irish explorer. He served in Robert SCOTT's Antarctic expedition, being invalided home in 1903. He commanded two further expeditions (1908–09, 1914–16), with one of his teams discovering the south magnetic pole in 1909. He died in South Georgia preparing for a fourth expedition.

**Shadwell, Thomas** (*c.*1642–92) English dramatist and poet. In the best of his 17 plays, comedies such as *The Virtuoso* (1676), he gives a lively and often

satirical account of contemporary life. He replaced
DRYDEN as poet laureate in 1689.

**Shakespeare, William** (1564–1616) English dramatist and poet. He was born and brought up in
Stratford-upon-Avon, where he attended the local
grammar school. He married Anne Hathaway in
1582, and they had three children by 1585 (their
last surviving descendant, a granddaughter, died in
1670). Nothing is known for certain of the circumstances of his move to London and entry into the
theatre, but in 1592 there appeared a reference to
him in a pamphlet by Robert GREENE. His plays are
generally divided into three groups. The first group
(late 1580s–*c*.1594) consists of histories, e.g. the
*Henry VI* trilogy, early comedies such as *The Two
Gentlemen of Verona*, and the tragedy of *Romeo and
Juliet*. The second group (*c*.1595–*c*.1599) includes
histories such as *King John, Henry IV Parts I and II*,
the comedies *A Midsummer's Night's Dream* and *As
You Like It*, and the tragedy *Julius Caesar*. The
third group (*c*.1600–*c*.1612) includes the great tragedies *Hamlet*, *Othello*, *King Lear*, *Macbeth*, *Antony
and Cleopatra*, *Coriolanus* and *Timon of Athens*,
the so-called "dark comedies," *Troilus and Cressida*,
*All's Well That Ends Well*, and *Measure for Measure*, and tragicomedies such as *The Winter's Tale*
and *The Tempest*. Shakespeare's other major works
are the narrative poems *Venus and Adonis* (1593)
and *The Rape of Lucrece* (1594), and the magnificent *Sonnets*, which are known to have been in
private circulation in London in 1598 before being
published, possibly not with his approval, in 1609.
The sonnets feature a romantic triangle between
the poet (Shakespeare) a dark lady (identity un-

known) and a beautiful young nobleman (possibly the Earl of Southampton). Shakespeare's status as the greatest of all poets and dramatists has only rarely been challenged. The works have been translated into every major language and are among the greatest works of Western culture.

**Shankar, Ravi** *see* **Ravi Shankar.**

**Shankly, Bill** [William Shankly] (1913–81) Scottish footballer and manager. Regarded as one of the outstanding football managers of the century, he transformed Liverpool into one of the most successful clubs of modern times. A renowned football fanatic, he once notoriously observed that football was more important than life or death.

**Shaw, George Bernard** (1856–1950) Anglo-Irish dramatist and critic. He began his literary career as a drama, literary and music critic in the 1880s, and after a false start in novel-writing, began writing plays in the 1890s. The plays, e.g. *Man and Superman* (1903), *Major Barbara* (1905) and *Pygmalion* (1913), have been very successful thanks to Shaw's mastery of witty dialogue. He was awarded the Nobel prize for literature in 1925.

**Shelley, Mary Wollstonecraft** (1797–1851) English novelist. The daughter of two prominent social reformers, William GODWIN and Mary WOLLSTONECRAFT, she eloped with SHELLEY in 1814 and married him in 1816 after his first wife, Harriet Westbrook, drowned herself. Her masterpiece is *Frankenstein, or the Modern Prometheus* (1818), a Gothic fantasy that has also been hailed as the first science fiction novel. There have been innumerable (usually very loose) stage and film adaptations of the novel, which arose out of an agreement between

Shelley, BYRON and herself to write supernatural tales.

**Shelley, Percy Bysshe** (1792–1822) English poet. His talent for public scandal emerged at Oxford University, where he was expelled for co-writing a tract entitled *The Necessity of Atheism* (1811), in which year he eloped with Harriet Westbrook. Two years later, he published his poem *Queen Mab*, which celebrates a future republican millenium of free love and vegetarianism. In 1814, he eloped with Mary Godwin (*see* Mary Wollstonecraft SHELLEY) and her 15-year old step-sister, Jane "Claire" Clairmont. Harriet committed suicide by drowning in 1816, in which year he married Mary. Shelley and his entourage moved to Italy in 1818, where he drowned in a sailing accident in 1822. His poems were among the greatest of English romantic poetry. The highlights are: *The Revolt of Islam* (1817); *Prometheus Unbound* (1820); *Adonais* (1821), his elegy on the death of KEATS; and several of the finest poems in the English language, notably *Ode to the West Wind* and *To a Skylark* (both 1820). His essay *A Defence of Poetry* (1821, published 1840) concludes with the defiant assertion that "poets are the unacknowledged legislators of the world." His last great (unfinished) poem, *The Triumph of Life* (1824), is a very bleak work (the title is profoundly ironic). *See also* SOCRATES, BYRON.

**Sheridan, Richard Brinsley** (1751–1816) Irish dramatist and politician, noted for his superb comedies of manners, *The Rivals* (1775) and *School for Scandal* (1777), both of which are firm repertory favourites. His other major play is *The Critic* (1779), an extremely funny burlesque that mercilessly satirizes the conventions of tragedy and the sleazy aspects of theatrical production. He was also highly regarded for his oratory in parliament, especially during the impeachment of Warren HASTINGS.

**Sherrington, Sir Charles Scott** (1857–1952) English physiologist. He shared the 1932 Nobel prize for physiology or medicine for his research into reflex action. His works include *The Integrative Action of the Nervous System* (1906).

**Shevardnadze, Eduard Ambrosievich** (1928– ) Soviet politician. Appointed by GORBACHEV as foreign minister in 1985, he attracted much notice in the West with his formulation of the "SINATRA Doctrine," i.e. each country should peacefully construct its foreign policy on a "My Way" basis. He resigned in 1990, warning of the threat of a reactionary coup. During the attempted coup of 19 August 1991, he joined YELTSIN in defying the coup leaders from the Russian parliament building in Moscow.

**Shockley, William Bradford** (1910–89) American physicist. He shared, with BARDEEN and the Chinese-born American physicist **Walter Brattain** (1902–87), the 1956 Nobel prize for physics for his development of the junction transistor. Shockley was also a highly controversial proponent of the view that heredity determines intelligence.

**Shostakovich, Dimitri Dimitriyevich** (1906–75) Russian composer. Many of his works, notably the opera *A Lady Macbeth of Mtensk* (1930), were severely attacked by Soviet cultural apparatchiks for their disregard of the canons of socialist realism. His works include 15 symphonies, 15 string quartets and song cycles.

**Sibelius, Jean** (1865–1957) Finnish composer. His

works reflect his strong Finnish nationalism, e.g. the tone poem *Finlandia* (1900), and often draw on the Finnish traditional epic, *Kalevala*. He also composed 15 symphonies, a violin concerto, choral and chamber works, and theatre music.

**Sickert, Walter [Richard]** (1860–1942) German-born British painter (of Dutch/Danish parentage). After studying in Paris, he became a strong influence on many British artists, most notably on the artists forming the Camden Town Group. His subject matter was usually London low (or bohemian) life.

**Sidney, Sir Philip** (1554–86) English poet, soldier and courtier. His works include *Arcadia* (1590), the first major English pastoral poem; the sonnet sequence *Astrophel and Stella* (1591), which inspired a host of imitations; and *A Defence of Poetry* (1595), a spirited defence of English as a medium for writing great poetry. His gallant death in action against the Spaniards in the Netherlands was followed by a host of tributes from his many admirers throughout Europe.

**Sihanouk, Prince Norodom** (1922– ) Cambodian statesman, formerly (elected) king of Cambodia (1941–55). He abdicated (in favour of his father) to become prime minister (1955–60) after independence from France in 1955, becoming head of state in 1960. He was deposed by a military coup in 1970 and fled to China, forming an alliance with POL POT's Khmer Rouge, who seized Cambodia in 1975. He again became head of state in 1975 and was deposed by Pol Pot the following year. After the Vietnamese invasion of 1979, Sihanouk formed a government in exile, in an uneasy alliance with the Khmer Rouge.

**Sikorski, Wladyslaw** (1881–1943) Polish general and statesman. In 1940, he became premier of the Polish government in exile and commander in chief of the Free Polish armed forces. The Soviet Union ceased to recognize his government after the 1943 revelation that the Russians had been responsible for massacring thousands of Polish officers in the Katyn forest. Sikorski died in a plane crash.

**Sikorsky, Igor Ivan** (1889–1972) Russian-born American aeronautical engineer. He built (in 1913) the first four-engined aircraft, and emigrated to the US in 1918, where he established the Sikorsky Aero Engineering Company (1926). He built the first successful helicopter in 1939, the VS-300, which suffered from teething troubles (the first model was incapable of flying forwards).

**Simpson, Wallis** *see* **Windsor, Duke of.**

**Sinatra, Frank** [Francis Albert Sinatra] (1915– ) American singer and film actor. He became a highly popular "crooner" of romantic songs in the 1940s, and won an Oscar for his part in *From Here to Eternity* (1952). One of the highest paid entertainers of all time, he is regarded as one of the finest modern popular singers, with a finely tuned jazz-like sense of phrasing.

**Singer, Isaac Bashevis** (1904–91) Polish-born American Yiddish writer. Much of his fiction deals with the now vanished world of Polish Judaism, e.g. *The Magician of Lublin* (1960). He was awarded the Nobel prize for literature in 1978.

**Sisley, Alfred** (1839–99) French painter of English extraction. His early works were classical in style, but he came under the influence of the Impressionists Renoir and Monet while studying in Paris. He painted mainly carefully composed and sensitively coloured landscapes, e.g. *Floods at Marly* (1876).

**Skinner, B[urrhus] F[rederic]** (1904– ) American psychologist. Influenced by John B. WATSON, he developed various techniques of behavioural psychology to illustrate his theory of "learning laws." His "Skinner box," in which rats learned to pull particular levers in order to get food, is a famous example of his approach. His works include *Beyond Freedom and Dignity* (1971).

**Skryabin** *see* **Scriabin**.

**Smart, Christopher** (1772–71) English poet. His best-known works are his great, highly idiosyncratic religious poems *A Song to David* (1763) and *Jubilate Agno* (unpublished until 1939), a wonderfully original celebration of God's creation written while Smart was confined in a lunatic asylum (1759–63). The most quoted lines from the poem are those describing his cat Jeoffrey. Dr Johnson was an admirer of Smart's piety (if not his poetry), and his strange, beguiling verse has gained recognition only in modern times.

**Smith, Adam** (1723–90) Scottish economist and philosopher. His book *Inquiry into the Nature and Causes of the Wealth of Nations* (1776), with its advocacy of free trade and the social benefits of private enterprise was of huge influence in the development of modern capitalist societies.

**Smith, Bessie** [Elizabeth Smith] (1895–1937) American blues singer, nicknamed the "Empress of the Blues." She became very popular with jazz audiences in the 1920s, and made several classic recordings with Louis ARMSTRONG. She died in a car crash.

**Smith, Ian [Douglas]** (1919– ) Zimbabwean politi-

cian. He was prime minister of Rhodesia (1964–79),
and declared UDI (unilateral declaration of independence) from Britain in 1965 in order to maintain
white minority rule. Majority rule came in 1979,
with **Bishop Abel Muzorewa** (1925– ) serving as
caretaker premier (1979–80). MUGABE's Zanu party
won the 1980 election. Smith resigned his leadership of his party in 1987.

**Smith, Stevie** [Florence Margaret Smith] (1902–71)
English poet and novelist. Her graceful, melancholic, and occasionally fiercely funny verse has
been much admired, especially the collection *Not
Waving but Drowning* (1957).

**Smollett, Tobias** [George] (1721–71) Scottish novelist. He served in the Royal Navy as a ship's
surgeon and took part in an attack upon a Spanish
port in the West Indies. In the early 1740s, he set up
a surgical practice in London. His picaresque novels, of which the most important are *The Adventures
of Roderick Random* (1748), *The Adventures of Per-
egrine Pickle* (1751), and his masterpiece, *The Expedition of Humphrey Clinker* (1771), are cleverly
plotted satirical works rich in characterization,
which achieved lasting popularity. His works influenced DICKENS.

**Smuts, Jan Christian** (1870–1950) South African
statesman and philosopher. He commanded Boer
forces during the Boer War, and became prime
minister (1919–24, 1939–48). Respected worldwide
as a statesman of depth, the common epithet for him
among his own people was "tricky," particularly
when he joined with the Allies in World War II. He
devised the philosophy of "holism," explained in his
*Holism and Evolution* (1926).

**Sobers, Gary** [Sir Garfield St Auburn] (1936– ) West
Indian cricketer. Regarded as one of the finest all-
rounders of all time, he scored more than 8,000 runs
(26 centuries), also taking 235 wickets and 110
catches in Test cricket. He was knighted in 1975,
when he retired.

**Socrates** (470–399 BC) Greek philosopher, the tutor
of PLATO. The sources of his teachings are many and
widely varied, but it is Plato's Socrates, a rather
maddening genius with a gift for answering questions with another question, who has come down to
posterity in Plato's "Socratic" dialogues, e.g.
*Protagoras*. The central theme in Socrates' thinking
is a quest for truth through rigorous self-examination: "the unexamined life is not worth living" (Plato,
*Apology*). He was forced to commit suicide by the
Athenians for supposedly corrupting youths through
teaching them "impiety". SHELLEY paid him a very
high compliment in *The Triumph of Life*, describing
Socrates and Jesus as the only two humans to have
broken free of the murderous wheel of life.

**Soddy, Frederick** (1877–1956) English chemist.
He was awarded the 1921 Nobel prize for chemistry
for his discovery of isotopes during his research in
radioactivity.

**Solti, Sir Georg** (1912– ) Hungarian-born British
conductor. A student under both BARTÓK and KODÁLY,
he left Hungary for Switzerland in 1939 as anti-
semitic repression intensified. His recording of
WAGNER's Ring cycle was particularly renowned.

**Solzhenitsyn, Aleksandr Isayevich** (1918– ) Russian novelist and historian. His novella, *One Day in
the Life of Ivan Denisovich* (1962), was based on his
experiences in a Soviet labour camp and was pub-

lished in the USSR during a brief thaw in cultural restrictions. Subsequent works, e.g. the novel *The First Circle* and his study of the labour camp system, *The Gulag Archipelago*, had to be published abroad (1968, 1973–75). He was awarded the Nobel prize for literature in 1970, and was deported from the USSR in 1974. He settled in Vermont in the USA, but has announced his intention to return to Russia.

**Sondheim, Stephen [Joshua]** (1930– ) American songwriter and composer. He studied with HAMMERSTEIN and wrote the lyrics for BERNSTEIN's *West Side Story* (1958), before writing the music and lyrics for several musicals, e.g. *A Funny Thing Happened on the Way to the Forum* (1962), *A Little Night Music* (1973) and *Into the Woods* (1986).

**Sophocles** (*c*.496–406 BC) Greek dramatist. Seven of his *c*.120 plays are extant. He was the most popular of the three great Athenian dramatists (the others being AESCHYLUS and EURIPIDES). The plays include *Oedipus Rex* and *Oedipus at Colonus*, and *Antigone*.

**Sopwith, Sir Thomas [Octave Murdoch]** (1888–1989) English aeronautical engineer. He founded the Sopwith Aviation Company in 1912, and designed and built the Sopwith Camel, one of the most successful fighter planes of World War I.

**Southey, Robert** (1774–1843) English poet. Closely associated with WORDSWORTH and COLERIDGE, only a few of his large output of poems are now regarded as having much merit. Poet laureate 1813–14, he was heavily satirized by BYRON for abandoning his youthful radicalism.

**Spassky, Boris Vasilyevich** (1937– ) Russian chess player. He was world champion (1969–72), losing his title to Bobby FISCHER in a ludicrously over-publicized contest that was much more of a Cold War phenomenon than a chess match.

**Spence, Sir Basil** (1907–76) Indian-born Scottish architect. Famous for a few highly prestigious buildings, such as Coventry Cathedral (1951), and notorious for some disastrous council housing, such as his council flats in Glasgow, the merit of Spence's work is hotly contested. (He reputedly remarked to Glasgow housewives complaining about his work that he would not accept criticism from non-architects.)

**Spencer, Lady Diana** *see* **Charles, Prince.**

**Spencer, Sir Stanley** (1891–1959) English painter. An isolated figure in modern art, he is best known for his series of religious paintings, particularly *The Resurrection* (1923–27), which depicts the residents of his home village, Cookham, rising from their graves. He also produced portraits, landscapes, and, in his capacity as a war artist, his *Shipbuilding on the Clyde* series of panels.

**Spengler, Oswald** (1880–1936) German philosopher. His historicist study, *The Decline of the West* (1918–22), argued that civilizations rise and fall in inexorable cycles, and that Western civilization could thus be expected to decay according to the same immutable laws that destroyed previous civilizations.

**Spenser, Edmund** (*c.*1552–99) English poet, noted particularly for his huge allegorical poem *The Faerie Queene* (1590–96), which describes the adventures of 12 knights (who represent 12 virtues). Many of the adventures begin at the court of Gloriana, the Faerie Queen (an idealized version of ELIZABETH I).

**Spielberg, Steven** (1947– ) American film director and producer. His first film (for television), *Duel* (1971), won high praise for Spielberg's skilful manipulation of tension. His subsequent films include some of the most successful films ever made, e.g. *Jaws* (1975), *Close Encounters of the Third Kind* (1977), *E.T.* (1982) and *Raiders of the Lost Ark* (1981).

**Spinoza, Baruch** (1632–77) Dutch philosopher. He was expelled from the Jewish community in Amsterdam for what was deemed to be heretical theology, and became noted for his daring intellectual speculation. His great work is his posthumously published *Ethics* (1677), in which he rejects the dualism of DESCARTES and argues for a virtually pantheistic deity.

**Spock, Dr [Benjamin McLane]** (1903– ) American pediatrician. His book *The Common Sense Book of Baby and Child Care* (1946) had a huge influence on many middle-class parents of the postwar generation, with its advocacy of a "permissive," non-authoritarian approach to the raising of infants (later works made tactical withdrawals from the more extreme positions taken in the earlier work). A passionate opponent of the Vietnam war, he helped form the People's Party, and was a candidate in the presidential election of 1972.

**Stalin, Joseph** [Josef Vissarionovich Dzhugashvili] (1879–1953) Soviet dictator. Born in Georgia, he was expelled in 1899 from an orthodox seminary in Tiflis for expounding Marxism. He became an active revolutionary on behalf of the Social Democratic Party and was imprisoned several times, escaping with surprising ease each time. After the Bolshevik

Revolution, he was appointed commissar for nation
alities, and became general secretary of the Centra
Committee in 1922, a position he held until his
death. Despite LENIN's so-called "Testament"
listing his shortcomings, Stalin manoeuvred his
way into absolute power, shrewdly playing of
BUKHARIN and his "rightist" allies against TROTSKY
and other "leftists." He forcibly collectivized Soviet
agriculture in the 1930s and developed the Soviet
Union's industrial base, using (and killing) many
millions of "Gulag" prisoners as slave labour. His
purges of the 1930s destroyed most of the surviving
old Bolsheviks, such as BUKHARIN, as well as the
army leadership. He signed a peace treaty with
HITLER in 1939, and seized Poland's eastern territories after Hitler's September invasion. Hitler's invasion of the Soviet Union in 1941 was spectacu-
larly successful in the first year, with large
sections of the population welcoming the Germans
as liberators, but forceful resistance from the Red
Army, notably in the defence of Leningrad, the
battle of Stalingrad, and in massive infantry and
tank battles, led directly to the defeat of Hitler's
regime and the occupation of eastern Europe by
Stalin's forces. After Stalin's death, KHRUSCHEV
came to power and denounced Stalin's brutality
and "personality cult" in a secret—but leaked—
speech.

**Stanislavsky, Konstantin** (1863–1938) Russian director and actor, who was co-founder of the Moscow
Art Theatre in 1897. The influence of his theory of
acting, requiring an actor to immerse himself in the
"inner life" of the character he is playing and so
convey to the audience the hidden reality behind the

words, has been immense. His theory is contained in such works as *An Actor Prepares* (1929) and *Building a Character* (1950).

**Starr, Ringo** [Richard Starkey] (1940– ) English rock drummer and singer. He was the Beatles' drummer (1962–70), and occasionally sang on their records, notably "Yellow Submarine."

**Stauffenberg, Count Berthold von** (1907–44) German soldier. He was one of the chief conspirators in the 20 July 1944 assassination attempt on HITLER, shortly after which he was executed.

**Steel, Sir David [Martin Scott]** (1938– ) Scottish Liberal politician. He became leader of the Liberal Party in 1976, following Jeremy THORPE's resignation. He led the Liberals during their partnership with David OWEN's SDP (1981–88), and resigned his leadership when the Liberals merged with the SDP to form the Liberal Democrats under ASHDOWN's leadership.

**Steele, Sir Richard** (1672–1729) Anglo-Irish essayist and dramatist. He was a close associate of ADDISON, with whom he was chief contributor to *The Tatler* (1709–11) and *The Spectator* (1711–12). His plays, e.g. *The Conscious Lovers*, were determinedly moral, Christian responses to the excess of Restoration drama, and had a strong influence on 18th-century drama. Steele was a good man, much loved by his contemporaries.

**Steichen, Edward** (1879–1973) Luxembourg-born American photographer. He was a founder of the Photo-Secession group with STIEGLITZ and others, and organized *The Family of Man* (1955) photography exhibition, which was highly influential in its portrayal of the unity of mankind.

**Stein, Gertrude** (1874–1946) American author, who settled in Paris in 1902. There she became a focal point for a group of writers and artists, including HEMINGWAY, Sherwood ANDERSON and PICASSO. Her own best-known work is her autobiography, *The Autobiography of Alice B. Toklas* (1933), eccentrically presented as if it were the work of her life-long companion.

**Stein, Jock** [John Stein] (1922–85) Scottish footballer and manager. He was manager of Glasgow Celtic (1965–78), during which period his club won nine consecutive league championships and became the first non-Latin club to win the European Cup in 1967 (finalists in 1968). He was manager of the Scotland team, and died during a match against Wales.

**Steiner, Rudolf** (1861–1925) Austrian philosopher. Influenced by theosophy, he formed his own movement of "anthroposophy" in 1912, dedicated to developing the innate human capacity for spiritual perception, through self-expressing activities such as art and dance. Many "Steiner schools" have been established throughout the world to teach children according to Steiner's principles.

**Stendhal** [pseud. of Henri Beyle] (1783–1842) French novelist and critic, noted for his great mastery of character analysis in such historical novels as *The Red and the Black* (1830) and *The Charterhouse of Parma* (1839).

**Sterne, Laurence** (1713–68) Irish-born English novelist. He was ordained as an Anglican clergyman in 1738, and his learned, witty and off-beat sermons at York became very popular. His wildly eccentric novel *The Life and Opinions of Tristram Shandy*

(1759–67) created a sensation in the 1760s, with its deliberately disordered narrative, lack of plot, practical jokes on the reader, and mordant sense of humour. His other novel, *A Sentimental Journey Through France and Italy* (1768), recounts the adventures of Parson Yorick on holiday (he gets as far as Lyon).

**Stevenson, Adlai E[wing]** (1900–65) American Democrat politician. A noted liberal and intellectual, who was much respected abroad, he stood twice against EISENHOWER as the Democratic presidential candidate (1952, 1956). His campaign speeches were published as *Call to Greatness* (1954) and *What I Think* (1956).

**Stevenson, Robert Louis [Balfour]** (1850–94) Scottish novelist, poet and essayist. He trained as an advocate in Edinburgh, but decided in his twenties to be a writer. By the time his first important fictional work, *Treasure Island* (1883), had been published he had established himself as an author of note with essays, poems and two travel books, *Travels with a Donkey in the Cevennes* (1879) and *The Silverado Squatters* (1883). His masterpiece is *The Strange Case of Dr Jekyll and Mr Hyde* (1886), a strange, disturbing story of dual personality. Other works include *Kidnapped* (1886), *The Master of Ballantrae* (1889), and the unfinished *Weir of Hermiston* (1896). He settled in Samoa, where he died. The Samoan nickname for him was "Tusitala," i.e. "the Storyteller."

**Stewart, Prince Charles Edward [Louis Philip]** (1720–88) also known as "Bonnie Prince Charlie" or the "Young Pretender," he led the Jacobite revolt against the Hanoverian King GEORGE III in 1745, fleeing Scotland when his Highland soldiers were defeated at Culloden in 1746. He died in Rome.

**Stewart, Jackie** [John Young Stewart] (1939– ) Scottish racing driver. He was world champion (1969, 1971, 1973), retiring in 1973 to pursue a highly successful career in business and as a sports commentator.

**Stieglitz, Alfred** (1864–1946) American photographer. He formed the Photo-Secession group with Edward STEICHEN, which became a highly influential force for establishing photography as an art form. He also founded the magazine *Camera Work* (1903–17).

**Stockhausen, Karlheinz** (1928– ) German composer. Regarded as the leading exponent of twelve-tone—or serial—music, he also used electronic sounds in his work. His work includes *Gruppen* (1959), for three orchestras, and *Kontakte* (1960).

**Stokowski, Leopold** (1882–1977) British-born American conductor (of Polish-Irish descent). A noted showman and popularizer of classical music, he is best known for his collaboration with Walt DISNEY in conducting the music for *Fantasia* (1940) (in which he shakes hands with Mickey Mouse).

**Stopes, Marie [Charlotte Carmichael]** (1880–1958) Scottish scientist and birth-control pioneer. She was the youngest Doctor of Science in Britain (1905) and acquired an international reputation as a palaeobotanist. The breakdown of her marriage (annulled in 1917) led her to the study of sex education, in which field she soon became a world authority and household name. Her book *Married Love* (1918), a frank analysis of sex within marriage, became an international best-seller (banned for a while in the USA). She established a birth control clinic in Holloway in London (1920), which gave free contraceptive advice to the poor.

**Stoppard, Tom** (1937– ) Czech-born British dramatist. His plays, e.g. *Rosencrantz and Guildenstern are Dead* (1966), *The Real Inspector Hound* (1968) and *The Real Thing* (1982) have been very successful because of their sharp, witty wordplay and fast, cleverly plotted action.

**Stowe, Mrs Harriet [Elizabeth] Beecher** (1811–96) American novelist. She wrote several novels, but the one she is remembered for is her great antislavery novel *Uncle Tom's Cabin, or, Life Among the Lowly* (1852). The novel created a sensation when published, and has been described as a factor leading to the American Civil War.

**Strauss, Richard** (1864–1949) German composer and conductor. His works include a series of richly orchestrated tone poems, e.g. *Till Eulenspiegel* (1894–95) and *Also Sprach Zarathustra* (1895–96), operas, e.g. *Elektra* (1909) and *Der Rosenkavalier* (1911), and the *Four Last Songs* (1948). He collaborated with ZWEIG on *The Silent Woman* (1935), which was banned by the Nazis after four performances.

**Stravinsky, Igor Fyodorovich** (1882–1971) Russian composer. He composed ballet scores for DIAGHILEV, e.g. *Petrushka* (1911) and *The Rite of Spring* (1913), the first performance of the latter provoking a riot but now regarded as a milestone in modernist music. He later composed several austerely neoclassical works, such as the opera-oratorio *Oedipus Rex* (1927), which also displayed the influence of SCHOENBERG's serial techniques. Other works include the Symphony in C Major (1940), and the opera *The Rake's Progress* (1951), on which AUDEN collaborated.

**Strindberg, Johan August** (1849–1912) Swedish dramatist and novelist. His unremittingly bleak plays, in which the strongest element is a pathological fear and hatred of women, are powerful, highly innovative works that have influenced many 20th-century dramatists. The plays include *Miss Julie* (1888) and *The Ghost Sonata* (1907).

**Stubbs, George** (1724–1806) English painter and engraver, best known for his paintings of horses, of which he had an outstanding anatomical knowledge, as shown in his book *Anatomy of the Horse* (1766). His works are also distinguished by masterly composition and atmospheric rendition of landscape. His works include *Mares and Foals by a River* (1763–68) and *Horses Attacked by a Lion* (1770).

**Suckling, Sir John** (1609–41) English poet, regarded as one of the finest of the "Cavalier" poets. The best known of his lyrics is the charming "Ballad upon a Wedding," which often appears in a discreetly bowdlerized version. He was reputed to be the best card-player and bowler in England, and may have invented cribbage.

**Suharto, Thojib N J** (1921– ) Indonesian general and statesman. He launched a brutal campaign of repression against communists and other dissidents in the mid-1960s, and assumed executive power in 1967 after president **Achmed Sukarno** *or* **Soekarno** (1901–70), the first president of Indonesia, resigned in his favour.

**Sukarno, Achmed** *see* **Suharto.**

**Sun Yat-sen** *or* **Sun Zhong Shan** (1866–1925) Chinese nationalist leader and statesman. Influenced by MARX and by Western democratic principles, he organized a revolutionary league based on the "Three People's Principles" of nationalism, democracy and reform. He played a leading role in the overthrow of the Manchu dynasty and became first president of the Republic of China in 1911–12, resigning to lead a revolt against General Yaun Shih-kai. With Soviet help, he regained power in 1923. After his death, the Kuomintang under CHIANG KAI-SHEK split from the Communists.

**Surrey, Earl of** [Henry Howard] (*c.*1517–47) English poet, soldier and courtier. His translations of parts of VIRGIL's *Aeneid*, printed posthumously, are notable for being the first (printed) blank verse in English. Surrey's brave, unruly life ended in his execution for treason.

**Sutherland, Dame Joan** (1926– ) Australian soprano. She became one of the world's leading bel canto operatic sopranos in the 1950s and 1960s, and retired in 1990.

**Sutherland, Graham** [Vivian] (1903–80) English painter. He was an official war artist (1941–45) and subsequently became a portrait painter of note. His portrait of CHURCHILL (1955) was destroyed by Lady Churchill.

**Suzman, Helen** (1917– ) South African politician. She became an MP for the liberal United (later Progressive, then Democratic) Party in 1953, retiring in 1989. She has been a long and consistent campaigner against apartheid.

**Suzuki, Daisetsu Teitaro** (1870–1966) Japanese Buddhist philosopher. His works on Zen Buddhism, such as *Studies in Zen* (1955), played a key role in popularizing the principles of Zen Buddhism in the West.

**Swift, Jonathan** (1667–1745) Anglo-Irish divine poet and satirist. His first important satirical works published in 1704, were *The Battle of the Books*, a defence of the merits of classical literature against the claims of the moderns, and *A Tale of a Tub*, an attack on religious extremism. In politics, Swift began as a Whig but soon became a staunch Tory. He became Dean of St Patrick's Cathedral in Dublin in 1713 and published several tracts defending the Irish poor against their overlords, including the savage *A Modest Proposal* (1729). His masterpiece is *Gulliver's Travels* (1726), which culminates in Gulliver's voyage to the Houyhnhnms ("whinims") intelligent horses whose nobility is contrasted with the brutality of humanity. Swift died leaving money to found a hospital for imbeciles, and was much mourned by the Irish people.

**Swinburne, Algernon [Charles]** (1837–1909) English poet and critic, noted for his sensuous verse described by himself as having a tendency to a "dulcet and luscious form of verbosity." His poems e.g. *Poems and Ballads* (1866), created scandal not just for their sexuality, but for the author's clear dislike of Christianity.

**Synge, [Edmund] John Millington** (1871–1909) Irish dramatist, noted for his poetic rendering of Irish peasant speech. His masterpiece is *The Playboy of the Western World* (1907), a highly controversial comedy (the audience at the Abbey Theatre in Dublin rioted on the first night when one of the characters referred to female undergarments).

**Szasz, Thomas Stephen** (1920– ) Hungarian-born American psychiatrist. He became noted in the early 1960s as a fierce critic of orthodox psychoanalysis, and argued that mental illness is in reality a myth fostered as an agent of repression in such works as *The Myth of Mental Illness* (1961). He argues that the only true mental illnesses are "diseases of the brain" and that much of what passes for mental illness should be classed as "problems of living." He also attacked LAING and the anti-psychiatry movement in *Schizophrenia: The Sacred Symbol of Psychiatry* (1979).

# T

**Taft, William Howard** (1857–1930) American Republican statesman. He became the 27th president of the US (1909–13) in succession to Theodore ROOSEVELT. More conservative in his policies than Roosevelt, he alienated the reformist wing of the Republican Party. He was appointed chief justice of the Supreme Court (1921–30), and became a noted isolationist in the 1930s.

**Tagore, Rabindranath** (1861–1941) Indian poet and philosopher. Although known primarily as a poet, he also wrote plays, essays and novels and short stories. Regarded by many Bengalis as their greatest writer, he was awarded the 1913 Nobel prize for literature and became venerated as a sage in Western intellectual circles. He was knighted in 1915, but repudiated the title in 1919 as a protest against the Amritsar Massacre.

**Tambo, Oliver** (1917–93) South African politician. He joined the African National Congress in 1944, and when the ANC was banned in 1960 left South Africa to set up an expatriate section. During MANDELA's imprisonment, he was the ANC's acting president (1967–77) and president (1977–91).

**Tanaka, Kakuei** (1918– ) Japanese politician. He was the Liberal Democratic minister of finance (1962–64), minister of international trade (1971) and prime minister (1972–74). He established dip-

392

lomatic relations with Communist China, but was forced to resign following charges of taking bribes from Lockheed, for which he was tried (1983) and imprisoned.

**Tange, Kenzo** (1913– ) Japanese architect. Influenced by LE CORBUSIER and by traditional Japanese building styles, his buildings include the Hiroshima Peace Centre (1949–55) and St Mary's Cathedral in Tokyo (1965).

**Tansley, Sir Arthur George** (1871–1955) English botanist. One of the pioneers of the study of plant ecology, he was the first president (1913–15) of the British Ecological Society. His works include *Practical Plant Ecology* (1923) and *The British Islands and Their Vegetation* (1939).

**Tarkovsky, Andrei** (1932–86) Russian film director, with a distinctive elegiac and often enigmatic style. The simplest of his seven feature films is his first, *Ivan's Childhood* (1962), his films steadily becoming more complex and allegorical, e.g. *Andrei Rublev* (1966), his two remarkable science fiction essays, *Solaris* (1972) and *Stalker* (1979), and his two films made in exile from the USSR, *Nostalgia* (1983) and *The Sacrifice* (1986). Tarkosky also directed a production of *Boris Godunov* for the Royal Opera, which was taken to Moscow in 1990.

**Tati, Jacques** [Jacques Tatischeff] (1908–82) French actor and film director. An ex-rugby player, he became an international comedy star with his Monsieur Hulot creation, an engagingly incompetent character hopelessly at odds with the modern world. Five Hulot films were made, including *Mr Hulot's Holiday* (1953) and *Mon Oncle* (1958).

**Tatum, Art[hur]** (1910–56) American jazz pianist.

Blind in one eye and partially sighted in the other, he was largely self-taught on the piano and became an acclaimed virtuoso of jazz piano music in the "swing" mode.

**Tatum, Edward Lawrie** (1909–75) American biochemist. With the American geneticist **George Wells Beadle** (1903–89), he demonstrated that biochemical reactions in cells are controlled by particular genes. With LEDERBERG, he discovered the phenomenon of genetic recombination in bacteria. All three shared the 1958 Nobel prize for physiology or medicine.

**Tavener, John Kenneth** (1944– ) English composer. He studied under Lennox BERKELEY, and became noted particularly for his religious compositions, e.g. the cantata *Cain and Abel* (1965) and the opera *Thérèse* (1973–76).

**Taylor, A[lan] J[ohn] P[ercivale]** (1906–90) English historian. Often a controversial figure (he argued that World War II was produced by accident as much as by HITLER's design), he was admired by his peers for his research and insight into modern European history, and became the historian best known to the British public through his (often unscripted) live lectures to television audiences. His works include *The Origins of the Second World War* (1961) and *The Trouble Makers* (1957).

**Taylor, Elizabeth** (1932– ) English-born (of American parents) American stage and film actress. Her films as a child include *National Velvet* (1944)—*see also* Shirley WILLIAMS—and *Little Women* (1949). Regarded as one of the most beautiful film stars of her generation, her films include *Cat on a Hot Tin Roof* (1958), *Butterfield 8* (1960) and *Who's Afraid of*

*Virginia Woolf?* (1966), the last two earning her Oscars. The latter film also co-starred her 5th husband, Richard BURTON, whom she married twice.

**Tchaikovsky, Peter Ilyich** (1840–93) Russian composer. Notable for his strong melodic sense and rejection of an overtly nationalistic and "folk" approach to composition, his works include tone poems, a violin concerto, the operas *Eugene Onegin* (based on PUSHKIN's novel in verse, 1879) and *The Queen of Spades* (1890), the ballets *Swan Lake* (1876) and *The Sleeping Beauty* (1889), and the so-called "Pathétique" Sixth Symphony.

**Teilhard de Chardin, Pierre** (1881–1955) French Jesuit theologian, philosopher and palaeontologist. He developed a theory of evolution, described in *The Phenomenon of Man* (1955) and other works, which he claimed was compatible with Roman Catholic teaching. All creation, in his view, is evolving progressively towards what he called the "Omega Point" of unity in God. The Church refused to let his books be published in his lifetime.

**Te Kanawa, Dame Kiri** (1944– ) New Zealand soprano. She is regarded as one of the world's leading operatic sopranos, and is particularly noted for MOZART and Italian opera roles.

**Telemann, George Philipp** (1681–1767) German composer. A highly prolific composer of the Baroque era, his works include over 40 operas and over 40 passions, many songs and a large number of instrumental pieces.

**Teller, Edward** (1908– ) Hungarian-born American physicist. He studied in Germany and under BOHR in Copenhagen, leaving Germany in 1933 after HITLER's rise to power. He settled in the US in 1935, where he became one of the leading figures in the development of nuclear weapons at Los Alamos. He was dubbed the "father of the hydrogen bomb" (tested 1952), and was almost unique among his colleagues for having few moral qualms about his work.

**Temple, Shirley** (1928– ) American film actress and Republican politician. She became the world's leading child film star with films such as *Dimples* (1936) and *Wee Willie Winkie* (1937). She later developed a career in politics under her married name of Shirley Temple Black, her posts including Ambassador to Ghana (1974–76).

**Teng Hsiao-p'ing** *see* **Deng Xiao Ping**.

**Tennyson, Alfred Lord** [1st Baron Tennyson] (1809–92) English poet. He first came to public notice with *Poems, Chiefly Lyrical* (1830). Subsequent volumes, e.g. *Poems* (1833) established him as a highly popular poet, and he was appointed poet laureate in succession to WORDSWORTH in 1850, the year in which he published his great elegy for his dead friend A. H. Hallam, *In Memoriam*. Tennyson became a much respected public figure, with several of his poems, e.g. "Locksley Hall" (1842), being regarded as oracular statements on the spirit of the age.

**Tenzing Norgay** *see* **Hillary, Edmund**.

**Terry, Dame Ellen Alice** (1847–1928) English actress. Her remarkably long stage career began in 1856 at the age of nine in a SHAKESPEARE production by Charles Kean, and ended in 1925. She formed a long partnership in Shakespearian roles with Sir Henry Irving, and had a close friendship (and long correspondence) with SHAW, who wrote many roles for her, e.g. Lady Cicely in *Captain Brassbound's Conversion* (1905).

**Thackeray, William Makepeace** (1811–63) Indian-born English novelist and essayist, noted particularly for the witty social satire of both his novels and his non-fiction works, e.g. *The Book of Snobs* (1846–47), a wickedly funny description of the varieties of snobbery. His masterpiece is *Vanity Fair* (1847–48), a decidedly non-moralistic tale of the opportunistic "anti-heroine" Becky Sharp, set during the Napoleonic wars. His other works include the novels *Pendennis* (1850) and *Henry Esmond* (1852).

**Thant, U** (1909–74) Burmese diplomat. He succeeded HAMMARSKJÖLD as secretary general of the United Nations (1961–72), and was widely admired for his role as a tactful mediator, most notably during the Cuban missile crisis.

**Thatcher, Margaret Hilda** (1925– ) English Conservative stateswoman. She was much influenced by her father, Albert Roberts, a grocer who was twice Conservative mayor of Grantham. She worked as a research chemist after graduating from Oxford, then became a barrister specializing in taxation law. She became MP for Finchley in 1959 and, as secretary of state for education and science (1970–74), became a hate figure for many when she ended provision of free school milk. She defeated HEATH in the Tory leadership campaign of 1975, becoming the first woman to lead a major British political party. As prime minister (1979–1990), she launched an ideological crusade (dubbed "Thatcherism") against what she perceived as the entrenchment of socialism in Britain, the principal elements of her attack being free-market policies and the privatization of nationalized industries. Her period of office was marked by rising unemployment and by the Falklands War of 1982, the success of which many believed to be the decisive factor in the Conservative's huge election victory of 1983 over Foot's Labour party. Her relationship with the next Labour leader, Kinnock, was notably confrontational, and she gave strong support to Reagan's forceful anti-communist foreign policy. Her policies were widely disliked by her political opponents and by moderate Tories, the latter forming small resistance groups around figures such as Heath and **Michael Heseltine** (1933– ), and (in the House of Lords) Macmillan (who made a speech denouncing privatization as "selling the family silver"). Abroad, she was condemned by Soviet spokesmen as the "Iron Lady," a tag she adopted with great joy, and was reviled by many Third World leaders. Her reception abroad, however, was often very warm. For many women, particularly in Africa, where she was rapturously received, she became a powerful role model. She welcomed Gorbachev as a "man we can do business with," and was acclaimed by figures such as Havel for her part in bringing the Cold War to an end. Increasing dissension within her cabinet, over such issues as the highly controversial Community Charge (or Poll Tax) and the disarray of the Health Service, led to her resignation in 1990 and the election of Major as prime minister.

**Theresa of Calcutta, Mother** [Agnes Gonxha Bojaxhiu] (1910– ) Yugoslavian-born (of Albanian parentage) Roman Catholic nun and missionary. She became a member of the Sisters of Loretto and trained in medicine in Paris, founding her own Order of the Missionaries of Charity in 1950. Venerated by many people as a living saint, her work in Calcutta with orphans and with the dying led to her being awarded the 1979 Nobel Peace Prize. Her order now has over 200 branch houses worldwide.

**Thomas, Dylan [Marlais]** (1914–53) Welsh poet with a hard-drinking, boisterous reputation. His poems are exuberant, often florid and occasionally obscure. His best-known single work is *Under Milk Wood* (1954), a radio drama in poetic prose.

**Thomas à Becket** *see* **Becket, Thomas à**.

**Thomas Aquinas, Saint** (*c.*1225–74) Italian theologian and philosopher. Despite strong family opposition, he joined the Dominican order in 1243 and eventually became a teacher in Paris and Italy. His two great works, the *Summae* (1259–64 and *c.*1265–74), establishing the need for both reason and faith in Christianity, have become a cornerstone in the teachings of the Roman Catholic Church.

**Thompson, Emma** *see* **Branagh, Kenneth**.

**Thompson, Francis** (1859–1907) English poet. Rescued from opium addiction by the poet and fellow Roman Catholic **Alice Meynell** (1847–1922), Thompson produced three volumes of poetry in the 1890s, *Poems* (1893), *Sister Songs* (1895) and *New Poems* (1897). The best known of his poems, e.g. "The Hound of Heaven", are intensely spiritual, with elaborate imagery.

**Thomson, D[avid] C[ouper]** (1861–1954) Scottish newspaper proprietor. His Dundee-based group included *The Sunday Post*, a straight-laced paper with virtual saturation circulation in Scotland, and many children's comics, particularly the *Dandy*

(1937) and *Beano* (1938). Thomson was a notably conservative and paternalistic figure who refused to recognize trade unions. *See also* Dudley WATKINS.

**Thomson, Sir George Paget** (1892–1975) English physicist. He shared the 1937 Nobel prize for physics with the American physicist **Clinton Joseph Davisson** (1881–1958) for their (independent) discovery of the diffraction of electrons by crystals. His works include *Theory and Practice of Electron Diffraction* (1939).

**Thomson, James** (1700–48) Scottish poet and dramatist. His plays are bombastic tragedies of little interest, but his poems, e.g. *The Seasons* (1726–30), were much admired by Romantic poets such as WORDSWORTH, who saw him as a true nature poet.

**Thomson, James** (1834–82) Scottish poet, chiefly remembered for his poem "City of Dreadful Night" (1874), a long, nightmarish vision of a decaying city, through which runs a River of Suicides. Thomson died an alcoholic.

**Thomson, Sir Joseph John** (1856–1940) English physicist. He was awarded the 1906 Nobel prize for physics for his discovery (1906) of the electron, one of the most significant discoveries in physics. Seven of his assistants and pupils (e.g. RUTHERFORD) went on to win Nobel prizes, and many others became professors.

**Thomson, Roy [Herbert]** [1st Baron Thomson of Fleet] (1894–1976) Canadian-born British newspaper proprietor. He began buying radio stations and newspapers in Canada in the 1930s, subsequently expanding into the US and Britain. He bought *The Times* (1966) and *Sunday Times* (1959).

**Thoreau, Henry David** (1817–62) American philosopher, and friend of EMERSON, whose advocacy of self-sufficiency and passive resistance to tyranny has been very influential, GANDHI being his most notable admirer. The best known of his works is *Walden, or Life in the Woods* (1854), which describes his two-year retreat to live in a cabin in the woods. He was an aphorist of genius, e.g. "The mass of men live lives of quiet desperation".

**Thorndike, Dame Sybil** (1882–1976) English actress. Notable for her long acting career, from 1904 to the late 60s, she created many roles, including SHAW's *Saint Joan* (1924).

**Thorpe, [John] Jeremy** (1929– ) English Liberal politician. Leader of the Liberal Party (1967–76), he resigned after being accused of conspiring to murder a male model, Norman Scott, who claimed to have been Thorpe's lover. Thorpe was acquitted.

**Thurber, James [Grover]** (1894–1961) American humorist, cartoonist and essayist, much of whose work first appeared in *New Yorker* magazine, including his most famous story, "The Secret Life of Walter Mitty."

**Tiberius** [Tiberius Claudius Nero] (42 BC–37 AD) Roman emperor. A much respected soldier, he succeeded his stepfather AUGUSTUS in 14. His reign became increasingly despotic and he ruled Rome from his refuge on Capri from 26.

**Tiepolo, Giambattista** (1696–1770) Italian artist, the greatest decorative fresco painter of the Rococo period. His works include *The Marriage of Frederick Barbarossa and Beatrice of Burgundy* (1751).

**Tillich, Paul [Johannes]** (1886–1965) German-born American theologian and philosopher. He served as a Lutheran military chaplain in World

War I, and became a brave critic of the Nazis, who barred him from teaching in 1933. He emigrated to the US, becoming a citizen in 1940. His highly influential theological work addresses the problems of matching traditional forms of Christian belief with an increasingly secular, and doubting, modern society. His works include *The Courage To Be* (1952) and *Systematic Theology* (1951–63).

**Tinbergen, Jan** (1903– ) Dutch economist (brother of Niko TINBERGEN). He shared the 1969 Nobel prize for economics with the Norwegian economist **Ragnar Frisch** (1895–1973) for their work in the field of econometrics. His works include *Econometrics* (1941).

**Tinbergen, Niko[laas]** (1907–88) Dutch ethologist (brother of Jan TINBERGEN). He shared the 1973 Nobel prize for physiology or medicine (with LORENZ and Karl von FRISCH) for his ground-breaking studies of animal behaviour, which established ethology as a science. His works include *The Herring Gull's World* (1953) and *Animal Behaviour* (1965).

**Tintoretto, Jacopo** (1518–94) Venetian painter. Influenced by TITIAN and MICHELANGELO, his dynamic, highly imaginative use of lighting and highlighting, as shown in *The Last Supper* (1592–94), earned him wide critical acclaim.

**Tippett, Sir Michael** (1905– ) English composer. A pacifist, he was jailed for three months during World War II as a conscientious objector. His works include several operas, e.g. *The Midsummer Marriage* (1955) and *The Knot Garden* (1970), the oratorio *A Child of our Time* (1941), symphonies, song cycles and chamber music. His books include *Moving into Aquarius* (1959, revised 1974).

**Titian** [Tiziano Vecelli] (c.1490–1576) Venetian painter, one of the great figures of world art. He studied with Giovanni BELLINI and worked with GIORGIONE, whom he succeeded as the master of Venetian painters for some 60 years. From 1530 he was patronized by the Holy Roman Emperor CHARLES V and then by PHILIP II. His powerful and richly coloured works include *Bacchus and Ariadne* (1523), *Charles V at Mehlberg* (1548), and *The Rape of Europa* (1562).

**Tito, Marshal** [Josip Broz] (1892–1980) Yugoslav statesman. He fought with the Bolsheviks during the Russian civil war and became secretary general of the Yugoslav Communist Party in 1937. In 1941, after the German invasion of Yugoslavia, he organized a partisan force to fight the occupiers, and succeeded in diverting British aid from other guerrilla forces to his own. After the war, he established a Communist government and broke with STALIN, but maintained a repressive regime. He succeeded in preserving a fragile Yugoslav unity, but 11 years after his death the break-up of the Yugoslav state began with Slovenia, then Croatia, declaring independence from the Serbian-dominated state in 1991.

**Todd, Alexander Robertus**, Baron Todd of Trumpington (1907– ) Scottish biochemist. He was awarded the 1957 Nobel prize for chemistry for his research into the chemical structure of nucleotides.

**Togliatti, Palmiro** (1893–1964) Italian Communist politician. He helped found the Italian Communist Party (with GRAMSCI and others) and became party secretary (1926–64). He lived in exile in the Soviet Union during MUSSOLINI's rule, where a city on the Volga was named after him. He returned to Italy in

1944, and helped build the Italian communist party into the largest in Western Europe.

**Tojo, Hideki** (1885–1948) Japanese soldier. He became minister of war (1940–44) and prime minister (1941–44). He resigned in 1944 after losses in the Pacific theatre of war, and was executed as a war criminal.

**Tolkien, J[ohn] R[onald] R[euel]** (1892–1973) South African-born British fantasy writer and scholar. Probably the most influential (and best-selling) fantasy writer, the works on which his fame rests are *The Hobbit* (1937) and the three-volume *Lord of the Rings* (1954–55)

**Tolstoy, Count Leo [Nikolayevich]** (1828–1910) Russian novelist, dramatist, short-story writer and philosopher. His autobiographical trilogy, *Childhood* (1852), *Boyhood* (1854) and *Youth* (1857), is one of the most remarkable ever published by a young man. His spiritual self-questioning resulted in some of the world's greatest works of fiction, notably *War and Peace* (1863–69), a panoramic epic of the Napoleonic invasion of Russia, and *Anna Karenina* (1875–77), a tragic tale of adulterous love, which raises profound questions about personal and social morality.

**Tortelier, Paul** (1914–91) French cellist, conductor and composer. He performed with BEECHAM in 1947, after which he toured worldwide as a soloist. A renowned teacher of the cello, his pupils included Jacqueline DU PRÉ.

**Torvill, Jayne** (1957– ) and **Dean, Christopher** (1958– ) English ice-dance skaters. They became world champions (1981–83), European champions (1981–82, 1984) and Olympic champions (1984)

Their Olympic win was achieved with an unprecedented top score of 6.0 from all nine judges. Their best-known routine used RAVEL's *Boléro* as the score.

**Toscanini, Arturo** (1867–1957) Italian conductor. Regarded as one of the most authoritarian conductors of all time, he was renowned for his fanatical devotion to authenticity and disdain for showy interpretation of the score, and for his remarkable musical memory.

**Toulouse-Lautrec, Henri [Marie Raymond] de** (1864–1901) French painter and lithographer. The son of an aristocrat, an accident in which his legs were broken stunted his growth. Influenced by VAN GOGH and DEGAS, his subjects were café clientele: prostitutes and cabaret performers in and around Montmartre, as in *In the Parlour at the Rue des Moulins* (1894). He is best known for his posters and lithographs.

**Tourneur, Cyril** (*c.*1575–1626) English dramatist, author of *The Atheist's Tragedy* (1611), and possibly also the author of one of the greatest revenge tragedies, *The Revenger's Tragedy* (1607).

**Toynbee, Arnold [Joseph]** (1889–1975) English historian. His major work is *A Study of History* (1934–61), which compares civilizations past and present in terms of a rhythmic process of growth and decay. An abridgement of his work published in 1947 became a best-seller, with Toynbee acquiring the reputation of a prophet in the US, although fellow historians were often sharply critical of his methodology.

**Tracy, Spencer** (1900–1967) American film actor. He won two Oscars in a row, for *Captains Courageous* (1937) and *Boy's Town* (1938). He had a long personal and professional relationship with Katharine HEPBURN.

**Trevelyan, George Macaulay** (1876–1962) English historian. His highly readable works include *History of England* (1926) and *English Social History* (1944) and several biographies, e.g. *Grey of Falloden* (1937).

**Trollope, Anthony** (1815–82) English novelist, whose more than 50 books are dominated by two main novel sequences: the "Barsetshire" novels, which focus on the provincial lives of the gentry, clergy and middle classes, e.g. *Barchester Towers* (1857); and the "Palliser" novels of political life, e.g. *Phineas Finn* (1869). Trollope was also a highly industrious civil servant, with a formidable appetite for life and work. His mother, **Mrs Frances Trollope** (1780–1863), was also a prolific author, whose best-known work is *Domestic manners of the Americans* (1832).

**Trotsky, Leon** [Lev Davidovich Bronstein] (1879–1940) Russian revolutionary. Arrested at the age of nineteen for political agitation, he was exiled to Siberia, escaping to join LENIN in London in 1902. An advocate of "permanent revolution," he believed that socialism could not be built in one country alone, and supported the Mensheviks against Lenin's Bolsheviks. He returned to Russia in 1917, where he joined the Bolsheviks and was largely responsible for creating and directing the victorious Red Army during the civil war. His influence in the party declined after Lenin's death in 1924, and he was forced into exile by STALIN in 1929. He settled in Mexico in 1937, where he was assassinated by a Russian agent. A ruthless, charismatic figure,

Trotsky's influence as a focal point for Leninist dissent against Stalinism was large. Initially critical of Lenin's iron grip on the party leadership as undemocratic, he recanted this view after the Bolshevik revolution, arguing, with a fair measure of casuistry, that any resemblances between Stalin's dictatorship and Lenin's (and his own use of terror) were merely superficial.

**Trudeau, Pierre [Elliott]** (1919– ) Canadian Liberal politician. He became an MP in 1965 and, succeeding PEARSON, prime minister (1968–79, 1980–84). A member of a wealthy Montreal family, he was a strong opponent of the Quebec separatist movement. He retired from politics in 1985.

**Trueman, Freddy** [Frederick Sewards Trueman] (1931– ) English cricketer. A notable fast bowler, he played for Yorkshire for 19 years (1949–68) and played in 67 Tests, taking a record 307 wickets in one match. He was also a batsman, scoring over 9,000 runs (making three centuries). On retirement, he became a popular commentator.

**Truffaut, François** (1932–84) French film director, critic and actor. One of the *Cahiers du Cinema* group of film critics, his first film, the semi-autobiographical *The Four Hundred Blows* (1959), was widely praised. His other films include *Jules et Jim* (1961) and *The Last Metro* (1980). He has acted in several films, e.g. SPIELBERG's *Close Encounters of the Third Kind* (1977) and in his own charming *Day for Night ("La Nuit Américaine"* 1973), in which Graham GREENE had a small uncredited walk-on role.

**Truman, Harry S** (1884–1972) American Democratic statesman. He became 33rd president of the

US (1945–52) after Franklin D. ROOSEVELT's death, and authorized the dropping of the atom bombs on Hiroshima and Nagasaki. He initiated the change in US foreign policy towards the Soviet Union expressed as the "Truman doctrine," a policy of containment of communism and aid towards groups or nations resisting communism, and approved the MARSHALL Plan of aid for Britain and Western Europe.

**Tshombe, Moise Kapenda** (1919–69) Congolese politician. He declared Katanga's independence from the Congo (now Zaire) in 1960, but was forced to concede defeat in 1963. Exiled in Spain, he returned in 1964 to become Congolese premier, and was ousted by MOBUTO in 1965. He went back to Spain, was kidnapped and taken to Algeria in 1967, where he died under arrest.

**Turgenev, Ivan Sergeyevich** (1818–83) Russian novelist, short-story writer and dramatist. His novels, e.g. his masterpiece *Fathers and Sons* (1862), explore such major issues of Russian life as serfdom and revolutionary change. The best known of his plays is *A Month in the Country* (1850).

**Turing, Alan Mathison** (1912–54) English mathematician. Regarded as one of the most important computer theoreticians, he developed the concept of an idealized computer called the "Universal Automaton" (later called the "Turing Machine") in his paper "On Computable Numbers" (1937). The computer, he posited, would be able to modify its own program through a sequence on paper tape of 1s and 0s. Turing also took part in the vitally important code-breaking project at Bletchley Park in World War II, which deciphered the German "Enigma" codes. He committed suicide after being charged with a homosexual offence.

**Turner, Joseph Mallord William** (1775–1851) English painter. Precociously talented, he exhibited his first work at the Royal Academy aged 15. After a trip to Italy in 1819 he became more interested in gradations of shifting light and atmosphere, e.g. *The Bay of Baiae, with Apollo and the Sybil* (1823). The works of the next two decades represent his finest period, CONSTABLE describing paintings such as *The Fighting Téméraire* (1839) as "airy visions painted with tinted steam". He found an influential champion in RUSKIN.

**Twain, Mark** [pseud. of Samuel Langhorne Clemens] (1835–1910) American novelist, short-story writer and humorist. After training as a printer, he became a Mississippi river pilot, taking his pseudonym from the depth-sounding call meaning "by the mark take two fathoms". His two most famous novels, *The Adventures of Tom Sawyer* (1876) and (his masterpiece) *The Adventures of Huckleberry Finn* (1884), have become world classics of children's literature.

**Tynan, Kenneth [Peacock]** (1927–80) English theatre critic. As critic for *The Observer* (1954–63), he was noted for his sharp wit, often directed at stage censorship, and for his vigorous promotion of the new "kitchen sink" drama of the mid–1950s (e.g. OSBORNE's plays) and "socially useful" plays, such as BRECHT's. He is now principally remembered for his revue *Oh Calcutta* (1969).

**Tyndale, William** *see* **More, Sir Thomas**.

# U

**Uccello, Paolo** (*c*.1396–1475) Florentine painter. His fresco *In the Flood* (*c*.1455) demonstrates his fascination with perspective and foreshortening. He developed a synthesis between Renaissance ideas of spatial composition with a Gothic sense of detail, as in *The Battle of San Romano* (1455).

**Ulbricht, Walter** (1893–1973) East German Communist politician. He left Germany for the Soviet Union in 1933, returning in 1945 in the wake of the Red Army. As general secretary of the East German Socialist Unity [i.e. Communist] Party (1946–71), he supervised the sovietization of East German society, crushed the Berlin workers' rebellion of 1953 and built the Berlin Wall in 1961.

**Urban VIII** [Maffei Barberini] (1568–1644) Italian pope (1623–44). He developed his diplomatic skills as a papal envoy to France, befriended writers and scholars (among them Galileo GALILEI), established the papal summer residence at Castel Gandolfo, and used his influence to establish members of his family in important positions. Galileo dedicated his *Dialogue* on the movement of celestial bodies to him, but despite this Urban—reluctantly—forced Galileo to retract his theory on pain of death.

**Urey, Harold Clayton** (1893–1981) American chemist. He was awarded the 1934 Nobel prize for chemistry for his isolation of the heavy hydrogen isotope, deuterium. He worked on the production of heavy water during World War II.

**Ustinov, Sir Peter [Alexander]** (1921– ) British actor, director, dramatist and raconteur (of Russian-French parentage). His plays include *The Love of Four Oranges* (1951) and *Romanoff and Juliet* (1956). Other works include an autobiography, *Dear Me* (1977). He is best known as an engaging raconteur in one-man shows and on television.

**Utrillo, Maurice** (1883–1955) French painter. He was encouraged to paint by his mother, **Suzanne Valadon** (1867–1938), also a painter, but he was largely self-taught. He is noted particularly for his street scenes of Paris, and his "White Period" paintings of 1908–14 are particularly sought after.

# V

**Valadon, Suzanne** *see* **Utrillo, Maurice**.

**Valentino, Rudolph** [Rodolfo Guglielmi di Valentina
d'Antonguolla] (1895–1926) Italian-born American
film actor. He became the leading screen personifi-
cation of the romantic hero in such films as *The Four
Horsemen of the Apocalypse* (1921) and *The Son of
the Sheik* (1926). He died of peritonitis, his funeral
attended by hordes of hysterical women.

**Van Allen, James Alfred** (1914– ) American physicist. He discovered, through detectors on the US
satellite *Explorer I*, the Van Allen radiation belts
outside the Earth's atmosphere.

**Vanbrugh, Sir John** (1664–1726) English drama-
tist and architect, noted for his witty comedies, e.g.
*The Relapse* (1696) and *The Provok'd Wife* (1697).
He was also one of the finest architects of his day,
the most famous of his buildings being Blenheim
Palace.

**Van der Post, Sir Laurens [Jan]** (1906– ) South
African novelist, travel writer and mystic. His works
are strongly influenced by JUNG and display a strong
sympathy for the "primitive" peoples of the world.
His novels include *The Seed and the Sower* (1963),
based on his experiences a a prisoner of war of the
Japanese in World War II and filmed as *Merry
Christmas, Mr Lawrence* (1982). His travel books

include two African classics, *Venture to the Interior* (1952) and *The Lost World of the Kalahari* (1958).

**van Eyck, Jan** (*c*.1385–1441) Dutch painter. A master in the medium of oil painting, he was court painter to Philip, Duke of Burgundy from 1425 to *c*.1430, and all his dated works are from the 1430s, when he lived in Bruges. His paintings are both realistic and charged with a serene, spiritual atmosphere, as in the *Arnolfini Marriage* (1434).

**Van Gogh, Vincent** (1853–90) Dutch painter. He originally studied theology and was a lay preacher before taking up painting in 1880. Uncompromising from the start, his art was thoroughly unacademic in its realistic subject matter and bold, expressionistic style, e.g. *The Potato Eaters* (1885). He moved to Paris in 1886, where his work was influenced by DEGAS, GAUGUIN and SEURAT, without compromising his enigmatic use of colour and powerful impasto brushwork. He spent the last two years of his life in southern France, partly in an asylum at St Rémy; it was a time of intense creativity arising out of personal anguish, e.g. *The Cornfield* (1889), at the scene of which he shot himself. His work has been enormously influential.

**Varèse, Edgard** (1883–1965) French-born American composer and conductor. His (usually orchestral) compositions are noted for their combination of the extreme registers of instruments with taped and electronic sounds. His works include *Hyperprism* (1923) and *Ionisation* (1925).

**Vasari, Giorgio** (1511–74) Italian painter, writer and architect, noted particularly for his *Lives of the Most Eminent Painters, Sculptors and Architects* (1550, revised edition 1568), an invaluable source book for the lives of Renaissance artists from GIOTTO to MICHELANGELO. He also designed the Uffizi in Florence.

**Vaughan, Henry** (1622–95) Welsh poet, best known for his collection of mystical religious verse, *Silex Scintillians* (1650–1655). Several of his poems, like those of HERBERT, have startlingly vivid opening lines, e.g. "They are all gone into the world of light."

**Vaughan Williams, Ralph** (1872–1958) English composer. Like HOLST, he was heavily influenced by traditional English music, particularly English folk song. His works include the choral *Sea Symphony* (1910), *Fantasia on a Theme by Thomas Tallis* (1910), operas, ballet music and song cycles.

**Vavilov, Nikolai Ivanovich** (1887–1943) Russian botanist and plant geneticist. He developed a "principle of diversity," which states that the original source of a cultivated plant will be found to lie within the area containing the greatest diversity of the plant. His theories were attacked by LYSENKO, resulting in Vavilov's imprisonment and death in a Soviet labour camp.

**Veblen, Thorstein** (1857–1929) American economist (of Norwegian parentage). Regarded as the founder of the school of institutional economics, he drew a famous distinction between the industrial process, which tends towards efficiency of production, and the demands of business, which may restrict output in the name of profit. His works include *The Theory of the Leisure Class* (1899) and *The Theory of Business Enterprise* (1904).

**Vega Carpio, Lope de** (1562–1635) Spanish poet and dramatist. His eventful life included service in both the Spanish Armada of 1588 and, later in life, the Inquisition. He reputedly wrote around 1500 plays, of which a few hundred survive.

**Velàzquez** *or* **Velàsquez, Diego Roderiguez de Silva y** (1599–1660) Spanish painter. His earliest paintings were *bodegones*, a type of genre painting peculiar to Spain, consisting largely of domestic scenes, e.g. *An Old Woman Cooking Eggs* (1618). On RUBENS' advice he travelled to Italy in 1628, where he was influenced by TITIAN and TINTORETTO, developing a lighter palette and finer brushwork. His works include the portrait of *Pope Innocent X* (1650) and *Surrender of Breda* (1634–35).

**Verdi, Giuseppe** (1813–1901) Italian composer. His post-1850 operas, which include *Il Trovatore* (1853), *La Traviata* (1853), *La Forza del Destino* (1862), *Aida* (1871), *Otello* (1887) and *Falstaff* (1893), were hugely popular and remain constant favourites within the repertory of most opera companies. He became a deputy in the first Italian parliament of 1860.

**Verlaine, Paul** (1844–96) French poet, regarded with his friend and lover RIMBAUD as an early Symbolist. The affair ended when Verlaine shot and wounded Rimbaud, spending two years in prison for the deed. Collections of his verse include *Saturnian Poems* (1866) and *Romances Without Words* (1874).

**Vermeer, Jan** *or* **Johannes** (1632–75) Dutch painter. He is best remembered for his small-scale intimate interior scenes, carefully composed and lit, usually by daylight through a window, e.g. *Woman in Blue reading a Letter* (1662–64).

**Verne, Jules** (1828–1905) French novelist, whose innovative fantasy novels, e.g. *Voyage to the Centre of the Earth* (1864) and *20,000 Leagues Under the*

*Sea* (1969), are regarded as the earliest great science fiction novels.

**Veronese, Paolo** [Paolo Caliari] (1528–88) Italian painter. One of the outstanding decorative painters of his day, he was encouraged in his work by TITIAN. His works include *The Marriage at Cana* (1562–63) and *The Last Supper* (1573), the latter incurring the wrath of the Inquisition, and was renamed *Feast in the House of Levi*.

**Verrocchio, Andrea del** [Andrea di Cione] (1435–88) Florentine sculptor and painter. Possibly a pupil of DONATELLO, he trained as a goldsmith and became popular for sculptures such as *The Doubting of Thomas* (1465). He ran a large and busy workshop, and part of his painting *The Baptism of Christ* (*c.*1472) is attributed to his most famous pupil, LEONARDO da Vinci.

**Verwoerd, Hendrik Frensch** (1901–66) South African politician. Anti-British and pro-German, he opposed South Africa's entry into World War II, and became prime minister (1958–66). He fostered apartheid, banned the ANC (1960) and took South Africa out of the Commonwealth in 1961. He was assassinated by a deranged white man.

**Vicky** [Victor Weisz] (1913–66) German-born British cartoonist. He became one of the leading left-wing political cartoonists and caricaturists of his day, notably with the *Daily Mirror* and *Evening Standard*. His cartoon creations included "Supermac," his cruelly accurate parody of MACMILLAN.

**Vico, Giovanni Battista** (1668–1744) Italian philosopher. His *Scienza Nuova* (1725), a remarkably original work which posits a cyclical rise and fall for civilisations as human nature evolves through cultural and linguistic changes, was largely ignored until the 19th century.

**Victoria, Queen** (1819–1901) British queen. She inherited the throne on the death of her uncle, **William IV** (1765–1837), king of the United Kingdom (1830–37), and married **Prince Albert** of Saxe-Coburg-Gotha (1819–61) in 1840. Albert became the dominant influence on her life, and after his death Victoria withdrew from public life, her seclusion being strongly disapproved of by the public and resulting in a climate in which the desirability of a republic was much discussed. At DISRAELI's instigation, she was crowned empress of India in 1876 and re-established the monarchy's popularity.

**Vidal, [Eugene Luther] Gore** (1925– ) American novelist, dramatist and critic. His American historical fiction provides an unofficial and waspishly entertaining alternative history of the US and its leaders, e.g. *Burr* (1973) and *1876* (1976). His work includes several important essay collections, e.g. *The Second American Revolution* (1982) and *Armageddon* (1987).

**Villa, Pancho** [Francisco Villa, originally Doroteo Arango] (*c.*1877–1923) Mexican revolutionary. A former bandit, his forces aided ZAPATA in the seizure of Mexico City (1914–15). Villa's forces sparked off the US invasion of 1916–17 by killing some US civilians.

**Villa-Lobos, Heitor** (1887–1959) Brazilian composer and conductor. When he was 18, he joined an expedition up the Amazon to collect folk music. He settled in Paris (1923–30), where his work, combining elements of traditional Brazilian music with the European classical tradition, became highly popular. He composed over 2,000 works, including 12 symphonies, 16 string quartets, five operas and symphonic tone poems.

**Villon, François** (*c.*1431–*c.*1463) French poet. The little that is known of his life indicates a violent, unstable personality. A former student at the University of Paris, he was banished from Paris in 1463, and nothing is known of him after this date. Two main collections of his work survive, the so-called *Little* and *Greater Testaments*. The latter includes the remarkable "Ballad of Ladies of Long Ago," with its haunting refrain *"Mais où sont les neiges d'antan?"*

**Virgil** *or* **Vergil** [Publius Vergilius Maro] (70–19 BC) Roman poet. His works include the ten pastoral poems *Eclogues* or *Bucolics*; the *Georgics*, poems on agricultural subjects that celebrate the rural way of life; and his masterpiece, the *Aeneid*, an epic poem in 12 books that charts the progress of the Trojan hero Aeneas from the fall of Troy to the founding of the Roman state. Patronised by AUGUSTUS and the friend of HORACE, he was one of the most influential poets of all time.

**Visconti [di Modrone], Count Luchino** (1906–76) Italian film director. An aristocrat, he became a Marxist in the 1930s. He began his career as a stage designer, then worked as an assistant to RENOIR. His films include *The Leopard* (1963), *The Damned* (1969) and *Death in Venice* (1971), the latter two starring BOGARDE.

**Vishnevskaya, Galina** *see* **Rostropovich, Mstislav**.

**Voltaire** [pseud. of François Marie Arouet] (1694–1778) French philosopher, poet, historian, essayist, dramatist and essayist. Regarded as one of the most important of the French philosophers of the Enlightenment, his most influential single work is the *Philosophical Letters* (1734), a collection of witty, acerbic attacks on the tyranny of the *ancien régime*. His main theme was *"Écrasez l'infâme"* ("Crush the abuses") of religious, political and intellectual despotism, and his writings, with those of ROUSSEAU (with whom he disputed bitterly), are often described as the main intellectual roots of the French Revolution. His other works include the remarkable novel *Candide* (1759), which, like Dr JOHNSON's *Rasselas*, takes a markedly pessimistic view of human endeavour.

**von Braun, Wernher** (1912–77) German-born American rocket engineer. The technical director (1937–45) of the German rocket project at Peenemunde in World War II, he designed the V–1 and V–2 rocket bombs that were launched in random attacks against southern England in 1944. Captured by the US, he was put to work on US rocket research, including the development of the Saturn moon rockets.

**von Neumann, John** (1903–57) Hungarian-born American mathematician. He was one of the founders of the theory of games, i.e. the application of statistical logic to the choice of game strategies. He also made significant contributions to quantum theory and to computer research, and was a consultant on the development of the atom bomb.

**Voroshilov, Klimenti Yefremovich** (1881–1969) Soviet military leader and statesman. A Red Army commander in the civil war, he was commissar for defence (1925–40), in charge of the Red Army. He became president (1953–60) after his friend STALIN's death.

# W

**Wagner, [Wilhelm] Richard** (1813–83) German composer. He achieved great success with his third opera, *Rienzi* (1842). The operas which followed, *The Flying Dutchman* (1843) and *Tannhäuser* (1845) were not so popular, and, in trouble with the authorities for his radical sympathies, he fled to Paris where he wrote critical works, including the vilely anti-Semitic *Judaism in Music* (1850). He established his own theatre in Bayreuth in 1876, where he staged his *Ring of the Niebelung* cycle. Wagner's strongly Romantic works revolutionized opera, with their use of leitmotif and dramatic power.

**Waldheim, Kurt** (1918– ) Austrian diplomat. After service as a Nazi intelligence officer in World War II, he entered the Austrian diplomatic service and became secretary-general of the United Nations (1972–82) and president of Austria (1986– ). Revelations about his role in the Nazi genocide machine in Yugoslavia during the war surfaced in the late 1980s. Waldheim's critics have pointed out that his repeated claim that he knew nothing of the Holocaust can only mean that he was the worst intelligence officer in the Nazi apparatus.

**Walesa, Lech** (1943– ) Polish trade union leader and statesman. An electrician at the Gdansk Lenin Shipyard, he was dismissed several times for organizing strikes, and became the leader of the free trade union, Solidarity, in 1980, which forced substantial concessions from the Polish government. After the imposition of martial law in 1981, Solidarity was banned and Walesa imprisoned (1981–82). After his release, he was awarded the 1983 Nobel Peace Prize, in which year Pope JOHN PAUL II visited Poland. A skilled negotiator, Walesa succeeded in getting Solidarity re-legalized, and, in 1989, in the first free elections in eastern Europe since the 1940s, a Solidarity government was formed with Walesa as president.

**Wallace, Alfred Russel** (1823–1913) Welsh naturalist. Independently of DARWIN, he devised a theory of evolution by natural selection, which he sent to Darwin in 1858, thus prompting Darwin to arrange for the publication of his findings. (In a rare example of scientific cooperation, both parties involved honoured the other's work.) Wallace's works include *Geographical Distribution of Animals* (1876) and *Man's Place in the Universe* (1898).

**Waller, Fats** [Thomas Wright Waller] (1904–43) American jazz pianist and composer. Renowned for his sense of humour, he became one of America's favourite entertainers and a much admired exponent of the "stride" school of the jazz piano. His many compositions include "Honeysuckle Rose" and "Ain't Misbehavin'."

**Wallis, Sir Barnes [Neville]** (1887–1979) English aeronautical engineer. He designed the R100 airship, the Wellington bomber and in World War II the "bouncing bombs" used in the famous "Dambuster" bombing raid on the Mohne and Eder dams (1943).

**Walpole, Horace** [4th Earl of Orford] (1717–97)

English author, son of Robert WALPOLE, noted for his vast correspondence and for his fascination with the "Gothic," which expressed itself in his conversion of his house, Strawberry Hill, into a pseudo-medieval castle, and the Gothic novel *The Castle of Otranto* (1764), a very influential work that spawned a host of imitations.

**Walpole, Sir Robert,** [1st Earl of Orford] (1676–1745) English statesman, father of Horace WALPOLE. He became a Whig MP in 1701, and became Chancellor and First Lord of the Treasury in 1715. He was, effectively, Britain's first prime minister from 1721–42, GEORGE I having little interest in the government of Britain.

**Walter, Bruno** [Bruno Walter Schlesinger] (1876–1962) German-born American conductor. Noted for his concerts and recordings of the great German Romantic composers, he is particularly associated with the works of his friend MAHLER. He held various important posts in German and Austrian music, e.g. with the Salzburg Festival, but, being Jewish, was forced to leave Germany in 1933 and Austria in 1938. In the US, he conducted both the Metropolitan Opera and the New York Philharmonic.

**Walton, Sir Earnest** *see* **Cockcroft, Sir John Douglas.**

**Walton, Izaak** (1593–1683) English author, best known for his very popular *The Compleat Angler* (1653, revised 1655, 1676), which is both a treatise on the art of angling and a celebration of the quiet life. The work has gone into countless editions since the 17th century.

**Walton, Sir William** [Turner] (1902–83) English composer. His works include a setting of Edith

Sitwell's poem *Façade* (1921–22), a self-consciously off-the-wall piece for voice and instruments that failed to shock the English bourgeoisie as much as was hoped. His other works include the oratorio *Belshazaar's Feast* (1930–31), and several film scores, e.g. for OLIVIER's *Henry V* (1944).

**Warburg, Otto Heinrich** (1883–1970) German biochemist and cell physiologist. A member of a notably intellectual Jewish family, he was decorated while serving with the Prussian Horse Guards in World War I. His work on cell metabolism and respiration, with particular reference to cancer research, earned him two Nobel prizes for physiology or medicine (1931, 1944), but he was unable to accept the latter by HITLER's decree.

**Ward, Dame Barbara Mary** [Baroness Jackson of Lodsworth] (1914–81) English economist and conservationist. She became a highly influential advocate of conservation and fair distribution of the Earth's resources during the 1960s. Her works include *The Rich Nations and the Poor Nations* (1962) and *Spaceship Earth* (1966).

**Warhol, Andy** [Andrew Warhola] (1930–87) American pop artist and film-maker (of Czech parentage). He became the prime exponent of Pop Art in the early 1960s, with deliberately mundane works such as his reproductions of Campbell's soup cans and his repetitive portraits of contemporary icons such as PRESLEY, MAO and Marilyn MONROE. His films include the three-hour *Sleep* (1963) and *Chelsea Girls* (1966). In 1968, he survived an assassination attempt by one of his "starlets." His books include *From A to B and Back Again* (1975).

**Washington, George** (1732–99) American general

and 1st president of the United States (1789–97). An experienced campaigner against the French, he became commander of the American armed forces during the War of Independence in 1785, leading them to victory against the British in 1781. After the Philadelphia Convention of 1787, he became president of the new country in 1789, retiring in 1797.

**Watkins, Dudley [Dexter]** (1907–69) English cartoonist. He became the D. C. THOMSON organization's chief cartoonist in the 1930s (the first allowed to sign his name), creating such characters as Desperate Dan for the *Dandy* (1937) and Oor Wullie for the *Sunday Post* (1936). The strong surreal element in Watkins' work—Desperate Dan lives in a Wild West version of Dundee policed by British Bobbies—has been much commented on. Watkins was a deeply religious Protestant, very dapper in appearance.

**Watson, James Dewey** (1928– ) American biologist. He and Francis CRICK discovered the "double helix" structure of DNA, for which they shared (with Maurice WILKINS) the 1962 Nobel prize for physiology or medicine. His works include *The Double Helix* (1968) and *The DNA Story* (1981).

**Watson, John B[roadus]** (1878–1958) American psychologist. He became the leading theorist and proponent of behaviourism with his view that a scientific approach to psychology can only be based on studies of behaviour under laboratory conditions. His works include *Behavior—An Introduction to Comparative Psychology* (1914). *See also* SKINNER.

**Watson-Watt, Sir Robert Alexander** (1892–1973)

Scottish physicist. Asked by the Air Ministry in 1935 to develop a "death ray," he instead played a major role in the development of radar, thus equipping RAF pilots with a significant advantage at the onset of World War II.

**Watt, James** (1736–1819) Scottish engineer. His improvements from the late 1760s to the hitherto unreliable steam engine led directly to the rapid expansion of the Industrial revolution. The watt, a unit of power, is named after him.

**Watteau, Jean-Antoine** (1684–1721) French painter, an outstanding exponent of Rococo art. His works include *Embarkation for Cythera* (1717) and *Enseigne de Gersaint* (1721). His many admirers and imitators generally failed to achieve his delicacy of colour and sensitivity of composition.

**Watts, Charlie** *see* **Jagger, Mick.**

**Waugh, Evelyn [Arthur St John]** (1903–66) English novelist known for his brilliant satires, e.g. *Vile Bodies* (1930) on the brittle postwar world of upper-class England, *Scoop* (1938) on war reporting, and *The Loved One* (1948) on Californian burial practices. His work also had a deeper tone, resulting from his conversion to Catholicism in 1930. His best-known novel, *Brideshead Revisited* (1945), although still a satire displays a growing spiritual concern. His masterpiece is his *Sword of Honour* trilogy, i.e. *Men at Arms* (1952), *Officers and Gentlemen* (1955) and *Unconditional Surrender* (1961), based on his own experiences with the Communist partisans in Yugoslavia in World War II.

**Wayne, John** [Marion Michael Morrison] (1907–79) American film actor. The best-known member of the John FORD "family" of actors, Wayne's first major

role was as the Ringo Kid in *Stagecoach* (1939).
Other classic westerns he starred in are Ford's *The
Searchers* (1956) and *She Wore a Yellow Ribbon*
(1949) and HAWKS' *Red River* (1948). Despite never
having served in the Forces, Wayne, very much a
political right-winger, became identified in the public mind as the definitive tough and laconic man of
action. He was, however, when directed by Ford and
Hawks, capable of conveying rich and surprising
depth, as well as being a screen actor of outstanding
presence. He directed and starred in *The Green
Berets* (1968), which is notorious for closing with the
sun setting in the East, and was awarded an Oscar
for *True Grit* (1969).

**Webb, Beatrice [Potter]** (1858–1943) and **Webb,
Sidney James**, [Baron Passfield] (1859–1947)
English social reformers and economists. Married
in 1892, the Webbs were, with George Bernard
SHAW and H. G. WELLS, the leading propagandists of
Fabian socialism, Sidney Webb having been a
founder of Fabianism in 1884. Their books together
include *The History of Trade Unionism* (1894, which
LENIN translated into Russian), and *Industrial Democracy* (1897). They co-founded the London School
of Economics (1895), founded the *New Statesman*
(1913) and produced hordes of pamphlets and articles. Their *Soviet Communism: a New Civilisation?*
(1935), a gushing account of the wonderful achievements of STALIN, is one of the key bad books of
modern political thought. Beatrice's autobiography, *My Apprenticeship* (1926), has been highly
praised.

**Weber, Max** (1864–1920) German sociologist. Regarded as one of the founders of sociology, he de-

vised the concept of "ideal types" of real situations for comparative purposes, and emphasized the role of religious values and charismatic personalities in changing society. His works include *The Protestant Ethic and the Spirit of Capitalism* (1930).

**Webern, Anton von** (1883–1945) Austrian composer. He studied under SCHOENBERG and became one of the leading exponents of his teacher's serial form of composition. His works include *Three Little Pieces* (1914), for cello and piano, and *Five Pieces for Orchestra* (1911–13).

**Webster, John** (c.1578–c.1632) English dramatist, noted for two very powerful tragedies, *The White Devil* (c.1609–12) and *The Duchess of Malfi* (c.1613). Webster's bleak and chilling dialogue has rarely been matched by other dramatists.

**Weil, Simone** (1909–43) French philosopher. From an intellectual Jewish family, she chose to live as a farm and industrial labourer during the 1930s, and worked for the Republican forces during the Spanish Civil War. She later developed a strong interest in Roman Catholic mysticism. She left France in 1942 and worked for the French Resistance in London, where she starved herself to death in sympathy with the inmates of the Nazi camps. Her religious works, all posthumous, include *Waiting for God* (1951) and *Gravity and Grace* (1952).

**Weill, Kurt** (1900–1950) German composer, noted especially for his collaborations with BRECHT, e.g. *The Threepenny Opera* (1928). He fled from Germany in 1935, settling in the US.

**Weinberg, Steven** (1933– ) American physicist. He devised a theory of the unity of the forces operating on elementary particles (now called the Weinberg-

Salam theory) that was independently arrived at by the Pakistani physicist **Abdus Salam** (1926– ), and later developed by the American physicist **Sheldon Glashow** (1932– ). All three shared the 1979 Nobel prize for physics.

**Weismuller, Johnny** (1903–84) American swimmer and film star. He was the first man to swim 100 metres in less than a minute, 440 yards in under five minutes. He won five Olympic gold medals (1921–28) and achieved further fame starring as Tarzan in 19 films in the 1930s and 40s. He is credited with inventing the Tarzan "yodel."

**Weizmann, Chaim [Azriel]** (1874–1952) Russianborn chemist and Israeli statesman. A distinguished scientist, he became a British subject in 1910, developing a synthetic acetone that aided the production of explosives. He participated in the negotiations for a Jewish homeland that resulted in the Balfour Declaration (1917) and became first president of Israel (1949-52).

**Welles, [George] Orson** (1915–85) American stage and film director and actor. He achieved great notoriety with his radio production of WELLS's *War of the Worlds* in 1938, which sparked off mass panic in the US, many of his listeners becoming convinced that a Martian invasion was imminent. He cowrote, produced and directed one of the greatest films of all time, *Citizen Kane* (1941), based on the life of Randolph HEARST. His other films include *The Magnificent Ambersons* (1942), *Macbeth* (1948) and *Othello* (1951). His other acting roles include, most notably, Harry Lime in REED's masterpiece, *The Third Man* (1949).

**Wellington, 1st Duke of** [Arthur Wellesley] (1769–

1852) Anglo-Irish soldier and statesman, nicknamed the "Iron Duke". He distinguished himself as a commander in India, and was appointed commander of the British forces during the Peninsular War of 1808–14, and led the Allied forces to victory against NAPOLEON at Trafalgar in 1815. Internationally respected for his achievement in defeating Napoleon, he became Tory prime minister (1828–30) and opposed reform.

**Wells, H[erbert] G[eorge]** (1866–1946) English novelist and short-story writer. His science fiction works include several classics, e.g. *The Time Machine* (1895), *The War of the Worlds* (1898) and *The Shape of Things to Come* (1933). He was a propagandist with the WEBBS and others for Fabian socialism, and his novels on contemporary themes generally address their subject matter from a "progressive" viewpoint, e.g. *Ann Veronica* (1909), and sometimes with a comic or satirical element, e.g. *Love and Mr Lewisham* (1900) and *The History of Mr Polly* (1910).

**Wesley, John** (1703–91) English evangelist. The 15th son of the poet and clergyman, **Samuel Wesley** (1662–1735), he joined (under the influence of LAW's writings) a small group of devout Anglicans, formed by his brother **Charles Wesley** (1707–88), who subsequently became known as "Methodists," which name was used to describe the expanding movement, and which remained within the Church of England in Wesley's lifetime. He founded the first Methodist chapel in 1739 and travelled widely throughout England for over 50 years, preaching, it was said, over 40,000 sermons. Charles Wesley, who became his brother's helper in his evangelical work for the rest of his life, wrote over 5000 hymns, including "Hark, the Herald Angels sing."

**West, Benjamin** (1738–1820) American painter. He settled in London in 1763, where he was patronized by GEORGE III and where his studio became a focal point for American art students. His great innovative painting *The Death of General Wolfe* (1770) defied tradition by depicting its characters in contemporary dress.

**West, Mae** (1892–1980) American vaudeville artist, dramatist and film actress. Several of her plays were banned for obscenity, notably *Sex* (1926), for which she was also briefly imprisoned. She became a major star, renowned for her sardonic wit and powerful sexuality, with such films as *She Done Him Wrong* (1933) and *My Little Chickadee* (1940). Her autobiography is *Goodness Had Nothing to Do With It* (1959).

**Weyden, Rogier van der** (*c*.1399–1464) Flemish painter. His paintings include *The Deposition* (*c*.1435) and his masterpiece the *Last Judgement* altarpiece (*c*.1450).

**Wheeler, Sir [Robert Eric] Mortimer** (1890–1976) Scottish archaeologist. Noted for his excavations, especially in the Indus Valley, on Romano-British sites and at Maiden Castle, and for his innovative methodology, Wheeler, a flamboyant figure, became a household name in Britain in the 1950s through his many television appearances and popular articles. His works include *Archaeology and the Earth* (1954) and an autobiography, *Still Digging* (1955).

**Whistler, James Abbott McNeill** (1834–1903) American painter. He settled in London in 1859, where he was influenced by the Pre-Raphaelites and by Japanese art. He became famous as a portraitist, with works such as *Arrangement in Grey and Black*, a portrait of the artist's mother. He became involved in a notorious court case with RUSKIN, who had sneered at Whistler's work in a review of an 1877 exhibition (Whistler was awarded a penny damages). He published his collected writings, *The Gentle Art of making Enemies,* in 1890.

**Whitehead, A[lfred] N[orth]** (1861–1947) English mathematician and philosopher. With his pupil, Bertrand RUSSELL, he wrote *Principia Mathematica* (1910–13), a highly acclaimed work that was described as the most important contribution to the study of logic since ARISTOTLE. His other works include *Science and the Modern World* (1925) and *Process and Reality* (1929), the latter being an attempt at defining a new philosophy of science.

**Whitlam, [Edward] Gough** (1916– ) Australian Labor politician. He became prime minister (1972–75), and was dismissed by Sir John Kerr, the governor-general, for refusing to call a general election. Labor was defeated in the ensuing election, and Whitlam retired from parliament in 1978. His works include *The Italian Inspiration in English Literature* (1980).

**Whitman, Walt[er]** (1819–92) American poet. His collection, *Leaves of Grass*, was first published in 1855; eight subsequent revised and enlarged editions appeared throughout his life, and the book is regarded as the most important single volume of poems in American literature, with its celebration of America as the land of liberty and democracy, with a concurrent celebration of the poet himself, his sexuality, and the great world of nature. Ezra POUND said of him, "He is America."

**Whittier, John Greenleaf** (1807–92) American poet. His strong Quaker principles pervade his work, which, like WHITMAN's celebrates the common people of America. His anti-slavery poems, e.g. *Voices of Freedom* (1846), contributed significantly to the abolitionist cause.

**Whittle, Sir Frank** (1907– ) English aeronautical engineer. He designed the first operational jet engine for aircraft. The first successful flight was made in a Gloster in 1941. Whittle's first patent had been taken out in 1930, and it was not until 1939 that the British government took a reluctant interest in the project.

**Whorf, Benjamin Lee** (1897–1941) American linguist. Influenced by the German-born American linguist **Edward Sapir** (1884–1939), he devised what became known as the Sapir-Whorf hypothesis, i.e. the assertion that "users of markedly different grammars...arrive at somewhat different views of the world." His theory derives from his comparison between the Hopi language and "standard average European" language.

**Wiener, Norbert** (1894–1964) American mathematician. Advised by his tutor, Bertrand RUSSELL, to study mathematics, he coined the term "cybernetics" for the feedback mechanism in electronics, the theory of which is expanded in works such as *Cybernetics* (1948). His other works include *The Human Use of Human Beings* (1950) and the autobiographies, *Ex-Prodigy* (1953) and *I am a Mathematician* (1956).

**Wilberforce, Samuel** *see* **Huxley, Thomas Henry**.

**Wilberforce, William** (1759–1833) English philanthropist and politician. He became a member of parliament in 1784 and, despite being a close friend of PITT the Younger, soon acquired a reputation for independence and for evangelical sympathies. His long campaign to end the British slave trade led to its abolition in 1807, with slavery being abolished throughout the Empire in the year of his death.

**Wilde, Oscar [Fingal O'Flahertie Wills]** (1854–1900) Irish dramatist, poet, essayist and wit. He first came to notice in the late 1870s, and lived gaily up to the "Bunthorne" image of an aesthete presented in GILBERT and Sullivan's comic opera *Patience.* After the publication of *Poems* (1881), he made a highly successful tour of America, published his children's stories *The Happy Prince and Other Tales* in 1888, with his only novel *The Picture of Dorian Gray* following in 1890. The first of his great plays, *Lady Windermere's Fan* appeared in 1892. The succeeding plays, *A Woman of No Importance* (1893), *An Ideal Husband* (1895) and *The Importance of Being Earnest* (1895) established him as the most important dramatist of the age, with their superbly witty dialogue and biting satire. He was jailed for homosexuality (1895–57), and during his imprisonment wrote *De Profundis,* a bitter apologia addressed to **Lord Alfred Douglas** (1870–1945), a minor poet whose relationship with Wilde had resulted in his imprisonment. After his release, Wilde fled to France, where he wrote *The Ballad of Reading Gaol* (1898) and died in poverty.

**Wilder, Billy** [Samuel Wilder] (1906– ) Austrian-born American film director and screenwriter. He emigrated to the US in the 1930s, winning Oscars for *The Lost Weekend* (1945), *Sunset Boulevard* (1950) and *The Apartment* (1960). Other films include *Double Indemnity* (1944), *The Seven Year Itch* (1955) and *Some Like it Hot* (1959).

**Wilkie, Sir David** (1785–1841) Scottish painter. He settled in London in 1805, where he achieved great popularity with his genre paintings, which depicted rural festivities and domestic scenes with wit and humour. His painting *Chelsea Pensioners Reading the Gazette of the Battle of Waterloo* (1822) was an immediate success when exhibited at the Royal Academy.

**Wilkins, Maurice Hugh Frederick** (1916– ) New Zealand physicist and biologist. Originally a physicist, he turned to biophysics after working on atom bomb research. His and Rosalind FRANKLIN's research into DNA structure resulted in CRICK and WATSON's discovery of the "double helix" structure of DNA, for which Wilkins, Crick and Watson shared the 1962 Nobel prize for physics.

**William I** *or* **William the Conqueror** (1027–87) duke of Normandy and king of England. The illegitimate son of the Duke of Normandy, he claimed to have been promised succession to the English throne by EDWARD THE CONFESSOR, and to have received the pledge of the future HAROLD II to support him in that claim. After Harold became king, William invaded England and defeated the English forces at the Battle of Hastings. He launched a ferocious assault upon rebels in the North of England in 1069, and ordered the compilation of the Domesday book in 1086.

**William III** *or* **William of Orange** (1650–1702) King of Great Britain and Ireland. At the invitation of disaffected members of the ruling class, William landed in England in 1688 to claim the throne and usurp his father-in-law, JAMES II, who fled to France. In 1689 William and his wife, **Mary II** (1662–94), were crowned king and queen of Britain and Ireland in the so-called "Glorious Revolution." His forces defeated Scottish and Irish rebellions, and he instituted a degree of mild reform with public stability.

**William IV** *see* **Victoria, Queen**.

**Williams, Shirley** [Vivien Teresa Brittain] (1930– ) English politician. The daughter of the feminist writer **Vera Brittain** (1893–1970), she lost the lead role in the film *National Velvet* (1944) to Elizabeth TAYLOR. She became a Labour MP in 1964, and formed the Social Democratic Party with JENKINS, OWEN and Rodgers in 1981, becoming the party's first elected MP (1981–83). She retired from politics to become a professor at Harvard University.

**Williamson, Malcolm** (1931– ) Australian-born British composer. Master of the Queen's Music since 1975, his works include several operas, e.g. *Our Man in Havana* (1963), and music for film and television and for children.

**Wilmot, John** *see* **Rochester, 2nd Earl of**.

**Wilson, Sir [James] Harold** [Baron of Rievaulx] (1916– ) English Labour statesman. He served in World War II as a civil servant and became an MP in 1945. He held various ministerial posts before succeeding GAITSKELL as Labour leader in 1963. He became prime minister (1964–70, 1974–76). Originally on the soft left of his party, he became a strong defender of US policy on Vietnam and imposed a statutory incomes policy to deal with the country's balance of payments crisis in the mid–1960s. He unexpectedly resigned in 1976, with CALLAGHAN succeeding him as prime minister.

**Wilson, Harriette** (1786–1846) English author and courtesan. Her *Memoirs of Harriette Wilson* (1825) created a public scandal by naming and discussing her various "protectors," associates and acquaintances, many of them prominent men. The work is not reliable in detail (WELLINGTON responded famously, "Publish and be Damned," to a request from the publisher for money to suppress details of his meetings with Harriette), but is written in a lively, restless prose that modulates into captivating pastiches of contemporary prose styles, with, for example, her meeting with BYRON being described in a suitable "sentimental" manner.

**Wilson, [Thomas] Woodrow** (1856–1924) American Democratic statesman. He became 28th president of the USA (1913–21). Re-elected in 1916 on a policy of neutrality, he declared war on Germany following the sinking of US vessels by U-boats. His "fourteen points" speech of January 1918 set out US conditions for ending the war, including the disbandment of the German, Austro-Hungarian and Ottoman empires and their replacement by nation states, and imposed the armistice with Germany on Britain and France. His last months in office were much troubled by ill health.

**Windsor, Duke of** [formerly Edward VIII] (1894–1972) English monarch, (1936). He succeeded his father, GEORGE V, to the throne, and became highly popular with the British public for his apparent concern at the lot of the unemployed ("something must be done"). He abdicated to marry the American divorcée, **Wallis Simpson** (1896–1986), after

BALDWIN had made plain his opposition to the notion of Mrs Simpson becoming queen. He married her in 1937, after which they lived in exile, the Duke becoming governor of the Bahamas during World War II.

**Wingate, Orde [Charles] Major-General** (1903–44) English soldier. An ardent Zionist, he became proficient in irregular tactics while aiding Jewish settlers in Palestine in the mid–1930s. In 1942 he organized the "Chindits," specially trained jungle troops who caused much disruption to the Japanese supply lines during the Burma campaign in World War II. Notably erratic in his behaviour—he attempted to commit suicide in 1941 and habitually received visitors while cleaning his body with a toothbrush—Wingate became a national hero. He died in a plane crash.

**Wittgenstein, Ludwig [Josef Johann]** (1889–1951) Austrian-born British philosopher. He studied under Bertrand RUSSELL (1912–13), who observed that he was soon learning as much from his pupil as he had taught him. On the outbreak of World War I, Wittgenstein returned to Austria to serve as an artillery officer, and was captured on the Italian front in 1918. While a POW, he wrote and sent to Russell his *Tractatus Logico-Philosophicus* (1921), a series of aphoristic propositions on the boundaries of language and philosophy in relation to the world. During the 1920s, influenced by TOLSTOY's asceticism, he gave his considerable inherited wealth away and worked as a schoolteacher. His posthumous *Philosophical Investigations* (1953) retracts the confident assertions of the *Tractatus*, focusing instead on the concept of language as a series of games in which "The meaning of the word is its use in language."

**Wittig, Georg** (1897– ) German chemist. He made several important contributions to organic chemistry, and shared the 1979 Nobel prize for chemistry with the English-born American chemist **Herbert Charles Brown** (1912– ) for their work on boron compounds.

**Wodehouse, P[elham] G[renville]** (1881–1975) English novelist and short-story writer who became a US citizen in 1955. His most famous creations, in e.g. *The Inimitable Jeeves* (1923) and *Carry on Jeeves* (1925), are Bertie Wooster, a giddy young upper-middle-class man, and his butler Jeeves, a shrewd and immensely competent man. Wodehouse also wrote lyrics for musicals in collaboration with composers such as Jerome KERN and Irving BERLIN. Interned during World War II, he foolishly made some innocuous broadcasts from Germany, which led to his being branded a traitor. He was given an honorary knighthood.

**Wollstonecraft, Mary** *see* **Shelley, Mary Wollstonecraft**.

**Wolsey, Cardinal Thomas** (c.1475–1530) English cleric and statesman. After studying at Oxford, he became chaplain to HENRY VII and was made a privy councillor (1511) by HENRY VIII, who then appointed him archbishop of York (1514–30) and lord chancellor (1515–29). Ambitious to make England powerful in world affairs, he negotiated a successful peace in 1518, but followed this by involving England in an alliance with CHARLES V in 1521, which led to an unnecessary and expensive war with France. Instructed by the king in 1527 to negotiate with the

Pope the annulment of the king's marriage, his failure after two years of pressurizing Rome led to his dismissal as lord chancellor (being succeeded by Sir Thomas MORE). He died on the journey from York to London to face charges of treason.

**Wood, Sir Henry [Joseph]** (1869–1940) English conductor. He founded the London Promenade Concerts (the "Proms") in 1895, which he conducted until his death. He published an autobiography, *My Life of Music* (1938).

**Woolf, [Adeline] Virginia** (1882–1941) English novelist and critic. She married (1912) the novelist and social reformer **Leonard [Sidney] Woolf** (1880–1969), and their home became the centre of the so-called "Bloomsbury Group" of writers and artists. Her novels, e.g. *Jacob's Room* (1922), *To the Lighthouse* (1927) and *The Waves* (1931), are written in a fluid, poetic style, and are recognized as being among the most innovative of the 20th century. She suffered greatly from mental illness, and drowned herself.

**Wordsworth, Dorothy** (1771–1855) English author, sister of William WORDSWORTH. She lived with William from 1795 until his death, and kept journals which were not published until after her death. The most famous of these is the *Grasmere Journal*, which contains many superb descriptive passages that were used by her brother as the basis for some of his poems.

**Wordsworth, William** (1770–1850) English poet, brother of Dorothy WORDSWORTH. Like many men of his generation, he was a great admirer of the French Revolution, and became disillusioned with revolutionary principles when the Terror began in 1793.

He met COLERIDGE in 1795, and they published their great joint volume *Lyrical Ballads* in 1798. Wordsworth's contributions reflect his view that poetry should be plain and accessible to all men and defined poetry as "emotion recollected in tranquillity". The book is regarded, with BLAKE's works of the 1790s, as the first great products of the English Romantic movement. Other great poems include "Resolution and Independence" and the "Intimations of Immortality" ode, and such sonnets as his stirring tribute to Toussaint L'Ouverture. His masterpiece is the long narrative poem *The Prelude: or, Growth of a Poet's Mind*, the first version of which was finished (but not published) in 1805 (revised version published 1850). Few other poets have so successfully blended, as here, the personal with the natural and social worlds into a coherent whole. Wordsworth became poet laureate in 1843, succeeding his friend SOUTHEY. Like Southey, he had become a staid conservative, much derided by BYRON and by young radicals such as BROWNING (who attacked him in "The Lost Leader"). KEATS, SHELLEY and BLAKE, however, while disagreeing strongly with many of his views, agreed that Wordsworth was a great poet.

**Wren, Sir Christopher** (1632–1723) English architect. One of the founders of the Royal Society, he was commissioned to rebuild St Paul's cathedral (completed 1710) after the Great Fire of London in 1666. He also designed many other new London churches.

**Wright, Frank Lloyd** (1869–1959) American architect. Regarded as one of the greatest modern architects, he sought to develop an architecture with traditionally American "organic" values of harmony between a building and its environment. His buildings include the Tokyo Imperial Hotel (1916–20) and the Guggenheim Museum of Art in New York (1959). His books include *Autobiography* (1932).

**Wright, Joseph** ["Joseph Wright of Derby"] (1734–97) English painter. His works include genre paintings, portraits and landscapes, the outstanding features of which are his extraordinary lighting effects, e.g. *An Experiment on a Bird in an Air Pump* (c.1767).

**Wright, Orville** (1871–1948) and **Wright, Wilbur** (1867–1912) American aviators and brothers. Cycle manufacturers, they designed and built the first heavier-than-air flying machine, a 12–horse power biplane, *Flyer I*, which flew for 120 feet in 1903. They formed an aircraft production company in 1909, in which year the US Signal Corps purchased one of their models.

**Wyatt, Sir Thomas** (1503–42) English poet and diplomat. He spent most of his adult life in the service of HENRY VIII, when he was not being imprisoned by him. Wyatt was very probably the former lover of Anne Boleyn, and how he escaped execution remains a mystery. He was a powerful and original poet, and wrote several striking love poems, e.g. "They flee from me that sometime did me seek."

**Wycherley, William** (1641–1715) English dramatist. His plays are regarded as being among the most licentious of Restoration comedies, and include *The Country Wife* (1675) and *The Plain Dealer* (1676). His witty dialogue and sardonic mockery of social conventions still works very well on the stage.

**Wyman, Bill** *see* **Jagger, Mick**.

# X

**Xenophon** (*c*.435–354 BC) Greek soldier and historian. A follower of SOCRATES, he enlisted as a merce-
nary leader in Persia in 401 and led the Greek forces
back through Persian territory in its 1500–mile
march to the Black Sea, a journey described in his
*Anabasis*. His other works include a history of
Greece, *Hellenics*.

Country Wife* (1675) and *The Plain Dealer* (1676).
His witty dialogue and sardonic mockery of social
conventions still works very well on the stage.

Wyman, Bill ▶ Jagger, Mick

# Y

**Yeats, W[illiam] B[utler]** (1865–1939) Anglo-Irish poet and dramatist. His early works include several important collections of poems, e.g. *The Wanderings of Oisin* (1889), which reflect his concern with Irish myth and legend. His play, *Cathleen ni Houlihan* (1902) demonstrated his support of Irish patriotism, and he later feared it had sent men to their deaths against the British. Following Irish independence, he became a member of the Irish senate. He was awarded the Nobel prize for literature in 1923. His brother, **Jack Yeats** [John Butler Yeats] (1870–1957) was an illustrator, particularly of comic strips and children's books, before turning to painting and writing.

**Yeltsin, Boris Nikolayevich** (1931– ) Russian politician. A member of the Communist party since 1960, he was brought into the Soviet Politburo by GORBACHEV in 1985, in which year he was appointed head of the Moscow party organization. His subsequent assault on the ingrained inefficiency and corruption of that body resulted in his demotion from the post and from the Politburo. In the free elections of 1989, he was elected to the Congress of People's Deputies, and won an overwhelming majority of votes in the Russian presidential election of 1990. Although widely distrusted by many Western observers, who dismissed him as a rabble-rouser, he gave strong moral support to the Baltic states in their move for independence and called for the liberalization of the Soviet state and establishment of a decentralized and market economy. During the abortive coup against Gorbachev of August 1991, he evaded capture and took refuge in the Russian parliament building, where he and his allies, such as SHEVARDNADZE and YEVTUSHENKO, publicly defied the organizers of the coup. In the aftermath of the failed coup, Yeltsin emerged as the most powerful figure within the disintegrating Soviet Union.

**Yevtushenko, Yevgenii Aleksandrovich** (1933– ) Russian poet. Regarded as the most influential post-Stalinist poet in Russia, he attracted huge crowds to his public readings in the 1950s and 60s, which often included outspoken denunciations of Stalinism, and was allowed to travel freely in the West. His best-known poem is *Babi Yar* (1962), a denunciation not only of the Nazi crimes against the Jews, but also of Russian anti-semitism (SHOSTAKO-VICH set this and other Yevtushenko poems to music). He also gave public support to SOLZHENITSYN. *See also* YELTSIN.

**Yonge, Charlotte M[ary]** (1823–1901) English novelist. The only one that is still regularly published is *The Heir of Radclyffe* (1853), in which, as in the rest of her work, the dominant theme is her strong belief in the transforming power of Christianity.

**Yukawa, Hideki** (1907–81) Japanese physicist. He became the first Japanese to be awarded the Nobel prize for physics, in 1949, for his prediction (in 1935) of the meson within the atomic nucleus.

# Z

Zeffirelli

**Zanuck, Darryl F[rancis]** (1902–79) American film producer. He began his Hollywood career as a scriptwriter, becoming a producer in 1927, and was one of the founders of 20th-Century Fox (1935). The many films he produced include *The Jazz Singer* (1927), *Little Caesar* (1930) and *The Grapes of Wrath* (1940).

**Zapata, Emiliano** (1879–1919) Mexican revolutionary. An Indian tenant farmer, he led (1910–19) a guerrilla campaign against the Mexican government in the name of land reform. He succeeded in occupying Mexico City three times (1914–15), and was assassinated by a government agent. *See also* VILLA.

**Zappa, Frank** (1940– ) American rock musician and Czech diplomat. Founder of the rock band Mothers of Invention, his songs include "Weasels Ripped My Flesh" and "Hot Rats." Noted for his witty observations on popular entertainment ("rock journalism is people who can't write interviewing people who can't talk for people who can't read"), HAVEL's government appointed him Czechoslovakia's "cultural liaison officer to the West" in 1990.

**Zátopek, Emil** (1922– ) Czech athlete. One of the greatest long-distance runners of all time, he won the 5,000 and 10,000 metres and the marathon in the 1952 Olympics.

**Zeffirelli, Franco** (1923– ) Italian stage and film director and designer. His films include *Romeo and Juliet* (1968), *Brother Sun, Sister Moon* (1973), in which St Francis and St Clare are portrayed as proto-hippies, and the TV film *Jesus of Nazareth* (1973), a highly reverential work once described as "Christ Among the Guest Stars."

**Zhivkov, Todor** (1911– ) Bulgarian Communist statesman. He became prime minister (1962–71) and president (1971–89). Under his rule, Bulgaria became the most servile of the satellites of the Soviet Union, at whose disposal Zhivkov placed his notoriously ruthless secret service. He was deposed in 1989, following the collapse of Soviet hegemony.

**Zhou En Lai** *see* **Chou En-Lai.**

**Zhukov, Georgi Konstantinovich** (1895–1974) Russian soldier. Appointed army chief of staff by STALIN in 1941 following the German invasion, Zhukov's forces repulsed the Germans from the suburbs of Moscow in December, successfully defended Leningrad and captured the German 6th Army at Stalingrad. He took Warsaw in September 1944, delaying his assault while the Germans eviscerated the Polish resistance, and took Berlin in May 1945.

**Zia ul-Haq, Mohammed** (1924–88) Pakistani general. He led the military coup against Zulfikar BHUTTO in 1977 and became president (1978–88). His refusal to commute Bhutto's death sentence was condemned worldwide. He opposed the Soviet invasion of Afghanistan (1979) and pursued a domestic policy designed to make Pakistan a totally Islamic culture. His death in a plane crash is generally assumed to have been due to sabotage.

**Ziegfeld, Florenz** (1869–1932) American theatre manager. His spectacular revues, the "Ziegfeld Follies," which were produced annually (1907–31), were designed as an American equivalent of the *Folies Bergères* in Paris. The revues featured music by composers such as BERLIN and KERN, and were important stages in the careers of many entertainers, e.g. W. C. FIELDS and Fred ASTAIRE.

**Zinoviev, Grigori Yevseevich** (1883–1936) Russian politician. He became chairman of the Comintern (1919–26) and Politburo member (1921–26). He allied himself with STALIN against TROTSKY following LENIN's death, and was subsequently himself purged by Stalin in 1927 and executed in 1936 after a show trial. The so-called "Zinoviev letter" allegedly written by him to the British Communist Party contributed to the electoral defeat of Ramsay MACDONALD's Labour government in 1924.

**Zola, Emile** (1840–1902) French novelist. Regarded as the most prominent exponent of Naturalism in the novel, his sequence of 20 novels, entitled the *Rougon-Macquart* series, describes the history of the Rougon and Macquart families within the setting of what he called the "natural and social history" of Second Empire France. He was also a highly able propagandist for socialism and for social justice. He had to flee to England following the publication of his letter "J'Accuse," a brilliant defence of DREYFUS, who had been falsely accused of treason.

**Zuckerman, Solly, Baron** (1904–83) South African-born British zoologist. He was chief scientific adviser to the British government (1964–71) and served on many government committees. He was also noted for his work on primates. His books include *The Social Life of Monkeys and Apes* (1932), the essay collection *Man and Aggression* (1968), and *Nuclear Reality and Illusion* (1982). His autobiography is *From Apes to Warlords* (1978).

**Zurbarán, Francisco** (1598–1664) Spanish painter. He painted mainly religious works, apart from a few still lifes. His starkly lit figures of monks or saints were painted in an austerely realistic style, as in his *St Francis*.

**Zweig, Stefan** (1881–1942) Austrian biographer, dramatist, essayist, poet and novelist (British citizen from 1938). Highly regarded as a translator and for his psychoanalytic biographies, e.g. of DICKENS and BALZAC, he also wrote the libretto for Richard STRAUSS's opera *The Silent Woman* (1935). He was Jewish and a pacifist, and died by his own hand.

**Zwingli, Huldreich** or **Ulrich** (1484–1531) Swiss religious reformer. After LUTHER and CALVIN, Zwingli became the most influential of the Protestant reformers. His movement was based in Zurich, from where it spread throughout Switzerland. He disagreed with Luther on the presence of Christ in the Eucharist, asserting that Communion was a commemoration of Christ's sacrifice and rejecting the doctrines of transubstantiation and consubstantiation. He died in battle against the Roman Catholic cantons.